The Global Indies

THE LEWIS WALPOLE SERIES IN
EIGHTEENTH-CENTURY CULTURE AND HISTORY

The Lewis Walpole Series, published by Yale University Press with the aid of the Annie Burr Lewis Fund, is dedicated to the culture and history of the long eighteenth century (from the Glorious Revolution to the accession of Queen Victoria). It welcomes work in a variety of fields, including literature and history, the visual arts, political philosophy, music, legal history, and the history of science. In addition to original scholarly work, the series publishes new editions and translations of writing from the period, as well as reprints of major books that are currently unavailable. Though the majority of books in the series will probably concentrate on Great Britain and the Continent, the range of our geographical interests is as wide as Horace Walpole's.

The
Global
Indies

*British Imperial Culture and the
Reshaping of the World,*
1756–1815

ASHLEY L. COHEN

Yale UNIVERSITY PRESS/NEW HAVEN & LONDON

Published with assistance from the Annie Burr Lewis Fund.

Yale University Press books may be purchased in quantity for
educational, business, or promotional use. For information,
please e-mail sales.press@yale.edu (U.S. office) or
sales@yaleup.co.uk (U.K. office).

Set in Minion type by IDS Infotech, Ltd.
Printed in the United States of America.

Library of Congress Control Number: 2020936896
ISBN 978-0-300-23997-3 (hardcover : alk. paper)

A catalogue record for this book is available from the British
Library.

This paper meets the requirements of ANSI/NISO Z39.48-1992
(Permanence of Paper).

10 9 8 7 6 5 4 3 2 1

For my parents,
Michael Cohen and Hara Borger Cohen

Contents

The Global Indies

Introduction

The Indies Mentality

On a winter evening a man sits by his fireside, waiting for the serene quiet of his country retirement to be interrupted by the delivery of a London newspaper. So opens "The Winter Evening," Book 4 of William Cowper's long poem, *The Task* (1785). The set piece is, without question, mundane; but therein lay its charm. Cowper's careful attention to the oft-overlooked minutia of daily life is what made him the most popular poet of the English middle classes. In *The Task*, in particular, he delighted readers by capturing a level of experience at once familiar and uncharted: the things said, thought, seen, felt, and done so often that they fade without notice into the barely registered background of everyday life. Take, for example, the occasion of waiting for a newspaper and wondering what news will be inside. When Cowper's paper finally does arrive, his survey of the chaotic landscape of "its map of busy life" forms one of the most memorable (and most critically commented upon) passages in *The Task*. But the interval of waiting that precedes this survey is worth dwelling upon. For in the pause of suspension just before Cowper receives his folded-folio paper "map," we get a mental "map" of his speculative anticipations:

> . . . who can say
> What are its tidings? have our troops awaked?

> Or do they still, as if with opium drugg'd,
> Snore to the murmurs of th' Atlantic wave?
> Is India free? and does she wear her plumed
> And jeweled turban with a smile of peace,
> Or do we grind her still? (4.24–30)

In the "Advertisement" that prefaces *The Task,* Cowper explains that he composed the poem through a process of free association, connecting one subject to another by "pursuing the train of thought to which his situation and turn of mind led him." Whether or not we take Cowper at his word, it is significant that the "train of thought" he pursues in this passage leads straight from one side of the globe to the other. In physical space, oceans and continents separate India from North America, the battlegrounds of the American War from the conquered territories of the East India Company. But in Cowper's mental map these regions are adjacent to one another: only the briefest of end-stopped pauses lies between them.[1]

Cowper's collapse of the vast distance between India and the Atlantic world captures a collective habit of mind that would have felt familiar and intuitive to his readers. They too expected to see Britain's most distant colonies paired with one another, not only when they opened a newspaper, but also when they read a poem, or attended a play, or debated politics at a dinner party, or stopped to look at a satirical cartoon in a print-shop window. In 1785 this expectation was a commonplace one; today it is an artifact of a whole view of the world utterly remote from our own. The aim of *The Global Indies* is to reconstruct one way in which late Georgian Britons viewed the world, and to see what new insights this perspective might have to teach us about the literary and cultural history of British imperialism. Thinking the two Indies together over the course of this book will prompt us to relearn much of what we thought we already knew about key topics in eighteenth-century colonial studies, including race, slavery, class, and sociability. In the more immediate context of *The Task*, the two Indies will help us recover a rich theoretical vein in Cowper's engagement with his global-imperial present.[2]

Very often in scholarship we unintentionally gloss over the strangeness of eighteenth-century ideas about the world. This is partly due to our sense that the globe is a "transparent," self-evident object of analysis. But, as Ayesha Ramachandran reminds us, the early modern "discovery" of a new continent across the Atlantic ushered in an epistemological crisis about the "intelligibility and scope of the known world." Early modern "worldmakers" solved this crisis by reshaping the world: synthesizing slivers of knowledge into a new "collective unity," a new "coherent world picture," a new "conceptual framework." Although the phrase does not appear in Ramachandran's account, "the Indies" was an important organizational device in the early modern period's new "system of order" for the globe. The age of discoveries first gave Asia and the Americas a common name: the "East and West Indies," "the two Indies," and, very often, simply "the Indies." As every schoolchild knows, this shared moniker for two places that could hardly be more distant was the result of a famous mistake: Columbus's misidentification of his so-called Caribbean discoveries as the East Indies. Yet this origin story obfuscates the more crucial point: the shared name stuck long after any misapprehension about the location of the two Indies had been rectified. Shakespeare's *Merry Wives of Windsor* illuminates one reason for the pairing's staying power: "I will be cheater to them both, and they shall be exchequers to me. They shall be my East and West Indies, and I will trade to them both." Asia and the so-called New World were both staging grounds for European fantasies about the accumulation of riches through trade and colonization. This is why the *Oxford English Dictionary* gives one definition of "the Indies" as "a region or place yielding great wealth or to which profitable voyages may be made." Fantasies of gain were load-bearing walls in the new conceptual structures fashioned by early modern Europeans to house and tame knowledge of the world. These fantasies only intensified in the ensuing centuries, as the bloody work of colonialism enabled dreams of wealth extraction to be materialized. Thus, even as the progress of geographical knowledge in the seventeenth and eighteenth centuries sundered the two Indies from one another in European cartography, they remained, in Jonathan Gill Harris's formulation, "conceptually proximate." Fast-forward to 1785 and they were still ever so close to one another in late Georgian mental maps of the world.[3]

Given its early modern pedigree, the pairing of the two Indies in *The Task* might be deemed, in Raymond Williams's terms, "residual." But it would be a mistake to dismiss the Indies as a dead cultural artifact, a fossil or relic of an earlier time. Marc Bloch, a historian of medieval France, said of the remarkable survival of "the royal touch" (the idea that a king's touch would cure scrofula): "Its longevity involves no degeneration. On the contrary, it retained a profound vitality; it continued to be endowed with a power of feeling that remained constantly active; it adapted itself to new political . . . conditions; and it assumed forms that had hitherto been unknown." Just as the royal touch survived and thrived centuries after we would expect such magical thinking to have lost its charm, the Indies found renewed influence at a time when we might expect to see it debunked and discarded. In Britain, the peak of its potency as an explanatory framework for comprehending the world occurred in the second half of the eighteenth century.[4]

A watershed in the history of the Indies pairing was the Seven Years' War (1756–63), which is also the historical jumping-off point for this study. Arguably the first global war, its battlefields spanned four hemispheres and five continents. After centuries of straggling behind other European powers in the race to lead the global economy and amass colonial possessions, Britain emerged from this conflict in a nearly uncontested position of geopolitical dominance. Most importantly for this study, victory over France and its allies secured Britain a worldwide empire whose outline traced the shape of the Indies. This was the source of the pairing's renewed "vitality." In the early modern period, the Indies had been amalgamated by virtue of fantasy. Post-1763, India and the Americas were densely interwoven in the fabric of the global economy, stitched together by the threads of British imperial policy. Within just a few years consensus dictated that the empire's most distant territories should be governed systemically, as a single unit. Above all this meant *thinking*—and *linking*—the two Indies together. Inevitably, the proliferation of economic and institutional ties endowed the pairing with new momentum, so that it seemed even more commonsensical and inevitable—hence, Cowper's "turn of mind." Once it was ingrained as a habit of thought, the conceptual pairing of the two Indies propelled more policies linking them in practice, which in turn generated more concrete ties, which further fueled conceptual linkages, which became more firmly entrenched than ever before. What we have here is not a tautology but a *mentalité:* what I call the Indies mentality.[5]

Although the study of *mentalités* never gained much traction in the United States outside medievalist circles, it is one of the twentieth century's great keywords in European scholarship. The term is a legacy of the *Annales* School. This loosely organized movement, established by Bloch and Lucien Febvre in the 1920s, eventually came to dominate the humanities and social sciences in the postwar shakeup of the French academy. The unusually low profile of the *Annales* School in the United States is unfortunate for several reasons, not least because it has distorted our reception of important French thinkers whose work took shape in or adjacent to its milieu, most notably Michel Foucault. More importantly, l'histoire des mentalités—which André Burguière calls the guiding *"spirit of the Annales"*—represents a powerful and underutilized methodological resource for cultural studies of the distant past. Two elements are particularly indispensable in the context of the present study. First, mentalités interrupt our natural tendency to assume that distant historical subjects perceived, thought about, and emotionally responded to the world in the same ways we do. Second, writing the history of any given mentalité involves simultaneously surveying multiple cultural registers. Instead of privileging one arena of experience or cultural production at the expense of all others, mentalités include everything from unconscious habit and common sense to affect and emotion, elite artistic practice and speculative thought, official policy and state-sponsored ideology—as well as the material conditions and institutional arrangements that subtend and result from all of the above. Much like the tradition of Marxist cultural studies pioneered by Stuart Hall in the 1980s, the study of mentalités tacks across and between all of these registers with the aim of "conceptualiz[ing] the ensemble of social relations which make up a whole society."[6]

To imagine that an outmoded method from the field of history might yield gains for literary scholars is already to enter into the mindset of Bloch and Febvre. Although both were historians, they rejected the "fearful schisms" of knowledge into "cloistered disciplines" in favor of a resolutely interdisciplinary approach. *Annales* School historians borrowed freely from economics, critical geography, sociology, anthropology, psychoanalysis, archaeology, and literary studies—any discipline that could help explain societal change was recruited to the cause. My return to the history of mentalités is undertaken in this spirit. Since revisiting an out-dated approach to historical analysis might seem akin to a rejection of more recent innovations in that field, let me emphasize that this is not the case. My point is not that we should turn back the methodological clock and erase a hundred-odd years of historiographical gains. To the contrary, this book is deeply influenced by recent trends in British imperial history. However, there is no reason that older historical methods may not be mined for new insights. A retooled and updated version of the history of mentalités might open a new path through a current methodological im-passe in literary studies. Before we can chart this path forward, we need to first get a better sense of what the study of mentalités entails.[7]

Mentalités and Non-Representationalism

Robert Mandrou defined mentalités (a term he helped popularize) as "visions of the world," and it is often glossed as "worldviews." An ocular metaphor is also used by Bloch in a passage from his methodological treatise that does not explicitly name its object as mentalités, but is help-ful nonetheless: "Clouds have not changed their shapes since the Middle Ages, yet we no longer see in them either magical swords or miraculous crosses. The tail of the comet cited by the great Ambroise Paré was prob-ably very little different from those which occasionally sweep across our skies. Yet, he thought he saw in it a full suit of curious armor. Compli-ance with universal prejudice had bested the habitual accuracy of his gaze; and his testimony, like that of so many others, tells us not what he actually saw but what his age thought it natural to see." To Bloch's ex-amples we might add another: the seven landmasses we call continents have not changed their arrangement on the surface of the planet, but when eighteenth-century Britons looked at the globe they very often saw the Indies, whereas we do not.[8]

When Bloch draws a distinction between what Paré "actually saw" and "what his age thought it natural to see," the implication is that men-talités are a distorting influence, perhaps even a kind of false conscious-ness. It would be easy to understand the pairing of the two Indies in this way: as a way of seeing the world that was, we now know, wrong. Yet I do not consider the Indies mentality to be a lesson in inaccuracy or a product of confusion. Instead, I take it as a reminder of the contingency of all geographical categories, including our own. In *The Myth of Continents*, critical geographers Martin Lewis and Karen Wigen point out that there is in fact no hard empirical basis for even the most seemingly self-evident geographical fact: our division of the earth's landmasses into seven continents. All geography, they suggest, ultimately boils down to "*metageography*": a "set of spatial structures through which people order their knowledge of the world." All geography is ideological. To use Henry Lefebvre's terms, the "production of space" occurs not only in man-made environments, but also on the largest possible geographical scales. Yet Lewis and Wigen's point is not that a social constructivist free-for-all is in order. Rather, they call for greater historicist attention to how different "metageographical categories" at once respond to and engender different ensembles of material and ideological conditions. The history of the Indies mentality is a veritable object lesson in how ideological conditions reshape material circumstances. In the sixteenth century, the Indies was a European fantasy; by the end of the nineteenth century, British imperialism had remade what Giovanni Arrighi calls "world *political-economic space*" in this fantasy's image. In this sense, we might describe the Indies mentality in the same way Doreen Massey characterizes contemporary globalization discourse: a "vision of global space" that "is not so much a description of how the world is, as an image in which the world is being made."[9]

How, exactly, does "an imaginative geography" like the Indies relate to the world "being made" in its "image"? Not, I would argue, via "representationalism." This is the term Karen Barad uses to name "the belief in the ontological distinction between representations and that which they purport to represent." The problem with representationalism, according to Barad, is that it—like the Newtonian physics it is based upon—is simply wrong. A theoretical physicist by training, Barad explains that "the heart of the lesson of quantum physics" is that "*we are a part of that nature that we seek to understand.*" Quantum physics proves beyond a doubt that "*No inherent/Cartesian subject-object distinction exists.*" Representations are not, in fact, ontologically distinct from "that which they purport to represent." Barad's ontological argument dovetails with Stuart Hall's important reformulation of Louis Althusser's recovery of Marx's "neglected

epistemological propositions." Taking onboard Marx's epistemology requires breaking with a positivist empiricism that would have us draw a
clean line of demarcation between abstract mental events and concrete
things in the word. For Marx, Hall clarifies, "ideas have a material existence." One implication of this stance is that the material world doesn't
exist outside ideology in a realm of pure concreteness. Here we find what
Gayatri Spivak calls "the necessity for de-fetishizing the concrete." Marxist
cultural critique is not a search through the rubble of false consciousness
to find a buried and obscured "authentic truth." To the contrary, it seeks to
understand how mental events become inscribed in material conditions.
Or, put another way, how ideology is implicated in the reproduction (with
a difference) of the world.[10]

Marx, Hall, Spivak, and Barad all share a commitment to philosophical realism. Their breaks with empiricist epistemology stem from
the belief that it simply cannot account for the complexity of the world
and our experience/knowledge of it. But there are other paths forward.
To return to Barad's framing of the issue, if we cannot stand "at a distance" and accurately measure or represent the world (since we are a part
of it), then we simply need to find "a way of understanding the world
from within and as a part of it." This is how I understand l'histoire des
mentalités: as a commitment to analyzing historically distant societies
"from the inside" of their own conceptual frameworks. Later in this introduction I spell out the resonances between this method and the most
compelling components in Althusser's structuralist Marxism. For now,
let's close the gap between Barad's diffractive methodology and l'histoire
des mentalités by updating Bloch's ontology. In the passage quoted above,
Bloch seems to suggest that mentalités are a distorting influence akin to
false consciousness. Burguière picks up on this strain of representationalism when he defines mentalités as "the filter of cultural arrangements"
through which the "natural world" passes as it is socially appropriated.
But we would be equally right to detect a hint of non-representationalism
in the passage quoted above, and in the project of the history of mentalités more generally. What would qualify as an *accurate* representation of
a comet? Bloch's first example does not even admit the posing of this
question: "Clouds" do not lend themselves to right or wrong, accurate
or inaccurate, representations. The medieval cloud-gazer is not "bested"

by "universal prejudice" when he sees "magical swords" float across the sky, nor do we succumb to delusion when we spot automobiles and personal computers in an imminent rain-shower. Clouds belie the central tenet of representationalism and point to a profound (but latent) challenge at the heart of l'histoire des mentalités: different historical, societal, and material conditions don't simply lead to different representations of the same world—they produce different worlds.[11]

The Global Indies is not a study of empirically verifiable representations of the world that turn out to be right or wrong in the end; nor is it a bid to recover how eighteenth-century authors reflected or represented the world as they stood apart from it. Instead, this book investigates how literature and other cultural productions participate in what Barad calls the "ongoing performance of the world in its differential dance of intelligibility and unintelligibility," and what Ramachandran and a number of other literary scholars call "worldmaking." In the field of British imperial history we have excellent scholarly accounts of the world-systemic transformations wrought by the rise of British imperialism post-1763. We understand fairly well how Britain reshaped the world at the level of military advances, parliamentary politics, forced migrations, and extractive economies. However, we have yet to put a fine enough point on the crucial question of how the discursive practice of linking Britain's colonies in India and the Americas relates to the proliferation of economic, political, and institutional linkages between them. To understand the remaking of the world, we must attend to literature's worldmaking capacities.[12]

Earlier, we saw that wringing sense out of even a few lines of Cowper's poetry requires reconstructing and fully re-inhabiting a view of the world very different from our own. Let us, then, return to those lines from *The Task* to stage a more thorough exposition of Cowper's Indies mentality.[13]

Cowper's Collective "Turn of Mind"

Although mentalités include everything from unconscious habit to high art, there is no better entry point to a historical mentality than its outmoded common sense. Because it operates under a "naturalistic illusion," common sense feels like "authentic truth" when it is in fact highly ideological: a conditioned (and usually collective) habit of mind. Like all habits, common sense is formed through repetition. That there is nothing more repetitive than the institution of the daily newspaper is a point Benedict Anderson made long ago. Like Julie Ellison, Kevis Goodman, and Daniel O'Quinn, I believe that the quickest path to making sense of "The Winter Evening" lies in the messy, untamed pages of the newspapers that were its source texts. During the winter of 1783–84, when Cowper was writing *The Task,* he was also avidly reading several London papers. If the poem's speaker expects to open his newspaper and find dispatches from America and India printed in vertical contiguity there, it is at least in part because Cowper (the poet) had done so many times before. In the final months of 1783, dispatches from India and North America were routinely printed in consecutive paragraphs. Cowper could open any issue of the *Morning Chronicle* (a London daily he read religiously) from the first week of October 1783, for example, and he would inevitably find a juxtaposition like the one he anticipates in "The Winter Evening." In the paper for Friday, October 3, a whole column of news about the cessation of hostilities in New York pivots without comment or explanation into a paragraph about a naval engagement between French and British fleets off the coast of Pondicherry. The transition is as abrupt as an end-stop; and, given the number of stray newspaper puffs that scholars have found laced through the stanzas of "The Winter Evening," it is entirely plausible that it—or another one like it—gave impulse to Cowper's poem. But to search for a single origin of these lines is to miss the point, which is precisely their non-singularity. If Cowper's "turn of mind" led him straight from America to India it is because this itinerary had become routine not only in newspapers but also in print, visual media, and performance.[14]

Now a word of caution is in order. The landscape of the late Georgian newspaper page is dizzyingly chaotic. Columns of news items are unsorted (thematically, temporally, or geographically), so that one paragraph follows the next seemingly (and in many cases truly) without any principle of order or selection. Thanks to the work of Donna Andrew, O'Quinn, and Goodman, we know that this pandemonium of paragraphs provided safe cover for reporting news that could not be openly printed. What's more, the disordered page provoked a playful eye: news-

paper "reading" was an active pursuit more reminiscent of *Emma*'s rid-
dles and today's crossword puzzles than the transparent paragraphs of
this morning's *New York Times*. The impulse to wring meaning out of
mayhem was thus one that all Georgian newspaper readers shared.
Reading diagonally across columns, or supplying connective tissue between subsequent but seemingly disconnected paragraphs, eighteenth-
century readers turned what Cowper called the newspaper's famine "of
no meaning" into a feast of signification.[15]

In "The Winter Evening," Cowper simulates this experience for
readers as he treks across the harrowing topography of the newspaper
page. By sneaking tidbits from the real papers into his poem, Cowper
invites readers to transpose interpretive practices across mediums. Scan-
ning the pages of the *Morning Chronicle* on October 3, 1783, readers
would have been expected to make the cognitive leap from New York to
Pondicherry. Although the connection between the two paragraphs
went unprinted, they would have little trouble supplying it: both cities
were battlefields in the American War. When Cowper transplants the
juxtaposition of "th' Atlantic wave" and India from the newspaper to *The
Task,* he invites his readers to take part in a simulated experience of
newspaper reading. He also trusts them to know the terrain well enough
to appreciate the reason for the abrupt change of direction: Cowper is
writing about a national trauma of loss whose emotional and material
geographies spanned the two Indies.[16]

To be clear, the terrain Cowper expects his readers to navigate
is not only the field of representational practices: it also includes the
grounds of material conditions. The juxtaposition of America and India
in the *Morning Chronicle*—or in Cowper's imagined newspaper of speculative musings—cannot be attributed to unconscious habit alone. The
Indies were "conceptually proximate" for eighteenth-century Britons at
least in part because they were economically, politically, and institution-
ally proximate as well. Although the pairing of the two Indies was a matter of habit, routine, and simple common sense, it was not merely floating
in the ether of mental life. Rather, this pairing was rooted in material
conditions: it existed in the world as well as in the mind. British troops
were simultaneously fighting a war in India and the Atlantic when Cowper paired the two in poetic verse. We get a concrete, if ethereal, sense of

this material proximity from the cloud of Indian-grown "opium" smoke that drifts across the Atlantic waters in Cowper's poem as if it were secondhand smoke from a neighbor close at hand, leaving British troops in America "drugg'd" and sleepy, "snor[ing]" toward defeat. Perhaps opium stands in here for the other East Indian food drug that, in historical fact, poisoned Britain's presence in America: tea. This global commodity lights up the complex circuitry erected between the two Indies in the years following 1763, when, as already mentioned, a consensus emerged to govern the empire systemically. The disastrous Tea Act of 1773 aimed to stabilize the finances of the East India Company—which were near collapse as a result of the insupportable speculation on its stock that followed its conquests in Bengal during the Seven Years' War—by turning North American markets into a captive outlet for £17 million-worth of unsold tea. The outcome of this legislation is well known: American colonists expressed their dissatisfaction with Parliament's systemic imperial bookkeeping by dumping £9,000-worth of tea into Boston Harbor. The empire's increasingly complex circuitry made it vulnerable to sudden conflagration from an isolated spark.[17]

As we have already begun to see, "mentalités" is best understood as an umbrella term that bundles together a number of discrete but related parts. The study of mentalités entails everything from unconscious habit, to highly speculative thought, to "structures of feeling"—as well as the institutional and material arrangements that subtend all of the above. So far, we have discussed the first and the last of these four components. In the next section I continue to use *The Task* as a base-camp to explore the remaining two, which, I believe, make a retooled version of l'histoire des mentalités especially indispensable for the current moment in eighteenth-century studies.[18]

Theorizing the Present

Perhaps the most useful critical reorientation entailed by the study of mentalités is not something it does but rather something it declines to do: contrary to popular currents in eighteenth-century studies, l'histoire des mentalités does not disentangle affect from cognitive activity. This is so important because recovering the role of the two Indies in late Georgian theorizations of empire and globalization requires working across and between conceptual structures, on the one hand, and structures of feeling, on the other.

In *Georgic Modernity and British Romanticism,* Kevis Goodman stages an admittedly persuasive case for a clean demarcation between thinking and feeling in the past, arguing that the global-imperial present was *affectively* accessible but *cognitively* inaccessible to Cowper and his contemporaries. Goodman locates the theoretical basis for her argument in Frederic Jameson's essay "Cognitive Mapping." There, Jameson argues that imperialism stretched the spatial boundaries of Euro-American social formations, engendering "a growing contradiction between lived experience and structure, or between a phenomenological description of the life of an individual and the more properly structural model of the conditions of existence of that experience." In other words, while lived experience was happening in London, the "structural coordinates" determinative of that experience were located in Bengal, or Jamaica. Jameson argues that this state of affairs was simply too much for historical actors to wrap their heads around: it was "often not even conceptualizable for most people." In *Georgic Modernity,* Goodman builds on this premise. If the present of global imperialism was unconceptualizable for someone like Cowper, then history must be "absent as *idea*" in *The Task.* But it *is* present in a different form, she argues—as "*feeling.*"[19]

Goodman's spin on Jameson has exerted an enormous influence over recent readings of *The Task,* particularly "The Winter Evening." Her reading of the poem hinges on two crucial lines that appear at the conclusion of Cowper's survey of the newspaper's "map of busy life" (whose speculative precursor I discussed at the opening of this introduction). At this moment in the poem, Cowper pauses to reflect on the task he has just completed, musing, "'Tis pleasant through the loop-holes of retreat / To peep at such a world" (4.88–89). The newspaper provides "loop-holes of retreat" for Cowper because it is the sensory passageway linking his isolated Olney existence to the outside "world"—and, thus, his present. Yet Cowper's need for such a prosthetic is not due to his retirement alone; it is, rather, the unavoidable result of living in an imperial age. For the "world" here is meant in two senses of the word: Cowper uses the newspaper to "peep" at the "world" of London politics and fashionable life, as well as the much larger "world" outside the metropole—what he a few lines later calls "the globe." Busy Londoners would likewise have needed the newspaper's "loop-holes" to "peep at" the latter "world" in 1784. Even with the newspaper's help, though, the phenomenological gap between metropolitan experience and global-imperial structure is never adequately closed, according to Goodman. Other scholars have tended to agree. Mary Favret's poignant reading of *The Task* as a meditation on modern wartime specifies that the poem's "haunting reminders" of the "larger world of suffering" are "affective rather than intellectual."[20]

I have taken the time to recapitulate Goodman's reading because, at the same time that it has revealed important affective dimensions of "The Winter Evening," it has also kept us from detecting a rich theoretical vein in Cowper's engagement with his global-imperial present. Tracing that vein leads us straight to the figure of the Indies. A heretofore unrecognized intertext is absolutely crucial for grasping the full scope—affective and cognitive—of Cowper's remediation of imperial affairs: Abbé Raynal and Denis Diderot's *Histoire philosophique et politique des établissements du commerce des Européens dans les deux Indes*. The *History of the Two Indies* (as it is often abbreviated in English) represents the late Georgian period's most important theorization of European imperialism. It is thus highly significant that Cowper engages with it in *The Task* at such length. We already know for certain that Cowper, like so many of his contemporaries, read this extraordinarily popular book with great keenness. Although he was initially resistant to what he thought would be "a History of rising & falling Nabobs," he soon discovered his error and spent the spring of 1778 reading all five volumes (more than three thousand pages!) aloud to his companion, Mrs. Unwin, in intervals of one hour at a time. He was so engrossed that he confessed in a letter to the friend who had lent him the book: "I have been in continual Fear lest every Post should bring a Summons for the Abbé Raynal, and am glad that I have finish'd him before my Fears were realized." Six years later, Raynal's influence had not yet waned. In January 1784, Cowper cites him as the source of his dislike of the East India Company and "all Monopolies." Perhaps, we might speculate, this reference reflects renewed interest, spurred by the publication of a new expanded English edition of the *History of the Two Indies* in 1783.[21]

In the very lines where Cowper elaborates the experience of peeping at the world through the newspaper, he also pays tribute to—and simulates—Raynal's "globally telescopic eye." In fact, the entire stanza following the famous "loop-holes of retreat" line echoes the opening pages of the 1783 edition of the *History of the Two Indies* so distinctly that the parallels can only be deliberate. It is fitting that readers have mistaken Cowper's paean to Raynal for an homage to an anonymous "news correspondent," since the *History of the Two Indies* anticipated the role the daily papers would later fill in Cowper's life. As he explained in 1778: "I am indebted to him [Raynal] for much Information upon Subjects, which, however Interesting, are so remote from those with which Country Folks in general are conversant, that had not his Work reached me at Olney, I should have been forever Ignorant of them." Just like the London papers would do some years later, Raynal supplemented Cowper's "conversable world," bringing "remote" subjects and places into retirement's reach. "The Winter Evening" reprises these early words of praise:

> He travels and expiates, as the bee
> From flow'r to flow'r, so he from land to land; ...
> He sucks intelligence in ev'ry clime,
> And spreads the honey of his deep research
> At his return, a rich repast for me (4.107–8, 111–13)

Tellingly, these lines also echo Raynal's own description of "the alarming task I have imposed upon myself" in compiling the *History of the Two Indies*. On page three of the 1783 edition, he describes calling "in to my assistance men of information from all nations," living as well as dead. While Raynal leaves the nature of the "information" he gathers unspecified, any reader of the *History of the Two Indies* would recognize Cowper's concise description as accurate: "The manners, customs, policy of all" (4.109).[22]

Conveniently, all of the material from the *History of the Two Indies* remediated in this stanza of *The Task* comes from the same single paragraph on page three, making the debt easy to trace. More helpful still, Cowper chooses some of the most memorable imagery from the *History of the Two Indies*, wherein Raynal imagines taking a virtual flight above the globe: "Raised above all human considerations" like "hope or fear, ...

we soar above the atmosphere, and behold the globe beneath us." Cowper remediates this imagery just as memorably when he describes removing to "a safe distance" from the "world" in order to better "view" it:

> Thus sitting and surveying thus at ease
> The globe and its concerns, I seem advanced
> To some secure and more than mortal height (4.93–95)

After he rises to a celestial viewing point, Cowper's flight continues to mirror that of Raynal. This is fitting, since Raynal takes his reader along with him on his virtual flight, writing in the first-person-plural case and present tense so that the passage in question reads like a guided simulation: "we let fall our tears ... upon virtue in distress ... we pour forth imprecations on those who deceive mankind, and those who oppress them and devote them to ignominy." Just as Raynal instructs, Cowper has an emotional response to what he sees looking down at the globe: "I mourn the pride / And av'rice that make man a wolf to man" (4.102–3). Clearly, Cowper found in the *History of the Two Indies* a template for responding to current events through feeling.[23]

But Cowper also found in the *History of the Two Indies* a sustained, self-conscious attempt to *theorize* the present. The experience the *History* held out to readers was both affective and cognitive, with an emphasis on the latter. From the very first words of its title page, which specify that it is a "*Philosophical*" history, the book's orientation is explicitly conceptual. Moreover, as Sunil Agnani argues, passages like the one quoted above reflect Diderot's desire to fashion the kind of "traveling philosophy" called for by Rousseau. In fact, even the emotional journey remediated by Cowper ends in thought rather than feeling. Raynal's virtual flight is a bid for *critical* as well as emotional distance. He soars into the atmosphere at least partly in order to gain enough perspective to pose questions that are truly global in scope: "It is from thence, in a word, that, viewing those beautiful regions, in which the arts and sciences flourish, and which have been for so long a time obscured by ignorance and barbarism, I have said to myself: Who is it that hath digged these canals? Who is it that hath dried up these plains? Who is it that hath collected, clothed, and civilized these people? Then have I heard the voice of all the enlightened men among them, who have answered: This is the effect of commerce." From a distant height, the East and West Indies—which, in Raynal and Diderot's usage encompass virtually all of the colonized regions of the globe—are brought into visual proximity. Now that the two Indies *look* as close as they already *sound,* Raynal can see new commonalities and systemic connections between them: it is evident that these distant "regions" are linked, in the present, by a shared history of colonial commerce. The intermingling of Raynal and Diderot's voices in this edition complicates the task of interpreting passages like this one. But whether "commerce" is being lauded for the cities it has founded or condemned for the suffering it has wrought, or a bit of both, the posing and answering of this question nonetheless represents an unmistakable attempt to *think,* on a *cognitive* level, the *idea* of global capitalism.[24]

Over the course of this book it will become evident that Raynal and Diderot's interest in theorizing the global-imperial present was one that many of their contemporaries in addition to Cowper shared. After all, thousands of Britons purchased and borrowed and read their books. O'Quinn's argument about the American Crisis holds true for the late Georgian period more generally: Britons, especially Londoners, were eager to "experience the present *critically."* Moreover, the period's newspapers, print media, theatrical productions, and visual culture—in short the entirety of its "mediascape"—were all geared toward facilitating such an experience. For Londoners, the experience of experiencing the present critically was quotidian. When Britons reflected critically on the present in the decades after 1763, they understood quite clearly that their everyday experience was being determined by forces located far away from their small North Atlantic island. Indeed, how could they not? It was an unavoidable fact of existence in these years. Late Georgian Britons sought, on an unmistakably cognitive level, to make sense of this complex state of affairs. Why not recover and learn from their theorizing?[25]

Past-Critical Reading: Close Reading from the Inside Out

The study of mentalités involves viewing past societies from inside their own conceptual frameworks. Given that the topic of this book is imperialism, some might fear that this method carries a risk of contamination.

Let me, then, clarify at the outset that this book is unequivocally anticolonial. Strategically inhabiting the inside of the Indies mentality does not
require merging with it or adopting its ethos. To the contrary, I believe
that the fear of getting too close to imperialist ideology may in itself pose
an obstacle to literary-historical analysis, as knowing something deeply
requires sustained intimacy with it. The latter idea is already enshrined
at the methodological heart of literary studies, in what we call close reading. What I am advocating here is simply a closer version of close reading: a kind of close reading from the inside out, or what I call *past-critical
reading*.

Past-critical reading is, like it sounds, almost post-critical but not
quite. While past-critical reading does part ways with what we might call
"strong" symptomatic reading—wherein the hero-critic uses his privileged powers of insight to unmask, expose, or rewrite a text—it does not
give up on critique entirely. It does not because it cannot: unlike post-
critical reading, past-critical reading doesn't see critique only as the alien-
able possession of the critic; it also recognizes critique as the inalienable
possession of many texts. Many but not all. Past-critical reading doesn't
see literary texts as inherently critical, as *necessarily* enacting critiques
whose latent politics merely need to be activated by the handmaid-critic.
Nor does past-critical reading seek to artificially "displace" the "conceptual activity" of critique from critic to text via a "strategic rhetorical
trope," an approach advocated by Nathan Hensley under the banner of
"curatorial reading." Past-critical reading's location of conceptual activity
in texts is not accomplished by a sleight of hand. Rather, it results from
the simple recognition that people in the past thought *critically* about
their present. Past-critical reading aims to harvest the insights of past-
critical thinking.[26]

I trace an important theoretical precursor of past-critical reading
to a text usually associated with suspicious depth reading, Louis Althusser's *Reading Capital*. Since Jameson identifies *Reading Capital* as
the theoretical basis for his argument in "Cognitive Mapping," it will be
doubly useful to spell out how I read Althusser differently than Jameson
does. The central premise of *Reading Capital* is that Karl Marx's *Capital*
needs to be read through the lens of its own theoretical perspective. Unfortunately, Marx never got around to formulating this perspective in

precise, stand-alone terms. Hence, Althusser argues, we must proceed symptomatically: on a first reading we excavate Marx's theoretical perspective (or "problematic") from *Capital;* and then we read *Capital* once again, this time through its own problematic. Jameson's take on *Reading Capital* has exerted a tremendous influence over this text's reception in North American literary studies. However, it is rarely noted how substantially Jameson modifies Althusser's method. Most notably, Jameson's symptomatic reading is not "double." Instead of excavating his "interpretive code" from a first reading, as called for by Althusser, Jameson substitutes a code supplied in advance: the "single vast unfinished plot" of Marxist history, "the history of class struggles." The resulting difference between Althusser and Jameson's methods is vast. Whereas Althusser "reads" a text (hence the title *Reading Capital*), Jameson "rewrites" it. The former approach is (or at least claims to be) minimally invasive, while the latter is maximally interventionist.[27]

All this means that, of the two critics, Althusser brings us closer to the kind of retooled historicist method I am calling past-critical reading. Given Althusser's reputation as the arch nemesis of historicism, this may come as a surprise. But Althusser is in fact highly sensitive to how the limits of the thinkable—or what he calls the *"mode of production* of knowledges"—shift over time, a process-event he refers to alternately as a *"change of terrain"* and a "transformation of the problematic." Such changes do not take place in a theory vacuum. Although Althusser's break with empiricism leads him to grant a semi-autonomy to knowledge production—meaning that knowledge is not simply, in Hall's words, "an empiricist reflection of the real in thought"—his *"mode of production of knowledges"* is nonetheless articulated to "the real world of a given historical society." It is constituted through a complex combination of "material," "mental," and societal ("economic, political and ideological") conditions. Put another way, a society's *"apparatus of thought"* is "a material as well as a 'mental' system, whose practice is founded on and articulated to the existing economic, political and ideological practices which directly or indirectly provide it with essentials of its 'raw materials.'"[28]

Apparatus of thought . . . Appareil des pensées. If this phrase has induced a mild spell of déjà vu it is probably because it echoes many of the keywords associated with the study of mentalités, most obviously

Bloch's *appareil conceptuel.* It takes only a little stretch of the imagination to see that what Althusser is describing in this passage is something very much like the study of mentalités, albeit transposed into a structuralist Marxist idiom. Althusser's kinship with the Annales School was no secret: out of only a handful of scholars mentioned by name in the text of *Reading Capital,* three are Annalistes. At some level, Althusser shared an intellectual project with them. The two fought a common enemy (positivist history) and worked toward a common goal: the systematic understanding of a whole society (Althusser's "mode of production" and the Annalistes' "total history"). Most importantly, both sought to supplant the history of ideas with a much more subtle and far-reaching study of how societies constrain and structure what is conceptualizable as thought in a given historical moment. What is Althusser's double reading if not a philosopher's version of inhabiting past mentalités? Why did Paré see armor where we see a comet? Why did Cowper see the Indies whereas we do not? In both cases, the answer has nothing to do with the myopia or farsightedness of what Althusser calls "any given thinking subject." Rather, what we have here is a collective phenomenon: the angles of vision alternately enabled or foreclosed by a given mentalité. Just as Althusser analyzes *Capital* from the inside of its own theoretical problematic, so the study of mentalités seeks to view past societies from the inside of their own mental frameworks.[29]

The Global Indies relearns the cultural landscape of eighteenth-century British imperialism by bringing the period's own conceptual apparatus to bear on it. While I hope this approach offers something new, it also takes inspiration from the cohort of mid-century literary scholars and historians known as the "British Marxists," sometimes referred to as the "British counterpart of the *Annales* group." Scholars like Raymond Williams, Eric Hobsbawm, and E. P. Thompson never regarded critique of even the highest order as the sole domain of the critic. Instead they insisted that the literature, thought, and social practices of the eighteenth century's laboring poor deserved to be taken seriously. They all sought, each in his own way, to recover the insights of historical subjects whose ability to reflect cognitively on their present had been denied by mainstream history. They sought, in Hobsbawm's words, "to restore to men of the past, and especially the poor of the past, the gift of theory."

My reading of "The Winter Evening" shares this motivation: I have sought to "restore" to Cowper the "gift" of theorizing his present—a task I complete in the next section.[30]

The Shape of the Global Eighteenth Century

Sometimes scholars working in the global eighteenth century treat this subfield's object of analysis ("the global") as something that is only visible in hindsight. One premise of this book is that eighteenth-century people were more preoccupied with theorizing global processes than we often tend to think; and I propose to use past-critical reading to recover and learn from this theorizing. In the past two decades the "global eighteenth century" has come to occupy a central place in the field of eighteenth-century studies, thanks to the work of Srinivas Aravamudan, Laura Brown, Catherine Hall, Suvir Kaul, Felicity Nussbaum, Roxann Wheeler, Kathleen Wilson, Chi-ming Yang, and many other scholars. The modeling of imperial and global space has also been amply treated in the wider field of British imperial history, where "south-south" connections between colonies have begun to garner as much attention as links between individual colonies and the metropole. This book would be unimaginable in the absence of Tony Ballantyne's work on the "webs of empire" or Alan Lester's "networked" model of imperial connections. To diffract the premise of this book through their terms, "the Indies" is shorthand for one particularly well-traveled web, or network, that linked the two most important colonies in Britain's empire.[31]

While I deeply admire all of the discussed work, I believe it might be improved by a more serious engagement with historical conceptualizations of global space. In today's terms we might name the subject of the *History of the Two Indies* as European imperialism, or global capitalism, or the modern world system. But Raynal and Diderot did not write in our terms, they wrote in theirs—so they wrote about the Indies. We should not mistake their lack of a modern theoretical vocabulary for an absence of serious theorizing. Although the figure of the Indies was already nearly three hundred years old, Raynal and Diderot turned it into a keyword by using it in a new way: as an analytic instrument for bringing geographically distant colonized regions into critical proximity. Take, for example, the very first sentence of the *History:* "No event has been so interesting to mankind in general, and to the inhabitants of Europe in particular, as the discovery of the New World, and the passage to India by the Cape of Good Hope." At first glance, this sentence appears to be a descriptive statement of fact. But an unstated theoretical problematic animates it. What might appear to be a minor grammatical error is in fact a major critical intervention. By referring to two distinct voyages (Christopher Columbus's expedition in 1492 and Vasco de Gama's in 1497) in the singular, as one "event," this sentence effectuates a radical perspectival shift, insisting that the history of the two Indies constitutes a single history: the history of global capitalism and European imperialism. The result is nothing less than a change of terrain. For Raynal and Diderot, the two Indies is much more than just a convenient shorthand. Like any good keyword, it performs crucial conceptual work, becoming the condition of possibility for a global, systemic critique of European imperialism.[32]

More than two decades ago, in *The Black Atlantic,* Paul Gilroy suggested that "cultural historians could take the Atlantic as one single, complex unit of analysis in their discussions of the modern world and use it to produce an explicitly transnational and intercultural perspective." Building on Gilroy's approach, as well as Lewis and Wigen's call for "a *creative cartographic vision* capable of effectively grasping unconventional regional forms," *The Global Indies* fashions a new "explicitly transnational" "complex unit of analysis": the Indies. In choosing to build a new analytic unit out of old recycled parts, I stress the importance of relearning the eighteenth century's own critical vocabulary for global imperialism. Only by so doing can we appreciate the extent to which global thinking saturates the period's literature.[33]

Take, for example, Cowper's pairing of "th' Atlantic wave" and "India" in the lines quoted at the outset of this introduction. It is still true, as I have argued, that this pairing reproduces an itinerary that by 1785 had become routine. But it is no less true that these lines represent an adept redeployment by Cowper of a cutting-edge conceptualization of global imperialism, which he imbibed from the *History of the Two Indies.* In pairing "th' Atlantic wave" and "India" in his imagined newspaper of speculative musings, Cowper prompts his reader to view current events unfolding at opposite ends of the empire as connected to one another. We might even say that he subtly teaches his readers to adopt a systemic perspective on Britain's global empire. Put another way, he prompts them to "peep" at the "world" through the lens of the Indies mentality. *The Global Indies* reactivates this way of looking in order to relearn the cultural history of British imperialism from a more historically attuned global perspective. Key discourses and conjunctures—from race and class to the Age of Revolutions—look fundamentally different when viewed from the capacious perspective of the Indies mentality.

The Plan of This Book

The chapters that follow are organized thematically, but they also proceed in chronological order, telling a diachronic story about changes in the culture of British imperialism between the Seven Years' and Napoleonic Wars. The story begins in the Prelude, where I set the scene for the chapters that follow. There, I try to capture the major cultural fallout of the Seven Years' War. In addition to radically disrupting the nation's socioeconomic status quo and altering the texture of metropolitan sociability, the war inaugurated a new way of seeing the empire: the Indies mentality.

Chapter 1 contributes to the ongoing scholarly reassessment of the so-called American Crisis, which I argue was actually experienced—and in many ways is still best understood—as a global crisis in imperial affairs. While the chapter discusses Edmund Burke's speech "On American Taxation" and Frances Burney's debut novel *Evelina*, its primary case study is Samuel Foote's neglected comic masterpiece *The Cozeners*. One of my goals in Chapter 1 is to show how the theater afforded playwrights especially complex representational practices with which to render the far-flung coordinates of Britain's globally stretched imperial social formation visible. At the theater, Londoners learned how to view the empire from the perspective of the Indies mentality; and they sought to make sense of current events within this global analytic framework.

In Chapter 2, I use the Indies mentality to relearn British racial discourse, which I argue formed in circulation between colonial India and the colonial Atlantic world. After exploring British drama's repertoire of racial character, I turn to the chapter's primary case study: Julius Soubise. Often overlooked by scholars today, during his own lifetime Soubise's celebrity rivaled that of his better remembered Afro-British contemporaries, Olaudah Equiano and Ignatius Sancho. Like Equiano's, whose travels took him to Turkey and the North Pole, Soubise's "life geography" overflowed the borders of the Black Atlantic: born in Saint Kitts, he grew up in London and spent the last two decades of his life in Calcutta. In the first half of Chapter 2, I attend to his time in London, where, I argue, he catalyzed tropologies of Eastern royalty in order to fashion himself as a "Black Prince," thereby carving out a racialized but still exalted place for himself in the beau monde. In the chapter's second half, I follow Soubise to Calcutta, tracing how his racial self presentation altered in his journey from metropole to colony, from the circum-Atlantic to India. While British ideas about race certainly traveled from the former to the latter, India's colonial racial formation was also shaped by Mughal precedents. Indeed, aspects of the subcontinent's Indo-Persian racial formation even migrated westward through imperial networks, influencing the evolution of racial ideologies in the British Atlantic world.

Chapter 3 builds on the critique of the Atlantic world paradigm initiated in Chapters 1 and 2. The chapter opens in Haiti, where, I show, revolutionary leaders like Jean-Jacques Dessalines opposed not only chattel slavery but also "political slavery," or subjection to the absolute rule of a foreign conqueror—namely, colonialism. From classical antiquity through the Age of Revolutions, political slavery was associated with Asia and Oriental despotism. This helps explain why eighteenth-century writers ubiquitously associated slavery with India even while they denied that actual chattel slavery was practiced there. The chapter traces the circuit of political slavery and Oriental despotism's global travels, around the world and in the "world" of metropolitan print. Picking up in the 1770s and ending in the 1790s, the chapter functions as a hinge between the post-Seven Years' War moment explored in Chapters 1 and 2, and the postrevolutionary, turn-of-the-nineteenth-century settings of Chapters 4 and 5.

Chapter 4 explores a contradiction at the heart of the mainstream abolitionist movement: colonialism in India was promoted as a solution to the problem of slavery. In her seminal study of nineteenth-century

US literature, *Scenes of Subjection*, Saidiya Hartman insists that we attend to forms of unfreedom that persisted across the *temporal* divide between slavery and emancipation. Building on Hartman, Chapter 4 focuses on forms of unfreedom that trouble the *geographical* divide drawn in abolitionist discourse between slavery and freedom *within* the British empire. The chapter begins with a brief discussion of Marianna Starke's pro-imperialism / antislavery drama (set in India), *The Sword of Peace*. Next, I turn to Maria Edgeworth's anti-Jacobin short-story collection *Popular Tales*, which features nearly identical scenes of slavery set in Jamaica and India. Edgeworth's fiction might seem worlds away from actual colonial policy; but by contextualizing her writing amid debates about the slave trade and proposals for the cultivation of sugar in Bengal, I show that her stories were important and highly regarded thought experiments in colonial governance. The chapter ends with a brief discussion of an important historical instantiation of the Indies mentality that falls outside the time frame of this study: the transportation of Indian indentured laborers to the Caribbean in the 1830s.

Chapter 5 explores one way in which the Indies mentality was reproduced at an institutional level: through the practice of rotating officials between postings in India and the Americas. A case study in colonial lives—which have become a crucial hermeneutic for imperial history in recent years—the chapter focuses on Maria Nugent, whose diaries and letters record her time in Jamaica and India, where her husband was governor and commander in chief, respectively. Though a woman's diaries might seem to offer only a limited perspective on imperial institutions, I argue that what Lady Nugent calls "the business of society" actually represents a crucial—but largely overlooked—arena of colonial governance. By painting a portrait of empire whose backdrop is a ballroom instead of a boardroom, I try to restore British women to the stories we tell about imperial rule.

In the Prelude and Chapters 1, 2, and 5, I spend what may seem like a surprising amount of time in what Hannah Greig shorthands "the beau monde." This reflects my belief that empire was pervasively present in London's fashionable world to an extent that does not always register in scholarship. Building on the work of Gillian Russell and Daniel O'Quinn, I argue that the history of sociability and the history of empire

need to be written together. Race, for example, played an underappreciated role in the making of elite class identities—even for Britons who
never stepped foot in the empire. In Chapters 1, 2, and 5 in particular, I
try to excavate the aristocracy's buried role in the making of the British
empire. By the turn of the nineteenth century, I argue, the Indies had
become a key site for the reproduction of the nation's ruling elite.[34]

What are the historical and methodological limits of the Indies
mentality? In the Coda, I jump forward in time to 1870 in order to witness the moment in time when the two Indies ceased to be thought together. I locate the swansong of the Indies mentality at the completion of
the first US transcontinental railroad to the Pacific, which was widely
hailed as an American "Passage to India." Next, I make a case for the por-
tability of my method, especially in the context of postcolonial studies,
where I hope it can be used to reconstruct and reinhabit non-European
epistemologies.

While this book brings together the literary and cultural histories
of Britain's Atlantic and South Asian colonies, my approach is not addi-
tive. The goal of this study is not, in other words, to combine everything
we already know about India with everything we already know about the
Atlantic world. Instead of merely trying to augment our knowledge in
this way, my aim is to shake up this knowledge's epistemological basis. I
do this by working with a different object of knowledge: the Indies. One
inevitable consequence of this approach is that the particularities of individual colonial histories are emphasized less than they tend to be in
other studies. This sacrifice is, I believe, worth making. We already have
countless studies detailing the singularities of South Asian and American colonial histories. What we lack is an account of how the fusion of
the two Indies into a single object of knowledge shaped the culture of
British imperialism, which, in turn, changed the shape of the world.

A Trip to Vauxhall

The Two Indies in the Fashionable World

T o picture how the Indies mentality manifested in Georgian London, let us take a trip to Vauxhall Gardens. From the time it opened to the public in the mid-seventeenth century, Vauxhall was in the vanguard of what we now call the entertainment industry. Like many of the cultural products discussed in this book, Vauxhall is not easily categorized. Nature and artifice came together in the gardens, where sculpted tree-lined paths echoed with the sound of artificial birdsong. Music, architecture, sculpture, and painting were all on display at Vauxhall, which was an especially important venue for visual art before the founding of the Royal Academy in 1768. Vauxhall was also a place to see and be seen: a venue for strutting and gawking, for gossip and celebrity sightings, for courtship and family outings. A multimedia entertainment experience that combined artistic consumption with sociability, Vauxhall represented a perfect epitome of late Georgian culture.[1]

One might think that the Seven Years' War would have dampened the gardens' festive mood. But in the early 1760s, Vauxhall's visitors actually had many reasons to celebrate. The Seven Years' War was a boon for British industry. Nancy Koehn estimates that, in today's dollars, Britain's victory came with "a $10 trillion price tag." This spelled bad news for the national debt, but it worked wonders for the national economy. Demand for manufactures and re-exports rose more than 33 percent during the war, and imports increased by 39 percent. The "power of commerce" helped power the nation to victory on the war's most important front: the battle for the global economy. Thanks to the wartime economic boom, many Londoners had a shilling to spare for admission to Vauxhall.[2]

The gardens' proprietor, John Tyers, was an astute entrepreneur who knew what his visitors expected in exchange for their entry fee: in the words of the *Gazetteer and London Daily Advertiser,* "novelty, improvement and variety." Every year, Tyers added "some new embellishing alteration" designed to re-captivate his customers. Unveiling these improvements on opening night, Tyers enticed Londoners to brave the chill spring air to see his latest wonders in person before the daily papers ruined the surprise. Pleasure, for Tyers, was always pedagogical. David Coke and Alan Borg emphasize that Tyers viewed Vauxhall as a kind of civilizing mission. By exposing his customers to "art, design and music of a consistently high standard" he hoped to improve their taste and virtue, thereby expanding the orbit of "polite society." More often than not, Tyers's lessons in taste took on a nationalist character: Vauxhall was littered with patriotic shrines to national achievement. In 1745, he commissioned Francis Hayman to paint four large Shakespeare paintings, thereby helping to inaugurate the Georgian cult of bardolatry. In 1748, when Tyers built an elegant Rotunda to compete with the main attraction at Ranelagh Gardens, he once again turned to the nation's literary and intellectual past for inspiration, installing busts of Milton, Dryden, Locke, and, of course, Shakespeare. Coke and Borg suggest that these busts provided an interactive experience. Thanks to the clever placement of mirrors and windows (visible in Figure 1), visitors to the Rotunda would "see sixteen reflections of themselves interspersed with the heads of famous figures from British literary history ... an early example of the ingenuity employed by Tyers' designers to intrigue and involve his visitors."[3]

During the Seven Years' War, Tyers's patriotism took on a martial cast. His pedagogical energies found vent in a new source of national pride: the empire. Around 1760, Tyers gave Hayman a new commission: to fill the four enormous frames that lined the walls of the Pillared Saloon, which was constructed as an addition to the Rotunda in 1751. The frames are visible at the center of Figure 1, in the square room

Figure 1. Henry Roberts (after Samuel Wale), *Inside of the Elegant Music Room in Vauxhall Gardens,* 1752. Line engraving, hand-colored. Yale Center for British Art, Paul Mellon Collection. The four empty frames are visible in the Pillared Saloon. Moving clockwise from the center, *Lord Clive Receiving the Homage of the Nabob* would have been in the second frame and *The Humanity of General Amherst* in the third. When a visitor to Vauxhall walked through the Saloon to the Umbrella, *Lord Clive* would have been on her left and *General Amherst* on her right.

attached to the round "Umbrella," or rotunda in the foreground. Originally, the frames were intended to hold tributes to Vauxhall's patron, the Prince of Wales. After the prince's unexpected death in 1751, they hung empty for a decade. Now, they were dedicated to a new topic: the ongoing war. The first of the four new paintings, *The Humanity of General Amherst* (see Figure 3), was hung in 1761. It portrayed Amherst's capture of Montreal, which, together with General Wolfe's success at Quebec, made Canada British. Next, in 1762, Hayman finished an allegory: *The Triumph of Britannia.* A decade and a half later, Frances Burney would poke fun at this painting during a trip to Vauxhall in *Evelina*. In

Figure 2. Francis Hayman, modello for *Lord Clive Receiving the Homage of the Nabob*, c. 1761–62. Courtesy of the National Portrait Gallery, London.

1763, a second history painting was hung directly opposite Amherst: *Lord Clive Receiving the Homage of the Nabob* (Figure 2). Fittingly, this painting was set on the opposite side of the empire, in Bengal. It pictured the aftermath of the Battle of Plassey, which secured the East India Company's first substantial territorial foothold in India. Finally, in 1765, the fourth painting was hung, another allegory: *Britannia Distributing Laurels to the Victorious Generals*. It is worth noting that three out of four of the paintings were up before the war was even over. One could hardly find a better example of the Georgian era's "culture of now" than commemorating battles in a war that had not yet been won.[4]

The unusual size of the Pillared Saloon's paintings suggests that they—like the Rotunda's busts—were designed to be an immersive

Figure 3. Francis Hayman, *The Humanity of General Amherst*, 1760.
Oil on canvas. Gift of The Beaverbrook Foundation. Collection of
the Beaverbrook Art Gallery. Accession number 1959.92.

virtual-reality experience. The paintings were, quite literally, massive:
each canvas measured twelve by fifteen feet, large enough that the figures in the painting were life-sized. As a former scene painter at Goodman's Fields, Hayman was used to filling a large canvas. His style might
be considered a halfway point between the workaday craftsmanship of a
scene painter and the more virtuosic artistry prized by later history
painters like Benjamin West. For this commission, Hayman's theater
background was more visible than ever. Douglas Fordham argues that,
to many of Vauxhall's visitors, *The Triumph of Britannia* "must have
looked like an elaborate stage set." The idea that Hayman's paintings
functioned like a theatrical mis-en-scène resonates with Gillian Russell's

argument that venues like Vauxhall and the Pantheon represented "the sublime of Georgian sociability": "a theatre without actors, in which the audience could most successfully perform itself." In the Pillared Saloon, this performance unfolded in the middle of the two Indies.[5]

The placement of the paintings in the frames is noteworthy in this regard. Hayman's two allegories hung opposite one another in the frames farthest from the rotunda. Visitors would therefore enter the Pillared Saloon through the gothic portal, walk past the allegories, and then, at the heart of the saloon and on the precipice of the Rotunda, they would find themselves surrounded by the Indies. On nights when the Pillared Saloon was full of guests bedecked in silks and high heads and diamonds, and the room was lit by candlelight, the boundary between guests and paintings, fashionable world and the world of global empire, would have blurred. Looking across the room from wall to wall, visitors would have noticed that the scenes in America and India mirrored one another: the figures of Clive and Amherst strike identical poses, lining up almost exactly. While their gestures of benevolence would have been familiar from Charles Le Brun's *The Family of Darius before Alexander,* in this context the two men might easily be mistaken for masters of ceremony, extending their arms out to Vauxhall's guests in a gesture of welcome, their open palms beckoning visitors to venture farther into the Rotunda. The gesture connected the colonial battlefields the paintings portrayed to the scene of sociability in which they were displayed: Amherst and Clive had won their battles overseas and were now distributing the riches of the Indies in London.[6]

Just as pedagogical as Vauxhall's other installations, Hayman's paintings taught Londoners a new way of seeing the world and their place in it. London was the center of a worldwide empire that stretched from the East to the West Indies.

Diagnosing the (American) Crisis in Foote's *The Cozeners* and Burney's *Evelina*

T he gargantuan size of Francis Hayman's Seven Years' War paintings fit the national mood. Much like the annus mirabilis of 1759, the year of the war's end, 1763, took on "mythical" proportions at the very moment of its unfolding: it was a time of intense optimism and rare national unity. The trouncing of France inspired an outpouring of patriotism; and since European rivalry had long since spilled beyond Europe's borders, imperial expansion was embraced as a necessary piece of this victory. But within less than a decade, the meaning of 1763 proved unstable. Initially lauded as a triumph, it was now bemoaned as a catastrophe. The catalyst for this reversal was the burgeoning conflict with the thirteen colonies.[1]

In scholarship and popular history alike, it has been customary to think of the American Revolution as a regional affair, a family dispute between near neighbors across the pond. But, coming as it did on the heels of the Seven Years' War, this event was actually experienced—and in many ways is still best understood—as a global crisis in imperial affairs. In this chapter, I reappraise the historical conjuncture of the so-called American Crisis from the perspective of the Indies mentality by attending to the neglected global dimensions of the crisis's remediation in literature, news media, political pamphlets, and parliamentary discourse.[2]

The text I consider at greatest length is Samuel Foote's rarely discussed comedy, *The Cozeners*. The play is an ideal case study for several reasons. Perhaps more than any other playwright, Foote epitomizes the late Georgian "culture of now." One opening-night review of *The Cozeners* predicted a limited shelf life on this count: "The Cozeners bids fair to raise a laugh, whilst the persons and circumstances laughed at are in the recollection of the public." Much as *Saturday Night Live* comedians do in the present, Foote turned the day's news—everything from high politics to low gossip—into grist for his comedic mill. Extreme topicality is what makes his plays so difficult to read today. Imagine trying to make sense of a *SNL* skit 245 years from now! But the effort is worth making on multiple counts. Although scholars tend to treat Foote like a minor playwright, he was in fact one of the most commercially successful entertainment icons of his age. He was also a comic genius; and humor's reliance on shared common sense makes it an inimitable "key to the cultural codes and sensibilities of the past."[3]

Foote's jokes in *The Cozeners* turn on the assumption that theatergoers were adepts at thinking the two Indies together, enabling us to lift this systemic perspective on empire from the play. *The Cozeners*' explanatory power is further amplified by its profound intertextuality. As a strategy to evade censorship Foote produced meaning by recycling media: he cited printed texts like newspapers, pamphlets, and poems, as well as visual media like mezzotint prints. The play therefore opens a portal onto the era's wider mediascape, revealing the Indies mentality to be a shared rather than an idiosyncratic perspective. Moreover, *The Cozeners* is not just a play about the colonies: it connects the mounting imperial crisis to everyday life in London. To use Jameson's Althusserian vocabulary discussed in this book's Introduction, Foote's play bridges "lived experience and structure," teaching his audience to conceptualize the "structural coordinates" of their daily lives by bringing the whole of Britain's imperially stretched social formation into the field of the visible. Put another way, *The Cozeners* staged the Indies mentality.[4]

In eighteenth-century studies, apart from a few important exceptions, the histories of imperial expansion and metropolitan sociability continue to be written largely in isolation from one another. But Foote insisted that the history of the two Indies was playing out right in the heart of the metropole. Nor was he the only Georgian writer to stake this claim. In this chapter's final two sections I extend my argument's explanatory range from theatrical stage to novelistic page by turning to Frances Burney's debut novel, *Evelina*. This may seem like an odd choice for a book about empire and a chapter about theater—but this is precisely the point. *Evelina* is principally concerned with metropolitan sociability, and in the late 1770s this topic was impossible to attend to within a purely domestic framework. Burney must—and does—address the issue of overseas expansion. This may be news to some critics: Burney's engagement with imperial politics continues to be vastly underestimated in scholarship. I believe this has a lot to do with how we read so-called domestic novels. Although Burney deploys the same mixed-media citational practices used by Foote, these intertextual references are short, easily missed, and therefore often ignored by today's readers. But if we read *Evelina* in the same way I recommend we read *The Cozeners*—alert to highly condensed topical signifiers—it becomes evident that Burney goes out of her way to locate her critique of Georgian metropolitan sociability within a global-imperial frame of reference that includes India and the Atlantic world.[5]

Finally, at the same time that this chapter uses the Indies mentality to relearn the American Crisis, it also uses the American Crisis to fill in the contours of the Indies mentality, a reconstructed perspective I carry through the book's remaining chapters.

The American Crisis: A Global Crisis in Imperial Affairs

Although this chapter attempts to do much more than merely enumerate the myriad linkages between the two Indies during the so-called American Crisis, a straightforward inventory of these linkages is a useful place to begin. The East India Company's best-known cameo in the American War is of course the Boston Tea Party, an episode that features in *The Cozeners'* opening scene. As mentioned in this book's Introduction, American Patriots chose tea as an emblem of their grievances for a reason: Parliament sought to use the North American tea market to balance the Company's books in the wake of the Seven Years' War. An American tea boycott was wise in strategic as well as symbolic terms.

Jonathan Eacott calculates that in the years leading up to the American Crisis, customs revenue collected on Company goods accounted for as much as one-third of customs income, which in turn accounted for 11 percent of government income from 1750 to 1781. The percentage was much higher in the 1760s and early 1770s, when customs revenue on Company goods doubled as a result of growing demand in the Atlantic colonies, where tea was consumed at a high per capita rate. Tea was also crucial to the solvency of the Company, which had become a pillar of the national economy. The Company's conquest of Bengal had raised false hopes of a windfall in agricultural tax revenue, leading to speculation on its stock and the inflation of its dividend payouts to 12.5 percent. When the promised bonanza never materialized, the Company was dependent on old-fashioned commercial revenue from goods like tea in order to pay its shareholders, fund military expenses, and stay afloat. In short, a tea boycott posed a grave threat to the entire British economy.[6]

An ongoing debt crisis escalated this situation from dire to catastrophic. In 1763, British national debt amounted to more than £133 million, one and a half times the gross national product. A heated debate began: How might the empire be made to pay for a war fought to secure its existence? Steven Pincus argues that this policy debate concerned the British empire as a whole, not just North America. One side of the debate was dominated by George Grenville, first lord of the treasury and chancellor of the exchequer. In 1763, he began implementing "a coherent and global vision" for the political economy of empire, paying down the national debt with revenue extracted from the colonies. This "vision" was not altogether new. Revenue extraction was the basis of other European empires; and it was central to East India Company operations in Bengal. What *was* new was Grenville's decision to implement extractive policies in North America.[7]

At this juncture, American colonists began looking ominously toward India for a preview of what their future in an extractive imperial system might hold. They did not like what they saw. Eacott identifies dozens of pamphlets, treatises, and newspaper items decrying plans to turn America into a second India. The colonists thought of themselves as Britons: they didn't want to be treated like "*Asiatics,*" dragged unwillingly into a new "imperial constitution" that was at once unrepresentative and extractive. These fears referenced the East India Company as well as the government. Patriots like John Dickinson warned that the Company, having conquered Bengal, was redirecting its ambitions westward: "they now, it seems, cast their Eyes on *America,* as a new Theatre, whereon to exercise their Talents of Rapine, Oppression and Cruelty." Dire prognostications like this one were fueled by the Bengal famine of 1769–70, a humanitarian outrage caused by Company mismanagement that resulted in the deaths of millions. Because the famine was partly to blame for Bengal's diminishing agricultural revenues—there simply weren't enough farmers left alive to till all of Bengal's arable land—it also contributed to the Company's economic imbroglio. In 1772–73, Select and Secret parliamentary committees were charged with investigating the Company's conduct in Bengal; and their inquiries were covered extensively in the American press. In his best-selling pamphlet *Observations on the Nature of Civil Liberty* Richard Price instructs his readers: "Turn your eyes to India: There, more has been done than is now attempted in *America.* There ENGLISHMEN, actuated by the love of plunder and spirit of conquest, have depopulated whole kingdoms, and ruined millions of innocent people by the most infamous oppression and rapacity." The American rebellion was motivated partly by the desire to avoid a similar fate.[8]

So far we have tracked the pairing of the two Indies in parliamentary policy and political discourse. India became even more materially entangled in North American affairs when France joined the war in 1778, thereby extending the conflict to the subcontinent, where France and England were rivals. Remember, this is one reason for Cowper's juxtaposition of "India" and "th' Atlantic wave" in *The Task:* the battle for the thirteen colonies was fought partly in India. American Patriots evidently followed news from India as closely as Cowper did, since they named a warship after the East India Company's fiercest adversary, the Sultan of Mysore, Hyder Ali. Like *The Task,* London news coverage collapsed vast distances in space and time. Colonel William Baillie's defeat at the Battle of Pollilur (in Mysore) in September 1780 had no causal connection to General Charles Cornwallis's surrender at Yorktown in October 1781, but the slow speed of communication from India meant they were reported with near simultaneity, feeding fears of imperial collapse on a global scale.[9]

In short, the ties binding the two Indies together during the crisis were far from obscure. They were in fact so numerous that it would have been hard for the average Londoner to remain ignorant of them. At the same time, representing the empire's systemic ties in all their complexity was difficult. Take, for example, Edmund Burke's speech "On American Taxation," delivered on April 19, 1774, four months after the Boston Tea Party and three months before the premiere of *The Cozeners.* Although it would be another year before the slow-simmering dispute with the colonies would reach the boiling point of civil war, the catastrophic dimensions of the crisis were already coming into focus. Ominously, Burke warned: the "prosperity of this whole empire" was at stake. Much of the speech is taken up with Burke's attempt to find a rhetorical vehicle capable of bringing "this whole empire" into view. Just as we did, he turns to "Tea": given "its necessary connections" with both Indies, Burke explains, tea "is perhaps the most important object . . . of any in the mighty circle of our commerce." The circle is an apt metaphor because it captures the global scale of Britain's trade as well as its fragility: a single fracture, and a circle is a circle no more. Next, he tries the figure of an unstable architectural structure, an image Cowper uses as well: "It is through the American trade of tea, that your East-India conquests are to be prevented from crushing you with their burthen. They are ponderous indeed, and they must have that great country to lean upon or they tumble upon your head. It is the same folly that has lost you at once the benefit of the West and of the East." Without America as a load-bearing beam for the weight of colonial India to "lean upon," the whole imperial edifice will fall to pieces, "crushing" Britain beneath it. Burke also mixes the two metaphors, warning: "so insignificant an article as tea" has "shaken the pillars of a commercial empire that circled the whole globe!" When he lands on a new metaphor, "that infinite variety of paper chains by which you bind together this complicated system of the colonies," Burke seems overwhelmed not only by the complexities of systemic governance but also by the task of rendering those complexities visible in the field of representation.[10]

Burke's task would have been easier had he been a playwright. The theater afforded more complex representational strategies than other mediums. On the narrow boards of the stage, vast distances were prone to sudden collapse. This was accomplished through juxtaposition (as in the newspaper) and through simultaneity, or the layering of multiple references overtop a single character or scene. Foote utilizes both strategies in *The Cozeners* in order to convey the multiple structural coordinates of the ongoing imperial crisis. In the play's climactic scene, for example, he uses burnt-cork blackface makeup to racialize a character as both East and West Indian, then juxtaposes this racist figure with another complexly layered satire: a blackface macaroni who represents a joint sendup of the politician Charles James Fox and Lord Chesterfield's natural son, Philip Stanhope. The sum total of the tableau is a searing critique of the nation's aristocratic leadership, with the corrupting influence of colonial wealth pinpointed as the cause of its decline. My reading of *The Cozeners* builds up to this complicated scene. First, I begin by exploring how—and why—Foote used the representational tools at his disposal to stage the Indies.

Staging the Indies in London

In *Entertaining Crisis,* Daniel O'Quinn argues that audiences flocked to London's theaters during the American Crisis in search of political and social "critique." Night after night, Londoners sought and found at the theater a complex remediation of the present: a "pedagogical revelation of the historical forces tearing apart the empire." I would argue that this urge to diagnose speaks to the very nature of a crisis. From the Greek *krisis* (decision, determination, judgment), "crisis" entered the English lexicon to describe a very specific moment of judgment: the turning point when an illness tips irreversibly toward recovery or death. "Crisis" shares an etymological root with "critique"—the Greek verb *krinein,* meaning to sift, separate, sort, judge, distinguish, and decide. This etymology imbues "crisis" with a meaning distinct from its seeming cognates—"disaster," "catastrophe," "calamity," and so on. A crisis is not a fitting appellation for any period of turmoil; it refers specifically to an event whose effect is to sift out insight from chaos. A crisis produces new clarity of vision; it alters perspective. In Althusser's terminology, a crisis might even initiate a "*change of terrain,*" radically realigning the horizon of the visible. Carrying on the shift begun in 1763, the American Crisis cemented a new way of seeing the world: the Indies mentality. The crisis pushed writers like Burke, Foote, and Burney to search out representational technologies capable of figuring the complex, systemic ties that increasingly bound the two Indies to one another and the metropole.[11]

Foote is not conventionally associated with the American Crisis, but he should be. After all, he gave the most dramatic episode in the crisis its name: the phrase *Tea Party* was first used by Foote in the 1740s to advertise *Diversions of the Morning,* a solo show that bypassed the Licensing Act of 1737 by selling cups of tea instead of tickets. Thanks to his 1772 play *The Nabob,* which has become a touchstone in scholarship, Foote is very closely associated with critiques of East India Company rapacity and corruption. Why, then, does *The Cozeners* go virtually unread today? One answer lies in the geographical scope of the play's critique. *The Cozeners* is more difficult to read—and deploy in scholarship—than *The Nabob* because it flouts our conventional critical divisions between the two Indies. Although it premiered smack in the middle of the American Crisis and discusses the Boston Tea Party in its opening dialogue, the play insists that events unfolding in the thirteen colonies be understood in a frame of reference that includes the Company's conquests in Bengal. More complex still, the fallout from both colonial disasters plays out onstage right in the heart of the metropole.[12]

The Cozeners' central plotline inverts the scenario portrayed in *The Nabob.* In the latter, a newly monied Company official threatens to destabilize a landed family by forcibly marrying into it. In *The Cozeners,* the "ancient" Aircastle family is desperate to shed their provincial squiredom and acquire the trappings of London fashion by selling their land in order to fund their son Toby's marriage to a newly moneyed colonial heiress. With this setup, Foote once again blames empire for upsetting the nation's traditional socioeconomic hierarchy; but, unlike in *The Nabob,* this time both of the two Indies are implicated. When the Aircastles roll into London ("the only spot for people to thrive in," Mrs. Aircastle tells us), their search for "a wife, with a suitable fortune" leads them straight into the clutches of a con artist, Mrs. Fleece'em, who is freshly returned from the Boston Tea Party, which she helped instigate by delivering "speeches at Faneuil-Hall, and the Liberty-Tree." Fleece'em and her henchman Flaw propose to match Toby with the former's supposed "niece," whom they describe as an heiress "lately arrived ... from the Indies" with a fortune large enough "to purchase the sceptre of Poland." Audiences would have instantly recognized this plot as a thinly veiled reference to a high-profile scam that exploded into public view in the winter of 1773–74, when a con artist named Elizabeth Harriet Grieve was charged with fraudulently selling public offices and sinecures. Her boldest scam was duping Charles James Fox—a lord of the treasury, compulsive gambler, fashion icon, womanizer, and the beau monde's most notorious all-around *enfant terrible*—into courting a mixed-race West Indian heiress, Miss Phipps, said to be worth £150,000. Given that Fox's debts of honor purportedly totaled nearly £200,000, the match would have been a convenient one. Unfortunately for Fox, Miss Phipps was a fiction of Mrs. Grieve's own making, just like Mrs. Fleece'em's niece in *The Cozeners*. Foote uses a dose of racist humor to further highlight his source material: when Fleece'em is forced to produce a stand-in for her fictional East Indian heiress niece, she commands Marianne, the slave she has brought back with her from Boston, to play the part, thereby restoring an Afro-diasporic woman of color to the center of the scam.[13]

In 1774, Fox's involvement with Grieve was viral news: the subject of salacious pamphlets, satirical poems, countless newspaper paragraphs, and gossipy conversations. But *The Cozeners* is much more than just another recounting of the Grieve affair. Fox is certainly central to the play's satire—its original title was reportedly "The Young Cub"—but Foote also uses Fox as the basis for a much broader critique of the present. Although Foote's early solo shows were personal satires, in the 1770s he was a theater manager, charged with writing plays for the Haymarket's ensemble cast. A wider canvas pushed Foote to anchor his satirical "take-offs" of individuals to larger social targets. Fox's well-known high-stakes gaming addiction made him a veritable poster child for "aristocratic vice" and corruption; and his resignation from the ministry in April 1774 aligned him with critics of the government's American policy. He was thus an ideal launchpad for Foote's evisceration of the nation's aristocracy for its failure of leadership during the crisis. Crucially, as we shall see below, Fox's family history also enabled Foote to root his take on the current crisis in the Seven Years' War.[14]

This temporal frame of reference is one condition of possibility for the play's capacious geographical reach. Since the Seven Years' War was associated with imperial expansion in both Indies, connecting the dots between the war and current events in the thirteen colonies enabled Foote to portray the so-called American Crisis as a global crisis in imperial affairs. Even though the Seven Years' War is never explicitly named in *The Cozeners,* it looms large over the play. Indeed, the play is in many respects a loose rewriting of Foote's 1765 indictment of wartime corruption, *The Commissary.* Many aspects of the latter will seem familiar to readers of *The Cozeners. The Commissary* also features a female con artist, Mrs. Mechlin, who, like Mrs. Fleece'em, capitalizes on her victims' desires for upwardly mobile marriages. Mrs. Mechlin's prime victim is her tenant, the eponymous commissary Zachary Fungus, who "brought home from the wars a whole cart-load of money, and who . . . went there from very little better than a driver of carts." Wartime profiteering leaves Fungus flush with cash, but this is not enough to satisfy his ambitions: "not content with being really as rich as a lord, [he] is determin'd to rival them too in every other accomplishment." In this desire he is not alone. The play alludes to a host of "new-fangled gentry" and "upstart nobility" whose fortunes all derive from the Seven Years' War. In order to realize his ambitions and "set up for a gentleman," Fungus hires a veritable army of tutors to teach him the necessary "accomplishments": fencing, dancing, riding, music, and oratory. Snippets of Fungus's lessons provide opportunities for Foote to satirize several celebrities and enable him to stage a broader critique of the commodification of aristocratic masculinity in post-1763 London (a topic discussed in Chapter 2). Apart from a seat in Parliament, Fungus's crowning ambition is "matrimony": a "grand alliance" with "a person of rank and condition." This comical desire sets the play's central plot in motion: Mrs. Mechlin tries to con him into marrying her supposed "niece," Dolly, a former "stroller" whom she passes off as a "woman of fashion." The parallels with Mrs. Fleece'em could hardly be clearer—indeed, *The Cozeners* picks up right where *The Commissary* left off. Why revisit *The Commissary* in 1774? Because the moment it documents was not yet over. The nation had continued on the same road to ruin—paved with fashion, runaway consumerism, upward mobility, and corruption—on a collision course with crisis. Just as

Burke does in his speech "On American Taxation," Foote pinpoints the origins of the present crisis to the end of the Seven Years' War: "the unfortunate period of 1764."[15]

The most concrete way Foote tethers his portrayal of the so-called American Crisis in *The Cozeners* to its prehistory in the Seven Years' War is by invoking Charles James Fox's father, Henry Fox, obliquely in the play text. In the character of Mr. Aircastle (the part Foote performed himself), he drops the following line about a West Indian heiress from his youth: "I remember Miss Patty Plumb of Jamaica . . . they say her grandfather was transported for robbing a hen-roost." The line might seem inconsequential, but it packs a big satirical punch. First, the activity of "robbing a hen-roost" recalls Fox's family name. Second, by mentioning an heiress from Jamaica, Foote references the Grieve affair. Third, by displacing the robbery to a previous generation, Foote evokes Fox's father, who did indeed rob "a hen-roost" when he eloped with Fox's mother, Caroline Lennox, in 1744. At that time, Henry Fox was a rising political star. Still, Lennox's father, the duke of Richmond, couldn't countenance a great-granddaughter of Charles II marrying a commoner (even the son of a wealthy financier), so the couple eloped. After his illicit marriage, Henry Fox acquired his fortune (and a barony) by becoming the Seven Years' War's most brazen profiteer. As paymaster general of the Forces, Fox was the army's personal banker: he received enormous sums of money from the exchequer and dispersed them to payees. In between, he held the money in personal accounts. Over the course of the war, he siphoned off hundreds of thousands of pounds into private investments, including speculations on the London stock market. In 1761–62 he made upwards of £100,000 by lending the government its own money, using exchequer funds to speculatively buy up and sell subscriptions on government loans. In 1766–69 he used at least £115,000 in public money to speculate heavily on East India Company stock in hopes of "raising the dividend," an event which, when it did take place, would have sunk the Company—and the entire national economy—if not for a government bailout. All this was very profitable. During a single year his profits from "unofficial" investments reached £54,851, not including his official salary, which totaled £400,000 over eight years. The scale of his enrichment was cartoonish: he was a Zachary Fungus in the flesh.

His reputation for unscrupulousness was so bad that he made the so-called English nabobs look good in comparison. In April 1773 a supporter of Lord Clive wrote in the *Public Advertiser:* "Let us compare the acquisitions of his Lordship with the purer transactions on this Side the Globe. Let us remember the . . . sums accumulated by John Calcraft, Esq; or Henry Fox." Imperial corruption started at home.[16]

Foote's evocation of Henry Fox's cupidity in *The Cozeners* serves several purposes. To begin with, in 1774 public resentment against Fox had not yet cooled. The nation was in the midst of a debt crisis, and he still owed more than a half million pounds to the public. His death two weeks prior to the play's premiere added insult to injury in the sense that his debts would now never be repaid. Meanwhile, his son's high-stakes gaming addiction poured salt in the wound. In April and December 1773, Henry Fox reportedly paid Charles's debts of honor to the tune of £83,000 and £140,000, respectively. The magnitude of these losses alone was sufficient to provoke public outrage. Even more incendiary, Charles James Fox was a lord of the treasury; and the money he was frittering away so carelessly had been stolen by his father from the public. One newspaper item found ironic solace in the latter consideration: "The extravagance and profligacy of the Young Cub produces at least one good effect, since it obliges the Old Fox to refund part of the ill-gotten wealth which he had collected together." Another paper ironically suggested that Fox would be "admirably qualified" to help his father put together his still unsettled paymaster accounts, since "a great deal of money has passed through his hands, and if he cannot tell us of any method to get it in, he can at least name a thousand ways by which it has been disbursed, to the knowledge of many a worthy gambler." This was not meant in jest: Sutherland and Binney estimate Fox used £118,718 of the public's money to pay his sons' gaming debts. By reminding audiences of the source of Fox's money, Foote draws a connecting line between the Seven Years' War and the American Crisis, encircling his diagnostic critique of the nation's ills in a geopolitical frame of reference.[17]

Foote also uses Fox and his father as a launchpad for a sweeping critique of the nation's aristocratic leadership. A host of scholars have shown that the aristocracy was widely blamed for the fiascoes unfolding on both sides of the empire in the early 1770s. Donna Andrew argues that the "aristocratic vice" of gambling was particularly implicated in this judgment. If MPs ruined themselves through high-stakes gaming, they would certainly ruin the nation at large through mismanagement and corruption. Fox was one of the beau monde's most notorious gamblers; and his involvement with the con artist Mrs. Grieve concretized these fears. At her trial, Grieve implied that Fox was not her unwitting victim but rather her accomplice. After all, she lent him a £300 advance on her fictional heiress's fortune. Fox needed the money to feed his gaming habit; and Grieve needed Fox in order to pull off her scam. Horace Walpole explains: "Her other dupes could not doubt of her noblesse or interest, when the hopes of Britain frequented her house." The press likewise blamed Fox for the scam's success: "the sight of gilt chariots almost perpetually at her door seemed to confirm her account of her great interest and connections." Some newspapers even suggested that Grieve was actually selling public offices—not merely defrauding victims by pretending to do so—and that the places were to be supplied by Fox.[18]

In *The Cozeners,* Foote amplifies Fox's personal perfidiousness into a symptom of his class's decay by combining his send-up of Fox with a lampoon of another gentleman whose incompetence was also headline news: Philip Stanhope, 4th Earl of Chesterfield. In March 1774, the publication of Lord Chesterfield's *Letters* made him the laughing stock of the fashionable world. Written in an attempt to groom his natural son (also named Philip Stanhope) for a political career, his epistolary advice epitomized the style of effete elite masculinity increasingly coming under fire in the 1770s. Worst of all, Lord Chesterfield's efforts were laughably ineffectual: Stanhope was by all accounts "a perfect Tony Lumpkin." Frances Burney judged him to be "a mere *pedantic* booby," whose stilted manners were inferior to the natural nobility of the visiting South Sea Islander Omai. By combining his satire of Fox with a send-up of Stanhope in the character of Toby, Foote braids together multiple strands of discontent with the nation's aristocratic leadership. Paired with their fathers, Fox and Stanhope feature in an intergenerational drama about the failure of the aristocracy to reproduce itself as a ruling class.[19]

This drama was seen to a much greater degree than it was heard. When audiences went to the theater, they didn't just *listen* to dialogue—they also *watched* a live performance. A master of embodied comedy and spectacle, Foote's comic genius exceeded his facility with words. If we merely *read* his play texts, we therefore miss a great deal of what audiences loved about his plays. Recovering *The Cozeners'* intergenerational drama requires delving into Foote's intertextual engagement with visual media.

"Every man knows what he sees": Visual Satire in *The Cozeners*

Like the law in general in the Georgian era, the legal apparatus regulating censorship in particular was designed to protect the rich and powerful. Charles James Fox was both. In the weeks before *The Cozeners* was scheduled to premiere, the play text "was twice returned from the Lord Chamberlain's office for revision." Matthew Kinservik argues that censorship worked principally by encouraging "playwrights to produce unobjectionable texts," making an outright rejection of this kind unusual. Foote thus represents an exception to Kinservik's rule. The only way he managed to secure the Lord Chamberlain's permission to stage *The Cozeners* was by stripping the play's dialogue of objectionable references to Fox. As Sir Walter Scott (who was told about *The Cozeners* by an unnamed "Lady ——," who had seen the play "in her youth") explains: "no express allusion to Charles Fox was admitted." This is one reason *The Cozeners* is so difficult to read: its opacity is intentional. In order to evade censorship, Foote's allusions to Fox had to be subtle. Yet live comedy depends on instant recognition: the audience needs to be able to follow jokes without too much effort. Foote thus had a tightrope to walk. In this section, I show how Foote managed to get his satire of Fox licensed while still making it legible to audiences, a feat he accomplished by harnessing the power of intertextuality and meme-like media tropes. Only by reconstructing these complex representational strategies can we piece together how the two Indies figure into the play's critique.[20]

To begin with intertextuality, *The Cozeners* is steeped in the print archive of the Grieve affair. Most notably, the names of the play's protagonists are lifted from this coverage. The source for the Aircastle family name is a satirical poem entitled *Female Artifice, or Charles Fox Outwitted,* which recounts Mrs. Grieve's fraudulent sale of government sinecures:

> The bait is swallow'd—fools in plenty come—
> They stipulate—agreed—they pay their sum—
> Then building high their castles in the air,
> Leave other simpletons their fate to share.

Mrs. Fleece'em's name also derives from print media. At the height of the Grieve affair, the *London Evening Post* printed the following: "In a conversation a few days since between the young Cub and a great man in administration, about imposing new taxes in the next sessions of Parliament, the former was heard to say, 'Let us fleece on, the wool will grow again, for the flocks are made for the use of the shepherds.'" By naming his con artist Fleece'em, Foote cites this paragraph's critique of the parasitical state and makes Fleece'em a stand in for Fox. Indeed, Fox's spectral presence in Fleece'em's character is brought out of the shadows with her final lines: "if all who have offended like us, were like us produced to the public, much higher names would adorn the Old-Bailey Chronicle than those of poor Fleece'em and Flaw." In addition to recalling the *Beggar's Opera,* these lines echo another satirical poem, "An Heroic and Elegiac Epistle from Mrs. GRIEVE, in Newgate, to Mr. C— F—":

> O *Charles,* thou vicious Culprit of these Times!
> Were we rewarded justly for our crimes,
> Many who thrive about a gentle King
> Would in their Ribbons upon Tyburn swing.

Fleece'em's last words also offer a metacommentary on censorship. Even though Foote promises in the Prologue (reprinted in the daily papers) to guard the public from "Vice," the most egregious exemplar of vice cannot be "produced to the public" onstage—or, as Foote insinuates, in a courtroom. But by thematizing his authorial impotence, Foote undoes it: in the very act of narrating his inability to take off Fox, he conjures him. The *Morning Chronicle* confirms this achievement: "To supply the defects of the law, and to lash with poignant ridicule those vices which cannot be legally punished, is the peculiar province of the comic satirist. Mr. Foote, on the present occasion, has amply fulfilled this idea."[21]

Foote's most creative and efficacious strategy for avoiding censorship was to *show* his audience what he couldn't *tell* them. As Andrew Benjamin Bricker explains, visual satire slipped through the cracks of the Georgian legal apparatus for prosecuting libel, making it much less risky than verbal satire. Foote could therefore salvage his satire of Fox by relocating it from the play's dialogue to its visual content. Two and a half centuries later, this visual satire is difficult to reconstruct; after all, it was deliberately effaced from the play text, and performance is ephemeral by nature. Thankfully, the newspapers give away Foote's game by cueing playgoers to *look* for the play's satire: "'To catch the living manners as they rise,' is the immediate duty of the comic satirist. His [Foote's] pieces are like Hogarth's prints, every man knows what he sees; the ridicule is therefore felt with a much greater degree of sensibility; the obvious truth of it rivets conviction, and although Mr. Foote's are rather rough sketches than finished pictures, there is something so striking in his manner and so bold in his figuring, that he gives us an infinitely larger share of pleasure and instruction." This remarkable passage instructs audiences to watch *The Cozeners* in the same way they would look at a satirical print. Most forceful is the suggestion that "every man knows what he sees." Fox might be all but missing from the play's dialogue, but readers were effectively told: *you will know him when you see him.*[22]

Foote produces Fox to the public, "figuring" him boldly, by turning Toby into a macaroni caricature. The narrative vehicle for this transformation is a two-step makeover that occurs in acts 2 and 3, prompted by Mrs. Aircastle's desire to make her son more fashionable and thus more desirable to his East Indian bride. In performance, Toby's post-makeover entrances were accentuated by Foote, who, in the character of Mr. Aircastle, delivered the lines: "Lord, Mrs. Aircastle, how you have altered the boy!" and "I tell you the boy is an absolute sight." Audiences were thus prompted to look long and hard at Toby; and it behooves us to do the same—or, at least, to try to reconstruct his appearance. Thankfully, the play's dialogue drops some breadcrumbs. After Toby's first makeover, Mr. Aircastle remarks "why, his face is as long as a fiddle stick! and then he has a bundle at his back, as big as a child!" Later, we learn that Toby's jacket is so wide-cut it "dangle[s] like a parcel of petticoats." The lengthiest description of Toby's new look occurs in a dialogue between his parents:

AIR. His whole figure is just like a spider, nothing but legs; a mere couple of stilts!—And then that top to his wig, my dear child—

MRS. AIR. Gives a fashionable turn to his face; and then adds to the height.

AIR. It has indeed, my soul, A prodigious happy effect.—A block, popping out of a hair-cutter's window, up two pair of stairs in the Strand.—And then that bunch at his back—

These clues are sufficient to puzzle out the crux of Toby's transformation. An exaggeratedly wide-cut coat, an enormous wig worn in a club or "bunch" on his back, and a high head culminating in a remarkable "top": Toby is dressed like a "macaroni," the 1760–70s incarnation of the perennial figure of the fop or beau.[23]

This was a stroke of genius, for it enabled Foote to conjure Fox onstage visually in a manner that the Lord Chamberlain could not have predicted by reading the play text. A macaroni was an excellent satirical vehicle for conjuring Fox, as he was well known as one of the very first macaronis—the "The Original Macaroni," to quote the title of Mary and Matthew Darly's 1772 caricature of him. Given all this, London playgoers might very well have recognized a caricature of Fox in Toby's act 2 makeover. Had any doubts lingered, Toby's act 3 makeover would banish them. As part of a multilayered racist joke whose complexities I unpack below, burnt cork is smeared across Toby's face and dabbed "on each of his eyebrows," thereby burlesquing Fox's most distinctive personal traits: a prominent five-o'clock-shadow and bushy eyebrows (Fox's nickname in Whig circles was "The Eyebrow"). The ever-helpful newspapers also cue playgoers to look for Fox in act 3: "A correspondent says, Mr. Foot's [sic.] New Piece was received last night with great applause. The character of C— F—, so justly expected by the public, was unfortunately bought off. The expectation of the audience was, however, kept up till the 3d Act, by an assurance that the honourable gentleman's finances could only afford to pay half price, and that he would appear towards the conclusion of the piece: but the dice of last night were propitious, it is supposed." Like Mrs. Fleece'em's final lines, this review trades in a variety of double-speak that would have been familiar to Georgian readers. On the one hand, the review implies that Fox's satire was "bought off," a practice common enough in the daily papers, where omission fees represented an important revenue stream. On the other hand, the review reports a humorous "assurance" delivered during the play—perhaps, we might speculate, by Foote—that Fox would still "appear towards the conclusion of the piece." Although it is then implied that Fox did not in fact appear—his "dice . . . were propitious," so he could afford to pay off Foote in full—this assurance is delivered with a nod and a wink. In the very same sentence, the paper tells the audience precisely when the "character of C— F—" *does* appear: in the play's "3d Act." When Foote uses blackface makeup to give his macaroni caricature bushy eyebrows onstage in act 3, Fox is conjured before the audience's eyes.[24]

Ultimately, Foote's macaroni caricature aimed at a larger target than Fox, who, we must remember, was only the penultimate target of *The Cozeners.* The macaroni fad's highly specific periodization enabled Foote to root his take on the American Crisis in the imperial expansion of the previous decade. Macaroni fashion was closely associated with the years directly following the Seven Years' War. Essentially an exaggeration of Continental styles, the macaroni trend was imported to England by young gentlemen like Fox returning from their grand tours, an institution put on hold during the war and resumed after its conclusion. As the *Macaroni and Theatrical Magazine* explains: "This dish was far from being universally known in the country till the commencement of the last peace." Only after peace with France had been established could the first generation of "macaronis" visit the Continent and come home outfitted in the style of their nation's recent enemy. Foote deploys the figure of the macaroni in *The Cozeners* to pinpoint 1763 as a watershed moment when the nation's traditional values, hierarchies, and fashions suddenly went haywire.[25]

In this book's Prelude we saw that Britain's ascension to the leadership of the global economy during the Seven Years' War was felt at home in the form of an economic boom that very quickly remade the texture of everyday life. In London and provincial cities, new venues of public amusement sprung up like mushrooms after a rainfall. Teresa Cornelys's Carlisle House, Almack's, the Pantheon, and Cox's Museum all opened during or after the war, forever altering London's entertainment land-scape. The dizzying pace of change is captured in Tobias Smollett's 1771 novel *The Expedition of Humphrey Clinker.* As Charlotte Sussman has argued, this novel helps "make visible the growing connectedness of English and colonial society" by documenting the domestic changes wrought by overseas colonialism. When the novel's country squire, Mat-thew Bramble, visits London for the first time in years he is flabbergast-ed: "London is literally new to me." The city, he finds, is flooded by a rising "tide of luxury" that has swept even "journeymen tailors, serving men, and Abigails" into the "gayest places of public entertainment," where they are "disguised like their betters" and pass as "fashionable fig-ures." "In short," he concludes, "there is no distinction or subordination left." Foote similarly indicts "places of public entertainment" as perni-cious sites of class masquerade in *The Cozeners.* Mrs. Fleece'em fools her victims into believing she is "is able to procure posts, places, preferments of all conditions of sizes" by having Flaw spread the word at "plays, op-eras, masquerades, and Pantheons, not to mention . . . most of the clubs, and coteries." To be clear, Foote was no enemy of fashion: he was a noto-rious fop in his youth, and by 1774 he was a fixture in London's most elite circles. The "real" beau monde is therefore not his target. What con-cerned him was the parroting of elite sociability further down the social ladder and the inundation of fashionable venues of amusement with pleasure-seekers from the middle and lower classes—concerns echoed by Burney a few years later in *Evelina.*[26]

The figure of the macaroni indexed precisely these fears. When macaroni style debuted in England it was outré, a mark of high fashion. It was therefore associated with aristocratic dissipation and excess, most especially gambling and promiscuity. Before long, though, the fad start-ed to become passé—even gauche—a sign of nouveau riche pretension. Dissipated sons of peers like Fox may have inaugurated the trend, but when even servants could afford to purchase a *high-street* version of the look, it lost its initial cultural capital and became a sign of class climb-ing. Macaronis were therefore closely aligned with anxieties about the commodification of aristocratic masculinity through the selling of gen-tlemanly fashions and accomplishments. Several of the macaroni carica-tures produced by the Darlys take aim at the sale of accomplishments parodied in *The Commissary*. Prints like "A Dancing Master Macaroni" and "The Catgut Macaroni" recall Zachary Fungus's army of tutors (his music master was even named "Doctor Catgut"). Another Darly print, *A Mungo Macaroni* (Figure 4), features Julius Soubise, the Afro-British

A MUNGO MACARONI.

Publish'd according to Act by MDarly 39 Strand Sept'r 10 1772

Figure 4. M. Darly, *A Mungo Macaroni*, 1772. Etching on laid paper. Courtesy of The Lewis Walpole Library, Yale University.

assistant of celebrity fencing master Domenico Angelo, whom I discuss at length in the following chapter. Soubise was a lightning rod for anxieties about the commercialization of elite masculinity, as *A Mungo Macaroni* attests. Moreover, this print exemplifies how the macaroni's competing significations—of aristocratic excess *and* imposture—could sit alongside one another, even within a single image. Although Soubise's race is signaled visibly via skin color, the image is not a racist caricature. Instead, it replicates an illustration from Angelo's fencing manual, a veritable textbook in the body techniques of aristocratic masculinity. "A Mungo Macaroni" therefore pictures Soubise as both insider *and* outsider. Likewise, the print portrays the macaroni as a symbol of elite breeding *and* class climbing.[27]

Foote also exploits the macaroni's multiple meanings in *The Cozeners*. While Fox was the epitome of fashion, vice, and excess, Stanhope was a pathetic example of aristocratic emulation gone awry. By caricaturing these men together in the character Toby, Foote lampoons both sides of macaroni character. In order to grasp the full depth of this satire, we need to look more closely at Foote's intertextual engagement with a specific macaroni mezzotint published in June 1774, just a month before the play's premiere, *Welladay Is This My Son Tom* (Figure 5). In this mezzotint, an uncouthly dressed "honest farmer" is shocked by the appearance of his son, Tom. Sent "to Town," Tom has shed his rustic simplicity in favor of full macaroni attire from the top of his laughably high-wigged head to the tip of his buckled heels. Toby's makeover reproduces the central drama of this image; and the bumpkinish Mr. Aircastle's above-quoted commentary on Toby's new look reads like a veritable description of it. The likeness is even more striking when we turn to the visual source of the macaroni pictured in *Welladay Is This My Son Tom*, another popular mezzotint published the previous summer entitled *The Macaroni, a Real Character at the Late Masquerade* (Figure 6). When Mr. Aircastle comments on the elongation of Toby's legs and face—"why, his face is as long as a fiddle stick" and "His whole figure is just like a spider, nothing but legs; a mere couple of stilts!"—he seems to be referring to these images. We might even speculate that actual "stilts" were used on stage to create a similar elongated effect. Or the joke could be a reference to Foote's wooden leg, whose comic potential he exploited routinely. In any case, both

Figure 5. R. Sayer and J. Bennett, *Welladay, Is This My Son Tom,* 1774.
Mezzotint with etching on laid paper. Courtesy of The Lewis Walpole Library,
Yale University.

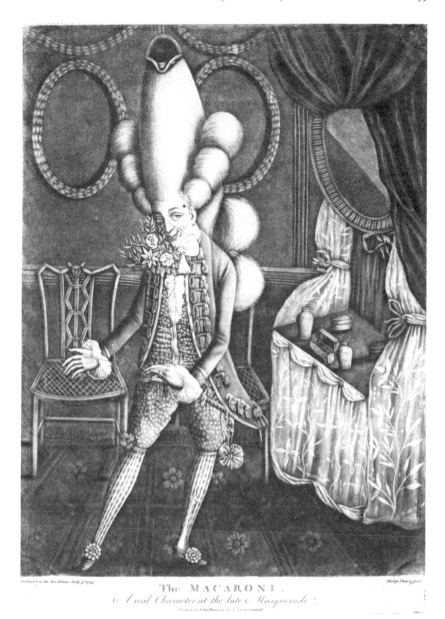

Figure 6. Philip Dawe, *The Macaroni: A Real Character at the Late Masquerade*, 1773. Mezzotint on laid paper. Courtesy of The Lewis Walpole Library, Yale University.

macaroni prints would have been familiar to London playgoers, who would have seen them displayed in print-shop windows.[28]

It may seem like a stretch to argue that Foote referenced specific mezzotints onstage; but scholars like Daniel O'Quinn and David Francis Taylor have taught us that print satire and drama were linked by a well-trafficked intertextual highway. Peter McNeil suggests that a multimedia approach is particularly crucial for understanding the pop-culture phenomenon of the macaroni, which cycled through the theater, visual satire, print discourse, and "real life" sociable interactions. By staging a visual tableau of *Welladay Is This My Son Tom,* Foote cites its critique of the rise of fashion and urbanization post-1763. He also uses its drama of intergenerational rupture to highlight the father-son pairs he parodies throughout *The Cozeners* (the Foxes and the Stanhopes)—the implication being that the aristocracy has failed to reproduce itself as a ruling class. The play's climactic penultimate scene pinpoints the corrupting influence of imperial expansion as the grounds for this failure, as I show in the next section.[29]

A Blackface Macaroni

The most memorable episode in *The Cozeners* occurs during act 3, scene 2, when the Aircastles' desire to meet Toby's East Indian bride leads Mrs. Fleece'em to command her slave or servant, Marianne, to play the part, thereby setting up a bed trick with a racist twist. Although this scene has been forgotten today (even by Georgian theater scholars), it was singled out for its comic genius well into the nineteenth century. In 1828, Sir Walter Scott described it as "one of the numerous hits that will be lost to posterity." It therefore deserves as much critical attention as the oft-discussed screen scene in Sheridan's *School for Scandal.* Whereas the latter scene captures Georgian anxieties about fashion and sociability, *The Cozeners* fuses such domestic misgivings to a global-imperial frame of reference that includes both of the two Indies, which are braided together from the scene's setup through its culmination.[30]

The episode begins with a lampoon of nabobery. In act 2, scene 1, the Aircastles agree to pay Flaw a finder's fee for Mrs. Fleece'em's niece: £5,000 plus "a few diamonds." Tillman Nechtman has established that diamonds were a hallmark of nabobery, as Company officials used them to transport their illegally acquired fortunes home. Foote doubles down on this implication when Flaw hints that the Aircastles should "purchase at the same time some presents for the young lady." After Lord Clive accepted a *jaghire* worth £27,000 per annum from Mir Jafar in 1759, "presents" became a byword for East Indian corruption. When Mrs. Aircastle is hesitant to bring a gift the "first time" she meets her prospective daughter-in-law, Flaw echoes Lord Clive's testimony before the Select Committee. "From time immemorial," Lord Clive testified, "it has been the custom of that Country, for an inferior never to come into the presence of a superior without a present." "Always the rule in the East," Flaw assures Mrs. Aircastle, "you never approach a superior without a suitable present." In case audiences missed the hint, Mr. Aircastle chimes in: "why, fool, that is the way the Nabobs have got all their wealth."[31]

In addition to building on his takedown of Clive from *The Nabob*, Foote also extends the geographical range of his earlier critique in *The Cozeners* by emphasizing the fungibility of the two Indies as a corrupting influence on the metropole. The most sensational token of this fungibility is Marianne's double racialization as a British actress playing an enslaved diasporic African playing an ambiguously racialized East Indian. As explained above, the setup for this double racialization is the Aircastles' eagerness to gift their soon-to-be daughter-in-law with diamonds as per Flaw's suggestion, requiring Fleece'em to produce her niece in the flesh:

> FLAW: . . . Who the deuce have you got?
>
> MRS. FL: Why, I considered that as a very ticklish point; it would be dangerous to trust, and difficult to find in this town a suitable subject: Don't you think that the black girl I brought with me from Boston—
>
> FLAW: The negro? zounds, her complexion will betray her at once!

In his discussion of *The Cozeners*, Sir Walter Scott identifies Marianne as the locus of the scene's humor: "Lady X tells me that, in her

youth, the laugh was universal so soon as the black woman appeared."
Fleece'em's attempt to pass off a "black girl . . . from Boston" as an heiress
from India is supposed to be funny on multiple counts, all of which index the racial (and racist) dimensions of the Indies mentality. To begin
with, there is the insinuation that the Aircastles are so hopelessly foolish
that they will not be able to tell the difference between a servant and an
heiress, or a West Indian and an East Indian. The joke can also be inter-
preted as yet another dig at nabobs, the implication being that Company
officials and their offspring are interchangeable with colonial subjects,
presumably as a result of exposure to the sun or miscegenation. The
term "East Indian" captures this ambiguity: it was used to describe both
Britons who resided in India and South Asians. Such slipperiness makes
it impossible to tell whether Mrs. Fleece'em's fictional niece has an Indian or a European mother, although Foote's penchant for racist humor
makes the former fictional scenario more likely. In that case, the Aircastles' presumed inability to distinguish between East and West Indians
might also convey a touch of metatheatrical humor: as I explain in the
next chapter, the same cosmetics were used to signify characters from
both Indies on the London stage. Finally, Mrs. Fleece'em's recourse to
Marianne reverses Foote's original substitution of an East Indian heiress
for Miss Phipps, such that the scene onstage now mirrors Fox's misad-
venture more precisely.[32]

By implicating Fox in this scene's racist humor, Foote sutures his
indictment of the corrupting influence of colonial wealth to his critique
of the nation's aristocratic leadership. This is accomplished in a number
of ways beyond Fox's mere involvement with Mrs. Grieve. Toby's imminent meeting with his fiancée is the occasion for his second makeover,
when, as mentioned above, Foote embellishes his macaroni caricature
with Fox's two signature features: a five-o'clock-shadow and cartoon-
ishly thick eyebrows. Remarkably, this transformation occurs onstage:

MRS. AIR: . . . You, doubtless, madam, know the taste of your
niece; may we hope that Toby has any chance of succeeding?
. . . But as to his figure, madam; do you apprehend it will
strike her? Toby, hold up your head!

MRS. FL: I can see no reason against it: Indeed, the young gentleman has rather a fairer complexion than what she has been commonly used to; the natives of India, from their climate, have rather a sallower hue.

MRS. AIR: True, madam.

MRS. FL: But, if necessary, that may be easily altered by art; some saffron, or snuff, just skimmed over his face—

MRS. AIR: Quickly!

AIR: I have a box of Scotch in my pocket: It may be done in an instant.

MRS. AIR: Their hair, too, is most commonly dark; but a little German blacking here on each of the eyebrows—

TOBY: If a burnt cork will do, I have one in my pocket.

Using blackface makeup, Foote conjures Fox right before the audience's eyes. Given the hurdles imposed by the Lord Chamberlain's censorship, this moment must have been a triumph. Audiences also found it funny on several counts. To begin with, the gag capitalizes on the lowest, least sophisticated form of racist humor: the implication that it is an insult to be Black. At the same time, the joke's barb was custom sharpened for Fox, who was maligned throughout his lifetime for his unusually dark complexion. Junius called him "Black Boy" and Edward Gibbon mocked him as a "black collier." Fox's skin tone invariably featured in retellings of his involvement with Mrs. Grieve. Walpole, for example, writes that the scam artist "once persuaded him [Fox] that, as Miss Phipps liked a fair man, and as he was remarkably black, that he must powder his eyebrows." A satirical poem mentions a similar detail:

> Will not your vengeance visit Arthur's Saint,
> And singe those eye-brows—I did only paint?
> Blast that black face—which I with pains improv'd;
> Which without aids like these no nymphs had lov'd.

Hic Niger est

Robbed between Sun and Sun

Figure 7. Anonymous, *Robbed Between Sun and Sun,* 1774. Engraving and
etching on paper. © The Trustees of the British Museum.

Foote recycles this incident from the textual archive of the Grieve incident, visualizing its crude racist humor for added comic effect.[33]

Foote's blackening of Toby's face onstage also contributes in crucial ways to his assassination of Fox's character. Once again, recovering
this element of the play requires an intertextual engagement with visual
satire. In a print entitled *Robbed Between Sun and Sun* (Figure 7), published six months prior to the premiere of *The Cozeners,* Fox, his brother
Stephen, and their father Henry are portrayed as anthropomorphized
foxes. Published on the heels of aforementioned rumors that Henry paid
off Charles's gaming debts to the tune of £140,000, the print pictures the
latter holding an open palm to his father, presumably asking for money,
while he uses his other hand to furtively steal his purse. Charles's motive
can be found on the floor in the form of dice, a dice box, and a rulebook
for games of cards. Encircling his legs is another motive of sorts: a chain
that is gripped by a black demon, presumably vice or greed. In sum, the

print is a damning judgment on Charles's character. Race is mobilized to convey this verdict. A caption above his head reads "Hic Niger est," or "He is black," an epigram that simultaneously cites Charles's personal appearance and condemns his moral character. Race is inseparable from morality here. While we tend to associate moral vocabularies of Blackness with the early modern period, Blackness's biblical connotations of evil were residual well into the eighteenth century. These residual connotations are fused with emergent Enlightenment ideas about race in the print's title, which invokes climatic theories of race, playing on their implication about the generational mutability of character.[34]

Like this print, *The Cozeners* interweaves the metropole and colonies in its indictment of Fox's character. Turning his caricature of Fox into a blackface macaroni is one way in which Foote accomplishes this interweaving. Macaronis were already symbols of aristocratic dissipation. By adding blackface, Foote at once visualizes the macaroni's moral decay (playing off Blackness's residual associations with evil) and ties this decay to the corrupting influence of colonial wealth (playing off Blackness's dominant racial connotations). The colonies and metropole are further intertwined in the scene's climax, when Toby brings his gift of diamonds to his East/West Indian bride, who is lying in bed, her face obscured by curtains. From one angle, this scene can be viewed as a topical comment on Fox's politics: an increasingly vocal supporter of the American Patriots, he rushes into the arms of his new political bedfellows, who are lampooned in the form of a Black enslaved woman. At the same time, the tableau Foote paints with this scene also needs to be viewed in a less strictly allegorical light. While "aristocratic vice" generated a near-constant stream of commentary in the 1770s, aristocrats could not be criticized openly. Censorship thus necessitated creative representational strategies, as Andrew, O'Quinn, Michael Gamer, and Terry Robinson have shown. Chief among these strategies was juxtaposition, as the newspaper coverage of *The Cozeners*' censorship evinces. Fox was never named in newspaper stories about the play's licensing battle. Instead, a seemingly unrelated paragraph about him was published in visual proximity to the censorship story, so that Fox and the play were juxtaposed on the newspaper page. For example, the *London Evening Post* placed reports about *The Cozeners*' censorship and Fox in the same vertical column (Figure 8). The item about Fox

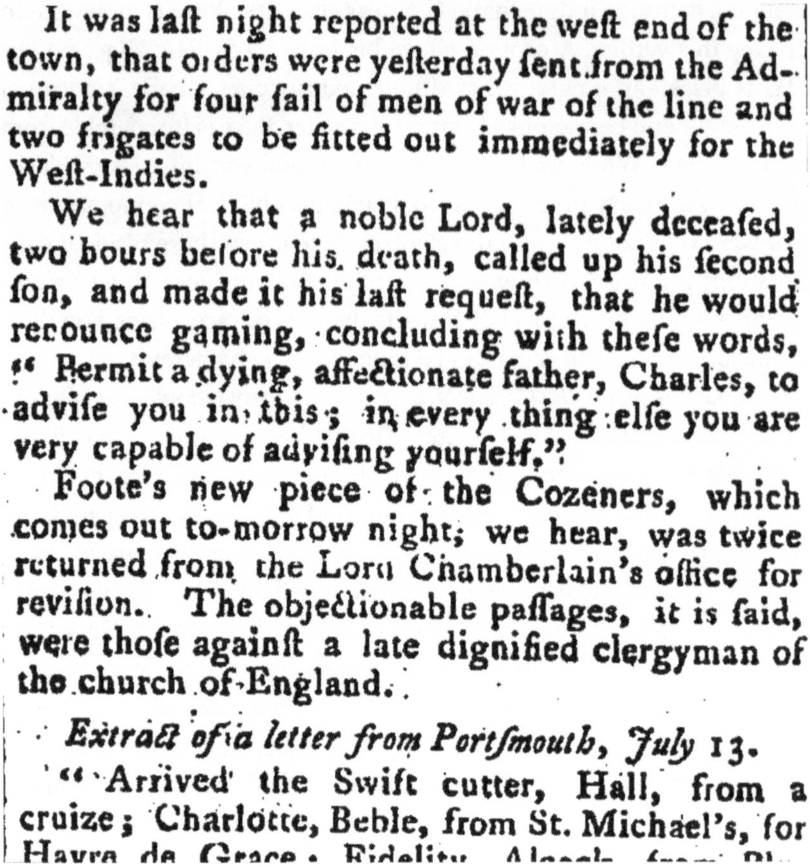

It was laſt night reported at the weſt end of the
town, that orders were yeſterday ſent from the Ad-
miralty for four ſail of men of war of the line and
two frigates to be fitted out immediately for the
Weſt-Indies.

We hear that a noble Lord, lately deceaſed,
two bours before his death, called up his ſecond
ſon, and made it his laſt requeſt, that he would
renounce gaming, concluding with theſe words,
'' Permit a dying, affectionate father, Charles, to
advife you in this ; in every thing elſe you are
very capable of adviſing yourſelf.''

Foote's new piece of the Cozeners, which
comes out to-morrow night; we hear, was twice
returned from the Lord Chamberlain's office for
reviſion. The objectionable paſſages, it is ſaid,
were thoſe againſt a late dignified clergyman of
the church of England.

Extract of a letter from Portſmouth, July 13.

'' Arrived the Swift cutter, Hall, from a
cruize ; Charlotte, Beble, from St. Michael's, for
Havra de Grace, Fidelity, Aleach, from Pl

Figure 8. *London Evening Post,* July 12, 1774, Issue 2859.
© British Library Board.

even references his father's death (which had occurred twelve days earlier),
thereby anticipating Foote's dual focus on father and son.[35]

Just like the newspapers, the penultimate scene in *The Cozeners*
uses juxtaposition to imply what Foote cannot say outright in the play's
dialogue. The scene does this by bringing multiple satirical targets into
suggestive proximity. When a blackface macaroni carrying a present
of diamonds approaches an American slave passing as an East Indian
heiress, the effect is a highly condensed tableau that brings all of the
geographically dispersed structural coordinates of the present crisis

simultaneously into view. The two Indies and the metropole collide on the world of the stage. While it has taken the entirety of this chapter to unpack and decompress the individual components of this scene's complex tableau, Georgian theatergoers would have grasped the many dimensions of Foote's satire with much less effort. They were already primed to view the play through the lens of the Indies mentality—a habitual way of looking that the play in turn reinforced.

After diagnosing the crisis, Foote engineers its cure: catharsis. The blackface macaroni Toby is purged from stage. When he pulls back the bed curtains and is shocked by the sight of Marianne's face—which would have been painted in blackface, mirroring Toby's own post-makeover look—Toby exclaims "Hey! what is this? Lord have mercy on me! she is turned all of a sudden as black as a crow! sure as can be, a judgment for forsaking poor Betsy," his country sweetheart. Toby's invocation of the moral connotations of Blackness is apt, for these lines represent a damning judgment on Fox's character that echoes the verdict of "Robbed Between Sun and Sun." When Fox's blackface stand-in is comically chased offstage by Marianne, one can only imagine that his rout was greeted with abundant applause.[36]

The Black Hole of Ranelagh? Empire and Sociability in Burney's *Evelina*

Like Foote, Burney is rarely associated with the American Crisis but should be. Her debut novel, *Evelina,* was published in January 1778, less than six months after Burgoyne's defeat at Saratoga and a month before France formally entered the conflict. Yet this context has figured little in scholarship on *Evelina*. Like the rest of Burney's oeuvre, *Evelina* has been analyzed within a domestic frame of reference that emphasizes home and nation over politics and empire. While the novel's subtitle indicates that it tells the *History of a Young Lady's Entrance into the World*, this is not the world of global empire, but rather the "World" of London public life. There are signs that Burney scholarship is beginning to expand in new directions. Ruth Scobie and Megan Woodworth have recently recovered neglected aspects of Burney's political engagements, including overseas exploration. Building on this work, I argue that *Evelina* needs to be understood in the political context of the 1770s. *Evelina* and *The Cozeners* might seem like an odd pairing, but they were written in the midst of the same seismic crisis in imperial affairs, and therefore share many of the same sociopolitical anxieties. Both are centrally concerned with class climbing and the erasure of rank distinctions in metropolitan spaces of amusement; and both harshly criticize styles of masculinity deemed dangerous to the nation. Foote's attack on effete macaroni masculinity in his satire of Stanhope finds its parallel in Burney's Mr. Lovel, a macaroni class climber. Meanwhile, Foote's attack on aristocratic excess in his send-up of Fox is mirrored in the dangerously dissipated Lord Merton, a drunken gamer and libertine who epitomizes aristocratic vice.[37]

It would be a mistake to dismiss the consonance between Burney's novel and Foote's plays as accidental. As already discussed, Foote was an entertainment icon in the 1760s and 1770s, the formative decades of Burney's youth. Margaret Anne Doody tells us that "Burney was fond of Foote's plays." This biographical fact finds clear expression in *Evelina,* when the novel takes us to the Haymarket. Evelina's visit to Foote's theater is a short and relatively fleeting incident in the novel, but it is jam-packed with politics. Of particular significance is the evening's program: she sees two of Foote's original productions, *The Minor* and *The Commissary.* The latter will already be familiar from earlier discussion in this chapter. The former strikes many of the same notes: it features the son of a mercantile family desperate to erase his low origins and climb the social ladder to gentility. Both of these plays must have been carefully chosen by Burney, as they resonate perfectly with her own critique of class pretension. Readers would have picked up on this resonance from the mere name-dropping of the plays' titles, which were cultural touchstones.[38]

Evelina's plot explores the same theme as these plays: the thin dividing line between class mobility and class pretension. The novel tells the story of a young woman raised in rural retirement who is unexpectedly thrown into London public life, where she must quickly learn the ways of "the World" without succumbing to them. The daughter of a baronet but unrecognized as such, Evelina must succeed on her own merits. Navigating a range of suitors who epitomize varying styles of masculinity, Evelina must discover—and endear herself to—the novel's ideal man, Lord Orville. In the process, she must differentiate herself from a host of class climbers and social pretenders, including her own mortifying middle-class cousins, the Brangtons, who mistakenly believe that the money generated by their father's silversmith business qualifies them as polite society. In short, *Evelina*'s portrait of 1770s London is entirely harmonious with the state of affairs portrayed in Smollett's *Expedition of Humphrey Clinker*, as well as *The Commissary, The Minor*, and, of course, *The Cozeners*. By naming two of these plays in her novel, Burney cites their critique. The citation is highly condensed but powerful, and it would not have gone unnoticed by contemporary readers trained to look for and unpack the slightest intertextual reference. Moreover, Burney's intertextual nod to Foote is doubly metatextual in the sense that she simultaneously cites Foote's plays *and his method of intertextual citation.*

The story of the "rise of the novel" may be one of the most enduring critical narratives we tell about the eighteenth century, but it is also one of the most misleading. In the 1770s, the novel was not the preeminent form of literary production in England; rather, that distinction goes to the theater. This is important insofar as the Georgian stage relied on a style of signification very different from the regime of "realist" representation that would become hegemonic with the Victorian novel. Theatergoers-turned-novelists like Burney—and, I would add, Jane Austen—exported the theater's representational strategies to the novelistic page. Reading *Evelina* past critically, according to its own interpretive protocols, therefore requires taking the reading methods we have honed on *The Cozeners* and bringing them to bear on Burney's novel. Doing so will illuminate facets of the novel that have long remained in shadow. For example, critics still struggle to come to terms with the novel's brutal treatment of its aberrant characters Madame Duval and Lovel. Although John Hart has shown that many of the novel's most violent scenes are lifted straight from mezzotint caricatures that depict English sailors—think Captain Mirvan (the husband of Evelina's London guardian)—in the act of assaulting macaronis, Hart is rarely cited in Burney scholarship. When we recall that recycling macaroni mezzotints was Foote's modus operandi in *The Cozeners*, Hart's argument takes on even more significance: Burney borrowed this page from Foote's playbook, transferring Foote's method from stage to page.[39]

When we read Burney's novel in the same way we read Foote's plays, *Evelina* overflows the domestic container it has been put in by critics. Take, for example, one of the novel's many debates about where to go for an evening's entertainment in London. Easily mistaken for a simple statement on metropolitan entertainment venues, this conversation also taps straight into the heart of imperial geopolitics. The exchange in question occurs in the latter half of volume 1. Having already visited and tired of one venue of public amusement (the Pantheon) and debated the merits of two others (Cox's Museum and the Opera), Evelina's party finally settles on a trip to the Ranelagh pleasure gardens. This decision is promptly overruled by the irascible Captain Mirvan, who "was quite in a passion at the proposal, and vowed he would sooner go to the *Black-hole in Calcutta*." With this line, Captain Mirvan compares London's most elegant pleasure garden to a colonial atrocity. The Black Hole of Calcutta was a tiny room where a hundred Britons were imprisoned overnight by Siraj ud-Daulah, the Nawab of Bengal, in 1756 during the leadup to the Seven Years' War. While the details of the incident remain unclear, dozens of the prisoners reportedly died of suffocation and heat exhaustion. Their deaths were publicized in England by John Zephaniah Holwell, whose daughter was an intimate friend of the Burney family.[40]

Burney's reference to this atrocity may be judged inconsequential when measured by dint of mere words, but under this deceptively tiny tip, an iceberg of colonial history lies concealed. Excavating it requires a reading method attentive to the potent signifying power of even the smallest citational reference. Unfortunately, our current interpretive strategies do not fit this bill. This is certainly true of our discipline's most well-known method for making sense of empire's brief appearances in domestic novels: Edward Said's "contrapuntal reading." Said's canonical reading of Austen's *Mansfield Park* famously focuses on a "mere half-dozen passing references" to the West Indian plantation that keeps the novel's English country house afloat, references that bear more than a passing resemblance to Captain Mirvan's remark. For Said, the brevity of these references to Antigua are symptomatic of a problem, even a short-coming, on Austen's part. His reading of *Mansfield Park* implies that because these references are brief and "passing," they are also unintentional and insufficient. The implication is that representation equals description: because the novel's eponymous English country is described ad nauseum, it is adequately represented, whereas the Bertram family's West Indian plantation is not. In all this, Said reads *Mansfield Park* as if it were a proto-Victorian realist novel. But Georgian readers approached novels armed with interpretive strategies they honed in the playhouse. Novel writers, too, employed representational strategies across mediums. Indeed, this debt could hardly be clearer in *Mansfield Park,* which thematizes theatrical performance. Moreover, thanks to Janine Barchas we now know that Austen's novels are steeped in topical media and celebrity culture, much like Foote's plays—and, of course, Burney's novels, which Austen openly admired. In Georgian theater, representation is not synonymous with description. As we saw in *The Cozeners,* highly condensed cues can carry enormous representational weight onstage. By reading Austen and Burney past-critically, through their own interpretive protocols, we can recover the full signifying power of passing references to empire.[41]

Reading *Evelina* past-critically requires, first and foremost, restoring it to the 1770s mediascape. Like the plays, newspapers, novels, and satirical prints alongside which it was encountered by readers, *Evelina* makes meaning through citational references. Captain Mirvan's vow that "he would sooner go to the *Black-hole in Calcutta*" is not a throwaway line intended to be ignored, but rather a highly significant recycled media trope—or what I shorthand as a "meme." Scholars like Betty Joseph have recovered how the Black Hole "captured the public imagination," helping to obscure—and thus enable—the East India Company's shift from merchant to ruler. But from the 1760s through the 1780s, the Black Hole also functioned in another way in metropolitan discourse—as the butt of a popular joke: Londoners routinely complained about overcrowding at the opera, theater, pleasure gardens, private assemblies, and even the royal court, by comparing them to the Black Hole of Calcutta. A few examples will illustrate the formula. In 1773, Horace Walpole complained that the French ambassador's ball was "approaching to Calcutta, where so many English were stewed to death; for as the Queen would not dis-Maid of Honour herself of Miss Vernon till after the Oratorio, the ballroom was not opened until she arrived, and we were penned together in the little hall, till we could not breathe." In 1774, a correspondent to the *Public Advertiser* decried overcrowding in the Pantheon's supper room on masquerade nights, writing: "the Black Hole at Calcutta is the only place I remember the Description of to bear any Resemblance to the suffocating Heat of this infernal Place." In 1776, another *Public Advertiser* letter bewailed the crowds at Garrick's final performance of *King Lear,* writing: "I am one of those who have survived being in the *Black Hole* at *Calcutta,* and I do assure you, the Play-house Passage at Drury-Lane, Yesterday Evening, was full as bad." In 1783, Drury Lane had evidently not improved: "To compare the situation of several hundred persons, broiling, and trampled almost to suffocation, in those avenues [leading to the pit], every night of Mrs. Siddons's performance, with the Calcutta Black-Hole, of horrid memory, is giving but a very inadequate description of the scenes of torture and distress I have there witnessed for five evenings successively." The formulaic joke also made its way onstage: in Arthur Murphy's 1778 comedy *Know Your Own Mind,* a private assembly is so stuffed full of gaming tables that "every room in the house was cramm'd like the black hole at Calcutta."[42]

In each of these instances, the joke turns on a humorous relocation of the Calcutta Black Hole to a London hot spot of polite amusement. Partha Chatterjee reads Holwell's famous Black Hole narrative along these lines, as an allegory for the capacity of "civilized" Englishmen to descend into savagery. According to Chatterjee, the narrative's true villain is not the Nawab of Bengal, but rather the "crowd of ordinary Europeans" who respond to their imprisonment by descending "into mindless disorder." I would argue that the Black Hole meme functions in much the same way. Invoked at moments when the pursuit of sociability turns in on itself and collapses into savagery, the Black Hole is deployed in metropolitan discourse to call into question the politeness of so-called polite society. Moreover, empire is implicitly blamed for this state of affairs. Echoing fears that Britain was following the example of imperial Rome's decline and fall—a widespread concern in the 1770s—the Black Hole trope implies that savage conquest overseas will lead to an undoing of civility at home. The spatial displacement of the Black Hole from Calcutta to London insinuates that the distance between the world of colonial warfare and the world of fashionable sociability is not so vast after all. Put another way, the Black Hole meme draws a solid connecting line between what Mary Favret calls the "*here*" of London's fashionable world and the "*there*" of colonial warfare. While Favret argues that the Revolutionary and Napoleonic Wars made wartime about "world systems" for the first time, "unlike the earlier Seven Years' War," what I am suggesting here is that Favret's argument is fully applicable to the American War, which was experienced in London as a global crisis in imperial affairs.[43]

In *Evelina,* Burney uses the Black Hole to signal precisely these fears about the incivilities of colonial warfare coming home to roost. What's more, Burney effectively doubles down on this meme's critique by voicing it through a naval war veteran, Captain Mirvan. To be clear, Captain Mirvan utters the Black Hole meme, but not as a metacommentary: he is also implicated in its critique. Indeed, his very presence in *Evelina* exemplifies the danger the meme flags. Shortly after the novel begins, the Captain returns from a long tour of naval duty in which he spent "seven years *smoked with the burning sun.*" We might speculate that the length of his absence is a reference to the Seven Years' War; or he could just as easily be returning from the American conflict. Either way, the crucial point is that even after his return to England the captain never ceases fighting. Waging "campaigns" against Evelina's Francophile grandmother, Madame Duval, and the macaroni Mr. Lovel, the captain turns Francophobic martial masculinity into a domestic import. The novel's verdict on this import is clear. Evelina sums up every reader's feelings when she writes: "I cannot bear that Captain; I can give you no idea how gross he is." Captain Mirvan's aggressive, uncouth style of masculinity makes him one of the negative examples—alongside Mr. Lovel, Sir Clement, Lord Merton, and Mr. Macartney—against which Lord Orville's masculinity is established as a prescriptive norm. Frustratingly, though, the captain is never banished from the fashionable world, even though his uncouthness renders him a fish out of water at genteel venues like the Pantheon. While other representatives of aberrant masculinity—for example, Lord Merton and Sir Clement—*are* eventually ejected from the novel's inner circle, Captain Mirvan remains stubbornly in place right through the novel's final scene.[44]

Captain Mirvan cannot be cast outside the pale of polite society *because he functions as a constant reminder of polite society's geopolitical coordinates.* Like Hayman's battlefield paintings hung in Vauxhall's pillared saloon, the captain reminds readers that the brave new world of London fashion documented in the novel is a product of imperial expansion in the two Indies. Whereas Hayman celebrated Clive and Amherst as noble and beneficent conquerors, Burney declines to sugarcoat colonial warfare. Writing from the disenchanted perspective of the 1770s, the victories of the 1760s now look to her like catastrophes. Instead of celebrating martial masculinity, Burney critiques toxic masculinity—a colonial strain of toxic masculinity that has arrived in London to plague her heroine. Empire thus plays an important—but easily overlooked—role in the novel's policing of elite class identities, as I argue in the next section.

Class, Race, and Empire in *Evelina*

Evelina could be described as a meditation on who has—and thus, what constitutes—class. Like *The Commissary* and *The Cozeners,* the novel sets out to expose and discipline class transgressions. While Evelina (who, we must remember, is a baronet's daughter by birth) is admitted to the beau monde, the novel keeps everyone else in their place. Socioeconomic stasis is therefore the condition of possibility for Evelina's ascension, which must be exceptional. Despite the novel's domestic setting, its class drama is a global story whose origin lies in the economic boom set off by imperial expansion during the Seven Years' War.

Just as Foote does in *The Cozeners,* Burney uses fashion to periodize the landscape her novel documents. After seven years at sea, Captain Mirvan, much like Smollett's Matthew Bramble, is mystified by how London has changed in his absence. The fashion trend that troubles him most is macaroni dress, which, as we have seen, was a post-1763 phenomenon. Like Foote, Burney connects her critique of macaroni masculinity to the forces unleashed by imperial warfare. Whereas Foote accomplishes this by painting his macaroni caricature in blackface, Burney connects hers to the Black Hole meme. In the same conversation wherein Captain Mirvan vows that "he would sooner go to the *Black-hole in Calcutta,*" Burney puts a finer point on his reasoning: he dislikes the macaroni fashions sported at Ranelagh. In particular, the captain objects to the emulation of macaroni style all the way down the social ladder. He complains: "before long, we shall ... see never a swabber" (lowly deck-cleaning sailor) "without a bag and a sword," the macaroni's two signature fashion accessories. Further challenged by Mr. Lovel, the captain issues his definitive statement on macaronis: "the men, as they call themselves, are no better than monkeys." This line presages Captain Mirvan's most shocking assault on macaroni masculinity when he literally sets loose a monkey on Mr. Lovel in one of the novel's final episodes. Dwelling for a moment with this earlier, often overlooked, monkey cameo will help throw into relief some of the subtleties of that later encounter.[45]

While Captain Mirvan's objection to macaroni style is undoubtedly rooted in his sense that it is a French import, his comparison of macaronis to monkeys should not be reduced to mere Francophobia. Monkeys were obviously not native to France: they were associated with exotic locations, principally India and Africa. They were also preeminent symbols of class climbing. If the Black Hole meme critiques class climbing while pointing an accusatory finger at empire, the monkey trope operates in much the same way. Nor was Burney the first writer to combine the Black Hole meme with a simian metaphor. In an anonymously published satirical sketch from 1762, George Colman the Elder describes a private assembly held by "Mrs. Marr-court," one of the many "Minor Dames of Second-hand Gentry, fond of aping the Vices and Follies of their superiors." Mrs. Marr-court's "publick-private" assemblies are so filled with gaming tables that "the Company are crouded [sic] together, as close as ... the poor Prisoners in the Black-Hole at Calcutta." The charge leveled here, that middling women were "aping" the habits of their social superiors, also echoes in Captain Mirvan's remarks. When he calls the men who frequent Ranelagh "monkeys," the implication is that venues of public amusement are sites for class masquerade (a charge also made in *The Cozeners*).[46]

Much like the Black Hole meme, Captain Mirvan's comparison of macaronis to monkeys is a highly condensed reference that taps into a viral stream of textual and visual media. In the 1770s, a number of visual satires of macaronis included monkeys as metonyms for class climbing. Ingrid Tague explains that monkeys—along with other exotic pets such as toy dogs and parrots and so-called pet African slave children—embodied

Brandoin pinx.!   Caldwall sculp.

THE MACARONY BROTHERS.

London, Printed for Rob.! Sayer, N.º 53, Fleet Street, & J. Smith, N.º 35, Cheapside, as the Act directs, 25 July, 1772.

Figure 9. James Caldwall, *The Macarony Brothers,* 1772. Line engraving,
stipple engraving, and etching on moderately thick, moderately textured,
blued white laid paper. Yale Center for British Art, Paul Mellon Collection.

"the worst excesses of fashionable consumption." One print satire discussed by Tague resonates particularly well with *Evelina. The Macarony
Brothers* (Figure 9) pictures an old tar standing with his back turned on
a macaroni, a contrast that recalls the juxtaposition of the honest father
and his foppified son in Figure 5. Meanwhile, a smartly dressed monkey

BOARDING SCHOOL EDUCATION, OR THE FRENCHIFIED YOUNG LADY.

Figure 10. M. Darly, *Boarding School Education, or, The Frenchified Young Lady,* 1771. Etching on laid paper, hand-colored. Courtesy of The Lewis Walpole Library, Yale University.

perched on the sailor's shoulder reaches out to the macaroni in a gesture of recognition. The monkey's dress calls attention to the effete artificiality of the macaroni's style, which is contrasted with the rough and unpretentious masculinity of the cobb-pipe-smoking sailor. The latter defends the empire overseas seas yet remains British in demeanor; meanwhile, the macaroni stays at home but is ridiculously outfitted in foreign fashions. Other prints demonstrate how the monkey was used in conjunction with other tropes to build complex multilayered portraits of class climbing. Tague identifies *Boarding School Education* (Figure 10) as one of many prints that pairs dancing masters with monkeys. Dancing masters were regularly ridiculed as facilitators of class climbing, including in *The Commissary.* The women pictured in Figure 10 represent Fungus's female counterparts: their comically high heads, modish dresses, and dancing lessons have done nothing to ameliorate their uncouth grotesqueness. In the foreground of the print, a monkey condenses this critique. Paired with another pet, a toy lapdog, he imitates the dancing master's lesson in sync with the two female pupils, the implication being that the women are merely "aping" the accomplishments of their superiors, and will never do better.[47]

Placed in this context, the famous monkey episode in *Evelina* represents one more addition to what was by 1778 a well-worn formula of pairing monkeys with macaronis for comic effect. The action of the scene is as follows: Evelina's party is sitting in happy conversation when they are interrupted by Captain Mirvan, who announces a "little gentleman visitor" for the macaroni Mr. Lovel, perhaps his "twin brother." When the visitor arrives he is "a monkey, full-dressed, and extravagantly *à la mode!*" The monkey proceeds to bite off Mr. Lovel's ear in a brutal disciplining of his class pretensions. The implication is that, compared to a real gentleman—like Evelina's fiancé, Lord Orville—Lovel is a mere monkey in man's clothes. Meanwhile, Captain Mirvan's cruelty places him at the other extreme of masculinity: he is an aggressive, violent, unhinged disturber of the domestic peace. With the captain as hyperaggressive perpetrator on one end and Lovel as helpless emasculated victim on the other, the ideal zone of normative masculinity is left to Lord Orville alone. Importantly, the violence done to Lovel also sets him apart from Evelina. In the moment right before Evelina's upwardly mobile marriage, Burney uses the monkey to distinguish her heroine definitively from social pretenders. Evelina is not, like Lovel (or the women in Figure 10), a monkey dressed up like a gentlewoman.[48]

The fact that an exotic pet is used to delineate the limits of class climbing in this scene is fitting, for, as we have seen many times over the course of this chapter, the empire and colonial trade were the most conspicuous sources for new wealth in the 1770s, and were therefore widely blamed for the destabilization of class boundaries. Burney would have been keenly aware of this fact. Thanks to groundbreaking research by Amy Louise Erickson, we now know that Burney's mother, Esther, "ran a highly successful business" selling "India and English fans," including "fans imported through the East India Company." Exploding the myth that Charles Burney was his family's sole provider, Erickson reveals that

Burney's mother "certainly earned the majority part of the household income" from trade—and colonial trade at that. Moreover, Charles Burney's profession as a young man was hardly more gentlemanly than that of his shop-owning wife. As a music teacher, he was a counterpart to the dancing master lampooned in *The Commissary* and print satires like Figure 10. Worse still, his brother *was* a dancing master. The fact that Esther and Charles met at a ball hosted by his dancing master brother gives us a good sense of their middling milieu. Years later, in the wake of his "transition from lowly musician to respected man of letters," Charles was eager to distance himself from these relatively lowly origins, as Sophie Coulombeau explains. According to Erickson, "laborious attempts [were] made ... to conceal the Burneys' trade connections in order to present an idealized self-image to posterity as a clan of genteel artistic professionals." Frances Burney was apparently as eager as her father to conceal her family's origins: she never mentions them, despite having been close with her maternal grandmother into adulthood. When Burney rose from the daughter of a fan maker to "Keeper of the Robes" in Queen Charlotte's court, she wished to conceal how very many rungs on the class ladder she had climbed to reach that station.[49]

Returning to *Evelina*'s final scene with this newly unearthed biographical information in mind, we can read it as an anxious meditation on the nature of class. The fact that an exotic imperial specter haunts Evelina's triumph might be read in light of Burney's own anxieties about her family's buried recent past in colonial trade. Laura Brown interprets Mr. Lovel's encounter with the monkey as an "encounter with alterity." She argues that Burney uses the monkey to pose the "question, 'What is man?'" I read this scene slightly differently, as posing a distinct but related ontological question: not *What is man?*, but rather *What is a gentleman?* Instead of probing the limits of the human, this scene stakes out the limits of upward mobility. Gentlemen, Burney insists, are born and not made. To make Mr. Lovel into a Lord Orville would be as difficult as turning a monkey into a man. Similarly, Burney uses the monkey to reign in any radical implications of her heroine's spectacular rise in rank, reminding her reader that one condition of possibility for Evelina's marriage is her birth. For the daughter of a baronet to marry a peer is a coup, not a scandal. The monkey thus allegorizes class boundaries by figuring them as just as impermeable as the boundaries between species—or between races.[50]

Evelina's meditation on class has important things to teach us about race. In visual and print media, the monkey was paired not only with other animal pets like dogs but with so-called pet slave children as well. Take, for example, Plate 2 of William Hogarth's *The Harlot's Progress* (see Figure 13), discussed in the next chapter. Another take-down of class pretension, Hogarth's print signifies the prostitute Moll's forays into fashion through two "pets": a monkey and a so-called pet African slave child dressed in an orientalized, vaguely Ottoman, costume. It is clear that these two form a pair in the print, as they occupy the same horizontal cross-section of the picture plane and lock eyes with one another. In addition to displaying his reaction to the general chaos of the scene before him, the boy's look of astonishment also registers a shock of recognition: his look reminds the viewer that his royal dress is no more ennobling than the bonnet sported by the monkey. Hogarth's print thus represents the boundaries between classes as akin to the boundaries between species and races—all of which are figured as impermeable.

In *The Cozeners*, we encountered another example of the articulation of race and class in the figure of the blackface macaroni. This figure might very well represent a caricature of the Afro-British celebrity Julius Soubise (pictured in Figure 4), who is the subject of the next chapter. Soubise was London's only Black macaroni, and in 1774 he was at the height of his fame. Utterly unique and sensational, Soubise was just the sort of celebrity Foote would be tempted to satirize. He also knew Soubise well, having dined with him many times at the home of Domenico Angelo, Foote's longtime friend and Soubise's employer. If Soubise was conjured onstage in *The Cozeners*, his presence would double down on the play's charge that the fashionable world was being invaded by outsiders—and that the empire was to blame. Soubise was a lightning rod for the kinds of anxieties about the mutability of class that animate *The Cozeners* and *Evelina*. His perfect mastery of aristocratic masculinity challenged the lesson at the heart of *Evelina*'s monkey scene: that class is immutably set at birth. More explicitly than *Evelina*, the archive of

Soubise's life ties these class anxieties to late Georgian conceptualizations of race.[51]

Delving into this archive in the next chapter, I show that answering the question What is a gentleman? requires attending to race as well as class, a task which, in turn, requires attending to both of the two Indies.

A Black British Racial Formation

Julius Soubise in London and Calcutta

I n the 1980s, Stuart Hall and others began using the term "Black British" to name the "common experience" of racism and margin- alization shared by South Asian and West Indian immigrants in the decades after decolonization. In a classic essay, he explores this pairing under the rubric "new ethnicities." Although Hall is concerned with horizontal racial solidarities formed from below, his insights can also be used to illuminate racial systems of classification applied from above. The road to a "common experience" of *decolonization* in the twen- tieth century was paved by a shared history of *colonization* in the eigh- teenth century. We have already encountered one example of how the expansion of British imperialism led to the fungibility of East and West Indian characters. *The Cozeners* culminates with a racist bed trick that humorously plays on the fact that blackface makeup was used to represent both Africans and South Asians onstage, rendering them visually inter- changeable. At the same time, there is another source for this scene's comedy: the ludicrous incommensurability of the enslaved African woman Marianne and the fictional East Indian heiress she is called upon to impersonate. *The Cozeners'* comic play of sameness and difference neatly captures a paradox in the representation of race in eighteenth- century Britain: while both East and West Indians contributed to the ranks of the "Black Poor," the astronomical wealth of Indian elites often exempted them from virulent racialization, and at times even prompted what Gerald MacLean, in a different context, calls "imperial envy." The two Indies were thus unevenly implicated in a peculiarly British version of "love and theft," to borrow Eric Lott's concept-metaphor for American blackface minstrelsy.[1]

Our current critical frameworks have made it difficult to grasp this geographically inflected push and pull between high and low, exalted and disparaged, envied and derided, racialized character. Paul Gilroy's call for cultural historians to consider the Black Atlantic as a "single, complex unit of analysis" has been instrumental in the emergence of Black Studies as a transnational field formation. At the same time, Atlantic-centric paradigms have also reinforced East/West hemispheric divisions in scholarship, thereby obscuring the global circulation of racial thinking between the Americas and Asia. W. E. B. Du Bois's "color-line" already traversed "Asia" as well as "Africa" and "America" by the late Georgian period. Understanding the internal contradictions that riddle this era's representations of race therefore requires a more capacious unit of analysis than the Atlantic world alone can provide; it requires the perspective of the Indies mentality. This chapter uses the two Indies to reconstruct the eighteenth century's Black British racial formation, showing how racial ideologies were formed in circulation between colonial India and the colonial Atlantic world. Along the way, I pay special attention to the role of Mughal elites—and the subcontinent's Indo-Persian racial formation—in the making of imperial Britain's racist common sense.[2]

As the theater profoundly shaped British racial ideologies, this chapter spends a good deal of time in the playhouse. After exploring the coexistence of the two Indies in the dramatic repertoire of racial representation, I shift my focus to the afterlives of theatrical characters in the world of fashionable sociability. Here I essentially reverse Chapter 1's direction of travel: instead of showing how the beau monde was caricatured onstage, I show how stage characters were used to represent race in the highly performative world of the beau monde. Like the mediation of the imperial crisis of the 1760–70s, the representations of race explored in this chapter crisscross visual, performance, and print media. Reconstructing the racial dimension of the Indies mentality therefore requires a mixed-media approach attentive to the highly generative interface between media and everyday life.[3]

The life of this chapter's primary case study unfolded on the very surface of that interface. Julius Soubise was Georgian England's most spectacular Black celebrity; and he remains vastly understudied in scholarship. Born on Saint Kitts in the mid-1750s to an enslaved African mother and European father, Soubise arrived in England in 1764 and eventually landed in the home of Catherine (Kitty) Douglas, duchess of Queensberry. A famous eccentric, the duchess raised Soubise in a manner very different from other enslaved boys kept as so-called pet companions. Instead of sending him back to the West Indies when he reached adolescence, she funded his education in the courtly arts of fencing, riding, and ballet. In the early 1770s, Soubise became a notorious fop and a fixture in the beau monde. His time in the limelight lasted until 1777, when the duchess's death necessitated that he flee to Calcutta, where he lived for the next two decades until his own death in 1798.

Several considerations make Soubise an ideal case study for this chapter. To begin with the obvious, his "life geography" spanned the two Indies. But even in London, Soubise fashioned a racial identity that drew on both Indies. Analyzing the archive of his life in London—which includes visual satires, gossipy manuscript letters, apocryphal print anecdotes, and newspaper stories—I show how he utilized tropologies of Eastern royalty in order to fashion himself as a "Black Prince." Next, I explore what happened when Soubise went from impersonating Eastern princes in London to rubbing shoulders with them in Calcutta. An untapped source for his life in Calcutta (the manuscript diary of his business partner, Richard Blechynden) enables me to follow Soubise's racialization from metropole to colony, tracking continuities as well as ruptures along the way.[4]

Soubise's chosen profession as a fencing and riding instructor made him a lightning rod for anxieties about how new wealth accrued in the empire was erasing class distinctions in the metropole. He therefore presents an invaluable opportunity to explore the role of race in the construction of elite masculinity in both London and Calcutta—and thus the articulation of race and class in Britain's domestic and imperial social formations. Like Chapter 1, this chapter excavates the neglected role empire played in the making of the British aristocracy, a topic I pick up once again in Chapter 5.

The Highs and Lows of Racial Representation on the London Stage

The winter of 1785–86 was particularly harsh in England. In January, the conspicuous distress of some of London's unhoused poor—shivering and starving on the streets of one of the world's richest cities—led to the founding of the Committee for the Relief of the Black Poor. Because this organization would eventually play a leading role in the colonization of Sierra Leone, a scheme initially supported by Olaudah Equiano (soon to become the era's foremost celebrity abolitionist), 1786 is often cited as a foundational moment in Afro-British history. But it is worth remembering that the "Black Poor" whose distress the Committee initially sought to relieve actually hailed from the East Indies. This is evident in the newspaper paragraph that brought about the Committee's inception: "Whereas there are now wandering about the Streets, in the greatest Distress, many Asiatic Blacks, who have been brought into this Country in the India Ships, being in want of the common Necessaries of Lodging, Cloaths, Fire, and Provisions, during the Severity of the Weather, some of whom have absolutely expired in the Streets, no Provision whatever being made for these un-happy Wretches; it is humbly recommended to the Public, to consider their hard Fate, and to provide for their Relief."[5]

Known as *lascars,* "Asiatic Blacks" hailed from all over the Indian Ocean world: present-day Bengal, Bangladesh, South India, Malaysia, Sri Lanka, and beyond. After arriving in London as sailors on East India Company ships, many were left without income or shelter until the following sailing season. Humberto Garcia argues that lascars were viewed as a "disposable" labor force and subjected to "slave-like conditions." Initially founded to aid "Asiatic Blacks," the Committee was subsequently alerted to the equally dire plight of "African and West India blacks." Many Black Loyalists (who served in the American War in exchange for freedom) were now unemployed and immiserated in London. Even after the Committee shifted its mission to focus primarily on this demographic, "Asiatic Blacks" still remained in its purview. Among those selected to participate in the disastrous colonization scheme were at least twenty lascars, one of whom—John Lemon, a literate twenty-nine-year-old born in Bengal—even served as a group leader on the mission. The fact that lascars were counted among the "Black Poor" and sent to Sierra Leone reveals the capaciousness of this era's geography of Blackness, which included both of the two Indies.[6]

The representation of race on the London stage reflects the same geographically capacious racist common sense that animates the category of the "Black Poor." Contrary to what we might expect, burnt-cork blackface makeup was not reserved solely for African characters in British drama, but was used to portray servants and slaves from both of the two Indies. On the London stage, visible Blackness was thus a geographically capacious category with room for South Asians as well as diasporic Africans. Take, for example, the instructions Thomas Rede gives for blackface cosmetics in his theater manual for aspiring actors *The Road to the Stage*. He instructs: "To produce the black necessary for the negro face of Hassan, Wowski, Mungo, or Sambo, the performer should cover the face and neck with a thin coat of pomatum, or ... lard; then burn a cork to powder, and apply it with a hare's foot." Notably, Rede's list of blackface roles includes two characters from outside the circum-Atlantic: Hassan and Wowski. While the former (from George Colman the Younger's Orientalist extravaganza *Blue-Beard*) reflects the non-European slaveholding practice of employing African eunuchs as harem guards (a subject I return to below), the latter is a more complicated case. Wowski belongs to another Colman play, *Inkle and Yarico*, whose sensational popularity was second only to Sheridan's *School for Scandal* in the last quarter of the century. In this well-known story, which cycled through various mediums and retellings, the hard-hearted English merchant Inkle sells his indigenous American Indian lover Yarico (who saved his life after a shipwreck) into slavery. Wowski is unique to Colman's version of the story, where she is Yarico's maid as well as the love interest of Inkle's servant, Trudge. Wowski's portrayal in burnt cork is noteworthy because a lighter cosmetic (probably Spanish brown or vermillion) was used to portray Yarico. The *Morning Herald*'s opening-night review complains about Wowski's appearance by contrasting it to that of Yarico: "We advise, also that *Wowski's* face not be so Jetty, and to agree in colour with her hands; she ought to be an American tawny, and not an African black." In the play text, we are told that Yarico is "a good comely copper," a color that, Nandini Bhattacharya argues, "has aesthetic as well as racial implications."[7]

The fact that two American Indian women appearing side by side in the same play would be painted different colors speaks (in Monica Miller's terms) to the "instability of the representational economy for black men" and women, and other racialized Others on the Georgian stage. In the case of Wowski and Yarico, the reason for their disparate appearance is not difficult to find. Put simply, while the servant Wowski belonged to the "Black Poor," Yarico did not. Yarico's visual differentiation from Wowski onstage flagged her higher status vis-à-vis her maid. Once again, Rede's manual is instructive. He distinguishes a series of racialized roles that should be played, not in burnt cork, but rather in the "tawny" color mentioned in the *Morning Herald*'s review of *Inkle and Yarico*: the "tawny tinge" of "Spanish brown" should be used to play "Sadi, Bulcazin, Muley, Rolla," "Bajazet, and Zanga." Like Rede's list of blackface characters, this list is geographically heterogeneous: it includes a Turk (Bajazet), a Peruvian (Rolla), and an African (Zanga). What do all of these characters have in common? In a word, status. They are all high-ranking royal or military figures. Repurposing Julius Soubise's "self-dubbed" nickname, we might refer to them as "Black Prince[s]." Like Yarico, the daughter of an Indian chief, they are racialized royalty. The lesson in all this is fairly clear: rank was a determinative factor in the representation of race. This was true both onstage and in London's wider mediascape. Prints depicting Yarico and Wowski also use color to visualize class difference. Figures 11 and 12 are typical of how these characters were portrayed. Yarico's skin tone is "copper" and her features are European, while Wowski is a racist depiction of lascivious African womanhood. In these prints, genre also plays an important role in shoring up the high and low poles of racialized character. Figure 11 portrays Yarico in a tragic idiom. Her robes evoke Greco-Roman statuary, embedding her within a classical aesthetic vocabulary. Meanwhile, in satirical prints Wowski always and only appeared as a racist caricature.[8]

Genre inflected the representation of race onstage as well. All of the Spanish brown parts mentioned by Rede belong to five-act tragedies.

Figure 11. Robert Pollard (after Henry Singleton), *Inkle and Yarico,
Plate 2d,* 1788. Engraving, aquatint, and roulette printed in dark sepia.
© The Trustees of the British Museum.

Meanwhile, Mungo and Hassan both hail from comic afterpieces. Once
again, Wowski is particularly instructive, as she belongs to the low-comic
subplot of a five-act comic opera (a precursor of musical theater). One
newspaper review linked Wowski's color to this consideration: "In point
of appearance, and in compliment we suppose, *Wowski* bore an under
part." The generic divide between low-comic blackface roles and tragic
roles racialized with lighter cosmetics was often rationalized on the basis
of acting technique. Rede takes this stance when he suggests that burnt

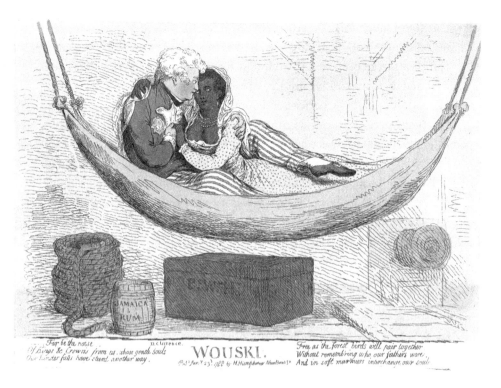

Far be the noise
Of Kings & Crowns from us, whose gentle souls
Our kinder fates have steen'd another way.

D. Clarence

WOUSKI.

Pub.ᵈ Jan.ʸ 23. 1788 by H.Humphreys NewBond St.

Free, as the forest birds well pair together
Without remembring who our fathers wore,
And in soft murmurs interchange our souls

Figure 12. James Gillray, *Wouski,* 1788. Etching, hand-colored.
© The Trustees of the British Museum.

cork "prevent[s] the possibility of the expression being observable." The
implication is that serious dramatic acting required visible facial features
whereas the performance of low-comic characters does not, as the latter
emphasized bodily movement, gesture, and, in the case of Mungo, parodied speech. (Mungo was one of the very first characters on the London
stage to speak in an imitation of West Indian dialect.) To blame blackface
for racist performance practices is, however, to mistake a cause for an
effect.[9]

The antipodes of high and low, tragic and comic, princely and
poor racialized character took shape within the Indies mentality. Robin
Kelley has compared Cedric Robinson's account of the European "creation of the Negro" in *Black Marxism* to Said's account of Europe's invention of the Orient as the Occident's foil in *Orientalism.* My point here is

that these inventions weren't merely similar, they were historically connected. Burnt-cork blackface was used to portray the servility of servants and slaves from both of the two Indies, just as lighter cosmetics were used to signal the comparative prestige of kings, emperors, and military generals from Africa, the Americas, and South Asia. But like all racist logics, the Georgian period's racist common sense was inconsistent. At the same time that blackface was used to represent a geographically capacious cast of servile characters, it was also associated more specifically with people of African descent, as the *Morning Herald*'s prescriptive comments about Wowski's color evince. Blackface was geographically portable on the world of the stage; but only because African slavery in the Americas made blackface such a powerful visual metonym for poverty, servility, and low status. Even when it was applied to a phenotypically diverse cast of characters, burnt-cork blackface always retained its connotations with African descent. Whereas only servile South Asian characters were portrayed in blackface, burnt cork was deemed suitable for African tragic heroes—most notably, Othello—right up until the early nineteenth century.[10]

Like Wowski, Othello offers an illuminating case study in blackface's competing valences. From 1604 through the end of the eighteenth century, Othello was played in burnt-cork blackface. Looking back from the vantage point of 1827, Rede explains that, in the past, Othello "wore the same sables as Mungo, in the 'Padlock.'" Othello's appearance changed in 1814, when the actor Edmund Kean inaugurated Othello's so-called Bronze Age. Writing a decade after this shift, Rede recommended that actors follow Kean's innovation—now prevailing custom—by using the "tawny tinge" of "Spanish brown" to play the "gallant Moor." Othello's color change reflected a newly dominant racist common sense. In the first decades of the nineteenth century it suddenly seemed evident that a Shakespearean tragic hero could not possibly be a Black African—or "a barbarous negro," as Samuel Taylor Coleridge vehemently insisted. Usually, Coleridge's comments are understood as a presage of the hardened racism of the Victorian era, which turned Othello's "blackness" into a "problem," to borrow Kim Hall's formulation. But in light of my discussion here, Coleridge's racism also looks like a back-formation of the Indies mentality. If late Georgian production practices made color a function of status (both social and generic), then Coleridge made status determinative of color and geographical origin. Put more simply, Othello's color change was symptomatic of friction between blackface's competing connotations.[11]

Another example reveals this friction as emergent at least six decades prior to Othello's color change. When David Garrick debuted as Othello in March 1745, his rival, the actor James Quin, purportedly shouted from the audience: "Here's Pompey—but where is the teakettle?" Apocryphal as it is, this joke is worth unpacking for the same reason we attended to Foote's obscure topical jokes in the previous chapter: it indexes a shared mentality. The most obvious reference for Quin's quip is a *Tatler* letter written from the comic perspective of an enslaved "blackamoor boy" named "Pompey," who is forced to play the part of a lady's so-called pet companion. He complains that, though a Christian, "I am obliged to dress like a Turk, and wear a turban." An African slave in orientalized costume, Pompey conjures both of the two Indies. This is clear in a visual intertext for the *Tatler* letter, Plate 2 of William Hogarth's *A Harlot's Progress* (Figure 13), which satirizes the prostitute Moll's pretensions to gentility by accessorizing her with an enslaved pet companion decked out in full Orientalist garb, turban and all. Quin's joke would have doubtless brought this print to mind, so much so that it has led generations of theater historians to argue that Garrick departed from conventional costuming in order to play Othello, not in Venetian or English military costume as was custom, but in *costume à la turque* with a high plumed turban. In fact, it seems unlikely that Quin's comment referred to Garrick's costume. Instead, the joke probably referenced his short stature, which, Quin implied, made him an inadequate stand-in for the imposing noble Moor. The joke may have also contained a bawdy allusion to Garrick's split from the actress Peg Woffington the previous summer, since another apocryphal anecdote tells of Woffington being gifted an enslaved child named Pompey by another paramour. The implication is that Garrick looked more like a scrawny enslaved boy than a powerful military hero—and the same was true, perhaps, of his sexual prowess. In short, Quin's joke worked by skipping across what should have been an unbridgeable gulf separating Shakespeare's noble Moor from the enslaved child Pompey. Like *The Cozeners'* bed-trick scene, Quin's disruption of Garrick's performance crossed the sand-drawn line between high and low, tragic and comic, noble and enslaved, rich and poor, Black character—and it did so for comic effect.[12]

Figure 13. William Hogarth, Plate 2 of *A Harlot's Progress*, 1732.
Etching and engraving on laid paper. Courtesy of The Lewis Walpole Library,
Yale University.

Put another way, the proximity of the "Black Prince" and the "Black Poor" made the former vulnerable to ironic inversion. This is the takeaway of Srinivas Aravamudan's brilliant reading of *Oroonoko* in *Tropicopolitans*. A royal slave, Oroonoko bridges the two poles of racialized character. On the one hand, he has all the hallmarks of a "Black Prince." Like Yarico (as pictured in Figure 11), Oroonoko's aestheticized features recall Greco-Roman taste: his nose is described by Aphra Behn as "rising and Roman," or aquiline. Chi-ming Yang points out that Imoinda's beauty is also aestheticized in a global idiom by Behn: her body is "carved . . . in fine Flowers and Birds . . . as if it were Japan'd." Asia is likewise present in

Behn's Africa. The African royal court of Oroonoko's father recalls contemporary English depictions of Ottoman seraglios, thereby aligning Oroonoko, once again, with the globally capacious "Black Prince" category. After his arrival in Surinam, however, Oroonoko is enslaved. Even though Behn and some of the other colonists continue to acknowledge his royal status, they also treat him like a pet. Oroonoko becomes, in Aravamudan's words, a "pet-king." Made into a lady's plaything, Oroonoko's royal dignity is transmogrified into cuteness. Theorizing outward from this example, Aravamudan argues that *Oroonoko*—both Behn's prose fiction and Thomas Southerne's stage adaptation—operates according to a "logic of parodic subversion."[13]

Production practices support Aravamudan's argument. In the second half of the eighteenth century, Southerne's Oroonoko was a blackface part, making his tragic status vulnerable to farce. Worse still, burnt cork was frequently used as a cloak of anonymity by aspiring actors testing the theatrical waters. Even David Garrick donned the blackface part of Oroonoko for one of his earliest performances (on a provincial stage). Left to amateur actors, Oroonoko became even more difficult to take seriously. Perhaps this contributed to the declining popularity of Southerne's play, which was staged only ten times between 1776 and 1800. Meanwhile, James Watt points out, Sultans proliferated on the London stage during these very same decades. Below I give one explanation for their continued vogue: the sheer volume of the wealth flowing from colonial Bengal perpetuated the mystique of Indian royalty.[14]

Julius Soubise in London

It was on this slippery, irony-suffused terrain that Julius Soubise made his fabulous London debut. Brought to England at the age of about ten by a Royal Navy captain, Soubise soon charmed the captain's cousin, the duchess of Queensberry, and was given to her. Perhaps Soubise's companionship was intended to console the duchess for the recent loss of her two sons to suicide and illness in tragically quick succession. Whatever the motive for bringing Soubise into the Queensberry household, the boy's status there was ambiguous, then and now: Was he free or enslaved? A companion or a servant? A pet or an adopted ward? When the duchess educated Soubise in the courtly arts of fencing, ballet, and riding, she may have been gratifying his own wishes, as Henry Angelo, the son of Soubise's fencing master, implies when he writes that Soubise "manifested a disposition for gallantry" and "talked of becoming a general." Or, the famously eccentric duchess may have simply been playing out the logic of slave-pethood to its logical conclusion, grooming Soubise to be her personal pet prince. This is certainly the implication of the racist and sexually suggestive satirical cartoon about the duchess and Soubise discussed below (see Figure 14). Anecdotes about Soubise's childhood recall Oroonoko's confinement as a "pet" of the ladies of Surinam. Like Behn's hero, Soubise regaled his patroness with displays of martial masculinity. Whereas Oroonoko hunted tigers, Soubise entertained the duchess and her friends with exhibitions of horsemanship. Like Oroonoko, Soubise was also subjected to parodic subversion—for example, when the duchess renamed him after the French war hero Charles de Rohan, Prince of Soubise. Like Oroonoko, the pet slave figure's tropological power derives from a "parodic subversion" of Black royalty. The pet slave evokes the "Black Prince" only to symbolically neuter him and cannibalize his power for the benefit of a white European audience. In the beau monde's theater of real life, Soubise was conscripted to perform the role of the "pet king" for an audience of white peers.[15]

In his late teens, Soubise suddenly began stylizing himself as a "Black Prince," effectively reverse engineering the Royal Slave's descent into indignity. Monica Miller captures this transformation perfectly: "around age nineteen, Soubise transformed himself from a black in fop's clothing to a fop who was black." If Behn stood the Black Prince figure on its head, Soubise landed him back on his feet. Ironically named for a prince, Soubise now started acting like one. He fenced and socialized with the sons of peers at Eton and Angelo's Academy. And he lived as if aristocratic excess was his birthright. Impeccably styled in the same macaroni fashions sported by Charles James Fox, Soubise was the Black counterpart of this aristocratic bad boy, as *The Cozeners'* blackface macaroni caricature seems to imply. Henry Angelo's memoirs paint a vivid picture of his libertine dissipation: "Soubise, even whilst at my father's, had private apartments, unknown to the family, where he assumed the habits of an extravagant man of fashion. He had a constant succession of visitors, and his rooms were supplied with roses, geraniums, and other expensive green-houseplants, in the spring. He was equally expensive in perfumes, so that even in the lobbies at the theatres, the fops and the frail would exclaim, 'I scent Soubise!' He was no less extravagant in nosegays, and never seen, at any season, without a *bouquet* of the choicest flowers in his bosom." Soubise was a familiar face in London's fashionable world. He "frequented the Opera, and the other theatres," attended masquerades at Vauxhall and the Pantheon, joined fashionable clubs, took the air in Hyde Park with "a fine horse and groom," and cruised Windsor in a post chaise and four attended by liveried servants. In Angelo's understated words, he "made a figure."[16]

Portrayals of Soubise in the late Georgian mediascape are centrally preoccupied with his balancing act on the razor's edge of high and low racialized character. Depictions of him routinely subvert his subversion of the pet slave figure so that it topples into parody once again. Take, for example, the first of two chapters on Soubise in *Nocturnal Revels.* Published in 1779 (two years after Soubise fled London for Calcutta), *Nocturnal Revels* is a salacious semi-fictional, semi-factual, semipornographic guide to London's "nunneries," or high-end brothels. The book's chapters on Soubise open with a revealing scene of reception, wherein a befuddled Londoner sees Soubise on "the *surface* of the *Ton* ... parading the streets of this Town, in an elegant equipage, servants in superb liveries, and drawn by fine dun horses." Struggling to guess the identity of this "extraordinary personage," the bystander flips through the "Black Prince" Rolodex: "it is not Omiah; no, nor the Prince of—of—Oroonoko, who was here some years ago:—he is a Prince of Ana—Ana—maboe.... Remember the story of *Zanga,* and we must tremble." Here we find a global cast of racialized royalty that includes three Africans (Oroonoko, Zanga, and William Ansah Sessarakoo) and a South Pacific islander (Omai). Notably, the roll call includes real-life celebrities in addition to fictional characters. Recall from Chapter 1, Omai was the toast of the Town in the 1770s, when he was brought to England by Captain Cook. As Kathleen Wilson argues, his racialization is an example of the global circulation of racial discourse in miniature, since the early modern trope of the "noble savage" was transposed from the New World to the South Pacific islands. Frances Burney's quip about the superiority of Omai's manners vis-à-vis those of Philip Stanhope (quoted in Chapter 1) turns on this trope, the implication being that Omai's nobility was natural in comparison to Stanhope's stilted, artificial, and outdated style of aristocratic masculinity. Sessarakoo, too, was a real-life prince. In 1748, he was rescued from an English slave trader who had promised to carry him to England to be educated but instead sold him into slavery. Like Soubise, Sessarakoo was viewed through the prism of Black stage character. When he attended a performance of Southerne's *Oroonoko* at Covent Garden, the tearful reaction of this real-life royal slave to his fictional counterpart's plight was more closely watched by audience members than the action onstage. Ultimately, *Nocturnal Revels* assembles this cast of princely characters only to deny Soubise a place among them. Replaying *Oroonoko's* "logic of parodic subversion," *Nocturnal Revels* flips the Black Prince coin once again, landing it this time on the side of the Black Poor: "This extraordinary character is neither more nor less than the son of a servant of the Prince of S—se," in fact, his "Negro domestic." Soubise is not a royal slave but the slave of royalty. By identifying his supposed owner as the prince of Soubise, *Nocturnal Revels* duplicates the barbed irony of the duchess's renaming of her child "pet-king."[17]

The second chapter on Soubise in *Nocturnal Revels* is also centrally concerned with pulling the rug out from under his performative self-stylization as a Black Prince. Once again, Soubise's ritual humiliation implicates both of the two Indies. The setup for the scene is as follows: after deciding to cement his place in the beau monde with a strategic marriage, Soubise begins to pay his addresses to "*a Lady of Beauty, Rank and Fortune,*" "the Honourable Miss G—, a celebrated toast, with a fortune of 30,000l." In a romantic epistle, he declares his love in terms that recall the pet slave figure once again, adding a twist of sexual innuendo (thereby taking a stab at the duchess, Soubise's former owner and rumored lover): "Madam, you have seized my heart, and I dare tell you I am your *Negro Slave.*" Miss G—'s irony-laden response is designed with the express intent to wound. Her letter uses the lash of "ridicule" to discipline "so impertinent, so vain, so presumptuous a *Black.*" Addressing her letter to "your Highness," Miss G— parodies Soubise's pretensions, which she ironically pretends to entertain. The stage is scripted into her takedown when she explains her partiality for Soubise by confessing, "I

never yet saw either OROONOKO or OTHELLO without rapture." Whether
this line is read as a parodic subversion of English drama's most famous
Black Princes, or as a more targeted attack on Soubise's aspirational self-
stylization in their mold, the import of Miss G—'s words is the same:
rejection. Her acerbic letter sent, she determines to have a "still more
complete revenge upon the Prince in person," at the "next Pantheon
masquerade."[18]

In the climactic Pantheon scene that follows, the world of global
empire is palimpsestically layered over London's fashionable world, producing the same effect as the Seven Years' War paintings displayed in
Vauxhall's Pillared Saloon. In *Nocturnal Revels* the mechanism for this
global palimpsest is the masquerade, a Georgian institution that, Terry
Castle taught us long ago, is synonymous with boundary crossing. Castle's argument that the disguise afforded by masquerade costumes facilitated the subversion of class, sexual, and racial identities is borne out in
Nocturnal Revels, where Soubise and Miss G— dress up as a "Sultan" and
"Sultana," respectively. More recently, Gillian Russell has textured our
understanding of masquerade by describing the Pantheon (a frequent
masquerade venue) as a virtual "theatre without actors, in which the audience could most successfully perform itself." *Nocturnal Revels* takes
pains to establish the Pantheon as a social stage, bearing out Russell's
argument. Miss G— and Soubise's confrontation is presented as a performance, whose diegetic audience is the fashionable world:

> S—se happened to choose the dress of a Sultan, and by some
> accident Miss G— fixed upon that of a Sultana: They were
> both splendid, and attracted the attention of the whole Ro-
> tunda. No sooner had Miss G— cast her eyes upon S—se,
> than she knew him by the discoveries made through the ap-
> ertures of his mask. The elegance of her figure, added to the
> sumptuousness of her dress, soon made him accost her, as his
> favourite Sultana of the night.
>
> Nothing could have more happily occurred, for the dis-
> play of her raillery. Upon his saying some civil things to her,
> and amongst others, that he had dropped his handkerchief to
> her; she bid him stand off, he was an impostor—she could

perceive he was only a black Eunuch in disguise; that she should acquaint the Grand Signior of the indignity offered his Sublime Highness by such a wretch, and have him flayed: "But," added she in another tone of voice, "that may be an attempt you have already made upon yourself, in order to promote a farther disguise; in that case, I would send you some of my own cosmetics, that you may not make too horrid an appearance in the Seraglio for human eyes to behold!"

For Georgian audiences, part of the pleasure of reading this scene must have been the interpellation of the reader as belonging to the fashionable world depicted therein. The reader's inclusion comes at the cost of Soubise's exclusion, which, remarkably, turns on the reader's familiarity with varieties of African enslavement endemic to the Islamic world. When Miss G— exposes Soubise as "only a black Eunuch in disguise," she alludes to the Ottoman and Mughal practice of employing enslaved African eunuchs as military advisors and harem guards. By recasting Soubise from the "Sultan" to the Sultan's slave, this scene repeats the insult implicit in the fabricated racist origin story told earlier in *Nocturnal Revels* (wherein Soubise is revealed to be the son of the prince of Soubise's "Negro domestic"). In one way, Soubise's choice to play the role of the Sultan recalls Hall's argument about "new ethnicities": it can be seen as a horizontal practice of identification that "engages rather than suppresses *difference*" in the interest of racial solidarity. At the same time, it is important to recognize *why* Soubise aligns himself with the Sultan: to foreclose his alignment with the Sultan's African slave. The gesture is therefore a complicated one that involves racial affiliation *and* disidentification across different "ethnic" lines.[19]

The masquerade scene is far from the only occasion when Islamic slaveholding practices surface in the archive of Soubise's life—or British representations of race more generally. Two decades ago, Robin Blackburn argued that Christian European attitudes toward race and slavery were "deeply marked by confrontation with Islam." In the years since, scholarship by Nabil Matar, Gerald Maclean, Humberto Garcia, María Elena Martínez, James Sweet, Ronald Segal, Ehud Toledano, and others has sketched out the contours of this "confrontation," as it played out in

Spain and on the Ottoman Empire's European frontier. It is worth noting that Shakespeare's *Othello* was deeply shaped by the latter context; and Mungo, who epitomizes the opposite pole of racialized stage character, was just as deeply shaped by the former. Mungo hails from Isaac Bickerstaffe's *The Padlock,* the smash hit of 1768. Although he is generally identified as the first blackface character to speak in a caricature of West Indian dialect, Kingston from *High Life Below Stairs* predates him. Mungo is rightly remembered, though, on account of his sensational popularity: he was a viral cultural phenomenon, the Georgian stage's most iconic West Indian slave character. Yet Mungo's literary origins also tie him to Muslim Spain and slaveholding practices associated with the Levant and East Indies.[20]

The Padlock is based on "The Jealous Husband," a 1613 story by Miguel Cervantes about Carizales, a sixty-eight-year-old gentleman who returns to Spain from the West Indies in possession of a considerable fortune, and marries a fourteen-year-old bride, Leonora, in the hope of producing heirs. While the story's primary reference points are located in the Atlantic world, one key detail bridges the two Indies: Carizales's "old Negro" groom is "an *Eunuch,*" making him the perfect guard for Leonora, whose chastity is fretted over by her "Jealous" older husband. Although enslaved Africans were employed in a variety of capacities in the Islamic world, in the English imagination they were primarily associated with the role of harem guard. Recall, Hassan (from Rede's instructions), who occupied this role in Colman's *Blue-Beard.* The fact that Carizales's "old Negro" groom is "an *Eunuch*" is therefore not a trivial detail; it is a crucial plot point. It is also the tip of the iceberg of a global history of literary circulation between East and West. *The Padlock* is essentially a harem play transposed onto a Spanish setting. While Mungo isn't a eunuch, and in fact explicitly indexes West Indian plantation slavery, he is nonetheless placed in the structural position of a harem eunuch in the play's plot, just as Don Diego (the play's stand-in for Carizales) occupies the structural position of the Sultan, whose absurd age relative to that of his bride makes him a figure of both predatory sexuality and impotence. Generically, and at the level of form, *The Padlock* fuses the two Indies. Mungo's enslavement therefore evokes *both* West Indian chattel slavery *and* the so-called "political slavery" of Oriental despotism.[21]

Given that Mungo was, like the Sultan, a popular masquerade costume, it is even possible that readers may have read Miss G— and Soubise's showdown with Mungo and *The Padlock* in mind. Even if this was not the case, *The Padlock*'s fusion of the two Indies is replicated in the masquerade scene. Miss G—'s accusation that Soubise is only a "black *Eunuch* in disguise" transports the pair to the vaguely Levantine setting already evoked by their costumes. Her threat to have Soubise "flayed" as punishment for his imposture likewise invokes the absolute power that Oriental despots supposedly exercised over life and death. At the same time, this threat also unmistakably brings a West Indian plantation setting to mind, recalling the torture—particularly whipping—that was inflicted on enslaved Africans by the enslavers given absolute, tyrannical authority over them by English law. Even Miss G—'s recasting of Soubise in the role of eunuch can be read with reference to English slaveholding practices in the circum-Atlantic, in the sense that it replicates the logic of the pet slave figure. I have argued that the pet slave's tropological power derives from a symbolic castration of the figure of the Black Prince. Here, that symbolic castration is literalized. Certainly a general attack on Black masculine virility, this moment also speaks more specifically to Soubise's reputation as a womanizer. Angelo's aforementioned claim that Soubise kept "private apartments" where he entertained "a constant succession of visitors" clearly implies that his guests were members of the fair sex. Soubise's very presence in *Nocturnal Revels*—a book about prostitutes and brothels—indicates that sexuality was a dominant theme in his remediation in the Georgian mediascape. Macaroni dress and African masculinity were both associated with hypersexuality, and Soubise combined the two. Indeed, he ultimately fled London because one of the duchess's maids accused him of rape, an accusation that is obviously impossible to confirm or deny. What is undeniable is that Soubise's sexuality was surveilled (and at times policed)—symbolically in *Nocturnal Revels* and in real life in London and Calcutta. Because Soubise occupies both the Sultan and the eunuch positions in *Nocturnal Revels,* he is simultaneously pilloried for his hypersexuality and emasculated.

The push and pull of racialized character animate Miss G—'s confrontation with Soubise in equal parts. Her denial of Soubise's suitability for the role of the Sultan stems from her own desire to play the Sultana.

It is not difficult to see why this would be a desirable role. The East Indies were associated with phenomenal wealth, particularly in the wake of the conquest of Bengal, when low-born Britons returned from India with fortunes fit for royalty. In the *Wealth of Nations,* Adam Smith reports: "The retinue of a Grandee of China or Indostan accordingly is, by all accounts, much more numerous and splendid than that of the richest subjects in Europe." The Sultana masquerade costume was likewise associated with the riches of the East, a factor that helps to explain its popularity among women eager to show off their resources. "Masquerade Intelligence" columns from the 1770s reveal that a small fortune was required to pull off this costume with any flair. In February 1770, for example, Miss Monckton reportedly attended a masquerade at Teresa Cornelys's Carlisle House dressed as an "Indian Sultana" laden with jewels valued at £30,000. In the spring of 1772, Lady Villiers purportedly equaled, or even outdid her, attending "the Pantheon Masque Ball" dressed as a "Sultana, with an astonishing quantity of diamonds, supposed to the value of 30,000l." (Another report raises the estimate to £100,000.) These reports may be apocryphal, but they are revealing nonetheless. Samuel Rowe argues that Oriental despotism was associated with "consumptive opulence" at this time, a connotation that often goes overlooked in scholarship. Clearly, bejeweled Sultanas circulated in metropolitan discourse as figures of superabundant wealth in the aftermath of Britain's imperial expansion on the subcontinent.[22]

Meanwhile, Soubise's shunting from the Sultan part also plays on color-based notions of race. When Miss G— threatens to unmask him as merely a "black Eunuch in disguise," the implication is that his skin color reveals his African ancestry, thereby disqualifying him from playing the role of the Sultan, who must be white. Indeed, Indian royalty were often represented—in English and Indo-Persian discourse alike—as white vis-à-vis their "black" Indian and/or African subjects and slaves. This implication is concretized in a running joke about cosmetics that begins with Soubise and Miss G—'s correspondence and crescendos at the Pantheon. In his initial love letter, Soubise is made a mouthpiece for color prejudice when he confesses, "I am of that swarthy race of Adam, whom some despise on account of their complexion." He then goes on to explain that new "discoveries" in "the researches of medicine" promise "to remove the tawny hue of any complexion, if applied with skill and perseverance. In this pursuit, my dear Miss, I am resolutely engaged." In her response, Miss G— ridicules Soubise's futile quest to "wash a Blackamoor white," writing, "I have inclosed a little packet* (some of which I use myself when I go to a Masquerade), which will have the desired effect." A note following the asterisks explains that the "packet" is "A parcel of Carmine, and Pearl Powder," cosmetics used as rouge and for whitening, respectively. Miss G—'s pointed reference to the masquerade reflects historical practices during this period, as aristocratic women often wore white paint to the Opera and masquerade. It also cues readers to visualize the masquerade scene that follows with these cosmetics in mind. When Miss G— dons her Sultana costume, her look includes a visage painted an artificial shade of white.[23]

Miss G—'s white paint carried the heavy symbolic load of her racial *and class* identities. Race and class are articulated here. Art historian Angela Rosenthal argues that the growing popularity of white paint among aristocratic women during the 1770s and 1780s reflects the emergence of whiteness as a "visually racial category." This is borne out in *Nocturnal Revels,* where Miss G— uses Soubise's Blackness as grounds to cast him in the role of a slave, to symbolically castrate him, and to threaten further violence all the while her own suitability for the Sultana role turns on her visually conspicuous whiteness. But it is important to remember that the pure-white complexion achieved by pearl powder and lead paint was not available to all British women. Rather, it was associated specifically with actresses, courtesans—and, in the final decades of the century, aristocrats and other female elites. Pearl powder was thus the opposing counterpart of burnt cork: in the performative theater of fashionable sociability, it functioned as a racialized marker of class identity. To borrow Frantz Fanon's phrasing: "You are rich because you are white, you are white because you are rich." For burnt-cork blackface characters like Wowski, the inverse of Fanon's dictum is equally applicable.[24]

Representations of Soubise's race in the Georgian mediascape are suffused with class connotations. The aristocratic pastime of fencing is especially significant in this regard. In addition to the duchess of Queensberry, Soubise had another important patron: the Italian-born fencing master Domenico Angelo. At the height of his celebrity, Soubise lived at

Angelo's Soho Square home and fencing academy, Carlisle House. He was so closely associated with Angelo that a 1789 news item identifies him simply as "the black assistant, some years since, at Mr. Angelo's Academy," making no mention of the duchess whatsoever. Largely forgotten today, Angelo's academy was a cultural touchstone from the 1760s through the turn of the nineteenth century. Elsewhere I have argued that Carlisle House was much more than a fencing academy: it was a well-trafficked hub in the beau monde, a masculine counterpart to Teresa Cornelys's Carlisle House, which was located right across Soho Square. Living at Angelo's Academy, Soubise brushed shoulders daily with celebrity actors, musicians, painters, politicians, and even royalty. David Garrick, Eva Marie Veigel, John Bannister, Thomas Sheridan, Samuel Foote, George Colman the Elder, Richard Brinsley Sheridan, Joshua Reynolds, Thomas Gainsborough, Benjamin West, George Stubbs, Johann Christian Bach, Elizabeth Ann Linley, John Wilkes, John Horne Tooke, the chevalier d'Eon, and the Prince of Wales all visited Carlisle House regularly. This celebrity guest list helped make it into a veritable finishing school for the sons of peers. Henry Angelo explains: "Garrick, the elder Colman, Sir Joshua Reynolds, and many illustrious foreigners also, were constant visitors at the house; hence the pupils had the advantage of conversing in many living languages, and acquiring that general knowledge of society, which no other house perhaps could afford. Indeed it was considered a school of politeness, and the best to rub off that shyness of habit, so common to youth from sixteen to eighteen, on quitting their studies, either in a public or private school, and an useful and agreeable probation, previously to entering either of the universities, or commencing their travels." For the steep sum of "100 Guineas per Annum," pupils could lodge at Carlisle House, study fencing and horsemanship, and hone their skills in the art of elite masculine sociability. Angelo's business model was resoundingly successful. At the height of Carlisle House's popularity, his income reached £4,000 a year.[25]

But the academy was not without its critics. While it is true that Angelo was the riding instructor of choice amongst the peerage and royal family—his pupils included ten Hanoverian princes—it is also true that he taught the courtly arts to any pupil who could afford his fees, including Soubise. While John Zephaniah Holwell's daughter was socializing with

Burney's music-teacher father (see Chapter 1), his son boarded at Angelo's Academy, where he was the only pupil ever to refuse to sit at table with Soubise. Nor was Holwell the only nabob who used his Indian fortune to fund his children's education in English gentility. In the post–Seven Years' War economic boom, Angelo's Academy functioned as an engine of upward mobility, where imperial fortunes could be domesticated. All this made Angelo a subject of controversy. And Soubise was the perfect poster-child for fears that Angelo's commercialization of the courtly arts was contributing to the erasure of class distinctions. The very ease and seamlessness with which Soubise inhabited the corporeal habitus of rank revealed rank to be a learned performance, unmasking the performative nature of aristocratic masculinity. In this context, we might read Miss

Figure 14. William Austin, *The D_ of [blank] playing at foils with her favourite Lap Dog Mungo after Expending near 10,000 to make him a—*, 1773. Etching on laid paper, hand-colored. Courtesy of The Lewis Walpole Library, Yale University.

G—'s unmasking of Soubise's African Blackness at the masquerade as an attempt to re-sharpen the increasingly blurry line between noble birth and noble breeding.[26]

Certainly, this is how we should read the most famous satire of Soubise: a print published in 1773 that pictures him fencing with his patroness, the duchess (Figure 14). Scholars have recognized this cartoon as a racist caricature: Soubise's physiognomy is grotesque, and the duchess is polluted by association, hence a fencing mask darkens her face. But in addition to indexing fears about racial miscegenation, this cartoon also captures fears about what Russel calls "miscegenation of rank." Angelo and fencing are crucial to this aspect of the satire. Indeed, the cartoon is a spoof of an illustration from Angelo's fencing manual *L'Ecole des Armes* (Figure 15). Except for the dress and countenances of

Figure 15. Charles Hall (after James Gwin), "Position pour la garde en tierce et le coup de tierce," Plate 5. Engraving, from *L'Ecole des Armes,* by Domenico Angelo (London: R. & J. Dodsley, 1763). Yale Center for British Art, Paul Mellon Collection.

the fencers, it exactly reproduces Plate 5, "Position pour la garde en tierce et le coup de tierce." Given that Angelo served as a model for his book's illustrations, he too is conjured in this satire. The cartoon's motto lambasting the duchess for "Expending near 10000 to make him [Soubise] a —" implicates Angelo as well. The duchess may have *spent* a small fortune trying to make "Her favorite Lap Dog" Soubise answer— both her call and her purposes—by making him a gentleman, but Angelo is equally guilty for having *earned* a small fortune in this pursuit. In other words, part of what is under attack in this cartoon is the whole economy of class aspiration. By replacing the handsome models from Angelo's fencing manual with a racist caricature and a woman, the cartoon takes aim at the heart of Angelo's philosophy and business model: the idea that fencing lessons had the power to transform his pupils— whoever they might be—into gentlemen. Like contemporary satires of dancing masters, this image attempts, in Ingrid Tague's words, "to reinforce the social hierarchy by demonstrating the futility of attempts to challenge its bounds." The cartoon's racist caricature of Soubise's African ancestry implies that race is immutable, like the boundaries between species. It also implies that Soubise's Blackness is immutably opposed to the noble mien he cultivated so assiduously.[27]

But Soubise is not this cartoon's *ultimate* target. After all, he was an anomaly—one of only a handful of Afro-Britons to make it past the velvet rope of the fashionable world as a participant. (Plenty of African servants and enslaved workers were present in a menial capacity.) The cartoon uses race to represent class difference in order to argue that class is *like* race: a matter of birth that cannot be changed through education. I have spent much of this chapter trying to tease out the underappreciated function of rank in race's representational economy. Here, my point is that this argument could easily reverse directions. Race was a crucial ingredient in the making of elite class identities in the metropole. Soubise therefore is not of interest *only* to scholars of race and empire: he is, rather, a profoundly important case study for anyone investigating the construction of elite masculinity in Georgian Britain. Indeed, Soubise was a flashpoint for this issue in London, and he participated in the transplantation of aristocratic masculine ideals to India, as we shall see in the remainder of this chapter.[28]

Soubise in Calcutta

The location of Soubise's long final act has stymied scholarship on him. When he left the circum-Atlantic, he also exited the geographical framework used by scholars to study him, effectively going offstage. The available archival record is also to blame. In London, Soubise was a cause célèbre; his life was well documented. In India, the paper trail runs dry: the only glimpses into his life come from a handful of newspaper paragraphs. Given this, it is entirely understandable that scholars have ended Soubise's story with his embarkation for India. However, a new discovery has radically altered the material record. Peter Robb's extensive work on the eighty-volume manuscript diary of Richard Blechynden—an architect and surveyor who lived in Calcutta from the 1780s until the 1820s—has revealed that Blechynden's on-again, off-again business partner and friend was none other than Soubise, who appears in his diary dozens of times between 1794 and 1798. In fact, Blechynden's diary contains over twenty thousand words about Soubise, illuminating many details of his life in India for the first time. Elsewhere, I have written extensively about the information we can glean about Soubise's life from Blechynden's diary. In what follows, I limit my discussion of Soubise's time in India to focus on the guiding theme of this chapter: the interdependence of the two Indies in imperial Britain's racial ideologies.[29]

A sketch of Soubise's life in Calcutta is a useful place to begin. When Soubise arrived in India he established himself as a fencing and riding master. Unfortunately, success eluded him. The newspapers that document these years are a chronicle of financial instability. Puff pieces placed by Soubise to advertise new ventures—fencing lessons, horse dressing, a mare for sale—are followed at regular intervals by notices of insolvency. Yet whether he was imprisoned for debt, hounded by creditors, or suffered the sale of his stables at auction, Soubise inevitably bounced back with new ventures. Then, in 1789, he survived a brush with death when a French neighbor took a razor to his throat. After recovering, he disappeared from the Calcutta record for three years. He may have traveled to Lucknow to visit the Nawab of Awadh's famed stables. Then, in 1794, he suddenly entered Blechynden's social orbit—and diary—when he married the daughter of Blechynden's friend William Pawson.[30]

The social milieu Soubise entered after his marriage was a world away from the exalted circles he had frequented at Angelo's Academy. Pawson, who joined the East India Company in 1765, was the son of a London wine merchant. Although he eventually rose to a position of some note as Military Paymaster General, he was removed from this office for financial irregularities sometime after 1780, and never fully recovered from this disgrace—it was simply too difficult to thrive in Calcutta outside Company employment, especially during the economic downturn caused by war with France in the 1790s. In 1791, Blechynden remarked of Pawson, "his debt is desperate." Like her father, Catherine Pawson can be counted as a member of Calcutta polite society, even though she was not always altogether polite. Upon making her acquaintance in 1793, Blechynden "thought she was very forward for a young lady," an opinion later confirmed by a mutual acquaintance, who "had a long talk with me about Miss Pawson over which it is as well to draw the veil." The implication is that she was either sexually promiscuous or not particularly protective of her reputation. A newspaper poem published by one of her admirers gives a similar impression, as does her penchant for acting, an activity considered out of bounds for gentlewomen. Although "respectable" European women were held to looser standards in Calcutta than in England, Blechynden gives the impression that Miss Pawson was skirting the boundaries of respectability. Despite all this, he was still shocked to learn of her relationship with Soubise. As he records in his diary: "Breakfast to Tiretta's he told me that Soubise the Coffree was to marry Miss Pawson. I stared at this but only said that I had seen so much of human nature that I was *surprised* at nothing—and that *this Country is famous for extraordinary marriages.*" Later he repeated this sentiment to the bride's father, insensitively telling him, "I had heard" about the marriage "but *scarcely knew how to believe it.*"[31]

The only way to account for Blechynden's shock and disbelief is anti-Black racism. While interracial matches between European men and Indian women were common enough in Blechynden's milieu—he himself established long-term relationships with several Indian "bibis"— Soubise's marriage was judged by Blechynden to be beyond the pale. As Pawson was quick to point out, his daughter's marriage would not have been unheard of in England: Pawson "inquired if Black people did not marry white women in England &c. &c. I replied in the affirmative and endeavored all in my power to sooth the old man as the matter is past remedy." While such matches did take place—Equiano, for example, married a white woman—they were most common among servants and the laboring poor. Blechynden and his friends did struggle with debt, but they still considered themselves genteel. Blechynden kept a garden residence outside the city where he spent his leisure time hunting in the manner of an English squire. Perhaps he reacted so strongly to Catherine Pawson's marriage because he believed it undermined her class identity and social standing. Or perhaps he simply found affection between a white woman and Black man difficult to countenance. After his first dinner with the couple, he seemed displeased to find "Mrs. Soubise's Bosom ornamented with a Portrait of Soubise" and compared the couple to "Othello and Desdemona," a comparison that echoes Hester Thrale's biting remarks about Francis Barber's marriage to a white woman. In both cases, the Shakespearean reference seems to imply that the marital unions were libidinally charged. Indeed, Pawson openly speculated as much, saying "to someone who was expressing his surprise at his daughter marrying Soubise, that he supposed the Coffree *screwed her up tight*—and that was the reason she preferred him—from which we must understand that he tried if matters would fit before marriage!" Here we find the same tropes about hypersexual African masculinity we encountered earlier, in London, now transported halfway around the world to Calcutta.[32]

In other passages, too, Blechynden's diary reveals that British racism traveled on the same global networks that connected the colonies to the metropole and each other. He was clearly wary of doing business with Soubise on account of his race. When Soubise and Pawson approached Blechynden about building commercial stabling for them in 1794, Blechynden wrote in his diary, "I do not wish to have anything to do with Soubise." To be fair, this was partly due to Soubise's reputation for insolvency, since "*Creditors* might seize it [the stabling] if known to be his property." But Blechynden's wariness also sprung from racism. Other Europeans in Calcutta apparently shared his prejudices. In a conversation with Pawson that took place in 1795, Blechynden explained why he thought Soubise's stabling did not have more subscribers despite its superiority to other available options:

I happened to observe that *perhaps* many persons might give the preference to an European to Soubise—he [Pawson] called it illiberal—I therefore asked him if Soubise were not his Son in law—& he had a Horse to Stand at Livery which would he prefer—Soubise's or Fewell's on the Supposition that both places were equally good—he said *Soubise's*! I then said—we will not speak of Horses & Stables—but suppose that a Europe Shop Keeper and a China Bazar man had Goods of equal quality and the same price to dispose of—to which would he give the Preference? he said the *Bazar-man!* on my staring at him he added under certain Conditions—I replied I presumed those Conditions would be that he had married his daughter he said no—I told him ... Providence has wisely implanted this Partiality in us—for we first prefer our Parents—then we add to them our Brothers & Sisters after them our more distant relatives—next our fellow Associates (or *friends* as the world in general call them)—our fellow Parishioners Our Townsmen—Our Country-men—then other Countries in preference and lastly all the world—and when our Philanthropy was so enlarged—we might then term ourselves Citizen of it—but that that man *lied* who pretended that all men were alike to him—he that did not prefer his parents & kindred was a monster—! x^c x^c—after similar commonplace remarks he said—well "I wish the Stable was full"—As this was adequate to saying I am of your opinion at the bottom I squeezed his hand and said "And so do I, with all my Heart."

Many of the sentiments expressed here were commonplace in the eighteenth century, especially in an international city like Calcutta, where the presence of English, French, Swiss, Italian, Armenian, Persian, East Asian, and African people, as well as Indians from all over the subcontinent, fostered both a degree of cosmopolitanism and a preference to stick with one's own community when possible. That said, it is noteworthy that Blechynden excludes Soubise from the circle of his "Townsmen" or "Country-men." Even though Soubise was raised largely in England,

and lived completely in the style of a European, Blechynden classes him alongside "a China Bazar man." Once again, the only explanation for this snub is anti-Black racism.[33]

In India, Soubise thus encountered a world that was at once new to him and not so very different from what he had left behind. Like Blechynden, Calcutta's other European residents cast Soubise in the same old roles he had been conscripted to play in London. A facetious playbill published in a Calcutta newspaper in 1780 advertised Soubise's supposed appearance in the avatars of both high and low racialized character: "Mr. SOUBISE will appear . . . in the Character of Othello. And afterwards perform the part of Mungo in the entertainment." In addition to facing more of the same, Soubise also encountered new varieties of racism in India. There he became what he had never been before: a "Coffree." Understanding this term requires some familiarity with the subcontinent's Indo-Persian racial formation, the subject of the next section.[34]

Translating Race in Late Mughal / Early Colonial India

Race was not a strictly European import to India. If, as Shruti Kapila tells us, "the importance of race in the history of ideas of British India and India itself has been consistently underrated," this is partly due to the ongoing denial that racism exists in India in the present, a denial that persists in the face of reams of evidence to the contrary, as Ania Loomba argues. The issue of race and racism in India is complicated, Loomba explains, by the importance of caste, which functions as "a racial ideology." I will have more to say about caste in Chapter 4. For now, I wish to emphasize three interrelated points about India's "ideologies of difference": first, they predated European colonialism; second, they included color prejudice; third, they "collided and intermeshed for many hundreds of years" with European racial ideologies, beginning with the Portuguese arrival in Goa in the mid-sixteenth century at the latest. In the remainder of this section, I flesh out these three points. I then return to Soubise, in order to locate him in the context of British India's hybrid European/Indo-Persian racial formation.[35]

Although rarely presented as such in scholarship, race was a component of the Mughals' self-conception of their rule in India. Originally

Chaghta'i Turks, the Mughals established their dynasty on the subcontinent in the mid-sixteenth century with the help of Iranian forces. Over the next three centuries, the Mughals adapted to the subcontinent, engendering a new fusion of Central and South Asian, or Indo-Persian, culture. When the British arrived in India, they consistently differentiated between Mughal rulers and the population they ruled. Religion was one axis of difference separating so-called Mahometan (or Muslim) and Gentoo (or Hindu) Indians. But color also factored into this perception. If Europeans drew a color line between the Mughal state and the people they ruled over, they could find precedent for such a color-coded logic of conquest in Indo-Persian sources. Persian was the bureaucratic and artistic language of the Mughal court, and therefore the elite lingua franca of the subcontinent until the middle of the nineteenth century. In Persian poetry and literary classics—sold, as Muzaffar Alam tells us, by every bookseller at every bazaar in Agra, Delhi, and Lahore—readers encountered a racial economy of representation that in many ways mirrored that of the London stage. Annemarie Schimmel points out that, from the days of Hafiz, and even earlier, "Hindu" was used in Persian poetry as a "synonym for 'black.'" The implied color difference between Central and South Asians was also visualized in art. In Persian and Mughal miniature paintings from the early modern period onward, Indians and slaves are represented as "blackish in color" in comparison to lighter-skinned elites. As in English, so too in Persian, Blackness signified across several registers simultaneously. Hindus were "black" in the sense that they were dark-skinned, "lowly," "treacherous," and, notably, "slaves." The "contrasting pair 'Turk and Hindu,' 'ruler and slave'" was a tropological touchstone in Persian literature. It would be odd for a trope of this kind to spring up in the absence of historical practice. Therefore, it should come as no surprise that, as Richard Eaton explains, "the Mughals actively participated in an ancient trade with Central Asia in which slaves figured prominently." From the late thirteenth century through Akbar's reign in the early seventeenth century, defaulters on revenue payments, "rebels," and other captives were enslaved and exported "to Central Asian markets, where they were exchanged mainly for war horses, on which the Mughal military system was strategically dependent." I will have more to say on the subject of slavery in India in the following chapter. For now, the relevant point is that in Asia, as in Europe and Euro-America, racism was a pretense for enslavement as well as a historical product of slavery.[36]

Like racism, the African presence in India predates colonialism. Some Africans in India were enslaved—brought by Arab slavers operating in East Africa and around the Red Sea. Others were free, and worked as artisans, traders, and military commanders. Europeans also brought Africans to India by way of the Atlantic world. Other West Indians, like Soubise, traveled to India of their own accord. It may seem surprising, but Soubise wasn't the only former resident of Saint Kitts to sail to India on the *Bessborough*. Also present was Ignatius Sancho's friend Charles Lincoln, a musician who went to India in search of work. The presence of two free West Indians on the same ship bound for the East Indies is a reminder of the density of global networks laid down by British imperialism.[37]

It is well known that during the first decades of East India Company rule in India many Europeans openly admired Indian culture, adopting Indian mores to an extent that some Britons (including Lady Nugent) found alarming. Sometimes scholars have used this fact to suggest that racism was absent from early colonial India. David Cannadine, for example, cites English fascination with and occasional friendliness toward Indian elites as evidence that "social ranking was as important as (and perhaps more than?) colour of skin." The unstated assumption here is that high-ranking Indians considered themselves—and were viewed by Britons—as nonwhite. In other words, English elites *overlooked* race in order to recognize Indian elites as peers. But this assumption was true neither in metropolitan Britain nor on the ground in India. Miss G—'s conspicuous whitening of the "Sultana" in *Nocturnal Revels* demonstrates that high-ranking South and Central Asian characters were color-coded as white in metropolitan discourse. Meanwhile, color was equally important in the Mughals' ideological self-conception of their rule. Company officials stationed on the ground in India were exposed to this ideology and embraced it. The idea of light-skinned conquerors ruling over dark-skinned slaves jibed with British sensibilities, primed as they were for race-based conquest by the long history of European colonialism in the Americas. Moreover, the British desire to replace the Mughals facilitated a psychic identification with them. Sudipta Sen captures this dynamic nicely: "there was an emerging consensus that the East India Company was a reluctant heir to a long tradition of ... Moorish or Islamic conquests or repeated invasions of the subcontinent." Certainly, this consensus involved a critique of the Mughals as "Oriental despots," but it also reflected a psychic affiliation—one made all the more attractive by the enormous wealth commanded by Mughal rulers.[38]

In the decades after Plassey, Company officials translated the subcontinent's Indo-Persian racial formation into an Atlantic idiom, rendering it legible for British colonizers. Persian language-learning tools were one site where this translation occurred. The importance of Persian for the business of commerce and government in India made it necessary for a substantial number of Company employees to develop a working proficiency in the language. Walter Hakala reveals that many of the lexicons produced by and for Company officials relied heavily on prominent Indo-Persian multilingual vocabularies used "to teach Indian children Persian through a Hindu-Urdu medium" in preparation for bureaucratic careers in the Mughal empire. Take, for example, John Richardson's *Dictionary [of] Persian, Arabic, and English,* published in 1777. Hakala shows that it incorporated entries from two important Indo-Persian sources: the late seventeenth-century *Ghara'ib al-Lughat* (Marvels of words/languages), and the eighteenth-century *Nawadir al-Alfaz* (Wonders of words). These works were not like our dictionaries today, mere alphabetically arranged lists of word glosses that aim for total lexical coverage. Instead, Hakala explains, Persian dictionaries were thematically organized: they presented "a stable set of concepts with cultural significance embedded within a shared cosmographic representation of the universe." To a much greater extent than is true in the present, dictionaries in eighteenth-century India "served as vessels carrying cultures across both physical and cultural divides." Richardson mined these profoundly ideological Persian sources for his own dictionary. As a result, his language aids taught Britons much more than Persian: they initiated readers into an Indo-Persian "ideological framework" that included race.[39]

Richardson's *Dictionary* replicates a cosmography wherein Mughal rule is conceptualized and represented in racialized terms. This is particularly evident in Richardson's glosses of English racial vocabulary. For example, Richardson glosses "BLACK" as "hindé fam," or Indian colored.

The direction of translation (from English to Persian) is noteworthy here. Company officials were effectively prompted by Richardson to transpose their racial vocabulary from one Indies to the other. Even more noteworthy are Richardson's Persian glosses for "A NEGRO." While East and West Indians were both commonly referred to as "black" in the Georgian period, the term "negro" was always more specifically associated with African ancestry. Yet Richardson translates this Atlantic-world diction into a South Asian idiom, glossing it as "hindé," "hindoo," "hind," and "hindoo-é"—all terms that refer to either the people or the land of India. Other lexicographic works pushed this equivalence even further. Take, for example, the etymology for "*Hindoo*-stan" (or Hindustan, meaning India) proposed by John Gilchrist in his 1787 *Dictionary of English and Hindoostanee:* "[*Hindoo*-stan] was first introduced in its derivative form by the M*oo*sulmans, from the Persian. It implies simply Hindoo-*land,* formed exactly as Scot-*land,* and like it, comprising clearly both the partial, and national appellative in the country's name alone. *Hind,* the ancient term for *India,* perhaps signifies *black, niger* which with the common adjunct *oo,* produces *blackey, negro,* &c. so that we might even venture to translate *Hindoo*-stan, at once *Negro*-land." In this remarkable passage Gilchrist presents a view of India as a conquered land from the perspective of the victors. The subjection of "*Hindoo*-stan" is rendered in racialized terms: Indians are "black" and India is "*Negro*-land." Gilchrist's telling reference to "Scot-*land*" reminds us that his perspective on Persian is being filtered through a British worldview, the Indies mentality. Citing "Asiatick Researches," he later argues that "*Ethiopia* and *Hindustan* were peopled or colonized by the same extraordinary race." Projecting his own act of racial translation onto history, and stretching this era's Black British racial formation to its logical breaking point, he suggests that Indians and Africans are one and the same.[40]

In his diary, Blechynden repeatedly uses the word "Coffree" to describe Soubise. Originally an Arabic term meaning infidel (*kafir*), "coffree" was used by Europeans in India and the Cape Colony to differentiate Africans from themselves on the one hand and from East Indians on the other. The need for such a label testifies, once again, to the presence of a significant number of Africans in British India. In Blechynden's usage, the term "Coffree" is clearly pejorative. Whether or not it predated colonialism,

racism against Africans existed in India in the 1780s. Later, in the nineteenth and twentieth centuries, Indian color prejudice was exported on a
global scale when diasporic Indians brought it with them to British colonies in Africa and the Americas. Arundhati Roy explains that elite Indians
often saw themselves as partners in the Raj, equal to Britons and certainly
superior to the empire's Black African subjects, a dynamic Antoinette Burton calls "brown over black." Mohandas Gandhi expressed this view during
his time in South Africa. Far from opposing colonial segregation there, his
primary political project was petitioning authorities to give Indians their
own segregated facility so that they would not be forced to share a post-
office entryway with Black South Africans. The "Indian is being dragged
down to the position of a raw Kaffir," he complained. Sadly, this aspect of
Gandhi's legacy is still alive and well: anti-African racism and violence are
common in India today.[41]

Soubise and the Nawab

In *The Black Atlantic*, Gilroy argues that whenever "racist, nationalist,
or ethnically absolutist discourses" prevail, then "[s]triving to be both
European and black requires some specific forms of double consciousness." In British India, the psychic effort required to be both Black and
British was even more demanding and complex, as the black-and-white
color divide was complicated by the presence of Indian elites who fell
somewhere in between these two poles. Capitalizing on this ambiguity,
Soubise navigated anti-African racism in Calcutta by aligning himself
with Indian royalty.[42]

   This strategy is on full display in one of the most revealing passages about Soubise in Blechynden's diaries, written in November 1794,
when Blechynden was working full-time for Pawson and Soubise con-
structing commercial stabling (in what would eventually turn out to be
yet another doomed business venture). Blechynden habitually recol-
lected long conversations in his diary. The following passage records a
story told for his benefit by Soubise at dinner:

   To Timber Yard and to the Stabling Soubise and Pawson both
   called there and tiezed [sic] me so much to dine with them

that I was obliged to Comply . . . Soubise sent for me so went. Pawson a Hindostanny Girl and myself sat down to dinner with them—Soubise mentioning my Grey Horse Bucephalus to me as he often does, told me the following Anecdote about him—He purchased him for 1800 Rs at Lucknow. The Nabob soon after came to his Stables examined them all over and enquired where this Horse was whom he described very accurately. On Soubise informing him he had sent him down to Calcutta he disbelieved him—then offered him 1800 Rs. and any 2 Horses in his stud after he had taken out two favorites which were by no means his best Soubise declined the offer as the Horse had been gone a fortnight and might for all he then knew be dead or lamed He then increased the price to 2000 Rs and 2 Horses after taking away his 2 favorites and lastly to 2000 Rs and *any* 2 Horses of his he chose [*sic*] into the Bargain—Soubise still declining he enquired of whom he had purchased him? this Soubise also declined telling him— and he in angry mood asked if he could so accurately describe the Horse he had never seen and yet miss further intelligence respecting the dealer from the same quarter? and went away. In less than 48 hours the poor man came to Soubise *without his Nose*—the Nabob having ordered it to be cut off for presuming to sell a Horse in his Country without first making him an offer of it! what tyranny!!

This passage is remarkable in a number of respects. To begin with, it paints a vivid picture of Soubise's milieu in India, where his dinner table includes Europeans and Indians. The story Soubise tells is also extraordinary—so extraordinary, in fact, that it tests the limits of believability. In the 1790s, the Nawab of Awadh, Asaf al-Dawla, was a powerful ruler, second only to the Mughal emperor in symbolic political authority. Soubise's soon-to-be business partner, the Chevalier de l'Etang— Virginia Woolf's great-great-grandfather and a rumored lover of Marie Antoinette, who was waiting out the French Revolution in India—was employed for a time in the Nawab's stables, which were among the largest on the subcontinent. It is therefore not inconceivable that Soubise did trade horses from the Nawab's stables in Lucknow. What is slightly more difficult—although by no means impossible—to believe is that Soubise would provoke and exasperate one of the richest men in India to such an extent. Exaggerated or not, Soubise's narration of his standoff with the Nawab amounts to an extraordinary act of self-fashioning. Perhaps the most remarkable aspect of the passage is the extent to which it recalls and reverses Soubise's apocryphal face-off with Miss G— in *Nocturnal Revels*. Aggrandizing himself vis-à-vis the Nawab, Soubise cannibalizes his power, reversing the parodic subversion he was subject to again and again in the London mediascape. Face-to-face with a real-life incarnation of the kind of Eastern royalty parodied in the pet-slave figure, Soubise comes out on top. The symbolic castration he suffered at the hands of Miss G— is now doled out at his suggestion, when he goads the Nawab into punishing the horse dealer, who loses his nose as a result. Here Soubise exercises the power to maim that constitutes a hallmark of Oriental despotism.[43]

Soubise's besting of the Nawab draws on his European aristocratic education. Thanks to Donna Landry and a number of other scholars, we know that horsemanship was absolutely central to the performance of aristocratic masculinity in Britain from the early modern period onward. A horse's appearance, its bloodlines, the way it was ridden and trained, and the type of tack with which it was saddled were all indicators of the pedigree of its owner. During the seventeenth and eighteenth centuries especially, as practices of horsemanship diverged along class lines, the horse a man rode and the style in which he rode it were as indicative of his social status as the clothes he wore or the street where he lived. In a symbolic register, too, horses were central to the political ideology of Britain's upper classes. Landry points to the frequency with which horsemanship was invoked as an analogy for governance: "To ride a horse well was to possess the virtues necessary for social authority and even political rule."[44]

To a remarkable degree, all of this was also true in India. As already mentioned in relation to the Central Asian slave trade, the horse was the foundation of military power in South Asia. From the Delhi sultanate of the thirteenth century to the Afghan Durrani empire of the eighteenth century and the Punjabi Sikh empire of the nineteenth century, political dynasties rose and fell on the subcontinent on the basis of their cavalry's military "horsepower." In addition to being a crucial instrument of warfare, the horse was also a potent source of symbolic political authority. Given that horses were never used for agriculture or transportation by peasants in India, they were associated exclusively with military campaigns, religious and courtly ceremonies, and conspicuous consumption. Well-bred horses were extremely expensive in India thanks to a shortage of arable pastures. (In 1813, a major was dismissed from the East India Company army after thirty years of service in India by a special order of the Supreme Council of Bengal for the offense of trying to sell a horse to the Nawab of Murshidabad for the "extravagant price of a Lack of Rupees," the equivalent of about £400,000 today.) Equestrian connoisseurship therefore served as an index of class training, elitism, and rank throughout India. Jagjeet Lally explains that Indian royals often chose to be represented in portraits in the act of inspecting an exceptionally magnificent horse. The privilege of being painted actually astride a horse was reserved for the Mughal emperor alone. Equestrianism was the source for much of the Mughals' metaphorical vocabulary for political power. The emperor was "the imperial stirrup," and horses were important signifiers of the hierarchical ordering of the court. Events like the annual reading of the stables' muster rolls were made into ritual state occasions. In the 1780s and 1790s, Lucknow, in particular, was a hub of the Indian horse trade thanks to the efforts of the Nawab, who was a renowned horseman. When Lady Nugent visited the "Nawab's stud of horses" in 1812 the stables were already past their prime, but they still contained "fifteen hundred [horses]; they are chiefly Arab, but some are English." This number is doubly impressive when we consider that a single fine Arabian horse could easily sell for upwards of £200 at this time.[45]

In short, the horse was one of the few signifiers of aristocratic masculinity that translated seamlessly across the cultural divide between Mughal and British elites. Meeting the Nawab on the shared ground of elite equestrianism, Soubise outdoes him. His reward is more than a horse: he also claims the elite masculine power the horse symbolizes. This symbolic power is epitomized in the name of the horse in question. Bucephalus was the famed steed of Alexander the Great (known in

Persian as Iskander), whose prowess was as legendary in Central and South Asia as it was in Europe. He was a potent symbol of military valor and conquest, and was particularly associated with India, as he died during the Battle of Hydaspes, a turning point in Alexander's conquest of what is now Punjab. Bucephalus was also a token of Alexander's exceptional horsemanship: he was a famously unmanageable stallion who refused to be governed by any other human. In managing to secure this symbolism-laden horse, Soubise wins a totem of the Nawab's elite masculinity. He also makes himself a middleman in the fantasized transfer of power from Mughal elites to Britons.[46]

The anecdote also consolidates Soubise's power at a more mundane level. The setup for Soubise's tale is a business deal: Soubise sold Bucephalus to Blechynden for the handsome price of 1,800 rupees. Viewed in this light, Soubise's heroic ordeal reads like the tall tale of a used-car salesman who wants to make his customer feel good about a very expensive purchase. When Soubise lets fall the crumb that the Nawab was prepared to give "2000 Rs and *any* 2 Horses" of Soubise's choice for Bucephalus, the implication is that Blechynden got a very good deal. Soubise would have made a larger profit by allowing the Nawab to keep his horse! Blechynden is thus the great winner of the story, since at little trouble to himself he secured a horse fit for a king. By selling Blechynden the horse Alexander the Great used to conquer India (at least in name), Soubise sells him a fantasy, connecting him to one of the great Asiatic empires of antiquity. Soubise also wins the prize of Blechynden's friendship with this anecdote. At the outset of this diary entry, Blechynden admits that he did not want to socialize with Soubise, and accepted his dinner invitation only after being "tiezed." In the months following this dinner party, Blechynden and Soubise began to socialize regularly, until they had a falling out a few months later.[47]

The anecdote about Soubise and the Nawab tells us a lot about the former's survival strategy in Calcutta, which involved putting the aristocratic education he had received under Angelo's tutelage to good use. Borrowing a page from Angelo's playbook, Soubise operated a manège that traded in class training as much as it did in horses. He essentially offered the same service Angelo made available to nabobs like Holwell in London, but he sold it on location, teaching Calcutta's class-aspirational

Europeans how to act like gentlemen. This business model could hardly be advertised in clearer terms than in a newspaper puff that was printed in the *Calcutta Chronicle* in 1788. Since the piece was in all likelihood printed at Soubise's expense, it is fair to read it as yet another act of self-fashioning:

> Yesterday morning, early, the manly exercise of horse-manship was practiced at the Menage, by the scholars of Mr. Soubise, before a very numerous assembly.
>
> After the practice was over, near two hundred of the principal people of the settlement sat down to an elegant breakfast provided on the occasion.
>
> Breakfast being over, a ball was given, and the ladies and gentlemen were so highly delighted, that it was not without evident signs of regret, they relinquished such a pleasing and health-giving source of amusement.

Evidence suggests that Soubise taught his pupils the same "eclectic hybrid" style of riding he had learned from Angelo, which combined the practical techniques used in hunting and racing with the more ornamental form of dressage traditionally practiced in the manège. This blend of horsemanship-as-country-squire-pastime and horsemanship-as-aristocratic-art was perfectly suited to Soubise's "scholars." Riding, and particularly hunting, were popular pursuits among Europeans in Calcutta, not least because these pastimes represented a grade of polite leisure culture that would have been closed to many of them at home. Moreover, from the above puff it is clear that, like his mentor, Soubise combined instruction in gentlemanly arts with the opportunity to practice genteel sociability. The description of the entertainment that follows the scholars' display of their equestrian learning recalls the salon-like atmosphere of Carlisle House. Soubise's manège taught more than horsemanship: it offered the opportunity to take part in a simulative performance of gentility.[48]

There is, of course, something incongruous about a formerly enslaved Afro-Briton teaching Europeans to act like gentlemen in India. Or perhaps it only seems incongruous because we have paid far too little attention to the roles played by race and empire in the making of the British upper classes. Georgian racial and class ideologies look different when viewed from the perspective of an analytic framework that includes both India and the Atlantic world. The next chapter argues that the same is true for another key topic in imperial history: the rhetoric of slavery.

Political Slavery and Oriental Despotism from Haiti to Bengal

I n autumn 1804, the most sensationalized episode in the Haitian Revolution was already old news. Reports of the massacre of Saint-Domingue's remaining French colonists first reached London by way of New York in April of that year. Three months later *The Morning Post* published a translation of the proclamation issued by Jean-Jacques Dessalines, General of the Armée Indigène, announcing the massacres with his epoch-defining utterance: "I have avenged America." Then, in late September, another "Proclamation of Dessalines," this one dated May 2, splashed across English newspapers. Addressed to the "Inhabitants of the Universe," this proclamation justified the massacres, now a fait accompli, to the world: "The Republic of Hayti wishes to live in peace with all mankind, except with the White slaves of a Buonaparte; to them they swear an eternal hatred, destruction and death. ... Let Frenchmen prove themselves worthy of freedom, by chastising their foreign tyrant, and by crushing the degrading yoke he has imposed upon them; and then, and not until then, will we treat with them as one independent state does with another equally independent."[1]

The May 2 proclamation displays all the hallmarks of "Dessalinean rhetoric." Literary scholar Chelsea Stieber characterizes Dessalines's discursive modus operandi as "rescripting dominant terms that circulated in the eighteenth-century Atlantic print public sphere to perform and legitimize Haitian statehood while simultaneously calling into question the putative legitimacy of those dominant systems." Calling the French "the White slaves of a Buonaparte" and taunting them to recover their "freedom" from the "foreign tyrant" who has imposed slavery's "degrading yoke" on France, Dessalines deftly invokes and rescripts two key concepts from European discourse: political slavery and despotism. These paired keywords were used to justify colonialism in both Indies. They also circulated on a global scale in the eighteenth century, from the "Atlantic print public sphere" to the "paper war" over East India Company rule raging halfway around the world in India. Extremely important in the history of imperialism, but vastly understudied in scholarship, political slavery and despotism are the subjects of this chapter. Using the perspective of the Indies mentality, this chapter recovers the key roles played by these concepts during the Age of Revolutions as they circulated between India and the Americas, and within the world of metropolitan discourse.[2]

Originating in classical antiquity, the concepts of political slavery and despotism made their first appearance in Europe during the sixteenth century's humanist Greco-Roman revival and rose to prominence in English writing shortly thereafter, during the political upheavals of the seventeenth century. In the ancient world and early modern Europe alike, the twin concepts of political slavery and despotism belonged to mentalities that conceptualized freedom as structurally interdependent on its opposite, slavery. For the Greeks, political slavery named the collective condition of a polity conquered by an outside invader. Meanwhile, despotism represented the flip side of this coin: the kind of government— absolute, arbitrary, extractive, tyrannical—imposed on the conquered. Because the gravest existential threat to the Greek city states was the powerful Persian empire, despotism was associated first and foremost with Asia—hence the well-known geographically inflected variation of this keyword, Oriental despotism. If subjection to the Persian emperor would turn free Greek citizens into slaves, then the emperor's current subjects must be slaves already. This logic saturates Herodotus's history of the fifth century BCE Persian wars. Classicist Page Dubois explains: "The great conflict between Asia and Europe is posed as a struggle between slavery and freedom: Europe metaphorically marked as free, Asia as enslaved. The Greeks as a people, united in opposition to the Asians, fight for what they understand as freedom, against enslavement, against incorporation into an empire in which only the emperor is free." Edward Gibbon evinces that this attitude was imbibed by Georgian students of the classical past. In his *History of The Decline and Fall of the Roman Empire,* he refers offhandedly to "the slaves of oriental despotism."[3]

In a number of disciplines, political slavery has traditionally been understood as a metaphor that operates independently of histories of chattel slavery. Dubois explodes this neat division between slavery's rhetoric and practice in the context of classical studies. "Literal and metaphorical slavery are inextricable here," she writes of Herodotus's history of the Persian wars, "as the struggle for Greek freedom was understood both as the preservation of a way of life, and as a escape from the fate of literal enslavement," a fate that befell war captives in the ancient world. Mary Nyquist extends Dubois's disciplinary critique to political theory. In scholarship on classical republicanism and its revival during the English civil wars, "political slavery appears to stand free of significant ties to actual, human bondage or to Euro-colonialism." Nyquist's point is that this appearance is misleading: slavery was ubiquitous in Greco-Roman society, and the Stuarts aggressively pursued a colonial policy whose cornerstone was the expansion of slavery.[4]

Meanwhile, political slavery's "ties" to "actual" practices of chattel slavery and "Euro-colonialism" are thrown into sharp relief in Dessalines's May 2 proclamation. "The Republic of Hayti" is an "island of liberty" not only because the revolution liberated individual Haitians from chattel slavery, but also because the republic is collectively free from the despotic rule of a "foreign tyrant," France. A master of weaponizing Enlightenment revolutionary rhetoric against Europe, Dessalines plays on the friction between slavery's rhetoric and practice in order to call out French hypocrisy and portray Haiti as the French Revolution's last stronghold. He reminds his listeners (and readers) that Haiti is the only place in "the Universe" where freedom from *both* political slavery *and* chattel slavery prevails. Nor is the May 2 proclamation unique in this respect. Julia Gaffield argues that political and chattel slavery are likewise fused in the Haitian Declaration of Independence. In this monumentally important document, Gaffield explains, Dessalines and his generals declared "*liberté*" not only "from individual enslavement—which had been abolished in the colony in 1793," but also from the "dominion" of France and "the metaphorical or political slavery of colonialism." Our collective scholarly neglect of political slavery has a lot to do with our fear that this concept minimizes the singular and incomparable unfreedom of chattel slavery, perhaps even with racist undertones. But Dessalines's reliance on the rhetoric of political slavery in his conceptualization of Haitian freedom and in his indictment of Euro-colonialism clearly indicates that we don't need to choose between chattel slavery and political slavery in our own critiques. To the contrary, reading political slavery *past-critically* requires attending to the variegated practices of unfreedom that always subtend this figure's deployment in rhetoric.[5]

This, in turn, requires an analytic framework that includes both of the two Indies. In the wake of the conquest of Bengal, especially, ancient Greek ideas about Oriental despotism were reactivated. From the Georgian period through the Age of Revolutions, British writers consistently —even ubiquitously—associated political slavery with Asia. From the 1770s onward, this notion was a well-worn fact: "The kingdoms of the east ... have always been despotic in their nature." Political slavery and Oriental despotism provided a convenient lens through which to view the subcontinent's history and justify its future: naturally servile, Indians were easily invaded by the Mughals, who ruled their conquered territory despotically, turning Indians into political slaves. The East India Company's conquest was thus justified as liberation, and the nonrepresentative character of its colonial government was rationalized as inevitable. Writing in 1784, during the debate over Fox's India Bill, Alexander Dalrymple put the matter simply: "a *conquered* people ... *must* still be *slaves,* however light the yoke; slaves can only be Governed by despotic power."[6]

Paying attention to this rhetoric doesn't mean choosing political slavery over chattel slavery, or India over the Atlantic world. Political slavery and despotism showed up in the Eastern and Western theaters of European colonialism in equal parts. In portraying India as a land of "perpetual slavery" (to borrow Adam Ferguson's turn of phrase), Britons employed the very same conceptual framework utilized by Dessalines to proclaim Haiti an "island of liberty." Void of any *inherent* politics, political slavery and despotism were mobilized in the service of divergent political ends, from Dalrymple's colonial project to Dessalines's radical anticolonialism. Political slavery and despotism were portable categories, in geographical as well as ideological terms. This chapter therefore divides its time between the two Indies. In the next section I begin where Chapter 2 left off, in colonial Bengal, where political slavery and Oriental despotism are ubiquitously present in policy debates about Company rule. In this section, and throughout the chapter, I take a genealogical approach. Surveying the sedimentary layers of meaning acquired by political slavery and Oriental despotism over the *longue durée* is necessary in order to grasp how and why these concepts were mobilized to advocate various policy positions in late eighteenth-century India. Many features of Oriental despotism attributed to the Mughal empire actually accrued to the concept whole centuries (if not a millennium) earlier, during classical antiquity and the seventeenth century, when the structural position of the "Orient" was filled by the Persian and Ottoman empires, respectively.[7]

Tracing the circuit of political slavery and despotism's global travels next brings me back to the scene of Chapter 1, the American War. Protesting Grenville's extractive revenue policies as tantamount to slavery, American colonists recycled a formulation honed in the East India Company pamphlet wars of the previous years. In the very different context of the thirteen colonies, however, such rhetoric reeked of hypocrisy: how could the Americans complain about political slavery when their economy was dependent on the practice of chattel slavery? In response to the Patriots' use—and abuse—of this rhetoric, "slavery" shed its more capacious meaning, becoming synonymous with chattel slavery, as it still is today.

Finally, I turn to metropolitan discourse to show how the charge of despotism was leveled against anticolonial enemies in both Indies in the 1790s and 1800s. Despotism's Asian associations did not prevent the London press from characterizing Dessalines and Henry Christophe, King Henry I of Haiti, as tyrants who needed to be deposed so that their subjects could be liberated from political slavery. This same logic was applied to Tipu Sultan of Mysore, the Company's most formidable enemy on the subcontinent. Yet these charges of despotism were a double-edged sword. The Persian, Ottoman, and Mughal empires were smeared as Oriental despotisms in very different contexts; but in each context, the insult derived from fear. The Greeks, English, and Company feared that these powerful "Asian" enemies represented an existential threat to "Europe." So-called despots were therefore ripe for recuperation as figures of anticolonial resistance and circulated in this capacity on a global scale. Previewing Chapter 5, this chapter concludes in Jamaica, where Lady Nugent watched enslaved West Indians perform a drama that included, in a starring role, the children of Tipu Sultan.

To a greater extent than in any other chapter, my analysis in what follows cycles through many different genres and types of writing, from political theory, to poetry, ethnography, travel writing, and political pamphlets. This is partly because the study of mentalities requires a broad and varied data set. But I also wish to make another point. Political theory involves just as much creative license as fiction and therefore calls for the same interpretive practice: close reading. The stories told about political slavery and Oriental despotism often appeared in "serious" treatises about politics and government, but they were stories nonetheless.

The "Perpetual Slavery" of the East

Late Georgian writers consistently associated slavery with the East Indies. Scottish Enlightenment philosopher Adam Ferguson encapsulated his era's reigning common sense when he observed, in *An Essay on the History of Civil Society,* that the "chains of perpetual slavery . . . appear to be rivetted in the East." Alexander Dow, a Scottish army officer in the East India Company, endorsed this verdict in his *History of Hindostan:* "Asia, the seat of the greatest empires, has always been the nurse of the most abject slaves." Such sentiments were repeated often enough during the crisis years of the 1770s to become clichéd. The hack poet Richard Clarke recycled this well-worn truism in *The Nabob: or, Asiatic Plunderers,* writing, "In *Asia's* realms let slavery be bound, / Let not her foot defile this sacred ground." Today, these verses read like a mistake: *didn't he mean the West Indies?* But for this era's writers, India featured prominently in slavery's mental map, which was a global one.[8]

When Ferguson, Dow, and Clarke spoke of slavery in India, they did not have actual practices of bonded labor in mind—although they would not have been wrong if they had. Indrani Chaterjee, Richard Eaton, Anjali Arondekar, Richard Allen, Rupa Viswanath, along with a number of other scholars, have established that an abundance of unfree labor practices and legal conditions thrived in early colonial India, including domestic slavery, slave concubinage, and agrestic caste-based slavery (which survived into the twentieth century under the pretense of debt peonage). Enslaved Africans were also imported into India, as we learned in Chapter 2. Meanwhile, enslaved and indentured Indians were transported to destinations in Central Asia, Mauritius, the Indian Ocean World—and, beginning in the 1830s, the British West Indies. That said, Company officials declined to admit the existence of most of these practices. Andrea Major describes this conspiracy of silence: "references to the existence of slavery in India remained conspicuous primarily by their absence." However, Major speaks only of *chattel* slavery here; references to *political* slavery were, by contrast, conspicuously *present* in English writing about India.[9]

Our failure to recognize political slavery as an important conceptual framework in colonial discourse has turned the ubiquity of slavery in eighteenth-century writing about India into a puzzle in scholarship. Madeleine Dobie offers one solution to this puzzle in *Trading Places,* where she argues that French writers "regularly projected or 'displaced'" the problem of African slavery from the West Indies to "the Oriental world." Dobie's psychodrama is compelling because it syncs with our instinctive tendency to read slavery as a metaphor when we encounter it outside the circum-Atlantic. Paul Ricoeur and Paul de Man explain that the "epistemology of metaphor" turns on displacement. Sensing that metaphors work by transplanting meaning away from where it "really belongs," our instinct is to curtail the "epistemological damage" by trying to "control figuration by keeping it, so to speak, in its place"—in this case, by returning slavery from India to its "proper" place, the West Indies. Ultimately, Ricoeur and de Man both argue that this understanding of metaphor is wrong because it fundamentally misapprehends the nature of language, which is inescapably figurative. More recently, Brad Pasanek and Amanda Jo Goldstein have established the existence of a similarly complex take on the figurative ontology of language—and so-called empirical reality—in the eighteenth century. To be clear, references to slavery in India without question derive some of their rhetorical power from the specter of African chattel slavery. But if we reduce the former to metaphors whose only referent is the latter, then we risk foreclosing the crucial conceptual and rhetorical work performed by the figure of political slavery in English writing on colonial India.[10]

The rhetoric of political slavery was used by European writers to depict India's conquest and subjugation by foreign powers—including the East India Company—as a calamity of monumental proportions. Instead of reading this language as an exaggeration vis-à-vis chattel slavery, we might read it as a welcome corrective to today's whitewashed histories, which far too often depict the Raj as benevolent in intent and harmless (if not even beneficial!) in effect. Late Georgian writers were far more willing to admit that, from the perspective of the conquered, colonialism always spelled humiliation, if not outright immiseration. In using "political slavery" to name this affliction, English writers followed classical precedent. In her account of slavery's use "as a figure for political oppression" in Western thought, Nyquist explains that, in ancient Greece, "slavery" referred to two conditions: the subjection of individual chattel slaves to their owners and the collective subjection of the entire polis of free male citizens to a tyrannical ruler such as a foreign invader. The very word "despot" (from the Greek *despotes*) fuses these two meanings: it refers at once to a master of slaves and to "the absolute ruler of a non-free people." Aristotle used *despotes* in both of these senses in his *Politics,* so that the difference between political slavery and chattel slavery boils down to a matter of scale: the household master of slaves rules over a polity in miniature, while the despot reigns over a country of slaves. Dubois insists that the rhetoric of political slavery in classical political philosophy was powerful only because of the ubiquitous presence of actual enslaved people in daily life in ancient Greece. "Manipulating the fears and anxieties of the free Greeks by threatening them with the status of their chattels" was only possible, Dubois explains, because those chattel slaves "were insistently, troublingly present." Political slavery was "one of the most potent of tropes in the rhetoric of this culture" precisely because the "awkward, ugly, brutalized slave body" was a daily reminder of slavery's ignominy.[11]

Like slavery in eighteenth-century Euro-America, slavery in ancient Greece was racialized, partly as a result of imperial expansion. After the

Persian wars, Nyquist explains, the slave population of Athens came to be numerically dominated by non-Greek "barbarian" adult males, resulting in the de facto racialization of chattel slavery. Meanwhile, the supposed "acquiescence of barbarians" conquered by Athens to "absolute, monarchical rule was deemed tantamount to 'slavery'" of the political variety. Once again, Aristotle is an apt reference point. Writing in the wake of the Persian wars, he declared "spiritless" Asiatics to be natural slaves, "more servile in character" than both "Hellenes" and "Europeans," and therefore vulnerable to conquest. It's worth pointing out just how ideological this rhetoric really was. Victory in the Persian wars wasn't easy: the Persian empire was a military powerhouse in the ancient world, and a feared opponent. Remember, the Persian wars stoked the rhetoric of political slavery because defeat would mean actual enslavement for the conquered—and defeat was a real possibility. Aristotle obfuscates these historical anxieties. In Asia, the emperor might be despotic, but the populace was weak: their "slavish nature" rendered them "the slave of every invader." Aristotle's seeming description is actually prescriptive. In Plutarch's *Lives,* he tells his pupil Alexander the Great to "behave as a leader (*hegemon*) towards Greeks but as a *despotes* towards the Barbarians conquered by his victories." Despotic rule was deemed "natural" for "Asiatics," but it would, Nyquist clarifies, "represent a demeaning, traumatic loss" for the free male citizens of Athens.[12]

In the 1770s this trope retained all of its potency, thanks to the two Indies. British America (like ancient Greece) was a slave society; and colonialism in India (as in Greece) was justified by a racist worldview that portrayed Asia as inferior. It would be difficult to overstate the importance of classical ideas about the natural servility of Asiatics in eighteenth-century conceptualizations of Company rule in India. One reason these ideas were transposed with such ease to the subcontinent is that the Mughals already conceived of their rule in racialized terms, a point I elaborated upon in the previous chapter. Company officials proved eager to view India's history of conquest in terms of slavery. Robert Orme summed up the common sentiment in his *Historical Fragments of the Mogul Empire,* where he describes the "Tartars who conquered this country" as "the lords" and "the Gentoos," or Hindus, as the "slaves of this empire." Conveniently, this perspective was entirely harmonious with the

prospect of India laid out in classical texts. Even Europeans in the position of eyewitnesses still insisted on viewing India through the lens of the
classical past. François Bernier—whose 1670 memoir of his time as a
physician in the service of Dara Shikoh (a son of Emperor Shah Jahan)
was enormously influential in eighteenth-century France and England—
was advised by Jean Chapelain (a founding member of the Académie
française) to inform himself "of the history and the revolutions of that
kingdom, not merely since Tamerlane and successors, but *ab ovo* and
since Alexander."[13]

Montesquieu helped merge ancient and modern perspectives
by updating Aristotelian natural slavery with new Enlightenment ideas
about the climatic origins of race. For Montesquieu, "the nature of the
climate" was primarily to blame for India's descent into "political servitude": in his view, "great heat enervates the strength and courage of men,"
leading to effeminacy and conquest. Not quite biological determinism,
Montesquieu's theory locates climate's effects—and therefore, slavery's
cause—in culture: "The customs of an enslaved people are a part of their
servitude." Roxann Wheeler argues that Montesquieu was particularly influential in Scottish Enlightenment circles; and since Scots were overrep-
resented in East India Company service, climate theory is omnipresent in
company writing about India. "Mild, humane, obedient, and industrious,"
India's "Hindoos" were, according to Dow (a Scotsman), "of all the nations on earth the most easily conquered and governed. Their government, like that of all the inhabitants of Asia, is despotic." Orme repeats
clichés about Indian slavishness so often in his *Historical Fragments* that
he finds it necessary to "apologize for reminding the reader so often, of
the gradation of slavery which subsists throughout Indostan; without carrying this idea continually with us, it is impossible to form any idea of
these people." Slavishness represented ground zero of Indian character.[14]

Taken together, the subcontinent's long history of supposedly despotic rule, on the one hand, and the natural slavishness of Indians, on the
other, provided a strong double-pronged rationale for the Company's
conquest of India and for the despotic character of its government. While
some commentators held out hope that "the rod of Moorish despotism"
would be "contrasted with the milder attributes supposed to characterize
an English administration," others argued that India could only be gov-

erned despotically. According to Montesquieu, the natural servility of India's "Gentoos" meant they would inevitably be ruled by a foreign invader: "A free nation can have a deliverer; a nation enslaved can have only another oppressor." This being the case, an English company was a better choice than Muslim conquerors—or so the logic seemed to go. Indian unfreedom was therefore judged to be the cause as well as an effect of the Company's despotic government. Sudipta Sen explains: "The notion of the unfreedom of colonial subjects in India was profound among British administrators."[15]

While retooled Aristotelian notions about natural slavery represented one source for this opinion, there were others. For instance, it also owed a great deal to Oriental despotism's association with landlessness. As "liberty and property" were "inviolable and mutually dependent qualities" in British thought, Sen argues, a landless people couldn't possibly be free. To my knowledge, there is no precedent in classical writing for the idea that political slavery entailed dispossession. Rather, I argue in the next section, this notion came into being during the seventeenth century, when the paragon of Oriental despotism was the Ottoman empire.[16]

Despotism as Dispossession

Before the Mughal empire became the paradigmatic example of Oriental despotism in European writing, this honor belonged to the Ottoman empire. In the seventeenth century, the Ottomans were a geopolitical powerhouse, the "terror of the world." Today the possibility is confined to the domain of counterfactual history, but it often seemed as if the Ottomans might conquer all of Europe. In 1683 they waged a two-week siege of Vienna; and as late as 1699, Gottfried Wilhelm Leibniz still feared a new wave of invasions from Central Asia. In short, the Ottomans occupied a structural position very similar to that of the Persian empire vis-à-vis ancient Greece. Classical ideas about Oriental despotism thus provided European and English writers a compelling lens through which to view their neighbors to the east. In 1603 Richard Knolles published the first "major original English account of the Ottomans," his *Generall Historie of the Turkes*. Anders Ingram argues that the *Generall Historie* remains faithful to Aristotelian precedent in general and on the subject of despotism in particular. To name just one example, Knolles recalls Aristotle's twofold usage of *despotes* when he describes the Ottoman state as despotic, "altogether like the government of the master over his slave."[17]

At the same time that classical ideas about Oriental despotism shaped Knolles's view of the Ottoman empire, the information he published about Ottoman society also seeped into and warped the conceptual framework of Oriental despotism. Our projection of disciplinary divisions onto a past that simply does not conform to them has obscured important connections between political theory and historical/ethnographic writings on Ottoman society. Ingram is one of the few scholars to insist that Knolles's *Generall Historie of the Turkes* should be read alongside another text he worked on contemporaneously and published three years later: his translation of Bodin's apologia for absolutism, *The Six Bookes of a Commonweale*. To my knowledge, landownership is not a perquisite of conquest in classical political theory. Perhaps this is because pre-European empires extracted tribute or taxes instead of annexing conquered lands outright. But in Bodin's influential retooling of Aristotle in *The Six Bookes of a Commonweale,* dispossession and propertylessness are introduced as essential features of political slavery. Nyquist suggests that Bodin found precedent for this idea in Hebraic law. While that may be the case, historical and sociological accounts of Ottoman society seem like an equally plausible influence. For Knolles and many other early modern European writers, the hallmark of Ottoman society was a supposed lack of private property rights. Knolles critiques this state policy for disincentivizing industry: "the subjects despairing to enjoy the fruits of the earth, much lesse the riches which by their industrie and labour they might get unto themselves, doe now no further endeavour themselves either to husbandrie or traffique." Even without delving into the complexities of Ottoman property rights, it is not difficult to recognize a classic example of Saidian Orientalism here. If "liberty and property" were the interlinked cornerstones of English identity, then Knolles portrays the Ottoman empire as England's Other by making the absence of property the crux of Ottoman society.[18]

Bodin turns this quintessential feature of Ottoman society into a key feature of despotism. In the process, he also traces the historical path of despotism's migration out of Asia and into Europe. Writing in the midst of a crisis in the political legitimacy of absolute monarchy, Bodin's primary purpose was to rehabilitate despotism by neutralizing its negative connotations. One way he did this was by splitting despotism into two categories, "lordly Monarchie" and "Tyrannical Monarchie." While both types of monarchs establish their hereditary rule through conquest and enjoy absolute power over their subjects, the former obeys divine and natural law while the latter does not. Given that Bodin's new distinction was a purely partisan effort to rehabilitate absolutism by rebranding it as benign and legitimate, early modern readers would have recognized "lordly Monarchie" as despotism by another name. Indeed, Bodin retains despotism's classical geographical association with Asia, dating its arrival in Europe to the fifth century AD invasions of the Huns: "But the people of Europe were courageous, and better soldiers then [sic] the people of Africke or Asia, could never endure the lordly Monarques, neither had ever used them before the incursions of the Hunnes into Europe.... But after that ... Englishmen, and other Northren people had tasted the manners and customes of the Hunnes, they began to make themselves Lords, not of the persons, but of all the lands of them whom they had vanquished." In this remarkable passage, Bodin achieves two contradictory purposes: he leaves Asia's natural inferiority and slavishness vis-à-vis Europe intact, and he implies that Europeans are nonetheless still vulnerable to political slavery.[19]

Bodin's origin story for "lordly Monarchie" is a testament to Cedric Robinson's argument in *Black Marxism* that modern "racial capitalism" is continuous with early modern feudalism, not a rupture from it. In his genealogy of European feudalism, Bodin projects ancient Greece's geo-ethnic division between free Greeks and servile Asians onto Europe's class hierarchy, so that the servility of the poor is, in a sense, Asiatic. Bodin's racialization of poverty is especially significant in light of my discussion of Mughal India's Indo-Persian racial formation in Chapter 2, as it points to continuities between European and non-European (and, therefore, colonial and metropolitan) status-inflected ideas about race. Bodin's account of feudal Europe is distinctly colonial in flavor: lords rule the servile poor by right of conquest. It is also applicable to the colonies: Bodin cites the conquest of the "great country of Peru" by "the

emperour *Charles* the first" as an example of lordly monarchy established through warfare. He also leaves the colonial connotation of foreign invasion intact in his transposition of despotism to England. Chief
among the "Northren people" who acquire a taste for "the manners and
customes of the Hunnes," in Bodin's telling, is England's first Norman
king: "*William* the Conqueror, having conquered the realme of England,
by force of armes, called himselfe not only lord of that realme, but also
caused it to be proclaimed, that the soveraigntie and propertie of all his
subjects goods, movable, and immovable unto him belonged." Although
Bodin eventually backpedals on this point, arguing that de facto property rights survived William's de jure abrogation of them, opponents of
absolutism were less forgiving in their verdicts.[20]

During the English civil wars, radicals applied Bodin's projection
of despotism onto England in the service of very different ends. Gerrard
Winstanley and the Diggers blamed their landlessness squarely on the
Norman Conquest, and they argued that their alienation from landownership "constituted slavery." Political slavery's relatively new association
with dispossession bore radical ideological fruit when Winstanley took
a stance against enclosure and argued for the redistribution of agrarian
land. Vittoria Di Palma paraphrases this position: "in order to fulfill
Cromwell's promise to liberate the English people from the monarchy
and its abuses, parliament was obliged to return to the commoners the
land that was rightfully theirs ... freeing England ... from the thievery
and despotism of its Norman conquerors." From this period onwards,
landlessness was a key feature of political slavery in English discourse,
and one of the burdens of the "Norman Yoke" protested by English radicals across three centuries, from the civil wars through Chartism.[21]

Bodin's transposition of despotism onto class was also picked
up and used for radical purposes across the Channel. In Revolutionary
France, Emmanuel Sieyès vilified the aristocracy as despotic invaders
who were foreign to the nation and could thus be expunged from it.
Retaining despotism's Asiatic associations, Sieyès lambasted the Third
Estate's acquiescence to the present social order "like a pack of Orien-
tals," and compared France's class hierarchy to India's caste system.
When Frenchmen read about caste in "stories of travels in India," Sieyès
wrote, "we describe the same kind of conditions as despicable, mon-

strous, destructive of all industry, as inimical to social progress, and above all, as debasing to the human race in general and intolerable to Europeans in particular." *So why do you put up with it?* he effectively asks his readers.[22]

During the Age of Revolutions, this rhetoric traveled to the two Indies. Dessalines picks up right where Sieyès leaves off when he portrays the French as political "slaves," subject to the "degrading yoke" of a "foreign tyrant." Meanwhile, in British India, despotism and political slavery's new connotations of landlessness were mobilized in important policy debates. Ranajit Guha argues that Oriental despotism played a key role in the Permanent Settlement of 1793, when Bengal's zamindars were given property rights in their landed estates. Dow—whose statements on Oriental despotism and political slavery I have already quoted multiple times—was a participant in the debates leading up to the Permanent Settlement, which began in the 1770s. Marshaling tropes of political slavery to assuage his critics' fears, he assures his readers: "To make the natives of the fertile soil of Bengal free, is beyond the power of political arrangements.... To give them property would only ... make them more our subjects; or if the British nation prefers the name—more our slaves." Unlike Dow, most of the Company officials who invoked Oriental despotism in the ensuing century did so as a rationale for dispossession. If the Mughal emperor was an Oriental despot, then he owned all India's land. The implication was that *zamindars* and *talukdars* didn't own their estates but merely held them at the pleasure of the emperor, collecting revenue for him from tenant farmers. Charles Grant tows this line in his *Inquiry into the Nature of Zemindary Tenures in the Landed Property of Bengal:* in "all the native States of Asia . . . the *Sovereign* is *sole,* universal *proprietary Lord* of the land." Others disputed this position. In his *Dissertation concerning the Landed Property of Bengal,* Charles William Boughton Rouse insists that Mughal India is no different from contemporary Britain, as "the rise and progress of private property in land have been nearly similar throughout the world." For Rouse, the emperor's supposed ownership of all property amounts to a boast that "gratified the vanity and ostentation of a Mogul emperor, the descendant of a race of Tartar conquerors; who called himself the shadow of God, and his viceregent upon earth." If "European travellers"

like Bernier, "dazzled by the splendor of his court, when they were humbly soliciting service under his nobles, may have been inclined to believe" this idle boast, then their gullibility should not be made the basis
for colonial policy. In the end, the temptation to flatter the emperor's
"claim of universal property" proved too strong to resist, since this
claim's logical end result was the transfer of all land to the emperor's
usurper, the East India Company—or, later in the nineteenth century,
the British Crown. For example, Lord Canning's "Oudh Proclamation,"
issued in the wake of the Mutiny of 1857, used the tenets of Oriental
despotism as a rationale for the confiscation of nearly the entirety of this
province's land. Here, once again, political slavery's association with dispossession turned out to be more prescriptive than descriptive—an alibi
for colonialism.[23]

In the next section, I return once again to the 1770s. Although political slavery was honed as a keyword in policy debates about colonial
India, during this crucial decade it traveled westward, to the thirteen
colonies.

Revolutionary Anti-Despotisms I: The American Crisis

It is well known that Greco-Roman republicanism enjoyed a full-scale
resurgence during the American Crisis. Political theorist Philip Pettit
has written at length on this subject. Calling the "opposition between
liber and *servus,* citizen and slave," republicanism's "single most characteristic feature," he argues that American colonists revived this tradition
from dormancy in order to cast non-representative government as political slavery. Missing in Pettit's work on the subject is any sense that
this rhetoric was filtered through colonial India on its way to the thirteen colonies. Given the profound entanglement of the East India Company in American affairs, it seems fair to speculate that the colonists'
complaints of political slavery were expressly calculated to dovetail with
charges that the Company was despotic. Jonathon Eacott states the matter plainly: "Britons on both sides of the Atlantic . . . associated the East
India Company with enslavement." Contrary to Peter Dorsey's claim, the
American colonists therefore did not invent a new "hyperbolic rhetorical device," when they compared taxation without representation to

slavery. Rather, political slavery and despotism were already being used to characterize, and at times protest, extractive revenue policies in India. When Joseph Priestley warned in his 1769 pamphlet on *The Present State of Liberty in Great Britain and her Colonies* that taxing the Americans without granting them adequate representation in Parliament "would make them the most abject slaves, of which there is any account in history," it seems very likely that he had "Asia . . . the nurse of the most abject slaves" in mind. In his best-selling pamphlet *Observations on the Nature of Civil Liberty* Richard Price makes this point with an Ottoman flourish that reminds his readers of political slavery's imaginative geography: "If . . . like the different provinces subject to the *Grand Seignoir,* none of the states possess any independent legislative authority; but are all subject to an absolute monarch, whose will is their law; then is the Empire an Empire of Slaves."[24]

It is a widely held misconception that the Americans' protests against political slavery were deemed perfectly compatible with their practice of chattel slavery. But this contradiction did not, in fact, sit easily with friends of the rebellious colonists, let alone their enemies. Gary Nash has shown that many British radicals who supported the colonists (including, for example, Price and Thomas Day) expected, or at least hoped, that emancipation would follow independence. Both men seem to have been blinded by their optimism. When emancipation failed to take root in the new republic, they worked to remedy the wrong they had helped bring about, collaborating with English abolitionists to pressure their American friends to extend liberty to all. French veterans of the American War likewise pressured their former allies to make good on their rhetoric and end slavery. "I would never have drawn my sword in the cause of America," the marquis de Lafayette wrote in a letter to George Washington, "if I could have conceived that thereby I was founding a land of slavery." Opponents of the American cause arrived at this conclusion much earlier than its proponents. Critics of Price and the position on American affairs he championed were quick to point out that if the British empire was "an Empire of Slaves" (as Price put it) it was so on multiple counts. Samuel Johnson captures this sentiment succinctly: "How is it that we hear the loudest yelps for liberty among the drivers of negroes?"[25]

The rhetoric of political slavery survived so long in British writing only because its usage was tethered to actual practices of unfreedom. The hypocrisy of the American colonists cut this tether; and the very meaning of slavery changed as a result. The word "slavery" was used to signify political slavery as well as chattel slavery throughout the seventeenth and eighteenth centuries. The American Revolution contributed to the demise of this common usage. Richard Hey voices an emergent common sense in his response to Price's *Observations on the Nature of Civil Liberty:* "It might be of use, in considering the nature of Slavery, to distinguish carefully between the *proper* sense of the word, and the *figurative* senses. Perhaps, the original and only proper meaning of it is, Domestic Slavery; including what Montesquieu speaks of under the names of Domestic and Civil Slavery, but not what he calls Political Slavery." Given how strongly Hey's prescription for a careful distinction between "the *proper* sense of the word" slavery "and the *figurative* senses" resonates with our twenty-first-century sensibilities, it is easy to mistake his chiding of Price for simple common sense. After all, the definition of slavery we have inherited is the one Hey proposed. Hey's reasoning also resonates with Samuel Johnson's definition of metaphor: "The application of a word to an use to which, in original import, it cannot be put." But as we have seen over the course of this chapter, political slavery was not *exactly* a metaphor. Given that "slavery" had already been in use as a synonym for despotic rule for over a millennium by the 1770s, it is difficult to argue that this meaning should be excluded from the term's "original import."[26]

The unfreedom of chattel slavery certainly imbued political slavery with a good deal of its terror. But the opposite was also true: Oriental despotism gave abolitionists a template for opposing chattel slavery as a species of arbitrary rule. Granville Sharp, Christopher Leslie Brown reminds us, "likened American planters to Turkish despots. The slaveholder, he said, was 'an arbitrary monarch, or rather a lawless Basha in his own territories.'" Historian David Brion Davis attributes this position to the abolitionist movement more generally, whose common sense he sums up thusly: "Every petty planter in America was in truth an arbitrary monarch," whose "tyranny . . . subverted the British constitution." Davis's argument is borne out in one of the most important and best-selling antislavery publications of the eighteenth century, Olaudah Equiano's *Interesting Narrative*. Political slavery features prominently in this text in ways that haven't yet registered in criticism. At the crucial turning point when Equiano purchases his freedom from chattel slavery, he frames his manumission as a release from arbitrary power. The "form of my manumission," he explains, "expresses the absolute power and dominion one man claims over his fellow." This point was important enough to warrant the inclusion of the said manumission document as an appendix to *The Interesting Narrative*. Reading it for themselves, readers could plainly see that the legal document uses the rhetoric of political slavery to characterize chattel slavery. Equiano's enslaver, Robert King, grants "the said Gustavus Vassa, all right, title, dominion, sovereignty, and property, which, as lord and master over the aforesaid Gustavus Vassa, I had, or now have." Dominion, sovereignty, lord and master, were all terms associated with *despotes* and despotism. Before Thomas Hobbes reintroduced the word "despotism" into the English language, *despotes* and its derivatives were translated as *seigneur, seigneurial, masterlike sway, dominion, dominus,* or *dominatus.* Remember, Bodin translated *despotism* as "lordly Monarchie."[27]

Strikingly, the language of Equiano's manumission form recalls Bodin's argument that conquest granted the conqueror dominion over the conquered *and* ownership of their persons. On this subject, Bodin argued, "a soveraigne prince having in good and lawfull warre vanquished his enemies, should make himselfe lord of their goods and persons by the law of armes, governing them now his subjects, as doth the good householder his servants or slaves." Holly Brewer's research reveals these overlaps between political and chattel slavery to be no idle coincidence. She argues that the Stuarts were proponents of both political slavery—they subscribed to Bodin's absolute version of dominion—and chattel slavery, and in fact fused the two in rhetoric and law. To name just one example: "A 1677 high court of King's Bench case in which Charles II was indirectly involved, *Butts v. Penny,* cited feudal law to argue that 'negroes' were hereditary villeins, forever owned and attached to the land." Meanwhile, in the colonies, Brewer argues, "Virginia's post-1660 laws about bond slavery followed royal ideals that emphasized heredity.... Its language mimicked the thirteenth-century feudal law of Henri de Bracton." Historically, Brewer proves, the expansion of political slavery (or Stuart despotism) in England was inextricably linked to the expansion of chattel slavery in the American colonies.[28]

The more capacious usage of the term "slavery" favored by radicals like Price and Dessalines highlights this historical link between chattel slavery and political slavery (or absolutism). Meanwhile, the narrower definition proposed by Hey actively works to obscure it. This was precisely Hey's motivation: his sole objective in trying to curb Price's broad usage of "slavery" was to de-radicalize the term, and thereby neuter its power as a political keyword. Price's critics often complained about his reliance on the word "slavery." For example, in one response to *Observations on the Nature of Civil Liberty,* John Gray bemoans that the pamphlet's "incoherent paragraphs are so larded with the words Liberty and Slavery, and Slavery and Liberty, that I wonder the printer's stock of types was not exhausted in composing them." Adam Ferguson reveals the reason for Gray's grumbling when he complains of political slavery's rhetorical potency in his own response to Price, where he notes the "mighty effect" of the latter's choice "of words": "There is not an English gentleman, I believe, that would not shrink from the thought of reducing millions of his fellow-subjects to a state of servitude." Limiting the purview of the word "slavery" would therefore disarm radicals of one of their most persuasive rhetorical weapons.[29]

Revolutionary Anti-Despotisms II: The Global Jacobin Crisis

If Price's opponents were dismayed by his radicalism in the 1770s, they had even more cause for alarm on the eve of the 1790s. For Price, events in France heralded the dawn of a new millennium. In November 1789, on the occasion of the anniversary of England's Glorious Revolution, he praised the unfolding revolution in France in these terms in a speech (and soon, a pamphlet) entitled *A Discourse on the Love of Our Country.* One of the most radical elements of this speech was Price's insistence that events across the channel should be viewed through the lens of British history, as a French 1688. Dusting off seventeenth-century rhetoric, Price celebrated the Glorious Revolution "as a bloodless victory, [when] the fetters which despotism had been long preparing for us were broken." Now, in 1789, France was finally catching up, breaking the fetters of monarchical absolutism and political slavery. Viewed from this perspective, the revolution in France could not but be greeted with enthusiasm by all patriotic Britons.[30]

In *Observations on the Nature of Civil Liberty,* Price had argued that Englishmen were "enslaved *partially*" (compared to the colonists, who were "enslaved *totally*") due to the inadequacies of parliamentary representation. A decade later in *A Discourse on the Love of Our Country,* he dilated this point: "When the representation is partial, the kingdom possesses liberty only partially; and if extremely partial, it gives only a *semblance* of liberty." Events in France should be a wake-up call for England, Price argued. It was time to finish the unfinished business of 1688 and turn England's "partial" freedom into full-blown liberty. Price ended his speech with a stirring call for a global age of revolutions to depose despotism around the globe: "Behold, the light you have struck out, after setting AMERICA free, reflected to FRANCE, and there kindled into a blaze that lays despotism in ashes, and warms and illuminates EUROPE! Tremble all ye oppressors of the world! Take warning all ye supporters of slavish governments and slavish hierarchies!" Price's listeners—radicals and counterrevolutionaries alike—understood full well that the "oppressors of the world" included England. Price was calling for the toppling of England's "slavish government" at home as well as for the toppling of its "slavish hierarchies" overseas in the colonies. Soon enough Price's parishioner Mary Wollstonecraft echoed his call—later joined by Thomas Paine, William Godwin, and a host of other home-grown radicals.[31]

It would be difficult to overstate the fear Price's radicalism struck into the hearts of his more conservative countrymen. Edmund Burke's *Reflections on the Revolution in France* was written directly in response to this speech and intended as a personal takedown of Price and his patron, Lord Shelburne. He laid out his intentions in a revealing personal letter: "I mean to set in a full View the danger from their wicked principles and their black hearts . . . I mean to do my best to expose them to the hatred, ridicule, and contempt of the whole world." When his *Reflections* were finally published a year later, many of Burke's contemporaries judged it to be a profound overreaction. But history would prove

Burke right in at least one respect: the revolution *was* a monumental, epoch-defining event, and it would cost its weight in blood.[32]

No event better captured the revolutionary spirit's ability to over-turn "slavish governments and slavish hierarchies"—and turn the world upside down in the process—than the slave revolt on Saint-Domingue and the creation of a new independent postcolonial state, Haiti. In 1804, Dessalines called for a Caribbean age of revolutions in terms strikingly similar to Price's rhetoric from a decade earlier: "Unfortunate people of Martinique, could I but fly to your assistance, and break your fetters! ... Perhaps a spark from the same fire which enflames us, will alight into your bosoms: perhaps, at the sound of this commotion, suddenly awak-ened from your lethargy, with arms in your hands, you will reclaim your sacred and imprescriptible rights." If Price had been deemed dangerous in 1789, then by 1804 Dessalines looked like an existential threat to the very existence of Euro-colonialism in the Americas—and around the globe.[33]

The British press responded to the global Jacobin crisis by weapon-izing the rhetoric of despotism and political slavery against anticolonial enemies in both Indies. Much as in the 1770s, the supposed despotism of Indian rulers was cited as a justification for the East India Company's usurpation of their kingdoms. For example, the Sultan of Mysore, Hyder Ali Cawn, was described as "the despotic ruler of an empire" who "gov-erned Mysore with absolute authority." Such rhetoric helped rationalize the first two of three wars fought to annex Mysore. After the onset of the revolutionary wars, when the Company was faced with the very real possibility of being ousted from the subcontinent by either the French or Napoleon's sworn ally, Hyder Ali's son and heir Tipu Sultan, accusa-tions of despotism took on a newly hysterical pitch. "Hyder Alli, who was, when compared with the worst despots of the European world, a monster, must yet be considered, when put in comparison with his suc-cessor Tippoo, as mild and merciful," wrote a former Scottish captive of Tipu in 1796. "Tippoo," he continued, "was so perfectly savage, that cru-elty seemed to be, not only the internal habit of his soul, but the guide of all his actions, the moving principle of his policy, the rule of his public conduct, and the source of his private gratifications." Morally corrupt, politically oppressive, and sexually deviant, Tipu Sultan was the boogeyman of East India Company nightmares. As public opinion in England increasingly rallied behind the Company and Indian colonialism more generally in the 1790s, he became a villain in the public imagination too, brought to life on London stages.[34]

The very same rhetoric was also used to malign perceived enemies in the West Indies. George Nugent, then governor of Jamaica, quietly sought to establish friendly commercial relations with the newly declared état d'Hayti. Nonetheless, Dessalines and the leaders who rose and fell in the wake of his assassination were all persona non grata in the British press. Edward Corbet, a British agent sent to Saint-Domingue by Nugent to negotiate a trade treaty in 1804, declared that "the government of the island ... is perfectly despotic under the chief Dessalines." If Tipu Sultan was "was so perfectly savage, that cruelty" was the guiding virtue of his character, then Henry Christophe, later King Henry I of Haiti, was equally "cruel and determined" and "despotic," according to British newspapers. Lest the public overlook the similarities between the two men, writers made the comparison manifest. Tabitha McIntosh and Grégory Pierrot quote from "A December 1811 'letter from St Domingo' published across a range of British newspapers [which] warned that Christophe was the 'most violent and determined enemy that the British have in this quarter of the globe.'" The letter ends with a warning: "I do not think it improbable that he will shortly prove himself as formidable an enemy to the British interests in the West, as ever Tippoo Saib did in the East Indies." Like Tipu, Christophe was judged to be a "monster" and a "bloody tyrant." In Haiti, his rule had ushered in "a state of slavery and terror, never, perhaps, equaled in the history of the human race." Given that chattel slavery had been the rule of the day in Haiti only two decades earlier, this claim was truly outrageous. Like the American colonists, British critics of Dessalines and Christophe tried to sever the practice of chattel slavery from the rhetoric of political slavery; and, as it had in the 1770s, the attempt met with ridicule—at least in some circles.[35]

Radicals and revolutionaries in England contested the characterization of the empire's enemies as uniquely despotic. In *Pig's meat; or, Lessons for the swinish multitude*—a publication named after what E. P. Thompson calls Burke's "epochal indiscretion," namely his description of French revolutionaries as "the swinish multitude"—Thomas Spence questions the mainstream logic that equated Indian rulers with despotism and made despotism a pretense for conquest: "But let us ... admit Tippoo to be the greatest tyrant the world has produced, will this justify our destroying thousands of innocent people ... ? ... Or, if our *humanity* must be indulged with tyrant-hunting, was there any necessity for our travelling so far as India to find one?" Spence's rhetorical question played on a trope prevalent during the American War, when George III was portrayed by colonists as an Oriental despot. He was even pictured as such—turban and all—in a mezzotint that circulated widely during the war. Now, in the 1790s, radicals revived the implication. In doing so they drew on a long tradition whereby Oriental despotism was used to critique European rulers, a strategy that was particularly prevalent in ancien régime France. As Saree Makdisi reminds us, one target of Montesquieu's portrait of Oriental despotism was the European elite; and in the 1790s the same was sometimes true. Oriental despotism was "mobilized by the mainstream radical movement" to criticize Britain's ruling class. Following the lead of Price's *Discourse on the Love of Our Country,* English radicals like Spence insisted that any worldwide war against despotism must begin at home.[36]

Every good villain carries the seed of a Byronic hero, and non-European "despots" like Tipu Sultan were no exception to this rule. Reared from infancy by his father ("the great and despotic usurper Hyder Ally Cawn," to prize "ambition and ferocity"), Tipu was despotism incarnate. At the same time, his detractors couldn't help but admire his villainy—or at least admit that from the perspective of his Indian supporters his "cruelty" might look like dashing "heroism": "The bravest hero, as he is there called, but what we should term the greatest despot, is always the most beloved among the ladies." Moreover, some idea of Tipu's Byronic heroism must have traveled on what Julius Scott calls "the common wind" from India and Britain to Jamaica. For, during Christmas festivities in 1801, Lady Nugent, the wife of Jamaica's governor, was treated to a performance—put on by enslaved and free men, women, and children—that featured Tipu's children in a starring role. Her description is frustratingly sketchy: "Then there was a party of actors.—Then a little child was introduced, supposed to be a king, who stabbed all the rest. They told me that some of the children who appeared were to represent Tipoo Saib's children and the man was Henry the 4th of France.—What a *mélange!*" Jamaican theater historian Errol Hill speculates that the performance Lady Nugent witnessed was "the Actor Boy masquerade," an episode in a Christmas ritual known as "Jonkonnu," which Lady Nugent and many other Europeans mistakenly transliterated as "Johnny Canoes." According to Richard Burton, Jonkonnu is one of the most "complex" and "important" "West Indian cultural forms," whose "origins are without doubt African." Burton describes Jonkonnu as "the core of the oppositional culture of Jamaican slaves," as Christmas festivities provided enslaved people a rare opportunity to vent "repressed feelings."[37]

Today, it is simply impossible to decode the allegory of the performance witnessed by Lady Nugent with any certainty. But we might speculate that it celebrated "Tippoo" as an anticolonial hero. Even though Tipu Sultan had been killed a year and a half earlier, his children appeared to carry on their father's legacy by murdering a European king. Perhaps Tipu Sultan's sons were charged with avenging their father's death? Or perhaps "Tippoo" stands in for other anticolonial heroes much closer to home, on neighboring Saint-Domingue? Although Burton specifies that Jonkonnu was a "ritual of opposition rather than of resistance," it is nonetheless remarkable that the version of it Lady Nugent witnessed contextualized Jamaican slavery in a global anticolonial context that included India.[38]

In this chapter I have tried to recover the geographical capaciousness of political slavery and Oriental despotism in the Age of Revolutions. Right up until the end of the eighteenth century, Asia was located at the very center of Britons' "mental map" of slavery. This changed at the turn of the nineteenth century, when the abolitionist movement began to conceptualize India as inherently free vis-à-vis the Americas, and to champion East Indian sugar as a "free" alternative to its West Indian counterpart. In the next chapter I explore this shifting geography of freedom.

The Geography of Freedom in the Age of Revolutions

I know there are many who suppose us to be merciless oppressors in the
East Indies, as well as the West. But . . . the suspicion . . . is utterly unfounded.
There is no slavery in the dominions of the East India Company, unless
the condition of a few domestic life servants, may deserve the name; and
even these are so treated that their bondage can scarcely be distinguished
from freedom.

—*James Stephen, The Dangers of the Country, 1807*

James Stephen can be counted among Britain's most dedicated
abolitionists. A lawyer whose work often took him to Saint Kitts,
Stephen was the Clapham sect's primary source for up-to-date
information about on-the-ground conditions in the West Indies.
In 1796, he moved to Clapham to join William Wilberforce's inner
circle; and a few years later he joined his family circle by marrying Wilberforce's sister. Today Stephen is best remembered for his tactical genius:
in 1805 he wrote the draft of a bill that would de facto end three-quarters
of the slave trade by proscribing British subjects from selling slaves to the
French colonies. He also contributed to the abolitionist cause in print,
publishing a number of books and pamphlets. His longest work, *The
Slavery of the British West India Colonies Delineated*, "became the chief

textbook for supporters of the anti-slavery movement" in the decades
between abolition and emancipation. However, despite his impeccable
antislavery credentials, Stephen was complicit in the perpetuation of
slavery in British India. In the passage quoted above, he repudiates the
idea that chattel slavery was practiced in India by dismissing the "bondage" of domestic "life servants"—or what we would commonly call
slaves—as mild enough to be indistinguishable "from freedom." This was
hardly an idiosyncratic position: many abolitionists denied chattel slavery's existence in India, even when confronted with evidence to the
contrary. Such a denial was necessary in order to draw a clean line of
demarcation between the "merciless" oppressiveness of the plantation
system in the West Indies and the benign—perhaps even benevolent—
character of colonialism in India.[1]

Stephen's comments epitomize a new common sense about the geography of freedom that took shape during the Age of Revolutions. India, long deemed "the nurse of the most abject slaves," now began to be
lauded as the bridgehead of a new kind of imperial freedom. A number
of historians have written about this shift, which P. J. Marshall describes
as a "moral swing to the east." The British empire survived the loss of the
American colonies by engaging in a process of ideological reinvention. If
the American Patriots were hypocritical enough to complain about English despotism when all the while practicing chattel slavery, then Britain
would take the moral high ground by building a new, post-American
empire of liberty. Despite its many flaws, Vincent Harlow's schema of a
"first British empire" in the Atlantic and a "second British empire" in
Asia does help to capture the mood on the ground at the turn of the
nineteenth century. As David Brion Davis observes, the "emergence of
the second empire involved a repudiation of the first. The second . . . was,
by definition, a 'free world.'" Christopher Leslie Brown places the abolitionist movement in this context. Antislavery and anticolonialism might
seem like a natural pairing; but the Clapham sect championed abolition
as a means to *save* the empire not *end* it. To be successful, Brown explains, the mainstream abolitionist movement "required an alternative
concept of empire" wherein "the customary association of slavery with
imperial wealth and power" was broken. Imagining such an alternative
was the movement's greatest achievement *and* its most objectionable

legacy: it resulted in the end of chattel slavery in the West Indies but facilitated the expansion of political slavery, or colonialism, in India.[2]

Until fairly recently, scholarship tended to reproduce the nineteenth century's dualist geography of freedom. New research on the prevalence of slavery in British India has helped change this state of affairs by exploding the myth that "labour in India was inherently free." Thanks to Indrani Chatterjee, Richard Eaton, Rupa Viswanath, and a host of other scholars, we now have the hard evidence we need to call out Stephen's declaration that there "is no slavery in the dominions of the East India Company" as a factual error, if not an outright lie. But if we stop there—if we merely add India to the rollcall of slavery's global hotspots—then we miss an opportunity for a more radical relearning of the meaning of freedom. Only by thinking across the geographical divide between India and the Americas can we begin to detect important *continuities* between chattel slavery and so-called free labor as conceptualized by mainstream abolitionists and other liberal reformers.[3]

In troubling the *geographical* divide drawn between slavery and freedom within the British empire, this chapter takes inspiration from one of the most important studies of slavery in nineteenth-century US literature, Saidiya Hartman's *Scenes of Subjection.* In this book, Hartman refuses to adhere to American history's conventional periodization of slavery and freedom. Without minimizing the event of emancipation, she enumerates the many forms of unfreedom that persisted in its wake. Despite the "hypostatized discontinuities and epochal shifts installed by categories like slavery and freedom," Hartman writes, an "an amazing continuity" characterized the pre-and post-emancipation experiences of African Americans. In this chapter, I build on Hartman's work—and the subsequent insights of Lisa Lowe—by transposing her intervention from time onto space. There is no question that chattel slavery and colonialism were fundamentally different forms of oppression that involved incommensurable kinds and degrees of immiseration and dehumanization. At the same time, it is vitally important that we resist an overly facile construction of freedom's geography that would have us pit East Indian freedom against West Indian slavery. In this chapter I argue that the celebrated "freedom" of India was riddled with many of the same "problems" identified by Thomas Holt in his study of nineteenth-century

Jamaica. After emancipation, Holt writes, "the 'free' worker discovered that new forms of coercion lay at the heart of the new freedom." Sounding the true depths of freedom's problems requires a global analytic instrument that brings both of the two Indies simultaneously into view.[4]

In what follows, I begin in the 1780s, when India took center stage in metropolitan politics yet again, this time with the impeachment trial of Warren Hastings. After a brief treatment of Thomas Parker's rarely discussed *Evidence of Our Transactions in the East Indies,* I move on to this section's primary case study, Mariana Starke's *The Sword of Peace.* This play neatly captures a sea change in public opinion that took place over the course of the trial, which lasted almost a decade. As the 1780s gave way to the 1790s, Indian colonialism ceased to be an embarrassment and became, instead, a fledgling source of national pride. Because Starke combines pro-colonial East Indian politics with a resolute stance against West Indian slavery, her play is a perfect example of the emergent logic that made abolitionism compatible with imperial expansion.

This logic was strengthened during the chaotic decade of the 1790s, when the French and Haitian revolutions abroad and the Jacobin crisis at home (including, most dramatically, the Irish Rebellion) injected long-standing debates about slavery and freedom with new urgency. This is abundantly clear in the following sections, where I discuss the Anglo-Irish writer Maria Edgeworth's unpublished essay "On the Education of the Poor" as well as her anti-Jacobin short story collection *Popular Tales.* The collection's two most important stories, "Lame Jervas" and "The Grateful Negro," feature nearly identical scenes of slavery set in Jamaica and India. This consideration alone makes *Popular Tales* an ideal case study for this chapter. But Edgeworth brings us even closer to freedom's problems, for her protagonists in both stories ameliorate repressive slave regimes by instituting reward programs that trouble our customary association of wage labor with freedom. Like her admirer Jeremy Bentham, Edgeworth embraced an ontology of causation wherein human agency is inescapably encumbered by circumstances. Her strategies for so-called free labor management are thus rooted in a philosophical vision that denies the very possibility of free will.

While Edgeworth's fiction might seem worlds away from actual colonial policy, her labor management methods bear a striking resemblance to those promoted in pamphlets and books published around the
same time by proponents of East Indian sugar. The promotional literature touting "free" Bengal sugar as an alternative to slave-grown Jamaican sugar is fascinating for its systematic comparisons of the two colonies,
which offer a veritable object lesson in the Indies mentality. Most importantly, it opens a window onto the empire's new geography of freedom at
the very moment of its creation. Deeply invested in an absolute distinction between "free" and "unfree" labor, these pamphlets circumscribe
freedom almost beyond recognition in order to make it compatible with
colonialism. Although experiments in East Indian sugar production
never really caught on, they represent a crucial prehistory to the final
episode I touch on, briefly, in this chapter: the transportation of indentured laborers from India and China to the Caribbean in the wake of
emancipation. As Lowe argues, the history of indenture complicates liberal narratives of a clean break between slavery and freedom. It also exemplifies how the Indies mentality was woven into institutional practice,
thereby setting the stage for this book's next and final chapter.[5]

Antislavery Imperialism in the Hastings Impeachment Trial and *The Sword of Peace*

In the 1780s, the loss of the American colonies prompted a period of
soul-searching about the history, character, purpose, and future of the
empire. A tract compiled by an English lawyer, Thomas Parker, captures
the national mood. Published less than six months after Lord Cornwallis's defeat at Yorktown, *Evidence of Our Transactions in the East Indies
with an Enquiry into the General Conduct of Great Britain to Other
Countries, from the Peace of Paris, in 1763* spends more than three hundred pages rehearsing the past two decades of colonial history in order
to find an explanation for the recent defeat. As the book's title indicates,
Parker places the blame for Yorktown squarely on India—an example
par excellence of the Indies mentality. Even though a relatively small
number of English nabobs carried out Bengal's despoiling, Parker argues that Parliament's "total acquittal" of Clive in 1773 meant that the

nation as a whole condoned—and thus bears responsibility for—the East India Company's actions: "so long as the ... Company, continue[s] to have the sanction of the whole community, the conduct of the state stands in avowed opposition to the principles of natural justice: the penalties of which are, a return of equal injuries to the society offending against those principles ... they that destroy others must themselves be destroyed." Viewed from this perspective, the loss of the American colonies looks like just retribution for the conquest of Bengal.[6]

For evidence of the connectedness of the two Indies, Parker first turns to the Boston Tea Party, just as we did in previous chapters. He views this event as a classic instance of eye-for-an-eye justice: "The people of that country [America] threw it [the Company's tea] into the sea, with the same wrong, with which the possessions had been obtained, and the property taken away from the Princes and people of India." If the Tea Party is Parker's Exhibit A, then Exhibit B is General John Burgoyne, who, only five years after overseeing the Select Committee's investigation of Clive, "was made the first public witness of the fall of our power in America" when he surrendered to Patriot forces at Saratoga in 1777. Exhibit C was Parker's most unconventional evidence: a series of numerical parallels between Britain's crimes in India and its losses in America. Three million Indians were "'destroyed, starved, and drove away' by our oppression in the East," Parker tallies; and three million is exactly the number of American colonists "we have been endeavoring to prevent the loss of to ourselves in the West." Likewise, Britain's spending in America eerily mirrors the Company's ill-gotten gains in India: "the hundreds of thousands which we opened our treasures to receive out of the spoil of our war in India, we have, as a nation, been spoiled of by the expenses of our war in America ... the total of each would be nearly the same—an hundred millions of pounds Sterling taken away by the exercise of our national power over the people of India; and an hundred millions expended in endeavoring to maintain our national power over the people of America." Coincidence? Parker thinks not. Instead, he sees divine justice at work. In classic jeremiad style, he argues that doom and gloom will ensue unless the nation repents. The aim of *Evidence of our Transactions in the East Indies* is to facilitate such a course correction. By gathering together and reprinting documents and testimony from the

1772–73 Secret and Select Committee hearings, Parker tries to restage Clive's trial in the theater of public opinion. Toward the end of his book, after spending hundreds of pages on India, he returns to the circum-Atlantic, adding that the slave trade must also be stopped in order to avert ruin and save the empire from further losses.[7]

Despite his idiosyncrasies, Parker is an excellent barometer of the affective atmosphere of the early 1780s. This was the decade when slaveholding was cast definitively outside the pale of respectability, its practitioners deemed morally dubious deviations from the national norm. According to Marshall, Edmund Burke felt much the same way Parker did at the end of the American War: "In his most gloomy and overwrought moods, which seem to have been frequent in the summer of 1784, he believed that Britain was exposing itself to divine vengeance for its crimes in India." Burke cured his gloomy mood with precisely the medicine Parker prescribed: he restaged the 1772–73 hearings by putting the Company on trial once again, this time in the person of Warren Hastings, who served as governor general of Bengal from 1772 to 1785. The Company's territorial holdings grew considerably under Hastings's watch, thanks to several expensive and controversial wars. Whereas corruption took center stage in Clive's hearing, Hastings's aggressive expansionist (and extortionist) policies were the focus of the impeachment charges brought against him by Burke, who was assisted by Richard Brinsley Sheridan and Charles James Fox. Although the possibility of impeachment wasn't introduced in Parliament until 1786, Burke essentially ran the trial's first dry run in his "Speech on Fox's India Bill" in December 1783. An effort to bring the Company under greater governmental control, it sparked a full-blown constitutional crisis. The bill was defeated, bringing the Fox-North coalition down along with it. When Burke launched the impeachment trial three years later, a primary motivation was to vindicate his 1783 position by proving that the Company was in dire need of oversight and reform.[8]

Given that impeachment was an archaic process—last used in 1746 to prosecute a Jacobite rebel—the Hastings trial is best viewed as a symbolic act. As literary critics like Sara Suleri, Srinivas Aravamudan, Daniel O'Quinn, David Francis Taylor, and Sunil Agnani have taught us, the trial was highly theatrical. Burke's and Sheridan's speeches from the trial are routinely cited as the century's finest oratory. On one occasion, Mrs. Sheridan was so moved that she famously fainted in the ladies' gallery specially erected to accommodate female spectators. The trial can even be considered a continuation of the critiques of empire staged in the London theater during the 1770s in plays like *The Cozeners* and *The Nabob*. Sheridan, for one, fully recognized the trial's dramatic potential. Taylor argues that he borrowed representational strategies from "she-tragedies" in order to convey the violation of the begums of Oudh. After the trial ended, he reversed this direction of intertextual borrowing, returning to his speeches in 1799 in order to mine material for his dramatization of conquest on the other side of the globe in Peru—*Pizarro*.[9]

It is not exactly accurate to say that the impeachment proceedings put colonialism on trial. Instead, Hastings stood in for a particular *style* of colonialism: Company despotism. In the previous chapter, we saw that despotism was a keyword equally popular among the Company's supporters (who cited Mughal despotism as a justification for British rule) and its critics (who accused the Company of governing its Indian subjects despotically). Burke ridiculed the former position and rehearsed the latter in his marathon three-day opening speech for the trial. Addressing the House of Lords, he told them: "Mr Hastings comes before your Lordships not as a British Governor, answering to a British Tribunal, but as a Soubahdar, as a Bashaw of three tails. He says: I had an arbitrary power to exercise; I exercised it. Slaves I found the people; slaves they are.... I was unfortunately bound to exercise this arbitrary power, and accordingly I did exercise it. It was disagreeable to me, but I did exercise it, and no other power can be exercised in that Country." Portraying Hastings as a "Soubahdar" or "Bashaw"—Persian and Anglo-Indian terms for "governor"—Burke implies that this "British Governor" shape-shifted into a full-fledged Oriental despot in India. As we saw in Chapter 3, political slavery and Oriental despotism were almost always paired. Here, Burke follows this general rule, invoking political slavery and Aristotle's natural slavery in order to convey Hastings's attitude toward his colonized subjects. Echoing Alexander Dalrymple's maxim that "slaves can only be Governed by despotic power," Burke ventriloquizes an unapologetic apologia for Hastings's tyranny as the ineluctable consequence of Indian servility.[10]

Mariana Starke's mildly successful comic drama, *The Sword of Peace, or A Voyage of Love,* visualized Burke's critique of Hastings's despotism for London theatergoers. The play premiered in the summer of 1788, when the spectacle of the trial's first season had only recently wrapped up. In essence, Starke gave audiences the opportunity to continue consuming the impeachment trial drama in a different medium. To quote O'Quinn, the play "supplements Burke's critique of Hastings's accession to arbitrary power." In *Tropicopolitans* Aravamudan vividly describes how Burke's rhetoric achieves "a conflation of sublime aesthetics and unfettered tyranny in the figure of Hastings ruling over a fantasy space of tyranny and servitude." *The Sword of Peace* re-creates this "fantasy space" on the London stage, populating it with a Briton-turned-Oriental despot and a host of Indian slaves.[11]

The play is set on the Coromandel Coast, in Madras. It follows the trials and travails of two English cousins, Eliza and Louisa Moreton, who, the prologue stresses, have traveled to India for reasons that have nothing to do with matrimony. The fact that they both happen to make excellent marriages in Madras is a testament to the power of "*Love*" (versus greed) to provide an honorable basis for the empire's next act. Fittingly, Hastings's stand-in, the colony's corrupt and tyrannical Resident (or governor), constitutes the primary obstacle to the play's happy hymenal resolution. The Resident is despotism incarnate. He is described as "the old tyrant," and is compared to India's most notorious "real life" Oriental despot, "Tippoo Saib," or Tipu Sultan. The Resident's despotism takes concrete shape in the arbitrary power he exercises over his British and Indian subjects. Eliza and Louisa are told unequivocally: his "will is law here." Unfortunately, his will is to marry Eliza. In line with the English stage's many tropological despots and sultans, the Resident has already succeeded in turning the colony into a veritable seraglio. Eliza is thus only the latest victim chosen for the indulgence of his licentiousness.[12]

The Resident's despotism is rendered visually legible in the play in a manner that conjures both of the two Indies. Stage directions call for the Resident to be "*dressed in a Banyan and congee Cap.*" Eliza draws attention to this costuming when she sarcastically promises, "Oh yes, I shall prepare myself to make a curtsy to his Worship's honorable congee cap directly." An Anglo-Indian word for watery rice porridge *and* a

French term for ceremonious dismissal, "congee" neatly joins Oriental despotism with French absolutism. Like Foote does in *The Cozeners,* Starke also engages visual media in her theatrical caricature. O'Quinn argues that Eliza's comparison of the Indian marriage market to the slave trade in act 1 intentionally calls to mind James Gillray's satirical print of two years earlier, *A Sale of English-Beauties, in the East Indies* (Figure 16). The print features a slave market where indecently exposed English-women are being examined by potential buyers, or suitors, all of whom are either East Indians or Europeans dressed in Eastern style. One portly figure stands in the center of the print, with a phallic roll of papers

Figure 16. James Gillray, *A Sale of English-Beauties, in the East Indies,* 1786. Etching and aquatint, hand-colored. Courtesy of the National Portrait Gallery, London.

protruding from his pocket inscribed "Instructions for the Governor General." He is a possible stand-in for Hastings, and the visual equivalent of the "Resident" in *The Sword of Peace*.[13]

It is noteworthy that the slave market in Gillray's print is also a scene of political slavery. Like many of the texts discussed in Chapter 3, Gillray uses *chattel* slavery to portray its *political* counterpart. To this end, the "Governor General" is accessorized with a child attendant who appears to be a so-called pet slave, a standard inclusion in seventeenth- and early eighteenth-century portraiture used to index the dignity of the sitter. Here, the child's presence indicates the governor-general's pretensions to monarchical grandeur and absolute rule. The parasol the child holds over the governor-general's head serves a similar purpose in a non-European idiom. Parasols—as well as *chowrees* and *punkahs*—were used in Mughal portraiture to draw the viewer's eye to royal and noble sitters, a practice replicated in European paintings of Indian subjects. Joseph Roach has shown that the parasol was also an important prop on the Restoration stage, where it signaled non-European settings and characters from "all four corners of the globe," including both of the two Indies. In visual art, too, the parasol crossed hemispheric borders. In print satires of West Indian planters, parasols were sometimes used to liken slaveholders to Oriental despots. For example, in *A West India Sportsman* (Figure 17) not one but two planters recline under the shade of parasols held over their heads by Black enslaved workers. Remember, Granville Sharp compared every slaveholder to "an arbitrary monarch, or ... lawless Basha," presaging Burke's vilification of Hastings as "a Bashaw of three tails." Figures 16 and 17 trade in precisely this transcolonial tropological economy. Yet chattel slavery is not merely a means to an end here. By conflating a seraglio with a slave market, Gillray effectively couples the issues of chattel slavery and political slavery, abolition and Company reform.[14]

In *The Sword of Peace*, too, chattel slavery is simultaneously used to figure itself and to metonymically figure political slavery, implying that *both* Company despotism *and* the African slave trade need to be abolished for the empire to be reformed. In a number of scenes, stage directions call for a crowd of "Blackamoors" to parade across the stage. Some are possibly servants, others are specified as slaves, and all are described

Figure 17. J. F., *A West India Sportsman,* 1807. Aquatint, hand-colored.
Courtesy of The Lewis Walpole Library, Yale University.

as "*black*," implying they would be played wearing burnt-cork cosmetics,
the stage makeup used to portray servants and slaves from both Indies.
In one comic bit, Eliza and Louisa's English servant, Jeffreys, complains
"there are fifteen of these black gentry loit'ring about there, doing nothing." All are owned or employed by the cousins' corrupt landlady, Mrs.
Tartar. The excessive nature of her slaveholding is thematized when Jeffreys pulls out "a list of the servants and slaves that belong to the retinue
of Mrs. Tartar." We can imagine him unfurling a long scroll onstage, elic-
iting a hearty laugh from the audience. Since Mrs. Tartar is an ally of the
Resident, and tries to subject her tenants to his tyranny, the slaves in her
household function as a visual gauge of arbitrary power, just as in Gillray's print. Another indicator that chattel slavery is being used to signify
political slavery here is the fact that almost every Indian in the play is
enslaved. A free merchant is the exception that proves the rule, as he is
Muslim and therefore aligned with Mughal despotism. At the same time,

Mrs. Tartar's "retinue" of slaves also functions to malign her character by associating her with the practice of chattel slavery. Starke connects Mrs. Tartar's slaveholding to abolitionist strains of critique explicitly in the play's comic subplot, wherein Jeffreys purchases a slave named Caesar from her in order to emancipate him.[15]

Given the play's Indian setting, many critics have puzzled over the amount of stage time Starke dedicated to the issue of slavery and abolition. In trying to decide whether Caesar represents actual practices of Indian slavery or a geographical mix-up about the location of the West Indies, Jeffrey Cox calls the play a "theatre of racial confusion." To the contrary, I would argue that Starke knew precisely what she was doing. As Felicity Nussbaum rightly observes, "attitudes towards the Orient and its Eastern subjects overlap and are deeply enmeshed in attitudes towards abolition and the transport of African slaves in the eighteenth century." In other words, Starke's decision to combine the issues of abolition and Indian reform is not as anomalous as it might appear to us—trained, as we are, to think the two Indies apart instead of together. Brown makes a similar point when he notes that many antislavery activists viewed abolition as only one battlefield in a multifront war for imperial reform that included India. Sharp, for example, advocated for the establishment of a representative government in Bengal. Other abolitionists rallied behind Burke's assault on Hastings. Marshall suggests that the impeachment effort gained as much traction as it did only because abolitionist MPs saw the India question as intimately connected to abolition. "For William Wilberforce in particular," Marshall explains, "the affinities were very clear: both were issues of national morality."[16]

Starke's decision to tap into antislavery sentiment also made good commercial sense. The play's abolitionist subplot distinctly echoes the comic subplot of George Colman the Younger's *Inkle and Yarico,* the smash hit of the previous season. The latter subplot centers on Inkle's servant Trudge, who remains loyal to Yarico's servant Wowski even when his master tries to betray and sell Yarico. Circumstantial evidence suggests that the parallels between the subplots were deliberate. To begin with, Starke mentions *Inkle and Yarico* by name in *The Sword of Peace* play text, where a stage direction specifies that an Anglo-Indian woman should be "the Colour of Yarico." Recall from Chapter 2 that Yarico's color was rendered distinct from Wowski's onstage, a production decision discussed in opening-night reviews and replicated in visual media. Furthermore, Starke wrote the part of Jeffreys for the popular comic actor John Bannister, who originated as Inkle but eagerly switched roles as soon as the "death of [John] Edwin made a vacancy in Trudge." As Bannister's biographer explains, he "hated to play the part of a villain" and was willing to shift from a lead to a supporting role in order to avoid doing so. In short, Starke was very likely deliberately trying to ride the coattails of Colman's success—and secure a star actor to her production —when she decided to include an abolitionist subplot in her play about Indian reform.[17]

The Sword of Peace epitomizes how abolitionism was hitched to a pro-imperial agenda that embraced the expansion of British rule in India. The play's resolution turns on two kinds of liberation from slavery: Jeffreys frees Caesar from chattel slavery, and the Resident's ouster frees the settlement's Indian and British subjects from political slavery. Here, freedom from political slavery does not require the end of colonialism; it merely requires the end of arbitrary rule, an end that is achieved when the despotic Resident is deposed in favor of a morally upright and virtuous replacement, David Northote. These events represent a fairly transparent allegory for Hastings's replacement by Lord Cornwallis, who, Nicholas Dirks explains, inaugurated "a new phase" of Indian colonialism "predicated on the rule of property and the benevolent intent of a new 'postdespotic' state." Northcote ushers in this "'postdespotic' state" in the world of the play. Early on, he is set up as the Resident's foil, when the latter derides Northcote's "ridiculous notions about honor, generosity, benevolence, and stuff: as if that had anything to do with trade." This may sound like a standard list of English virtues; but they are all anti-despotic. The despot lacks "honor" because he follows no laws; and he lacks "generosity" as well as "benevolence" in the sense that he cares only for his own interests, monopolizing all private property (just as the despotic Company monopolizes the Indian trade). Northcote, in contrast, promises to protect "the lives and properties" of his subjects. Yet this mission is deemed perfectly compatible with colonialism. The abolitionist subplot does crucial ideological work in this respect by aligning English character with benevolence: "a true-born Englishman," Jeffreys tells

Caesar, "never lifts his hands against the oppress'd." For Starke, Indian colonialism passes this litmus test.[18]

The Hastings impeachment trial resulted in precisely this shift in public perception: airing empire's dirty laundry helped clear the air. As Dirks explains, by the trial's end the "imperial enterprise had been cleansed of corruption." Even though Hastings was acquitted, Burke's goals were therefore not entirely unmet. Although Burke is sometimes represented as anticolonial, his aim was never to end the British presence in India. What he really wanted was to reform empire by displacing the Company with the British government—just as the military officer, Northcote, replaces the commercial Resident at the end of *The Sword of Peace*. Although this did not officially come to pass until after the Mutiny of 1857, the slow displacement of the Company in fact commenced much earlier. In the 1780s and 1790s, the Crown began monopolizing top Indian appointments and staffing the upper ranks of colonial governments with military men, just as Starke fantasized (a development I discuss in Chapter 5). Of course, this was not due to Burke's efforts alone. But by appearing to purge rapacity from the business of empire the impeachment trial did play an important role in what Dirks calls "the regeneration of the imperial idea." Put another way, the trial achieved the same end that Brown attributes to the abolitionist movement: it "provided moral capital for the expansion of the British empire in the nineteenth century."[19]

As it happened, the Hastings impeachment trial began at the end of an era. The trial would drag on for nine long years, but in its second year the world changed instantly and forever with the fall of the Bastille. In November 1790, Burke called the French Revolution "the most astonishing that has hitherto happened in the world." Within a few years, he might have wished to revise that verdict: in 1791–93, the Haitian revolution overthrew colonial slavery, establishing the world's first committed antislavery postcolonial state. These events profoundly altered the politics of empire. In the 1780s, antislavery seemed like it *might* be compatible with imperial expansion. After the 1790s, this was a necessity if the abolitionist movement was to have any chance of success. Fueled by anti-French patriotism, Britain's "turn to empire" (to quote Jennifer Pitts) was almost complete by the turn of the nineteenth century.[20]

Managing the Global Jacobin Crisis in Edgeworth's *Popular Tales*

On June 13, 1804, the *Morning Chronicle* published detailed coverage of a debate in the House of Commons regarding a bill to abolish the slave trade. In "a speech of some length," George Ellis "opposed the principle of the Bill—a principle which was grounded upon a proposition similar to that maintained by the National Convention of France, when it affected the universal and immutable rights of man. Unless that proposition were contended for, and he fancied there were few who would now attempt to plead for it, he conceived that the idea could not be sustained that no men ought to be slaves." The son of a Grenada enslaver and grandson of a member of the council of Jamaica, Ellis came by his pro-slavery sentiments honestly. But the French Revolution presented an irresistible opportunity for men like Ellis to embellish personal greed with counterrevolutionary trimmings. In addition to being an ardent apologist for slavery, in the 1790s Ellis became a staunch opponent of revolutionary principles and a "constant contributor to *The Anti-Jacobin*." This political trajectory exemplifies a key challenge faced by abolitionists in the wake of the French Revolution. Men long invested in the plantation system could now couch their defense of slavery in counterrevolutionary "principle." To name just one more example, a "hysterical pamphlet" cited by David Brion Davis accused Wilberforce and his associates of being "the JACOBINS OF all England." Wilberforce was quick to apprehend the seriousness of the charge: he "sent word to Clarkson that any further talk of the French Revolution 'will be ruin to our cause.'" In this way, Davis argues, the Jacobin crisis prompted the mainstream abolitionist movement to rebrand itself as a conservative enterprise. Success would require carefully distinguishing between critiquing the slave trade and endorsing "the universal and immutable rights of man." A newly skeptical public needed to be convinced that abolition wouldn't spell a Jacobin bacchanal of unbridled liberty.[21]

Maria Edgeworth is a testament to the revolution's conservative influence on early nineteenth-century liberal reformers. Counterrevolution was the raison d'être of Edgeworth's political program. While it would be a mistake to reduce her politics to a psychological response to personal trauma, her experience during the 1798 Irish Rebellion does shed light on the evolution of her political sensibilities. Edgeworth's family belonged to the Anglo-Irish Protestant landlord class. The fact that her father, Richard Lovell Edgeworth, dabbled in radical politics and experimented with progressive estate management techniques did not fundamentally alter this fact. In 1798, the family still had targets on their backs; and in September, when French forces and Catholic rebels were on the march in the Irish countryside, they fled home in fear of their lives, heading for the town of Longford. While they were absent, rebels destroyed several neighboring estates, but left their home conspicuously untouched. Legend has it that a rebel leader recognized the Edgeworth's housekeeper as the very woman who had given his wife charity the previous year, leading him to declare that "he would stand her friend now." R. L. Edgeworth also took some of the credit, "boasting in 1798 that no tenant of his had ever been a Defender." Elizabeth Kim and Gary Kelly spell out the implication of this boast: his "modern" estate management methods secured him the loyalty of his tenantry. But peasant rebels were not the only mob the family had to fear. Edgeworth's well-known radical inclinations led his peers to doubt his loyalty; in Longford, a Protestant mob nearly lynched him as a traitor. Maria Edgeworth's 1798 was thus an experience of near calamity at the hands of *both* sides of the Revolutionary issue. Therefore, it is hardly surprising that she went on to chart a moderate course.[22]

Edgeworth's politics are difficult to convey using today's liberal/ conservative binary. Even the most reductive account of the 1790s calls for a tripartite division between those who embraced revolution, those who rejected revolution but supported reform, and those who dug their heels into the ancien régime status quo. Edgeworth falls into the middle category. Swerving far to the right of republican radicalism à la Paine, she also steered clear of Burke's brand of hard-line reactionary conservatism. We can see Edgeworth navigating this middle course in an unfinished essay she began in the aftermath of 1798 entitled "On the Education of the Poor." The essay opens with a firm statement of compassion for the plight of the poor and a "wish that we could at once render all classes of society equally happy." But Edgeworth tiptoes back from the edge of Jacobinism, explaining that "an equal division of property"—or what anti-Jacobins called the *leveling system*—"could not for any length of time continue in society," since nature's unequal distribution of strength and talents would soon upset any artificially induced equilibrium. "The disproportion between the actual happiness of the highest and of the lowest classes of society cannot be suddenly diminished by any measures of benevolent reformation," she concludes ruefully. Edgeworth goes on to trace a firm dividing line between revolution and reform. "The good sense of the English nation has drawn many useful lessons from the bloody scenes which have been acted in France," she writes: "They have learned that gradual improvements are better than insurrection, and revolution." While Edgeworth clearly believed that society's most egregious injustices needed to be ameliorated, she insisted that this be done without "overturning the present order of things" in the process. While she never printed her essay "On the Education of the Poor," Edgeworth translated its theories into fictional practice in the short-story collection she published a few years later, *Popular Tales.* Like Hannah More's *Cheap Repository Tracts,* Edgeworth's collection is best viewed as an intervention in the Revolutionary crisis, albeit one intended for middle-class rather than poor readers.[23]

One of the most remarkable aspects of *Popular Tales* is its geographical scope. The collection's two most important stories, "Lame Jervas" and "The Grateful Negro," take readers all the way from England's Celtic fringe to India to Jamaica. While some scholars have suggested that India and Jamaica merely provided safe cover for Edgeworth to write about Ireland, such a reading vastly overestimates her parochialism and vastly underestimates the global dimensions of the Revolutionary crisis. To begin with the latter, just like the so-called American Crisis, the Jacobin crisis looked markedly more global at the time than it does in scholarship today. "Tippoo Saib" makes a cameo appearance in *Part the Second* of Paine's *Rights of Man,* and with good reason: a self-professed ally of Revolutionary France, "Citizen Tipu" reportedly founded a Jacobin club in his capital city of Seringapatam. Recall from Chapter 3 that "Tippoo" also featured in the Jonkonnu festivities staged by enslaved Jamaicans for the benefit of Governor Nugent and his wife on Christmas day in 1801.[24]

While Edgeworth was not a personal friend of the Nugents—so far as we know; it seems fairly likely that they at least brushed shoulders when Nugent was commander of the northern district of Ireland in 1798 or adjutant general in Ireland in 1799–1801—her inner circle included a remarkable number of imperial governors. Her closest friends in Ireland were Catherine "Kitty" Pakenham and her neighbor Lady Moira. The former married Arthur Wellesley, who served in India under the command of his brother, Richard Wellesley (Bengal's governor general and commander in chief from 1797 to 1805). Meanwhile, Lady Moira's son, Francis Rawdon Hastings, was governor general and commander in chief in India from 1812 to 1822, where he served alongside Nugent and socialized with Kitty's brother, Thomas Pakenham, who was also in India from 1803 to 1835. Edgeworth's own brother, Michael Pakenham Edgeworth, went to India in 1831. Yet another Edgeworth family friend, Lord Cornwallis, spent the 1790s rushing from one corner of the empire to the other and back again, fighting Tipu Sultan in Mysore, and stamping out the rebellion in Ireland, where he was assisted by Nugent until 1801. In short, Edgeworth's social network not only ruled Ireland, they also governed the empire.[25]

The geographical scope of the revolutionary crisis was therefore perfectly clear to Edgeworth, as we can see from *Popular Tales*. In "Lame Jervas" and "The Grateful Negro," she stages and re-stages a thinly veiled version of her own experience in 1798 in every corner of the empire. Slavery features centrally in each of these counterrevolutionary *gedankan*. Repeatedly, enslaved laborers plot revolts only to renounce insurrectionary violence when unexpected kindnesses from masters kindle their gratitude, which inspires loyalty. To begin with "Lame Jervas," this novella-length tale narrates the rags-to-riches rise of its eponymous protagonist, who begins life as a child miner in Cornwall and grows into a leisured gentleman thanks to a residence in India. I discuss the story's frame narrative and opening sections (both set in Cornwall) in the next section; for now, I will focus on Jervas's time in India. After traveling to Madras to work under the real-life educational reformer Andrew Bell, Jervas is sent on a scientific embassy to the court of another real-life figure, "Tippoo" Sultan. When Tippoo learns of Jervas's mining background, he hires him to modernize and reform his tin and then diamond mines—a plotline that is also semi-realistic in the sense that Cornwall represented the "vanguard . . . of world industrialization" at this time, particularly in regard to mining technology. Chief among Jervas's challenges in India is learning how to effectively manage the enslaved laborers who staff the Sultan's mines. As in *The Sword of Peace*, almost every Indian character we meet in "Lame Jervas" is enslaved—excepting the despot Tippoo, his son Prince Abdul Calie, and a single Sikh merchant named Omychund (a fictionalization of Amir Chand, a fabulously wealthy trader who was defrauded of £2 million by Clive during the conquest of Bengal). Just as in Starke's play, chattel slavery's ubiquity in "Lame Jervas" reveals it to be—at least in part—an index of political slavery, and thus of Oriental despotism.[26]

Like the Resident in *The Sword of Peace*, Tippoo functions simultaneously as a caricature of a real-life figure and as a personification of Oriental despotism. The latter is clear from Jervas's very first meeting with him, when he is overwhelmed by the Sultan's sublimity: "Unaccustomed as I was to Asiatic magnificence, I confess that my eyes were at first so dazzled by the display of oriental pomp that, as I prostrated myself at the foot of the Sultan's throne, I considered him as a personage as high as human veneration could look." The real Tipu Sultan was a highly effective leader who modernized his military with new technology and stayed abreast of political developments in Europe; hence his appeal as an anticolonial hero as far away as Jamaica. But Edgeworth's fictional Tippoo is an overgrown child—easily distracted, impressed by mechanical tricks, and terrifyingly impatient. In Chapter 2 we saw that Britons fetishized the Oriental despot's supposed power over life and death. Jervas is horrified to see the arbitrary way in which Tippoo exercises this power. On one occasion, a minor mistake committed by "one of his blacks, a gentle Hindoo lad," is enough to turn the Sultan's "joy to rage": "he instantly ordered the slave's head to be cut off!"—a punishment averted only by Jervas's interference. This incident presages the story's resolution, which involves Jervas saving Indian subjects from an oppressive Indian ruler. More specifically, he bargains with Tippoo to secure the emancipation of enslaved diamond miners. Emancipation here is not just an end to chattel slavery; it also allegorically figures the end of Oriental despotism, an end achieved through the extension of British rule, which, it is fantasized, will benefit colonizer and colonized alike. By the time *Popular Tales* was published, a version of these events had actually come to pass: in 1799, Tipu Sultan was killed in the Fourth Anglo-Mysore War and his kingdom was annexed by the Company.[27]

At the same time, "Lame Jervas" also points to a more extended form of conquest promoted by all liberal reformers: education. In his classic study *The English Utilitarians and India* Eric Stokes glosses Thomas Babington Macaulay thusly: "The permanent and most profitable form of conquest was that over the mind." While Stokes acknowledges Macaulay's indebtedness to late Georgian thinkers like Wilberforce and Charles Grant, we should add Edgeworth to this list. Macaulay openly praised Edgeworth, rating her as "the second" "woman of her age" (behind Germaine de Staël and ahead of "Miss Austen"). *Practical Education* arguably made Edgeworth the foremost pedagogical expert in Britain at the dawn of the reform era. In her essay "On the Education of the Poor" she identifies education as the single most effective weapon in the counterrevolutionary reformer's arsenal. "[It is] in vain you expect that the poor should neither be discontented or seditious nor riotous," she scolds her reader, "unless you teach them how their happiness is connected with their obedience to the laws … those who would govern must instruct the people." Here Edgeworth anticipates Fanon's description of education's purpose in a capitalist/colonial society (albeit without a whiff of criticism): "[to] instill in the exploited a mood of submission and inhibition which considerably eases the task of the agents of law and order." Instruction, in this context, must not be confused with the pursuit of scholasticism: "To educate the poor and to make them scholars are not synonymous terms," Edgeworth writes. Nor is education an engine for upward mobility; instead, its purpose is "to fit them [the poor] for fulfilling the duties of their actual situation." By education, she clarifies, she means the "acquisition of those habits which tend to render men good subjects, and useful members of society." Education is subject formation.[28]

We can see this process of subject formation in action in Edgeworth's fiction. In one of her Irish novels *Ennui,* an exemplary estate manager credits the "school-house" as "the means of doing all the rest" he has accomplished in terms of "civilizing" his Irish-Catholic tenants: "We could not expect to do much with the old, whose habits were fixed; but we tried to give the young children better notions.... if we have done any thing, it was by beginning with the children: a race of our own training has now grown up, and they go on in the way they were taught, and prosper to our hearts' content, and, what is better still, their hearts' content." Education produces subjects who *desire* their own subjection: "their hearts' content" is brought into line with that of their masters. This is what makes education such an important instrument of colonial domination in Edgeworth's oeuvre: education transforms enemies into allies by shaping their desires in childhood. Take, for example, Prince Abdul Calie from "Lame Jervas." Although he is the eldest son of Tippoo Sultan, the prince shares none of his father's despotic inclinations. Unlike Tipu, who was reared into despotism by his father, Hyder Ali—or so the *Authentic memoirs of Tippo Sultaun* alleges—Prince Abdul Calie was shaped in the mold of his guardian, Lord Cornwallis, who educated Tipu Sultan's sons in real life. In Edgeworth's fictional universe, Jervas also tutors the prince, who is all "politeness" and "benevolence." These English virtues save Jervas's life when the prince betrays his father in order to rescue Jervas from jail when the latter is unjustly accused of stealing a diamond. Defeating Tippoo doesn't take winning a war in Edgeworth's book; it merely requires educating his son.[29]

In "Lame Jervas," the workplace represents the most important arena for colonial reeducation. Jervas frames his difficulties in managing Tippoo's enslaved miners as a pedagogical challenge: the task of "instruct[ing] his miners how to ... manage the ore according to the English fashion" is a "laborious and difficult undertaking," since "in no country are prejudices in favor of their own customs more inveterate, amongst workmen of every description, than in India." Even so, Jervas eschews violence. Rather than "have a poor slave tortured, or put to death, because he roasted ore in a manner which I did not think so good as my own method," Jervas explains, he overcame their resistance by introducing a reward system: "some few, who tried methods of my proposing, and found that they succeeded, were, by my directions, rewarded with the entire possession of the difference of profit between the old and new modes. This bounty enticed others; and in time that change was accomplished, by gentle means, which I had at first almost despaired of ever effecting." I will have much more to say about this rewards system in the next section. For now, I will make only two points. First, labor management is presented here as a form of adult education. In *Ennui,* the estate manager praises the benefits of "beginning with the children," but also admits that "it was a long time before we could bring" any change to bear—"Twenty-six years" to be exact. During the Jacobin crisis, this was simply too long to wait. In the absence of a more expedient solution, "the present order of things" stood little to no chance of being preserved. Jervas's reeducation of his enslaved workforce demonstrates that it is in fact possible to alter "the old, whose habits were fixed," by using reward-based incentives. Second, Jervas's "gentle" approach to labor management does much more than boost profits. In India, his life is twice saved by loyalty born of gratitude, recalling Edgeworth's experience during the Irish Rebellion (which her father credited to his progressive estate-management practices). Jervas narrates: "These slaves became so much attached to me that, although the governor of the mines, and certain diamond merchants, were lying in wait continually to get rid of me some way or other, yet . . . I was always apprised of my danger in time, by some of these trusty slaves; who, with astonishing sagacity and fidelity, guarded me whilst I lived amongst them." For Starke in the 1780s, benevolence was a means to stave off further imperial losses. For Edgeworth in the 1790s, it was a means to prevent insurrectionary violence—a matter of life and death.[30]

If "Lame Jervas" reveals Edgeworth's counterrevolutionary formula (rewards + gratitude = loyalty) to be efficacious in India as well as Ireland, "The Grateful Negro" adds Jamaica to this list. The story compares the management practices of two neighboring plantation owners, Mr. Edwards and Mr. Jeffries. While Mr. Edwards rewards good behavior (just like Jervas), Mr. Jeffries does not. When the story opens, the latter is in fact about to do the opposite: even though Caesar is "the best negro in [his] possession," he is preparing to sell him, thereby cruelly separating him from his wife, who would remain on Mr. Jeffries's plantation. Mr. Edwards rights this wrong by purchasing Caesar and allowing him to stay in place, in effect rewarding him for his work performance. In the end, this decision saves Mr. Edwards's life. The harsh treatment meted out on Mr. Jeffries's plantation by his overseer Durant—who "did not scruple to use the most cruel and barbarous methods of forcing the slaves to exertions beyond their strength"—had inspired Caesar to plan a revolt that he was on the brink of executing. But Caesar's gratitude to Mr. Edwards gives rise to loyalty so strong that he breaks what Alan Richardson calls "horizontal" ties of affiliation with his fellow enslaved Africans in favor of "vertical allegiance" to his enslaver. Even though Caesar was "bound to" his friend Hector "by the strongest ties," having survived the middle passage with him, he nonetheless turns on him, informing Mr. Edwards about the planned rebellion: "The principle of gratitude conquered every other sensation: the mind of Caesar was not insensible to the charms of freedom.... His heart beat high at the idea of recovering his liberty; but he was not to be seduced from his duty, not even by this delightful hope." In this passage, we can detect Edgeworth's eagerness to distinguish between liberal reform and Jacobin "liberty." Far from being based on revolutionary principles, Edgeworth's progressive management techniques are actually a safeguard *against* "the charms of freedom." As in India, so too in Jamaica, reform is proffered as a way to save empire, not end it. This is amply demonstrated in the fate of Mr. Jeffries, whose failure to inspire gratitude and loyalty in his slaves eventually compels him to give up his plantation. Unable to "shake off his constant fear of a fresh insurrection among his slaves," he leaves the island. Meanwhile, Mr. Edwards prospers.[31]

The idea that inspiring gratitude represents the solution to the Jacobin crisis may sound hopelessly naïve, the Pollyannaish daydream of a female novelist. But Edgeworth's conviction was actually shared by some of the era's most important politicians. On June 7, 1804, the *Morning Chronicle* covered another parliamentary debate about abolition. On this occasion, William Pitt, prime minister and chancellor of the exchequer, spoke out in favor of the bill, arguing that abolishing the slave trade would save plantation slavery by preventing revolt. Conjuring the specter of Saint-Domingue without daring to speak the former colony's name, Pitt reminds his listeners of "the danger of French Revolutionary principles coming in contact with the situation of Negro slavery." Then, in a series of lines that could have been pulled directly from the pages of *Popular Tales,* he expounds on the power of gratitude to engender loyalty and stave off rebellion: "It was by ameliorating the condition of the Negroes already in the Islands that some degree of attachment and fidelity to their masters was to be produced." "The old Negroes," or those born on the island rather than in Africa, "in many instances would have a degree of friendship for a master whom they had long served," and would therefore "shudder at the idea of any revolt against him." Like Jervas, who insists that "even in the most debased and miserable state of existence, the human heart can be wakened by kind treatment to feelings of affection and gratitude," Pitt believes that Jamaican slaves, "even in their degraded situation," would not rebel once they "had experienced their [master's] generosity," "kindness and humanity." Pitt's remarkable, perhaps willful, naiveté rivals Edgeworth's delusive hope that gratitude could outshine the Jacobin "charms of freedom." Reading Pitt's comments more generously, we might chalk up his self-delusion to deliberate and shrewd strategizing: he was determined to abolish the slave trade at any cost, even if it meant defending slavery itself.[32]

Usually, the idea that benevolence could save the empire was reserved for India. Pitt's speech and Edgeworth's story reveal how some sought to hitch the West Indies to the eastbound wagon of imperial regeneration. This is one way to understand the politics of amelioration—namely, as an attempt to include the West Indies in Marshall's "moral swing to the east." As Ramesh Mallipeddi emphasizes in his reading of "The Grateful Negro," the story exemplifies the ameliorationist position. In addition to being the favored course of Pitt, amelioration was also championed by Edgeworth's ideal planter, Mr. Edwards—and by his real-life model, Bryan Edwards, author of *The History, Civil and Commercial, of the British West Indies.* Unlike Pitt, Edwards did not pair amelioration with abolition. Instead of ending the slave trade, he was content merely to reform slavery's most outrageous abuses, a position seconded by his fictional doppelgänger in "The Grateful Negro." The story's omniscient third-person narrator explains: "He adopted those plans, for the amelioration of the state of the slaves, which appeared to him the most likely to succeed without producing any violent agitation, or revolution." These lines recall Edgeworth's essay "On the Education of the Poor," where she insists that reform must be accomplished without "overturning the present order of things," even if that order was slavery. In both texts, Edgeworth's position bears a striking resemblance to the political sensibilities expressed by emancipation's architects two and a half decades later. In *The Problem of Freedom,* Holt quotes a "Colonial Office staffer," who describes the goal of emancipation thusly: "to pass from bondage to freedom without overthrowing the existing apparatus of social order in the passage." Once again, at the risk of stating the obvious, "the existing apparatus of social order" in Jamaica was racial slavery. Nonetheless, in "the scale of Whig values," Holt explains, "liberty was conditioned by and subordinated to the maintenance of a traditional hierarchical order in society." In the 1790s, radicals like Richard Price were calling for a worldwide war against despotism and political slavery: the toppling of "slavish governments and slavish hierarchies!" Edgeworth and subsequent liberal reformers calculated the costs of revolutionary upheaval and the benefits of radical change differently. Although they sometimes championed freedom, their version of liberty looked nothing like the Jacobin variety.[33]

In the next section I take a closer look at the labor-management techniques Edgeworth proffered as a solution to the Jacobin crisis. Since her stories portray the implementation of the same techniques in Cornwall, India, and Jamaica, they prompt us to think across the usual divisions between the East and West Indies, and between chattel slavery and so-called free wage labor.

"Free" Labor Without Free Will

Rewards are the secret of Edgeworth's labor-management program. Indeed, the idea that loyalty should be rewarded is baked into the very motto of "Lame Jervas." In the story's frame narrative, an adult and gentlemanly Jervas visits the Cornish tin mine where he toiled as a child laborer. "Mr. R—," Jervas's former master and the mine's owner, throws a banquet in Jervas's honor where Jervas edifies the mine's current workforce with a recital of his life story, the telling of which brings us out of the frame narrative and into the main action. Right before Jervas's narrative begins, Mr. R— "filled a glass, and drank" to the following toast: "May good faith always meet with good fortune!" When the assembled miners complain that "none could guess" the meaning of these words and demand "an explanation of the toast," elucidation comes in the form of Jervas's life story, which functions as an advertisement for Edgeworth's reforms, the proverbial proof in the pudding that her reward system works.[34]

In the previous section, we witnessed Edgeworth's reward system in action in both of the two Indies, where Jervas and Mr. Edwards reward good behavior and are amply rewarded in turn when their lives are saved by "grateful" slaves. But the very first time the reader encounters this formula is on English soil, in Cornwall. The labor-management strategies Jervas institutes in "Tippoo" Sultan's diamond mines are inspired by his old master, Mr. R—. The resemblances between colonies and metropole do not end there. Mr. R—'s labor-management strategies are identical to those employed by Mr. Edwards on his model Jamaican plantation. The plotlines of "Lame Jervas" and "The Grateful Negro" also echo one another. The unexpected kindness Jervas receives from Mr. R— following an alcohol-fueled workplace accident (which leaves him with a limp, hence his nickname) fills Jervas with "gratitude—the first virtuous emotion I was conscious of having ever felt." Gratitude soon begets loyalty. Like Caesar, who "knelt down, and, in a transport of gratitude, swore that, with this knife, he would stab himself to the heart, sooner than betray his master!," Jervas declares himself "ready to die" for Mr. R—. Shortly thereafter, he risks his life to protect Mr. R—'s profits, just as Caesar risks his life to expose the rebellion. Betraying his fellow miners in the same manner Caesar betrays his fellow slaves, Jervas informs Mr. R— about a plot to conceal and secretly profit from a newly discovered vein of ore. Praising Jervas for his "fidelity," Mr. R— promises, "I will take good care of you, my honest lad." He keeps his promise, rewarding Jervas just as Mr. Edwards rewards Caesar. That very night, Jervas narrates, "I lay down, for the first time in my life, upon a feather-bed." The next morning, he is given "five guineas" and told he will be paid "an annuity of ten guineas out of the profits of the new vein." The lesson in all this is clear: "I only hope you will serve your next master, whoever he may be, as faithfully as you served me," Mr. R— tells Jervas when they part. Indeed, he has given him every incentive to do so, by making Jervas's betrayal of his coworkers the springboard for his meteoric rise from rags to gentlemanly riches.[35]

In nineteenth-century liberal ideology, wage labor is touted as slavery's inverse—its "absolute opposite," in the words of Najnin Islam. But in Edgeworth's stories there is "an amazing continuity" between so-called free wage labor and slavery. Following Hartman, we might even say that "attempts to assert absolutist distinctions between slavery and freedom" in *Popular Tales* would be "untenable." In addition to the parallels already noted, Jervas's childhood in Cornwall involves types of deprivation usually associated with slavery, such as natal alienation. Jervas narrates: "Where I was born, or who were my parents, I do not well know myself, nor can I recollect who was my nurse, or whether I was nursed at all." His earliest childhood memory is of labor: "being set, along with a number of children my own age, to pick and wash loose ore of tin." By any measure, his deprivation is extreme: "Buried under ground in a mine, as I had been from infancy, the face of nature was totally unknown to me." The similitude between Jervas's immiseration as a miner in Cornwall and the deplorable conditions endured by enslaved miners in India is even made explicit when he cites his own childhood as the inspiration for the reward system he implements in "Tippoo's" mines: "I have reason to know that, even in the most debased and miserable state of existence, the human heart can be wakened by kind treatment to feelings of affection and gratitude." Remarkably, Jervas experienced "the most debased and miserable state of existence" as *a wage laborer in England.*[36]

Other scholars have pointed to continuities between labor conditions in England and the colonies. In *The Problem of Freedom,* Holt contends that "the British experience with its own working class was a rehearsal for the formulation of policy for West Indian freed people." Like Hartman's *Scenes of Subjection,* Holt's study uses the post-emancipation experience of formerly enslaved people to illuminate liberal freedom's shortcomings. In the next section, I extend this argument to colonial Bengal and the production of so-called free East Indian sugar. For now, I want to dilate on the implication of Holt's comments about the British working class: reverse engineering his argument, we might say that the very same problems that bedeviled the post-emancipation freedom of "West Indian freed people" also severely curtailed the vaunted freedom of wage laborers in England. Hartman likewise points us in this direction when she notes "the role played by abolitionist and antislavery reformers in the conceptualization and dissemination of repressive free labor ideals." While she cites Bentham as an example of "continuities between the management of slave and free labor," we will find an even better example in Edgeworth, whom, it is worth noting, Bentham unabashedly admired.[37]

Rewards might seem like a fairly unobjectionable basis for labor discipline. Without a doubt, they are far less sinister than the punishments that were historically doled out in slave labor camps on America's cotton frontier, where, Edward Baptist reveals, labor management was synonymous with torture. Still, rewards were viewed as a mechanism for subjection by the liberal reformers who advocated them. This is perfectly clear when it comes to the thinker who popularized this view of social discipline in England, Thomas Hobbes. "*Reward* and *Punishment*" feature in the famous opening paragraph of *Leviathan,* where Hobbes unfurls an extended metaphor for the commonwealth as "an artificial man." Just as "the *Nerves*" cause movement "in the body natural," so "*Reward* and *Punishment,*" "fastened to the seat of the Sovereignty," are the means by which "every joint and member is moved to perform his duty" in the "artificial man," *Leviathan.* Edgeworth was not a professed admirer of Hobbes; indeed, during her lifetime almost nobody was. After coming out on the losing side in the English civil wars, "Hobbes was anathema in eighteenth-century England." His ideas "became respectable," James Crimmins tells us, only at the turn of the nineteenth century, thanks to the efforts of liberal reformers like "Bentham"—and, we can add, Edgeworth. Her pedagogical treatise *Practical Education* features a chapter entitled "On Rewards and Punishments," where she connects her philosophy of education to the questions of political philosophy explored by Hobbes. The primary purpose of education, Edgeworth argues, is to secure "an habitual, rational, voluntary, happy obedience" to "all the laws on which the prosperity of society depends." "How to induce" such obedience "is the question" she poses in *Practical Education*—and answers with three words taken straight from Hobbes, perhaps via Bentham: "Rewards and Punishments."[38]

Liberal reformers were attracted to Hobbes's political philosophy at least in part because its mechanistic account of human action offered a blueprint for political stability. This is evident in Bentham's *Introduction to the Principles of Morals and Legislation,* which was written in the 1770s but not published until 1789. The opening paragraph of the introduction unmistakably echoes the passage from *Leviathan* quoted above: "Nature has placed mankind under the governance of two sovereign masters, *pain* and *pleasure.* It is for them alone to point out what we ought to do, as well as to determine what we shall do. On the one hand the standard of right and wrong, on the other the chain of causes and effects, are fastened to their throne. They govern us in all we do, in all we say, in all we think: every effort we can make to throw off our subjection, will serve but to demonstrate and confirm it. In words a man may pretend to abjure their empire: but in reality he will remain subject to it all the while." The source of Hobbes's appeal for Bentham in this passage is fairly clear: he offers a foolproof recipe for securing obedience. No matter what "mankind" does "to throw off our subjection" to pain and pleasure, the effort is as useless as trying to unlink cause from effect: it is impossible to escape from their dominion, or "empire," even at the level of what "we think." Why this is the case is not spelled out here; but it is implied via a few carefully chosen keywords. In place of Hobbes's "*Reward* and *Punishment*," Bentham substitutes the experiences they elicit, "*pain* and *pleasure*," thereby emphasizing empiricism, particularly the empiricist doctrine of the association of ideas. Another addition is equally important: "the chain of causes and effects." For Georgian readers, these keywords would have flashed in neon lights. Unmistakably, they signal Bentham's position in a heated ongoing debate about the nature of causation, agency, and free will: the liberty and necessity controversy.[39]

The liberty and necessity debates are often described as a philosophical dispute about the existence of free will. While this is true, it is also misleading in the sense that the "topics" of "free will and political liberty" were not "isolated and distinct" in the eighteenth century, as Philip Pettit notes. Literary critic William Ulmer carves out an even more expansive purview for what might easily be mistaken for a niche concern: "the dispute between libertarians and necessitarians . . . became an important polemical coordinate and a recurrent point of reference throughout the intellectual life of late eighteenth-century England." As Ulmer implies, the debates were highly politicized, especially during the English civil wars and the Age of Revolutions. Although neither position has any *inherent* politics, they had strong political associations. In the English context, the belief in metaphysical liberty often correlated with radicalism; hence Burke's derision of Richard Price as the "professor of metaphysics" in *Reflections on the Revolution in France.* Necessitarianism (also known as determinism) was most closely associated with counter-revolutionary politics à la Hobbes. At the same time, some well-known English radicals were necessitarians—most notably William Godwin, but also Price's close friend and collaborator Joseph Priestley. Meanwhile, on the other side of the English Channel, the political fault lines of the debate were exactly reversed: in France, necessitarianism was synonymous with radicalism. This is another indication that each position was ideologically malleable. At the same time, there is no denying that necessitarianism was profoundly appealing to liberalism's architects, including Edgeworth.[40]

Although Bentham affected not to "care two straws about liberty and necessity at any time," necessitarianism forms the bedrock for his moral and political philosophy, which is deeply indebted to Hobbes. As noted, for most of the eighteenth century Hobbes was very unpopular. This changed during the Age of Revolutions. In the previous chapter, I argued that the American Revolution catalyzed a transformation in the definition of slavery; now, I'm suggesting that it triggered a corresponding sea change in the meaning of freedom. Pettit sketches out this historical trajectory: "Hobbes's notion of freedom [as noninterference] had little influence prior to the late eighteenth century.... It is as if the Hobbesian notion had been put on the shelf of historical curiosities, only to be reclaimed at a time when suddenly it promised to do important ideological work: to help in silencing complaints of servitude and domination—complaints of unfreedom." Pettit's historical narrative helps elucidate the ideological fault lines of the liberty and necessity debates in England. Proponents of metaphysical freedom insisted that liberty required the total absence of any "foreign" influence over actions, or what is often shorthanded as "domination." For radicals like Price this translated into a revolutionary agenda: the toppling of all "slavish hierarchies" in church, state, and private life. Meanwhile, some necessitarians argued that liberty was actually "compatible" with domination, as it only required the absence of outright restraint. Domination was perfectly fine, according to this definition of liberty, so long as agents weren't restrained outright from carrying out actions. This position easily lent itself to apologias for hierarchies of domination in government and other arenas. In seventeenth-century England, Hobbes used necessitarianism to defend monarchical absolutism. In the nineteenth century, a new generation of liberal reformers and colonial governors used it to draw out what Stokes calls liberalism's "latent authoritarianism."[41]

Now let's get a firmer sense of what the opposing positions in the liberty and necessity debates entailed. To begin with the "liberty" position in the debate, it is exemplified in a text we have already encountered twice before (in Chapters 1 and 3): Price's *Observations on the Nature of Civil Liberty*. This best seller stages its famous case for "civil liberty" only after a fairly long (and, today, usually ignored) disquisition on "physical," or metaphysical, "liberty." In his response to Price, Richard Hey clarifies the meaning of this term: "The Author's definition of Physical Liberty conveys nearly the idea which, I think, has been by the generality of writers affixed to the term *Free-will*." For Price and his interlocutors, free will was judged to be a matter of causation. "By PHYSICAL LIBERTY," Price specifies, "I mean that principle of *Spontaneity*, or *Self-determination*, which constitutes us *Agents*; or which gives us a command over our actions, rendering them properly *ours*, and not effects of the operation of any foreign cause." Price defines agency as a kind of ownership, or "command," over causes for acting. When no dominating presence or "foreign cause" influences our actions, then and only then can we be said to have agency. This might seem like a simple precondition; but necessitarians insisted it was utterly impossible to achieve. Priestley elucidates this position in a book-length exchange with Price entitled *A Free Discussion of the Doctrines of Materialism, and Philosophical Necessity*, published by Joseph Johnson (who also published *Popular Tales*) in 1778. According to Priestley, agents cannot possibly act in the absence of foreign causes because "every human volition is invariably directed by the circumstances in which a man is, and what we call *motives*." If every action happens in a context, then causes for acting must be located at least partly in the external world of "circumstances." Inevitably, the contexts within which we operate influence the causes for our actions by motivating us to avoid pain and seek out pleasure—Bentham's "two sovereign masters" of "mankind." Acting without foreign causes would require either living in a void or being utterly immune to pain and pleasure—both impossibilities.[42]

Priestley's rebuttal of Price epitomizes the determinist strain of thinking that Jonathan Kramnick calls "externalism." Externalist theories of causation relocate the causes of actions from the hermetically sealed internal world of subjects—the realm of intentions and desires—to the external environments that subjects inhabit. When Priestley argues that "every human volition is invariably directed by the circumstances in which a man is," the implication is that causes for actions are dispersed in contexts, not concentrated inside self-encapsulated selves. Externalism helps account for necessitarianism's popularity among liberal reformers. Kramnick makes this point in relation to Hobbes, who, he writes, "evidently found [it] convenient in a time of political uncertainty" to argue that the "contextual sources of action" inescapably "bind agents to external structures." In the midst of a civil war and a crisis in the legitimacy of monarchical government, "Hobbes finds in necessity the very basis of obedience and order." A century and a half later, counterrevolutionaries once again sought comfort in necessitarianism, especially in its political affordances. More specifically, they were consoled by the reliable manner in which motives govern human action. Motives are so foolproof that Priestley likens them to the laws of Newtonian physics: "rewards and punishments . . . are applied to, and influence or move the will, as much as external force moves the body. . . . Let the mind act contrary to motives, or the stone move contrary to the laws of gravity, and I shall then, but not before, believe that they are not the only and necessary causes." All this gives us a new vantage point on the rewards-based labor management program illustrated in "Lame Jervas" and "The Grateful Negro." The ease with which Edgeworth's reforms are transposed from Cornwall to India to Jamaica—and from scenes of wage labor to political slavery to chattel slavery—is no longer so remarkable when we consider that their philosophical basis lies in a theory of human action that claims to be universal to all mankind. From Edgeworth's perspective, there is no fundamental difference between a so-called free wage laborer and an enslaved laborer because she subscribes to a necessitarian view of humankind as fundamentally unfree.[43]

This is not the way we are accustomed to thinking of liberalism. In scholarship—especially scholarship on slavery—liberalism is most often equated with a *commitment* to agency, not a disbelief in it. Walter Johnson, a historian of US slavery, epitomizes this position in his important essay "On Agency." There, he argues that it is time to displace agency as "the master trope around which historians understand arguments about slavery" because, under this trope's sway, scholarship on slavery has become "saturated with the categories of nineteenth-century liberalism." In his account of liberalism, "the category of 'humanity' is conflated with the category of free will," a conflation that traps scholars in an endless loop of arguments for slave "humanity as indexed by the presence of acts of self-determination." Without minimizing the importance of Johnson's historiographical intervention, it is worth noting that his account of liberalism's view of agency is not, technically speaking, entirely correct. For political theorists it is a commonplace that liberalism inherited its dominant conception of liberty from Hobbes, a necessitarian. While Hobbes redefined liberty in an attempt to make it consonant with domination (a position known as compatibilism), other necessitarians openly admitted their doctrine's implications for human freedom. In his discourse with Price, Priestley puts the matter simply: "If *self-motion,* or *self-determination,* properly so called, be essential to liberty, I must deny that man is possessed of it; and if this, and nothing else, must be called *agency,* I must deny that, *in this sense,* man is an agent." For liberal reformers who subscribed to necessitarianism, humanity was not defined by agency, but rather by a lack thereof. Scholars of slavery might therefore leave behind the "master trope" of agency by means of a renewed engagement with the foundational philosophical categories of nineteenth-century liberalism, which in fact leave little room for our commonsensical conflation of humanity and free will.[44]

In "Lame Jervas" and "The Grateful Negro," Edgeworth translates liberalism's philosophical tenets into a counterrevolutionary game plan. If the ultimate determinants of human action are located outside human agents, then the best way to secure the subjection of potentially insurrectionary subjects is to shape the environment those subjects inhabit. This can be done by lacing "circumstances" with causes for acting, or motives, in the form of rewards and punishments. Priestley, whom Edgeworth read and admired, assumes the inevitability of this approach: "The governors will rule voluntary agents by means of rewards and punishments, and the governed, being voluntary agents, will be influenced by the apprehension of them." In Priestley's schema, the ultimate governor of human actions is in fact God, since providence ultimately dictates the circumstances of our lives. In Edgeworth's stories, enslavers take on this role, playing God for their subordinates. Recall that both Jervas and Caesar kneel down in prayer before their respective masters; and Jervas tells the reader that after Mr. R— showed him kindness, "I looked up to him as to a new sort of being." One could hardly find a purer expression of the ideology of benevolent paternalism: masters reign like gods in a divinely ordered hierarchy of dominance and subordination. "Tippoo" also plays an important role in this schematic, as a negative example. In *Practical Education*, Edgeworth warns that an inconsistent distribution of rewards and punishments has the power to spoil an education, ending with the maxim, "The favor of princes is an uncertain reward." This is exactly what Jervas learns during his time in the Sultan's service when he is alternately rewarded (with riches) and punished (with imprisonment), seemingly at random. Jervas, on the other hand, proves himself to be adept at playing God vis-à-vis the enslaved miners he manages: he rewards them consistently for good behavior, thereby securing their loyal submission.[45]

By the time Jervas reaches India, he is already prepared for the challenge he will face there, having practiced Mr. R—'s methods on a surrogate: the puppet laborers who populate a diorama mine he builds shortly after leaving Cornwall. If there are any doubts that *Popular Tales* represents a deliberate intervention in the liberty and necessity debates on the part of Edgeworth, Jervas's diorama of puppet miners should settle them. Necessitarianism is often associated with mechanical philosophies and mechanistic views of human nature. Edgeworth literalizes this equation when Jervas learns how to manage human laborers by first practicing with puppets on strings: "It was some time, even when all this was ready, before we could contrive to make our puppets do their business properly: but patience accomplishes every thing. At last we got our wooden miners to obey us, and to perform their several tasks at the word of command; that is to say, at the pulling of certain strings and wires, which we fastened to their legs, arms, heads, and shoulders; which wires being thin and black, were at a little distance invisible to the spectators." In this passage, Edgeworth materializes "the *Nerves*" of Hobbes's "artificial man" and Bentham's "chain of causes and effects" into "strings and wires" that only need be pulled in order to secure instant obedience.

With a little practice, Jervas overcomes all resistance, including a "stiff old fellow, whose arms . . . I could never get to bend: and an obstinate old woman, who would never do anything else but curtsy, when I wanted her to kneel down and to do her work." With no way to "throw off" their "subjection," each of Jervas's puppets is "moved to perform his duty." After these challenges, managing real-life laborers is as easy as child's play.[46]

If Jervas's diorama is the stuff of Hobbesian and Benthamite dreams, it is also a set piece from one of Price's nightmares. A bogeyman haunts all of Price's writing on liberty and necessity: the automaton. In the same way that the loss of political liberty turned men into slaves, according to Price, the denial of metaphysical liberty turned them into machines. If man is not "a *self-moving* being" endowed with "agency," he writes in his exchange with Priestley, then "he is nothing but a machine." Price wanted to believe that a "man invited by the hope of a reward"—like the characters in Edgeworth's stories—was altogether different from "a man dragged along like a piece of timber," because the former followed a motive with "*his own* agency." Priestley, on the other hand, insisted that both cases were one and the same: "man has no other liberty in following motives than water has in running downhill, or than the arms of the scale prest by weights, have in rising and falling." By rewarding enslaved laborers in India and Jamaica, Jervas and Edwards elicited the actions they desired with the same mechanical efficiency of pulled puppet strings. This was precisely the vision of humanity that Price abhorred when he accused Priestley of reducing men to "a system of conscious machinery," and God to "the mover and controuler of an universe of puppets." For Price, a "universe of puppets" was an incubus; for Edgeworth, it was a model of social order. These contradictory responses speak volumes about the revolutionary/counterrevolutionary divide.[47]

It is significant that in Jervas's diorama the chains (or, in this case, strings) that bind (and manipulate) the puppets are "at a little distance invisible to the spectators," rendering their submission undetectable. Necessity's ability to fly under the radar of awareness was a frequently discussed aspect of the necessitarian position. Priestley, for example, emphasizes that "though real, and important," necessitarianism "has nothing to do with anything that is within the apprehension of the bulk of mankind." "When men say that they are *free*," Priestley continues, "they have no idea of anything farther than a freedom from the control of others.... *Internal causes* are never so much as thought of, and much less expressly excluded, when they speak of this most perfect liberty." Kramnick draws out this point nicely in his discussion of a memorable "rhetorical flourish" in Hobbes: the figure of a spinning wooden top that thinks its motion "proceeded from its own Will" because it is unaware of the boys who "lasht it." Like Hobbes's spinning top, human actors are often unaware of the circumstances and motives that set their actions in motion. Kramnick extracts the relevant point here: "The feeling of freedom, in other words, does not accurately represent the experience by which it is engendered." This was an attractive proposition to colonial governors and liberal reformers in England who were eager to secure submission without seeming to curtail liberty.[48]

Once again, it is important not to dismiss *Popular Tales* as the naïve fantasy of a female novelist. Many of Edgeworth's ideas were lauded and embraced by men who were in a position to carry them out. Sir James Mackintosh, a Scottish jurist and MP who served as the chief judge of Bombay, "said he should require 'for Botany Bay a code from Bentham, and "Popular Tales" from Miss Edgeworth.'" Mackintosh's desire to send *Popular Tales* to a penal colony in the luggage of colonial governors is a powerful testament to its perceived value as a training manual for managing rebellious subjects. If, as Foucault provocatively wrote, "Bentham is more important for the understanding of our society than Kant and Hegel," then I believe the same might be said of Edgeworth.[49]

In this chapter's next and final section, I trace out echoes of Edgeworth's labor-management strategies in a series of policy experiments that sought to use so-called free Indian labor to solve the problem of West Indian slavery.

Buying and Selling from Cawnpore to Cheapside

In the final two decades of the eighteenth century, abolitionists and investors teamed up to promote East Indian sugar cultivation as a potential solution to the problem of West Indian slavery. As Eric Williams explains in *Capitalism and Slavery*, the East India Company began to take an interest in sugar in 1787, following Wilberforce's first proposal to abolish the slave trade. These efforts gained steam in the wake of the uprising and revolution on Saint-Domingue, when African slavery's days suddenly seemed numbered. In "Lame Jervas" and "The Grateful Negro," slaves and so-called free wage laborers are functionally inter-changeable. Proponents of East Indian sugar took a slightly different tack, in the sense that they touted the supposed differences between free Bengali peasants and enslaved Africans. But the deviation from Edge-worth ends there. Like her stories, the pamphlets and reports promoting East Indian sugar paint a picture of freedom that is simply indistin-guishable, in many ways, from slavery. Taking another page from Edge-worth's playbook, this literature argues that the supposedly universal attributes of humankind can be harnessed in order to secure obedience and extract labor in the absence of slavery's material whips and chains.[50]

At the outset of her essay "On the Education of the Poor" Edge-worth expressed her desire to discover a universal panacea for the Jaco-bin crisis that would be equally effective in "different countries" despite variations in "National character and climate National institutions and customs." In the previous section I argued that necessitarianism pro-vided Edgeworth with exactly this kind of master key to the human heart and mind since its principles supposedly transcended cultural dif-ference. East Indian sugar enthusiasts also embraced a transnational view of human nature. Or, more precisely, they included Bengali peas-ants in the category of mankind while excluding enslaved Africans from it. Here, I offer a slight emendation to Lisa Lowe's argument that "mod-ern liberalism defined the 'human' and universalized its attributes to Eu-ropean man" to the exclusion of non-European colonized subjects. A "Minute of the board of trade" from 1792 exemplifies how Bengali peas-ants were brought into the fold of mankind at the expense of West Indian slaves. The "Minute" begins with a virtual exercise in the Indies mentality: "a short comparison of . . . the cultivators of the ground in the West-India islands with those of this country [Bengal]." One of the most important differences between the two is that the Bengali peasant's free-dom renders him subject to the same motives that govern the rest of mankind. The problem with slavery, in this view, is that the "West-India slave has no interest in the success of his labour," meaning that "[t]her[e] is no cheering motive to animate his industry," or no hope of reward. Hence, the need for punishment: "the heavy charge of the establishment of overseers and superintendents" is "requisite for urging the labour of slaves."[51]

Liberal reformers were sensitive to the dangers of a disciplinary apparatus that relied solely on punishment. In "The Grateful Negro," the slave rebellion on Mr. Jeffries's plantation is chiefly attributed to the "tyranny" of the overseer Durant, who relied entirely on "brutality which he considered as the only means of governing black men." This philosophy costs him his life. During the uprising, "he died in tortures, inflicted by the hands of those who had suffered most by his cruelties." Meanwhile, the ideal planter Mr. Edwards better understood the power of rewards: "Those who are animated by hope can perform what would seem impossibilities to those who are under the depressing influence of fear." Edgeworth expounds the same principles in her chapter "On Rewards and Punishments" in *Practical Education:* "Hope excites the mind to exertion; fear represses all activity." Other liberal reformers agreed. In his plan for the *Panopticon,* Bentham admits that the chief weakness of his design is that it fails to balance rewards and punishments: it "*does* give every degree of efficacy which can be given to the influence of *punishment* and *restraint.* But it does nothing towards correcting the oppressive influence of punishment and restraint, by the enlivening and invigorating influence of *reward.* That noblest and brightest engine of discipline." This line of thinking is echoed in the 1792 "Minute of the board of trade," which emphasizes affect when it laments the lack of "cheering motive" among West Indian slaves. Meanwhile, the "Bengal peasantry are freemen," and as such, the "Bengal peasant is actuated by the ordinary wants and desires of mankind."[52]

In *Scenes of Subjection,* Hartman asks a provocative question: "Suppose that the recognition of humanity held out the promise not of liberating the flesh or redeeming one's suffering but rather of intensifying it? ... Or what if the heart, the soul, and the mind were simply the inroads of discipline"? While Hartman poses these hypotheticals in the context of the post-emancipation United States, they are equally applicable to colonial Bengal—or, at least, to the fantasy version of it presented in literature advocating East Indian sugar. In this fantasy, laborers toil without the lash; or, more precisely, they drive themselves to labor through internalized discipline, the hallmark of the industrialized wage laborer. The "ordinary wants and desires of mankind" turn out to be "the sharp eye of personal interest [that] guides his judgment." No artificial reward is needed to motivate the free laborer, who is naturally compelled by "personal interest" to seek out profit and accumulation. Living as we do at the tail end of centuries of liberal and neoliberal capitalism, it is sometimes difficult for us to recognize this vision of humanity as ideological. "The nineteenth-century conception of freedom is so much a part of our intellectual baggage," Holt writes, "that it requires effort to see it merely as an artifact of history rather than one of the givens of human nature and desire."[53]

While Holt's study focuses on the liberal architects of emancipation in Jamaica, many of his arguments translate perfectly to Bengal. The freedom of the free Bengali peasant is a freedom to accumulate. One of Holt's main arguments is that liberalism naturalizes capitalism by positing profit seeking as a basic instinct of humankind: it "makes market-governed social relations into *natural* phenomena." We could hardly find a more perfect testament to his argument than the 1792 "Minute," which contrasts the artificial motivation inflicted on the slave in the form of bodily punishment with the natural acquisitiveness of the Bengali peasant. Ranajit Guha quotes an early example of this outlook from a 1772 pamphlet on improving revenues in Bengal: "The minds of mankind we find are much the same in all countries, and actuated by the same views and desires . . . there can be no doubt that the acquisition of property will be as desirable to Asiatics as it is to Europeans." Stokes likewise cites the belief "that human nature was intrinsically the same in all races" as the basis for colonial policy makers' faith that Indians would eventually become consumers of British goods. A Select Committee Report quoted by Stokes takes this view of man as an article of faith: "We may be assured that in buying and selling, human nature is the same in Cawnpore as in Cheapside." Translating these insights into a more contemporary theoretical vocabulary, we might say that proponents of East Indian sugar, like the engineers of West Indian emancipation, were exemplars of what Stefano Harvey and Fred Moten call "governance": "the criminalization of being without interest." Or, to be more precise, we might say that in

Bengal we see the flipside of the postemancipation "criminalization" of unindustriousness documented by Hartman and Holt. The inclusion of Bengali peasants under the umbrella of humanity was contingent on their continued, supposedly voluntary, self-motivated labor.[54]

With almost unbelievable candor, proponents of East Indian sugar disclosed the source of the Bengali peasant's unforced "industry": extreme deprivation. Henry Thomas Colebrooke is today best remembered as a Sanskrit scholar; but he was also an important official, serving, most notably, as chief of Calcutta's court of appeal and a member of the Council of Bengal. One of his most influential publications was his *Remarks on the Husbandry and Internal Commerce of Bengal,* which was privately printed and circulated in 1795 and made available to the public in 1804 (when excerpts were featured in *The Anti-Jacobin Review*). In his *Remarks*—which were intended, in part, to stump for Bengal sugar— Colebrooke waxes poetic on Indian immiseration: "The necessaries of life are cheaper in India than in any other commercial country and cheaper in Bengal than in any other province in India. The simplest diet and most scanty clothing suffice to the peasant, and the price of labour is consequently low." Whereas "the West-Indian slave has no incentive for exertion; nor can he be roused to it, by the smart of recent chastisement or the dread of impending punishment," Bengali peasants "labour with cheerful diligence and unforced zeal"—unforced, that is, by anything other than the imminent threat of starvation. Indeed, Colebrooke hits the hard limits of the vaunted freedom of the Bengali peasant when he reveals that labor is rarely remunerated in wages—or, when it is, in wages so low they amount to nothing at all: the "price of their daily labour, when paid in money, may be justly estimated at little more than one ana sica, but less than two-pence sterling . . . or compare with it the still cheaper hire of labor by a payment in kind, a mode which is customary throughout Bengal. The allowance of grain, usually made to strong labourers, cannot be valued at more than one ana and does in reality cost the husbandman much less. The average would scarcely exceed a penny half-penny." Colebrooke's point is that free Bengali labor is cheaper than West Indian slave labor. But in making this point he throws into relief a liberal mentality in which extreme deprivation is judged to be consonant with freedom. P. J. Marshall reads moments like these with

critical generosity: "Underlying the apparent insensitivity of the abolitionists to Indian poverty was their passionately held conviction that
freedom redeemed any material condition however dire." Where Marshall sees passion and "conviction," I see convenience, callous disregard,
and greed. Men like Colebrooke stood to gain from the Bengali peasant's
immiseration. Indrani Chatterjee spells this out: "From the time of his
arrival in India in 1782, he had entrepreneurial ambitions of becoming
a plantation lord on the West Indian model; frustrated in South Asia he
ultimately bought land in South Africa for this purpose." Colebrooke's
personal motivations aside, it was precisely in order to distinguish between liberalism's anemic and emaciated conception of freedom, on the
one hand, and actual human liberation, on the other, that Marx differentiated between "formal" and "substantive" freedom—a practice adopted
by Hartman in *Scenes of Subjection.* Marx's point, and Hartman's, is that
the idea that wage labor is inherently free is an ideological fiction.[55]

In truth, the so-called freedom of the Bengali peasant often didn't
even meet the criteria for "formal" freedom. Colebrooke, who, like Stephen (quoted at the outset of this chapter), opposed slavery in the West
Indies, was complicit in perpetuating slavery in India. "In some places,"
Colebrooke admits, "the land-holders have a claim to the servitude of
thousands among the inhabitants of their estates." But, he assuages English consciences, this need not be considered slavery: "slaves of this description do in fact enjoy every privilege of a freeman except the name;
or, at the worst they must be considered as villains [*sic*] attached to the
glebe, rather than as bondmen labouring for the sole benefit of their
owners. Indeed, throughout India, the relation of master and slave appears to impose the duty of protection and cherishment on the master, as
much as that of fidelity and obedience on the slave, and their mutual
conduct is consistent with the sense of such an obligation; since it is
marked with gentleness and indulgence on the one side, and with zeal
and loyalty on the other." Colebrooke's description of the "mutual" feudal
bonds between enslaved people and their enslavers—with "fidelity and
obedience" owed by the former and "obligation" owed by the latter—
might easily be confused for one of Edgeworth's fictions. Indeed, it re-
sembles nothing so much as the model slave plantation from "The
Grateful Negro." In her book on agrestic caste-based slavery, *The Pariah*

Problem, Rupa Viswanath argues that this kind of rhetoric was pervasive in nineteenth-century India, and she shorthands it as the "trope of 'gentle slavery.'" "Repeatedly—indeed relentlessly," Viswanath writes, "officials re-assured their superiors in Britain that Indian slavery was not to be con-fused with its Atlantic counterparts, setting the terms for future discourse on servitude." In short, benevolent paternalism of the kind peddled by Edgeworth was deployed in policy as an alibi for slavery.[56]

Thanks to the efforts of Colebrooke and other liberal reformers, slavery in India survived the nineteenth century. Company officials "sought . . . to have India exempted" from antislavery legislation, includ-ing "the Empire-wide abolition of slavery that was passed in 1833." Cole-brooke played a significant role in this policy decision. Rosane and Ludo Rocher have uncovered a secret minute written by Colebrooke in which he argues against abolition in India. "I trust not to be considered an ad-vocate for slavery, nor indifferent to the miseries incident to the most degraded condition in human society," wrote Colebrooke, "when I ob-serve, that, in this country, Slaves are in general treated with gentleness and indulgence." An important "theorist for the conservative Bengal government" (in the words of the Rochers), Colebrooke effectively translated Edgeworth's apologia for slavery as a form of benevolent pa-ternalism into colonial policy and practice. Thanks in part to Cole-brooke's efforts, slavery was not abolished in India until 1843. Even then, Viswanath argues, in the Madras presidency "the British did nothing to challenge the condition of agrarian unfreedom." Instead, they allied with high-caste landowners in order to secure the continued subjection of Dalits or "pariahs," a "racialized subpopulation and the descendants of agrarian slaves," who were openly referred to in Tamil-language records as slaves—and sold as such—into the twentieth century.[57]

The slave revolt on Saint-Domingue gave birth to yet another idea as to how the East Indies might be made the savior of the West. Al-though the transportation of indentured Indian and Chinese laborers to the Caribbean did not begin until 1838, the plan was first hatched in a secret memorandum written in 1803, which speculated that "introduc-ing a free race of cultivators" to Jamaica might serve as a buffer against insurrection. In *The Intimacy of Four Continents,* Lowe argues compel-lingly that indenture irredeemably complicates liberal narratives of the nineteenth century as a triumphant transition from slavery to freedom. More recently, Najnin Islam has added to this picture, arguing that indentureship leads us away from classic conceptions of agency toward a "fractured notion of volition." One of Islam's most innovative arguments is that indenture's architects consciously exploited existing forms of caste oppression. Just as Colebrooke and other officials conspired to conceal caste-based forms of slavery in Bengal and Madras, so officials sought out low-caste recruits for transportation to the Caribbean, as they were already accustomed to hard labor and immiseration. All this leads Islam to argue that the figure of the "New World 'coolie'... needs to be apprehended in relation to British imperial discourses on caste" as well as race, adding that "race and caste were apprehended in relation to one another in this particular moment." Nearly thirty years ago, the pioneering historian of caste-based slavery, Dharma Kumar, connected low-caste immiseration in India to indenture in the Caribbean. Indenture "has been described as a 'new system of slavery,'" Kumar writes: "But one must consider the conditions the emigrants were leaving behind and the probability that they went willingly, though undoubtedly with insufficient knowledge." Laborers leaving India, Kumar continues, "went to free themselves from debt bondage and to escape miserable conditions at home." Colebrooke's portrait of Indian indigence makes Kumar's argument very easy to believe, albeit with one proviso: newer research by Viswanath proves that debt bondage was in fact a mere alibi for what can only be considered slavery. Far from leaving a peasant agrarian utopia for the horrors of plantation labor, indentured Bengalis traded in one form of slavery for another. All this further complicates the already "fraught" category of agency, to quote Islam once again.[58]

Abolitionists and other reformers may have believed that formal freedom redeemed even the most dire circumstances; but we can take a more nuanced view of things. Setting aside the logic of nineteenth-century liberalism, we can distinguish more carefully between freedom's formal and its substantive varieties. Taking to heart Johnson's appeal to move beyond the "master trope" of agency, we might use our own critical criteria to decide that an existence so onerous and contingent that it would lead people to indenture themselves voluntarily need not meet the requirements for freedom. This is merely one way in which the perspective of the Indies mentality can help us to relearn what we thought we already knew about freedom.[59]

One of the most remarkable things about indenture is how it reshaped material conditions—including places and populations—in the image of the Indies mentality. In the next chapter, I show that this seemingly exceptional event was in fact typical in at least one sense: colonial governors regularly wove the two Indies together in policy; indeed, institutional practice encouraged them to do so.

A Sociable and Aristocratic Empire

Lady Nugent's East and West India Journals

INDIES, *n.* . . . . 2. Used allusively for a region or place yielding great

wealth or to which profitable voyages may be made.

—*Oxford English Dictionary*

The diaries and letters written by Maria Nugent in Jamaica and India—where her husband was governor from 1801 to 1806, and commander in chief from 1811 to 1814—are a testament to the strength of the two Indies pairing as a "grid of intelligibility" for the business of imperial governance. In a letter written shortly after her arrival in Bengal in 1812, Lady Nugent explains her intentions for her "East India Journal": "I keep a constant Journal of everything which I mean to leave as a Legacy to my dear children. This added to my West India Volume will serve as a History of many years of our lives and with all its imperfections it will I am sure be interesting to them." Five years after her death, Lady Nugent's family published her East and West India journals privately as companion volumes. The two Indies gave shape and coherence to "many years" of her and her husband's lives.[1]

The same was true for many of their peers: by the turn of the nineteenth century, most high-ranking military officers would expect to spend time in more than one colony—and more than one hemisphere. Scholars have recently begun to pay more attention to this phenomenon, which David Lambert and Alan Lester call "imperial careering." By reconstructing how the institutionalized circulation of personnel facilitated the circulation of practices, policies, and ideologies around the globe, scholars have been able to prove just how often experiences in one colony informed decisions made in another. For example, Laurence Brown argues that the institution of indenture owes its genesis at least partly to the "global circulation of people and ideas"—more specifically, the global circulation of colonial governors.[2]

This chapter contributes to scholarship on "imperial careering," showing how the Indies mentality was reproduced at an institutional level through the practice of rotating high-ranking personnel between posts in the two Indies. This practice encouraged the men—and, I argue, women—who ruled the empire to adopt a holistic view of it. For colonial governors, the two Indies represented one and the same thing: both were "place[s] yielding great wealth" where in just a few years a fortune big enough to last a lifetime, or even longer, could be made. Spatially amalgamated fantasies of profit and wealth may seem to harken back to the dreams that put wind in the sails of the age of discoveries, but the *Oxford English Dictionary* definition of "the Indies" quoted as the epigraph to this chapter endured well into the nineteenth century. Jamaica and India were functionally interchangeable sources of monetary and social capital for Britain's upper classes. The Nugents and their peers saw the two Indies as fungible sources of liquidity, honors, and reputation. While most of the extant scholarship on imperial careering focuses on what colonial governors did for the empire, I am far more interested in what the empire did for colonial governors. Instead of spending this chapter showing how the Indies mentality was inscribed in practice at the level of official "public" policy, I thus explore how it shaped the "private" lives of the empire's governing elite—who, over the decades in question, increasingly belonged to the nation's most privileged families.[3]

In some measure, my focus on "private" life is dictated by the nature of this chapter's primary sources: Lady Nugent's diaries don't have a lot to say about policy decisions. But it also reflects my conviction that sociability represents a crucial and largely overlooked aspect of imperial governance. New work by Amanda Vickery and Hannah Greig explodes the myth that the business of politics was mostly business. Political men, they show, spent most of the day socializing. One implication of their argument is that the research tools and interpretive strategies developed for women's history can be just as usefully applied to the age-old subjects of History with a capital H—political men. Lady Nugent's journals are a testament to their argument, which in turn amplifies the use value of this kind of source. If socializing was a key component of politics and governance, it was an arena of the state where women could claim an equal—if not a leading—role. While Lady Nugent's balls and dresses might seem frivolous, they were in fact instruments of statecraft; and, as such, they represent an untapped source for Imperial History in the most serious sense of the term. Taking women's political work seriously can also help to address a notorious problem with the colonial archive. As Betty Joseph aptly puts its: "the records of colonialism for the most part teem with men." In this chapter I suggest that female life writing represents an underutilized source for colonial governance. Viewing it as such can help us to work with the same old colonial archive in new and creative ways.[4]

In the first half of this chapter, I argue that in the decades following the revolutionary crisis the institution of Crown patronage turned the two Indies into a veritable aristocratic social safety net. By re-spinning the elaborate kinship webs that connected Nugent to his patrons and clients I reveal how colonial appointments in the two Indies were utilized to serve the needs of what the sociologist Norbert Elias calls "Society with a capital S." Like many colonial governors, Nugent acquired and then spent his massive imperial salaries in the service of repairing his elite family's downwardly mobile fortunes. This included losses (and gains) of social capital as well as money. Only a few decades earlier, Jamaican and Indian fortunes were tainted with associations of corruption, rapacity, and new money; but now the colonies were becoming sources of outright social and political prestige, which manifested most tangibly in honors. The amount of attention colonial governors lavished on such seemingly trivial matters as etiquette, honors, and titles indicates that these matters deserve *our* attention as well.[5]

In the chapter's final section, I focus on the Nugents' parental patronage of young men in Jamaica and India. In Chapter 1, I connected the empire to anxieties during the 1770s about the aristocracy's failure to reproduce itself as a competent ruling class. Three decades later, attitudes had changed so drastically that gentry families now willingly sent their younger sons to the colonies, even leveraging personal connections in order to do so. However, if a sizeable number of elite young men were going to spend a good portion of their early adulthoods in the colonies, they had to be able to do so without destroying their manners, characters, health, reputations, and prospects—for example, through mixed-race liaisons. "Respectable" venues for courtship needed to be erected in the colonies. In this book's Prelude, I used Hayman's enormous history paintings to draw attention to the overlooked presence of empire in metropolitan spaces of fashionable sociability during the Seven Years' War. Here, I make a distinct but related point: during the Revolutionary and Napoleonic wars, Vauxhall ended up in the canvasses, as spaces of elite sociability sprung up in every important colony and the Indies began to function as a de facto extension of the fashionable world.

While social institutions like assemblies (or balls) might seem like sideshows from the actual business of imperial rule, they represented one condition of possibility for the reproduction of Britain's governing elite on the ground in the empire. This was an important dimension of the imperial project and an arena in which women claimed a leading part. Painting a portrait of colonial governance whose backdrop is a ballroom instead of a boardroom thus represents one way of restoring women to the stories we tell about imperial rule.

Colonial Lives, Patronage, and the Late Georgian Welfare State

These days, it seems that almost everybody in the field of British imperial history is writing about "colonial lives." It is not difficult to see why. Scholars are newly eager to cross conventional divisions between oceans, colonies, and hemispheres; and lives present a ready vehicle. Many colonial officials, both military and civilian, spent time in more than one colony, and often on more than one continent. Take, for example, Nugent's closest colleagues in India: Sir Charles Metcalfe, Sir Samuel Hood, General William Eden, General Miles Nightingale, Lord Moira, and

Sir Evan Murray MacGregor all previously or subsequently served in the West Indies or North America. Meanwhile, General George Hewett, Lord Moira, and General Nightingale served in Ireland, and many of these men saw action in the Mediterranean as well. Moreover, this list is far from complete.[6]

Along with many other scholars, I am also convinced of the critical utility of colonial lives; they are indispensable for lighting up the institutional circuitry that hardwired the Indies mentality into British imperial culture. At the same time, it is crucial that colonial lives not be used as a getaway car from structural history, as they sometimes have been. Since the past turns out to be riddled with relatively few incorrigible villains, refracting imperial history through the banal lives of individual colonizers can have the effect of rendering it bathetic, especially if it is paired with a turn away from structure. Suddenly histories of conquest, enslavement, colonialism, and the extraction of wealth cease to look so very bad after all. Thankfully, we do not need to choose between colonial lives on the one hand and the history of Empire with a capital E on the other. The two can be reconciled.

The discipline that has spent the most time wrestling with the relationship between individuals and structures is, arguably, sociology. Recent sociological paradigms like Bruno Latour's actor-network-theory (ANT) promise to undo the "actor/system," "micro/macro" binaries that pit "real life" against "structure," and "local interaction" against "global context." But I find an even more useful schematic in the (admittedly much less trendy) work of the mid-century sociologist Norbert Elias. More specifically, Elias's idea of a "court society" is a tremendously helpful hermeneutic for understanding the lives of colonial governors, and one to which I return throughout this chapter. Like Latour, Elias sought to dismantle the "antinomy" between "'individual phenomena' on one hand, and 'social phenomena' on the other." In order to do this, he turned to a historical case study: the ancien régime court of Louis XIV. When studying a court society, Elias argued, it is imperative to leave behind our own "bourgeois" sense of the divisions between "personal" and "professional" life, since the two were in fact coterminous for courtly elites. More recently, Dena Goodman, Hannah Smith, and Hannah Greig, have advanced similar arguments, demonstrating that what Elias calls "Society with a capital S" and the state were functionally interchangeable with one another in eighteenth-century England as well as France.[7]

Like many colonial governors, Nugent secured his appointments in Jamaica and India through family connections. Although he does seem to have been professionally competent, he was chosen for office principally because he needed the kind of cash flow that only a colonial salary could deliver. While his "professional" appointments obviously came from government ministers, the latter were acting in a "personal" capacity when they chose him for office. To put the matter simply, they were helping out a family member in need. During the 1760s, 1770s, and early 1780s, fortunes made in either of the two Indies were considered tainted in the metropole: "From West and East alike flowed luxury and potential corruption," in the words of historian P. J. Marshall. In Chapters 1 and 2 we encountered many instances where colonial wealth was characterized as morally and racially polluting. By the end of the 1790s, this taint had largely worn off. High-ranking colonial officials were now granted the benefit of the doubt by the public, especially in India. To quote Marshall once again, Britons who served there "claimed to do so with high professional pride, strict integrity and benevolence of purpose." Such claims would have been scoffed at only a few decades earlier, but now they went largely unchallenged. In this atmosphere, the younger sons of peers and other representatives of elite families fallen on hard times could safeguard their reputations *and* their bank accounts with a trip to the colonies. Empire was thus a springboard for the rebounding finances of many aristocratic families. The Nugents exemplify this general trend. Prior to his colonial appointments, Nugent was on the verge of going broke; after them, he could boast a baronetage, a red ribbon of the Order of the Bath, and a fortune substantial enough to secure his family's class position for generations.[8]

Nugent was a member of what has been called the "service elite." This term is meant to suggest a reformation in the nation's most privileged orders. Pivoting away from the excesses of the 1770s and 1780s, the greater aristocracy shed its associations with vice and regained a reputation for political leadership. The phrase "service elite" is intended to answer one question: How did the British upper classes survive the revolutionary 1790s intact? But it implicitly poses another: Whom, exactly, did the "service elite" serve? Was Nugent of service to the people of Ireland when he was tasked with "the suppression of the Rebellion" of 1798, when, Lady Nugent records, he was busy "holding courts martial, and signing the death warrants of very many" rebels? Whom did he serve as governor of Jamaica, when his chief priority was safeguarding the island for slavery? Who benefited from Nugent's later posting in Bengal, when the frontiers of the Company's dominions expanded under his watch? Like other members of the so-called service elite, Nugent served his own bottom line. Most "aristocratic imperialists" (a term I prefer) took up colonial postings not out of a sense of disinterested duty but because they needed the money. Plum postings could pay more than £20,000 per annum, not including emoluments. This is a staggering sum—so staggering that the upper ranks of imperial governance are best understood as an aristocratic social safety net.[9]

Accepting a position like governor of Jamaica or commander in chief in India meant drawing on the dole, albeit in a gentlemanly manner that protected—and even enhanced—the dignity of the recipient. In 1754, a dozen peers were recipients of what Lewis Namier calls "the aristocratic dole": a government handout of an average of £800 paid by the House of Lords to "men of rank in distress" in order to "maintain the dignity of the peerage." Men without titles received the proportionate sum of £500 from the House of Commons. Truth be told, these figures are Lilliputian in comparison to the number of peers who received aid dressed up in the form of a sinecure or salary. Well over half—and at times up to 70 percent—of the peerage received financial aid during the Georgian period. This came mostly in the form of "places," for example, in the royal household or about the king's person. Another source of aid were political appointments, a well-known bastion of "Old Corruption," which, E. P. Thompson insists, is "a more serious term of political analysis than is often supposed." Although the paymaster general of the forces certainly performed some work, one would be hard pressed to argue that his value to the nation justified a remuneration of £100,000 *p.a.* (the sum Henry Fox stockpiled during his term in this office), especially at a time when less than 3 percent of the population of England and Wales enjoyed a net income greater than £200 *p.a.* Nugent's patron, George Temple-Grenville, the first marquess of Buckingham (hereafter Lord Buckingham) offers another example of just how astronomically lucrative a position in the ministry could be. A man of middling talent at best, he collected £20,000 in a single year from his tellership of the exchequer, an office whose profits were calculated as a fixed percentage of all government spending and so tended to balloon in wartime. Absurdly inflated remuneration packages like these were precisely what William Cobbett had in mind when he denounced the aristocracy as "a prodigious band of spongers, living upon the labour of the industrious part of the community." To call the peerage parasitic was not to engage in empty rhetoric: the idle rich were the principal recipients of government money, which, we must remember, was collected through taxes that disproportionately burdened the laboring poor.[10]

In 1853, Karl Marx wondered aloud in the *New York Tribune* "whether the new Governors are made for Indian provinces, or Indian provinces for the new Governors." The latter proliferated, Marx observed, thanks to the "Whig invention of alleviating exhausted countries by burdening them with new sinecures for the paupers of aristocracy." While Marx's comments could easily be written off as mere polemic, Namier seconds his opinion, referring to aristocratic pensioners and place holders as "State paupers." Thanks to the "Legacies of British Slave-ownership" project, we now have a fairly good sense of how the nation's upper classes enriched themselves from the extracted labor of enslaved Africans. Lord Buckingham's son married a West Indian heiress, Anna Eliza (Brydges) Grenville (hereafter Lady Temple), who eventually became Lady Nugent's most intimate friend. During her first few months on Jamaica, Lady Nugent declared herself delighted to visit "the Hope estate," which, she records, "is very interesting for me, as belonging to dearest Lady Temple." (After a longer acquaintance with the sugar-industrial complex, she lost this sense of pride, writing "I would not have a sugar estate for the world!") But owning plantations wasn't the only path to profit in the West Indies. Colonial officials like Nugent also stood to gain; and if he could serve his patron's personal interests in the process, so much the better. Like Marx, reform-era British radicals understood empire to be a mechanism for the redistribution of wealth up the social ladder. *The Black Book; or Corruption Unmasked!*, published in 1820, dedicates an entire chapter to "The Influence of the East India

Company." In another *Tribune* article entitled "British Incomes in India," Marx puts a finer point on this line of critique. After asking, "What is the real value of their Indian Dominion to the British nation and people?" he effectively answers: it depends on what *class* of "people" one has in mind. While twenty million Britons paid for the empire via taxes, only sixteen thousand "individual British subjects" profited from it—in the form of patronage, salaries, and stock.[11]

As a case study, the Nugents bear out and add texture to Marx's analysis. Nugent exemplifies how colonial patronage benefited a slim stratum of the nation's class hierarchy. More specifically, it benefited families and individuals from the greater aristocracy who were in danger of slipping below the status of their birth. Maya Jasanoff puts the matter plainly when she explains that "India particularly appealed to ambitious but somewhat marginalized individuals, like down-at-heel gentry, Scots, Irish Protestants—and American loyalist refugees." To be clear, the "individuals" Jasanoff lists off here were in reality only marginally "marginalized." At a time when 9 percent of the nation's families enjoyed 50 percent of the national income, only families on the winning side of this wealth gap were well connected enough to secure coveted positions in the colonies. But, as Jasanoff indicates, without *some* degree of marginalization, however privileged, a trip to either of the two Indies was unthinkable. Everyone knew that overseas travel meant gambling with one's life, a risk that was only worth it if the reward was truly needed for survival. The Crown and ministers who controlled colonial patronage therefore doled it out in the manner of a lifeboat: it was extended to those who were in danger of sinking.[12]

At the turn of the nineteenth century, the Nugents found themselves in precisely this predicament. Born into privilege, they were both downwardly mobile due to fallen family fortunes. To begin with Sir George Nugent, his grandfather, Robert Craggs Nugent, first Earl Nugent in the peerage of Ireland, was one of the richest men in Britain. He even inspired Horace Walpole to invent a verb for his method of accruing his fortune (by successively marrying rich widows)—to "Nugentize." As the eldest son of Lord Nugent's eldest son, Sir George Nugent would have been his grandfather's heir; but after his father's death in 1771 he lost his patrimony when his grandfather used the Marriage Act of 1753 to have his father's marriage set aside, rendering Nugent illegitimate. With this blow Nugent (then fourteen years old) lost the prospect of an Irish earldom, a fortune of £200,000, and land with rents worth £14,000 *p.a.*, all of which instead passed to his half-aunt, Mary Nugent, the issue of one of his grandfather's later marriages. When she married George Temple-Grenville in 1775, the patrimony that would have been Nugent's passed to his new half-uncle.[13]

Maria Skinner's background was in many respects similar to that of her husband. The daughter of Cortlandt Skinner, the last royal attorney general of New Jersey, she was born in 1771 into a position of privilege that she soon lost when her childhood fell prey to the vicissitudes of wartime. Even though her father commanded some of the largest Loyalist units during the American War, the family still fell on hard times after 1783, when they fled across the Atlantic to safety. Despite his military service, Skinner was only partially compensated for his wartime losses: he abandoned £10,382 of assets in America, for which Parliament allocated him £5,169 and a £500 pension. (The latter figure is notably identical to the commoner's "dole" described by Namier.) Skinner eventually settled his family in Belfast, where they became reacquainted with Nugent, whom the Skinners had first met years earlier during the American War. Maria wed him in 1797.[14]

Even though the Nugents inherited far smaller fortunes than what they might have had, they were still rich in social connections, or what Elias would call "their wealth of personal contacts." Despite his illegitimacy, Nugent remained firmly within the family circle and was treated generously by his grandfather. A £500 annuity (again, identical to the commoner's "dole") ensured that he would at the very least remain a gentleman. He was also set on the path of a distinctly aristocratic career when his grandfather purchased him a commission in the 39th foot (at the cost of approximately £500). This was in 1773, when Nugent was sixteen. Fifteen years later, when Nugent's grandfather died, Lord Buckingham became his nephew's closest "friend," or patron. He was ideally suited for this role, since he headed an exceptionally prominent family. Lord Buckingham's father (George Grenville) had been prime minister, and his uncles (Richard Grenville-Temple and William Pitt the Elder) and brother (William Wyndham Grenville) were all formidable politicians. Lord

Buckingham was not a shining light in politics himself, but he did sit in Parliament and serve two terms as lord lieutenant of Ireland. Most importantly, as head of the family he was well placed to ask for favors.[15]

Patronage could make or break the life of a young man. Indeed, it is difficult to recover a sense of patronage's paramount importance at this time. Novels like Edgeworth's *Patronage* and *Vivian,* and Austen's *Mansfield Park* and *Persuasion,* probably do the best job of conveying its ubiquity as the oil that greased the wheels of men's careers. Patronage was especially decisive in professions dominated by members of the greater aristocracy—namely, the military, the Church, and politics. The army's purchase system literally made professional advancement contingent on a combination of personal connections and cash. As such, it was, in John Cannon's estimation, "the nearest thing in England to the sale of office which was so prominent a feature of the *ancien régime* in France." (The navy's lack of a purchase system is precisely what made it seem like a utopian meritocracy to Edgeworth and Austen.) Nugent's colonial appointments testify to the importance of patronage. Put simply, he would not have gained these posts without his relationship to Lord Buckingham. The termination of Nugent's career is equally telling in this regard. His tenure as commander in chief in India came to an abrupt and early end because someone better connected than himself wanted the office—or, more precisely, its salary. Likewise, India was Nugent's final appointment because the death of Lord Buckingham in 1813 cut off his access to government favors. Perhaps this is one reason why Lady Nugent described his death as a "sad disaster." It was a professional as well as a personal "calamity."[16]

While patronage was essential to professional advancement, it was also deeply personal. In the historical vocabulary of patronage, patrons and clients were most often referred to as "Friends." Lady Nugent uses this vocabulary, for example, when she writes to her children on the occasion of Lord Buckingham's death: "He was always your dear papa's best friend and has been to all of us the kindest and most affectionate friend we ever had, to you my darlings in particular." Naomi Tadmor argues that the term "friendship" should be taken seriously. It has something to teach us about the fundamental indivisibility of "webs of kinship, friendship, patronage, economic ties, neighborhood ties, and, not least, political ties." Lady Nugent's usage of the term attests to this overlap. Her journals contain countless instances of Lord Buckingham's kindnesses. When she traveled home from Jamaica several months before her husband, landing in London alone with her two children, Lord Buckingham sent a servant "to town ... to take charge of us down to Stowe," his palatial country residence. The servant also "brought a most kind and affectionate letter, from dear Lord Buckingham himself; offering even to come to town, if I could not immediately go to the country, and insisting upon my making Pall Mall [his London townhouse] my home, &c. and not going to an hotel." At Stowe, where Lady Nugent lived for eight months while she awaited her husband's arrival, she met with further kindnesses, including the surprise of a bust of Nugent in her bedroom, which occasioned "many jokes, by Lord Temple, on their giving me a husband of marble, &c." Certainly these displays testify to real intimacy and affection. Lord Buckingham was Nugent's friend and kin, and the men's families were also close. The Nugents always spent Christmas at Stowe, and Lady Temple was Lady Nugent's closest friend. For the queen's birthday in 1806, the two even went to court in matching dresses. (The queen "said ... they were the prettiest she had seen.") Lady Nugent was also close to Lady Temple's mother-in-law, an intimacy Lord Buckingham acknowledged when, after his wife's death, he enclosed "a pearl ring which Lady B. always wore" in a letter to Lady Nugent in India. Most revealing of all, during the Nugents' time in India, their children remained in England under the guardianship of the Grenville clan (a subject I return to below).[17]

It is impossible to understand how the empire came to serve as an aristocratic social safety net without an adequate sense of the extent to which kinship networks and patronage networks were one and the same. Today our ideal of "friendship" is disinterested, but in court societies, professional networks were fused with personal ones. For this reason, Tadmor warns against assuming "instrumentality to be in opposition to sentiments and affection." Lambert and Lester make a similar point regarding colonial officials: "Professional career, family obligations and love were intertwined, and a historiography that insists on separating them—especially on separating profession from emotion—is likely to be incomplete." Lord Buckingham's patronage of Nugent is telling in this regard; it is impossible to draw a boundary line where his patronage of a loyal client ends and his familial support of a beloved nephew begins. He cared for Nugent in a manner that was distinctly paternal, countenancing and cleaning up after the reckless mistakes of youth. For example, as a young man, Nugent decided he wanted to raise his own regiment as a colonel, a desire that Lord Buckingham judged "extravagant" but nonetheless passed along to Lord Amherst (commander in chief of the Forces), who opposed it outright. With his design quashed, Nugent set his heart on the no less exalted position of aide-de-camp (ADC) to the king, an honor usually reserved for the heirs of peers. By the time it became clear that no such appointment would be forthcoming from Pitt's ministry (probably due to Nugent's illegitimacy), he had already taken the rash step of resigning his commission in the Coldstream Guards, so that he was now unemployed. Like a harried father, Lord Buckingham picked up the pieces, pressuring the war office to allow Nugent to carry on with his original plan of raising a regiment. Moreover, "rather than *ask more favours*" from the ministry on Nugent's account, he personally recruited ninety men and bought three commissions for the new regiment, essentially paying for Nugent's foolhardiness out of his own pocket to the tune of thousands. Lord Buckingham was obviously committed to using his fortune and influence to take care of his nephew, doubtless because he had acquired some of it at the latter's expense. Over the course of Nugent's lifetime, Lord Buckingham secured him countless "*favours.*" Nugent earned £109 annually from an old Tudor sinecure Lord Buckingham secured him as "keeper of St. Mawes Castle." For four decades, he represented Lord Buckingham's interest in the House of Commons. When Lord Buckingham was lord lieutenant of Ireland, he appointed Nugent his ADC, a position that paved the way for the latter's subsequent Irish appointments as commander of the northern district and adjutant-general.[18]

In many ways this is a banal story. There is nothing out of the ordinary about families using available resources to help their own. What is extraordinary is the kind of resources available to Lord Buckingham as head of one branch of the Grenville family. To secure one's nephew the offices of governor of Jamaica and commander in chief in India represented impressive feats of patronage. Not many families were positioned well enough to serve their semi-marginal members in this way.

But Nugent wasn't the only beneficiary here: the illustriousness of the Grenville clan was also heightened by Lord Buckingham's patronage of his nephew. It would hardly serve the family's reputation to have shabby relatives in low places. Every advancement enjoyed by Nugent enhanced Lord Buckingham's reputation; it was a point of pride to be able to furnish the very best offices as a patron. Moreover, Nugent repaid Lord Buckingham in another fashion: by distributing his own patronage to Lord Buckingham's friends, clients, and kin. At the highest level, this involved taking responsibility for the career prospects and well-being of Lord Buckingham's nephew, George Matthew Fortescue, who served as Nugent's ADC in India. At the lowest level it involved small favors to Grenville family friends. During their fourteen-month tour of the upper provinces in India, the Nugents met Sir David Ochterlony, who, Lady Nugent notes, had been "recommended . . . to our notice" by Lady Temple. In addition to doing him the great honor of sitting next to him at dinner—how great an honor this really was will become evident—Lady Nugent provided an extensive report of the sociable encounter to Lady Temple in subsequent letters. "Sir G— . . . knew you were his *friend*," she explains, "and as *your friend* showed him every little kindness in our power." Ochterlony was so moved by this display of "kindness," Lady Nugent writes, that "he expressed much gratitude towards you and asked me whether I thought he might take the liberty of thanking you by Letter for the Introduction," a liberty Lady Nugent granted by proxy. Lady Temple was amply rewarded for the Nugents' attention to her "*friend*" when Ochterlony sent her thanks in the form of "a large parcel" containing, by Lady Nugent's report, "*12 shawls,* of the very best quality and indeed more beautiful and magnificent than any I have seen yet in India." The whole incident testifies to patronage's quid pro quo. Men like Ochterlony understood that their careers depended on patronage, and they were exquisitely sensitive to its minutest niceties.[19]

The Economics of Imperial Accumulation

The chief attraction of colonial appointments was their salary. The governorship of Jamaica, Philip Wright estimates, paid "about £8,500 per annum on the average in peacetime and almost double that during a war with Spain." While this may not seem like an extraordinary sum when compared to other elite postings, the island's low cost of living meant that governors could expect to bring well over half their earnings home in savings. As a point of contrast, the lord lieutenant of Ireland was expected to spend £15,000 a year *in excess of the position's salary* (£30,000) on table, dress, and entertainment. This was a prestige posting fit only for very wealthy peers like Lord Buckingham. Comparatively, the lieutenant governorship of Jamaica was a moneymaking office. As such, it attracted well-connected members of the greater aristocracy who were willing to risk a few years in the island's infamously insalubrious climate in exchange for a lifeline of cash.[20]

The dangers of a residence in Jamaica were such that only the truly desperate would take the risk of spending any time there. The hazards began on the sea journey to the island. The only reason the office of governor fell vacant in 1801, Wright explains, is that "the Governor designate, Major-General Knox, had been drowned at sea on his way out to take up the appointment." As soon as the Nugents arrived on Jamaica, the deaths of their friends and colleagues commenced. Only a month later, Lady Nugent wrote in her journal: "Rise at 6, and was told, at breakfast, that the usual occurrence of a death had taken place." Indeed, she records countless deaths (including that of her own brother), mostly due to yellow fever and other tropical diseases. At one point she complains, "there are, in fact, only three subjects of conversation here,—debt, disease, and death." So many mortalities created a confusion of anxiety and callousness. "The complaints in this country are, in fact, so rapid and so mysterious," Lady Nugent reflects, "that one cannot feel a moment's security." Eventually, Lady Nugent learned to steel herself against the losses of others, writing "I am determined not to lament, as I am too apt to do, for the illness and deaths I hear of daily, among various parts of our society." War presented another cause for alarm. At many times between 1801 and 1806 an invasion seemed imminent, thanks to the on-again, off-again war with France. Meanwhile, the prospect of a slave uprising perpetually terrified the white inhabitants of Jamaica. After the uprising on Saint-Domingue these fears were raised to a fever pitch. The fear of a revolt was one reason Lady Nugent left the island eight months prior to her husband's departure. On the eve of his departure, Nugent downplayed the danger: "The People of this Island are now perfectly convinced that they have nothing to apprehend from the Vicinity of a Black Empire ... the Island of St. Domingo is no more talked of here, than if it was in the East Indian Seas." It was easy for Nugent to be optimistic: he would soon be off the island. On the whole, the experience was harrowing enough that Nugent vowed to give up the business of colonial governance for good, writing to Lord Buckingham, "Really when I look back it astonishes me that I should have borne so long an Absence from all of my Friends, but I hope at length to make up for it, by never leaving England again as a Soldier." Five years in Jamaica had enriched him enough that he was able to stick to this determination in the short term, turning down an offer of the position of commander in chief in India in May 1806. In 1808, the Nugents purchased a home for £16,000, a sign of significant liquidity.[21]

Only a few years later, in 1811, Nugent reneged on his resolution. The cause for this about-face can be found in his finances. The first five years of the Nugents' marriage produced no pregnancies, leading Lady Nugent to fear that she might be barren. Then, during their second year in Jamaica, their first son was born. The birth of two more healthy children and one infant mortality over the next few years drastically changed the Nugents' financial outlook. Despite his illegitimacy and his wife's fallen family fortunes, they had been able to retain their hold on gentility. Now, in addition to maintaining their own standard of living, they faced the added duty of providing for at least three—and who knew how many more?—children. The only way to ensure that their children would enjoy the gains they had made was to secure another imperial salary. With his wife pregnant once again, Nugent took decisive action as soon as opportunity arose. In January 1811, General George Hewett resigned from the post of commander in chief of India. This was a senior posting, second in authority only to the governor general of India. While nominally filled by the East India Company's Court of Directors, in practice it was appointed by the Crown. With an annual salary and emoluments worth at least £20,000, it was the second most profitable office in the entire empire, and thus a valuable line of patronage to be leveraged by those in power. Nugent wasted no time in writing to Lord Buckingham's brother, Lord Grenville (then leader of the Whig Party), doubtless with his patron's blessing if not at his behest, requesting the same position he had refused five years earlier. In February, he "had an audience of the Prince Regent, at Carlton House." Since this was a matter of Crown patronage, and the king was ill, the Prince of Wales would ultimately decide the matter. Lady Nugent writes of the meeting: "he was most graciously received in his private apartment; but nothing new or satisfactory, about the Indian plan, was the result." By March, Nugent had finally secured the support of the prince regent, and the confirmation of the Company's Court of Directors. Lady Nugent, six-months pregnant with her fourth child, was given a mere four months to prepare to take the previously unimaginable step of venturing out to the colonies once more, this time without her children, on what she described as "our last Campaign."[22]

In Jamaica, Lady Nugent had learned that a colony was no place for English children. Just a few years on the island had been enough to creolize her eldest children, George and Louisa, as toddlers, suffusing "their little funny talk" with "Creole ideas and ways" that required a reparative education upon their return to England. After this experiment, she never again contemplated bringing her children to India. Despite the great emotional toll of a years-long separation, this was a decision she never regretted. In a letter sent home from India, she reported: "the children here are fat but deadly pale and sallow. Very few of them speak a word of English and I should imagine the indolent Habits and suspect Ideas instilled in them here would be very difficult to get the better of in England." All that said, the prospect of leaving their children behind for at least five years—and maybe forever—was heartbreaking for both of the Nugents. In the absence of dire concern about their children's future class positions, it would have been unthinkable. Indeed, Lady Nugent deemed the "sacrifice" of leaving home to be so very "great" that she was critical of Britons who turned to the business of imperial governance without sufficient compulsion in the form of children in need of inheritances. In a letter to Lady Temple sent from India she writes: "One thing astonishes me very much my dearest Lady T—and that is that the Nightingales who have *once been in this climate* should like to return to it. A Major General on the staff has to be some 7,000 a year but then they have no children and I would rather have as many Hundreds in England if I had only myself to take care of." For Lady Nugent, risking one's life for the sake of anything other than one's children was pure insanity. She even joked on this matter when setting off for India, writing, "indeed if we but live to return, we should desire to be sent off to Doctor Willis immediately if we even thought of quitting our Home again."[23]

In the synopsis appended to the beginning of her West India Journal, Lady Nugent feigns following the call of duty when leaving for Jamaica, writing that "General Nugent was surprised by his appointment" and "neither of us over well pleased; but, like good soldiers, we made up our minds to obey." In truth, Wright clarifies, Nugent could not have been surprised, since he applied for the appointment as soon as he learned it was available. Roughly a decade later, no sense of professional duty is apparent in the decision to go to India; instead, the Indian "Campaign" is characterized as a personal sacrifice. Despite her "great anxiety" at the thought of leaving home for so long, Lady Nugent admits that, "for the future benefit of our dear children, I ought to wish it." The intense grief she experienced in India as a result of the separation was mitigated only by her conviction that her children's future welfare was at stake, a perspective her husband shared. Only two weeks after her arrival in India, when she was still in the grip of a serious depression, she wrote in her journal: "At times I have been low, ill, and miserable; then ... comfort[ed] ... seeing that my dear Nugent's mind is satisfied, and consoled, with the prospect of this last campaign (I trust our last), being of service to our dear children. God grant we may see them once more; then I shall never repent the great sacrifice we have made."[24]

In the end, the personal benefits accrued from their "last Campaign" proved to be worth the risk. Before they left for India, Lady Nugent confessed to Lady Temple, "Sir G was overloaded with land and constantly in want of money and made a *press* about every expense." Only a few months after their arrival in Calcutta, their outlook had changed completely: "Sir G— ... is well—his affairs *most prosperous*. I wish I could be more explicit. Suffice to say if he remains the 5 years he proposes to himself the comfort and ease of the remainder of our lives as well as the perfect independence of our dear children in a pecuniary point of view will be perfectly and amply secured." In exchange for a few years' employment in India, the Nugents secured their family's hold on

gentility for at least another generation. Perfectly independent "in a pecuniary point of view," their children would be liberated from the need
to earn a living; they would, in short, be gentlemen.[25]

Indeed, Nugent's imperial salary transformed his children's lives
even while he was still in India. Lady Nugent inundated her husband's
extended family with letters about her children's care; and her evolving
instructions indicate a steadily rising standard of living. As soon as it
became evident how much money they would accumulate in India,
Lady Nugent called for escalations in the scale of her children's domestic
economy. As she explained to Lady Temple, her children's governess,
Miss Dewey, "is a most scrupulous economist and was lately taught this
lesson by me." Flush with Indian emoluments, Lady Nugent needed Miss
Dewey to unlearn "this lesson" in parsimony. Now, she entertained very
different "wishes upon the Subject of Economy": "Everything for the
children should be done in a gentlemanlike way. We wish them to have
good House, to keep a proper Table, to travel with Ease and Comfort and
not stuffed up and run the risk of breaking their Necks by the old Lan-
dau's tumbling to pieces etc. etc." For her eldest son, George, who was
enrolled in a small public school, Eton was now contemplated. Her
eldest daughter, Louisa, began instruction in the "accomplishments" expected of a gentlewoman destined for the marriage market: "For Louisa
order a riding master—music, dancing, drawing or what ever you please
in that you have carte blanche to do what you like with them all and be
assured where their improvement or welfare are in question we wish all
pecuniary matters to be totally disregarded." Money spent on the children's education, clothing, equipage, and table effectively translated Indian cash into British class.[26]

Cash might—and did—outfit the Nugents' children with the trappings of gentility; but finery alone cannot guarantee social standing. In
a court society, Elias explains, "property itself does not yet constitute a
social 'reality' independent of the opinion of others, as the recognition
of membership by others itself constitutes membership ... in this
'good society.'" For their children's admission into "good society," the
Nugents relied on their aristocratic kinsmen, the Grenvilles. Living in
close proximity to Stowe—which would shelter Queen Victoria as an
overnight guest only a few decades later—the children benefited from

an upbringing far superior, in social terms, to that which their parents could have provided them. George spent his school holidays with the future proprietor of Stowe, the Viscount Cobham, sharing lessons from his tutor. Meanwhile, Louisa was shepherded through adolescence under the supervision of a marchioness and a future duchess. Lady Nugent was particularly gratified by this aid, given what she considered to be the "deficiencies" of her own education. The American War had interrupted her childhood, robbing her family of their home, station, and fortune. As she explained in a letter to Lady Buckingham: "if anything could ever reconcile me to the misery of losing sight of my Children for such a length of *Time,* it would be the very great advantages I am sensible they will derive from being under your Care. My understanding is naturally good, but from the peculiar Situation of my Father and Mother deprived of their Future and traveling about the World, it has not been properly cultivated and many an Hour of unhappiness has the knowledge of my own Deficiencies occasioned me. Therefore I know I could not do our darling Louisa the Justice you can and I am most anxious she should escape the mortifications upon this subject that I have so often suffered." At Stowe, Lady Nugent's children recouped the losses of the previous generation by enjoying "the very great advantages" that only their aristocratic relations could provide them. Supervised by women of high rank, Louisa mastered the accomplishments and acquired the social graces expected of a gentleman's daughter.[27]

Available evidence indicates that this grooming was successful. In 1824, Louisa married Sir Thomas Francis Fremantle, a baronet. It is a testament to the strength of Grenvillite social ties that Fremantle's father was, like Nugent, a recipient of Lord Buckingham's patronage. Initially, Nugent worried that the children of two "placehunters" would have trouble finding sufficient income to marry, but all objections to the match were eventually resolved. Like his father-in-law, Fremantle was an MP for Buckinghamshire in Parliament thanks to patronage; but his political talents were such that he eventually joined the ministry. In 1874 he was rewarded for his political career with a baronage. The Nugents would not live to see it, but their grandson would enter the peerage as the second baron Cottesloe. Louisa's great-great-great grandson still holds the barony today, just as her brother George's descendant still holds their father's baronetcy. In short, the Nugents successfully reintegrated themselves into the nation's most privileged ranks, a feat that would have been impossible—or at least much more difficult—if not for the empire.[28]

The Accumulation of Social Capital

At the turn of the nineteenth century, the two Indies were important sources of prestige for Britain's ruling classes. Each time the Nugents traveled to the colonies, they returned with a tangible emblem of their gains in this arena, honors. If Nugent's imperial career was necessitated by his illegitimacy, then his appointments in Jamaica and India assuaged this injury in more than one way: by repairing his monetary fortune and by helping him regain social capital, thereby repairing the damage done to his reputation. As a teenager, Nugent had lost the prospect of an Irish barony. Now, he and his supporters were well aware, a detour through the empire represented his surest path back into the lower ranks of the peerage.

The British honors system does not always get its due in scholarship, probably because it seems faintly "ridiculous" from the perspective of "bourgeois-industrial societies," as Elias points out. But "if one respects the autonomy of the structure of court society," he continues, then court etiquette and honors reveal themselves to be "an extremely sensitive and reliable instrument for measuring the perceived value of an individual within the social network." The haggling over honors engaged in by Nugent and his Grenville relations during and after his time in the Indies bears out this argument.[29]

When his term as governor of Jamaica was coming to a close, Nugent began fishing for a nonmonetary reward for his time on the island: "some Mark of Distinction" from the Crown. In particular, he desperately wished to be admitted to the Order of the Bath, an honor which, he claimed, "the Duke of York promised to procure" him in 1803. When Lady Nugent reached home some months before her husband, she was put on the red-ribbon beat. A day spent in meetings at Downing Street convinced her it was a lost cause. She learned it was "the anxious wish of General N.'s friends in the Government, that he should accept of a baronetage *now,* as giving him claims for the *ribbon,* which General N. prefers . . . there are objections to his being made a Knight of the Bath at present, which makes all that espouse his interest, and the Duke of York in particular, anxious that he should accept of the favours now offered him." Years later—when Nugent was still nursing this old grudge—he implied that the "objections" in question stemmed from his being "a member of the opposition"; but the rumored (and more likely) cause of the snub was his illegitimacy. The strategy proposed by the duke of York is telling, for it reveals the extent to which angling after honors required playing the long game. Similar strategizing was taking place at Stowe: Lady Nugent records having "a great deal of talk with Lady B., on the subject of the *Peerage.* Lord B. thinks it is not the moment, but that it may be soon; and may then be pushed for." Such comments indicate that Nugent's concern with honors was not an idiosyncratic obsession, but a more general preoccupation of his social milieu wherein money alone did not make the man. In bourgeois society, Elias writes, "financial gains and losses plays a primary role, while in the court aristocratic type the calculation is of gains and losses of prestige." Nugent lived among peers and shared their prerogative; hence his yearning for a tangible sign of "prestige" gained in the Indies.[30]

On his return from Jamaica, Nugent remained in London for *an entire month* for the sole purpose of petitioning Lord Grenville to meet on the subject of his denied request for a red ribbon of the Order of the Bath. Apparently, Lord Grenville rejected Nugent's pleas for even a short audience at Downing Street, forcing him to record his grievances in a letter whose vehemence reveals that he believed his reputation to be at stake: "I hope Your Lordship will excuse the Liberty I take, in requesting most earnestly, that you would be pleased to make Use of your Influence to procure me . . . some Mark of His Majesty's Favor, as a Reward for the Services I have performed; that I may not appear to have incurred the King's Displeasure. . . . No General Officer thus circumstanced I believe, ever returned from that Government, without receiving some Mark of Distinction, and situated as I am generally supposed to be, with my best Friends in high Power, I beseech Your Lordship to consider in what Light I shall be viewed by the World." Clearly, honors were given on a quid pro quo basis. They were also, clearly, closely guarded by the Crown.

Why else would the Duke of York refuse the red ribbon to Nugent despite the latter's extensive pleading? It is worth noting that most of Jamaica's governors were either already peers at the time of their appointments or became so subsequently. Thus, Nugent's claim that a denial of his requested honor might look like a deliberate snub in the eyes of the fashionable "World" was not without basis, especially since his term as governor had been fractious. The fact that Nugent pressed for a red ribbon is equally telling. Perhaps this was a personal preference. More likely it was a calculated request. He probably knew that the peerage was a long shot, and the Order of the Bath was more exclusive than the well-populated ranks of baronets. In the end, he had to settle for a baronetcy. It wasn't a red ribbon, but at least it came with titles—this is when he became a "Sir" and Mrs. Nugent a "Lady." Still, his hankering for the red ribbon was not placated. Nearly ten years later, when the Prince Regent owed Nugent a favor after replacing him abruptly with Lord Moira, Nugent was finally made a Knight of the Order of the Bath, in Calcutta. In honors, as well as in money matters, the Nugents' East Indian "campaign" put an end to processes of accumulation begun in the West Indies.[31]

It might be tempting to dismiss Nugent's pining after honors as a foible, but there was nothing personal, or private, about titles: their purpose was to publicly locate people within hierarchies of power. Honors epitomize an important feature of court societies: "the intrusion of many aspects of what we consider private life into the public, social sphere." Very often, this "intrusion" goes overlooked in scholarship on colonial establishments, with the result that elite women are left out of the stories we tell about the business of colonial governance. Lady Nugent's journals reveal the extent to which she shared her husband's occupation. Take, for example, the entry she wrote when Nugent's appointment in Jamaica was confirmed. Using the first-person plural, she resolved, "we are soldiers and must have no will of our own." Though Lady Nugent was not making policy decisions, she absolutely shared her husband's governmental duties in other ways. Wright puts the matter plainly: "As the Governor's wife," Lady Nugent "found herself at the center of a slave-owning society, with a part to play there." Her "part to play" was "the *Governor's lady*."[32]

At first, occupying "a public situation" felt *unheimlich* enough that Lady Nugent navigated the distance between her private and public selves by referring to the latter in the third person. For example, when describing her husband's swearing-in ceremony she writes: "I then went to the drawing-room, and received all the ladies of Spanish Town, &c. the principal officers of the Navy and Army, the Members of Council, and the number of the gentlemen of the House of Assembly, who had come to compliment the new Governor and his Lady; bowing, curtsey-ing, and making speeches." The switch to the third person in this passage captures the cognitive dissonance generated by performing a public role. By the time she reached India a decade later, the Nugents had become accustomed to leading double lives "as public and private characters." At a farewell banquet in 1814, her departure from India was characterized as a return to private life: "the president [of the supreme council] pro-posed my health by itself, with a few kind words, about my going from the duties of public life, to fulfill those which were more congenial to a mother's heart." Wives shared their husband's careers and "duties."[33]

In both Jamaica and India, Lady Nugent's duties encompassed what she calls "the business of society." At times, this "business" could be quite amusing; indeed, it needed to be, since the Nugents and other of-ficials had no so-called real or personal social life apart from it. That said, the business of society was still business. Elias captures this dynamic nicely when he writes of the "characteristic double face" of "the social life of court people": "On the one hand it has the function of our own private life, to provide relaxation, amusement, conversation. At the same time it has the function of our professional life, to be the direct instrument of one's career." At important balls, Lady Nugent allocated her sociability diplomatically, with the care of an expert politician. On one occasion she divided her dances in order "to please both civil and military, army and navy," an exhausting undertaking that required, in her words, "danc[ing] myself almost to death." Similarly, on their diplomatic tour in India, the Nugents entertained "all the society of Delhi"—Society with a capital S, that is—a daunting task made easier by the resident Mr. Metcalfe, who "formed [it] in four divisions" to be entertained on four different eve-nings. In Cawnpore, a frontier outpost the Nugents visited during their aforementioned tour of the upper provinces, Lady Nugent "held an

assembly in the dining bungalow," the best building available for the purpose. Once again, she chose her partners diplomatically, opening the
dancing with the commanding officer, General Champagné. "[T]he evening went off very gaily," she reports, "but I was exceedingly fatigued."
The "business of society" was hard work, comparable to the duties of her
husband.[34]

As a public figure, Lady Nugent's private life was severely circum-
scribed in the colonies. When she attended church for the first time on
Jamaica, for example, it was not as a private worshipper, but "in state,"
with "All the world staring." Even undressing now became a public affair.
Recalling France's ancien régime—where the king's daily routine of
waking, eating, dressing, and so on was turned into a series of ceremo-
nial occasions—Lady Nugent often received women of color in her
private apartments while she undressed for the evening. Personal friend-
ships, she found, were also now out of the question. A few months into
her stay on the island she was dismayed to hear "a great deal of gossip
from some of our staff about favoritism; for I am such a great lady, that
all I say and do is remarked upon." From this point on she resolved "to
live alone in my private hours, and so put an end to these silly little jeal-
ousies." Occupying a "public situation" meant that even the smallest
friendly overtures were now politicized. When hostilities with France
appeared to be resuming, the Nugents "agreed it will be good policy" to
use her pregnancy as a pretense to remove her from Society in order to
avoid the potential disaster of wrongly acknowledging or snubbing
French officers' wives. She was therefore "declared unequal to society, till
after my confinement; and so all will be settled, and I shall know by that
time what ladies to receive." Maintaining this charade demanded a comical level of commitment. Passing a French party on the road one day,
she had to "Affect to lie back in the carriage, like an invalid, to keep up
the character I have politically adopted." Sociable intercourse with the
governor's lady was, fundamentally, "political." Lady Nugent's attention
was an instrument of statecraft; and, as such, it needed to be managed
with great care.[35]

Even Lady Nugent's sartorial decisions were politicized. On first
meeting her in 1800, Elizabeth Fremantle (Louisa's future mother-in-
law) described her as "an amazing dresser," who "never appears twice in

the same gown" and "seems not to care how much money she spends in dress." Lady Nugent's attention to fashion in both her journals bears this out. In the Indies, however, dressing was no mere personal amusement but an affair of state. In Jamaica she quickly learned that "every word, look, and action, and article of dress, is canvassed." For this reason, dressing demanded a good deal of deliberation. Lady Nugent was hardly exaggerating when she wrote that she "held a *council* with the ladies, to decide upon the dresses for the evening" on the day of an important ball. She also sent her "maid to work for the young people, to make them smart for the ball," a service she repeated in India when the sudden introduction of court etiquette at Government House mystified ladies who had never attended court in London. As court dress was, by this period, completely divorced from popular fashion, it required special knowledge. Lady Nugent was therefore "obligated, all the morning, to answer notes, about dress, and see various ladies, on the subject of feathers—gave Mrs. Lindsay a set of my own, Johnstone [her maid] helping to show how they must be placed, &c." Even men were not above playing ball-gown politics. In her West India Journal, Lady Nugent records giving an "audience to the old superannuated President of the Council, who wanted me to patronize a decayed milliner of bad character. Altogether it was an unpleasant business, and I got rid of it civilly, but decidedly." Perhaps Lady Nugent's eschewal was owing to moral considerations; or, it might have been due to the fact that she sourced her dresses from Europe. On one occasion in Jamaica she records, "dear Lord Buckingham has sent me a most beautiful lace cloak." About nine months later she received two more boxes, "one full of straw bonnets from dear kind Lady Buckingham, and the other, lace, veils &c. from dear, dear Lady Temple." When the state of the war with France allowed it, she also received dresses from a French fashion icon, "Madame le Clerc," sister of Napoleon and wife of the general sent to try to retake Saint-Domingue. Judging from Lady Nugent's description of these gowns, Danielle Skeehan argues that the "pink and silver dress" and "crape dress, embroidered in silver spangles" sent by Madame le Clerc were "likely made *in* France, but with a creole aesthetic in mind." Of course, aristocratic women's dress was politicized in England too. The duchess of Devonshire's adoption of the Whig colors blue and buff during the elections of 1784 is one obvious example. However, Lady Nugent was no duchess. Before leaving England in 1801, she was only Mrs. Nugent. While she enjoyed access to the fashionable world, she was not in its limelight. As soon as she landed in Jamaica, though, she ballooned in importance, becoming "a great lady."[36]

"If I were the Queen of Sheba," Lady Nugent writes in her West India Journal, "I could not be made more fuss with than I am here. It is really overpowering. A word from me decides everything with the ladies, and a look sets all the gentlemen flying to anticipate my commands." Embellishments aside, this was more true than not. In Jamaica, as "the Governor's lady," Lady Nugent was the highest-ranking woman in society. The same was true in India until the arrival of Lord Moira and his wife Lady Loudon in 1813, as the wife of the previous governor general, Lord Minto, did not accompany him to India. In both Indies, then, Lady Nugent stood at the very apex of colonial society, in the position that was occupied by the royal family and the upper ranks of the peerage in England. Indeed, Lady Nugent even outranked peers in the Indies, where colonial customs of precedence prevailed. In her West Indian Journal she writes, "I was obliged, As Governor's lady, to take rank of [Lady Margaret Cameron], but have promised her, her *revenge* in England, and shall be delighted to give it." Perhaps the sheen of this sort of honor had worn off a decade later, because in India Lady Nugent broke with local custom to "insist upon giving Lady H[ood] *precedency*." Along with a number of other ladies, she petitioned the prince regent to align Indian precedency with metropolitan standards. In the meantime, she continued to be treated like royalty. When the Nugents attended "the amateur play" in Calcutta, they "[w]ere received with 'God save the king.' Great applause, all standing up when we came into the theatre." In keeping with Company custom, they also adopted the trimmings of Indian royalty. Arriving "in great state" in Calcutta involved being preceded by a line of male attendants carrying ornamented "silver sticks," a badge of nobility in Mughal courts.[37]

No wonder Lady Nugent feared others might think "that I like being a great lady." Her standing in the colonies was worlds above her social station in England. To be clear, she did regularly attend court and take part in the beau monde in London, but her only distinction in such circles was her unusually good fashion sense. In the Indies, on the other hand, she occupied the role of the queen at such gatherings. The farewell ball given in the Nugents' honor gives us some sense of the splendor of elite Calcutta society. True to form, Lady Nugent was "very solicitous about my dress, and had many tailors and embroiderers working for me." Her shoes "were also embroidered," and her "own hair and diamonds" completed the "costume." The gentlemen in attendance were equally fastidious in their dress: they were "all wearing broad crimson ribbon, upon the left shoulder, across the breast, with the word 'Farewell,' in large gold letters." Lest the courtly tone of this event be in doubt, Lady Nugent was seated on "a little sort of a throne, a few steps above all the other seats, with a canopy over it, all of Chinese crimson satin and gold fringe." As at the theater, "God Save the King" was played at her entrance. In "the ball room ... several emblematical transparencies and mottos" completed the decorations. These were illuminated in a dramatic manner, as Lady Nugent explains: "The instant I took my place, there was lighted up, directly opposite to me, an immense transparency, representing the Indiaman we are to embark in, under full sail, with 'Farewell' on her colours." One could hardly imagine how the occasion could have been celebrated with more éclat.[38]

The social capital accrued by Lady Nugent in the two Indies traveled back with her to England. On her return from Jamaica, her maid "passed herself on the French valets de chambre for having been a maid of honour, in foreign parts, where, she assured them, I had been a queen!" In some respects, this was more true than not. A few months later, when Lady Nugent was still living at Stowe, she was given pride of place at the Grenvilles' New Year's Eve gathering: "All the parties staying in the house were arranged in the saloon, and formed a sort of line, to where Lord and Lady B. &c. stood. I was desired to stand first, as representing Lady Temple, who, unfortunately, cannot be there, on account of her illness." It is difficult to imagine Lady Nugent being asked to fill Lady Temple's place before her stay in Jamaica. It took a trip to the Indies for her to become a "public" person—a woman of some importance and distinction. Likewise, the request surely would have flustered her had she not been habituated to "stand first" there. Another measure of how the colonies enhanced Lady Nugent's prestige occurred right after her arrival at

Stowe when, in the middle of dinner, she narrates, "we were surprised by the sudden and unexpected appearance of General (now Sir Arthur) Wellesley. He was greeted with the greatest friendship and delight, and placed on the other side of dear Lord Buckingham, who is anxious to learn all about his Indian campaigns, &c. as soon as possible. . . . In short, the two people, from the east and west, both arriving the same day, afforded much mirth and amusement to the whole party." We see here another way in which capital was accrued in the Indies, in the form of information. Jamaica and India were hugely important in British politics at this time, and access to the latest news from each location was a boon to "dear Lord Buckingham," who could no doubt find some way to use it to his advantage. The parallel placement of Lady Nugent and Sir Arthur Wellesley is also telling. Both were honored as participants in the business of colonial governance.[39]

Up until now I have tried to demonstrate that the fashionable world was far more entangled with the colonies than is typically presumed. In the next section I extend this argument by showing how, at the turn of the nineteenth century, the colonies functioned as satellite campuses of London's fashionable world. Institutions for elite sociability were necessary if the colonies were to serve as the stomping grounds for fashionable young gentlemen from the nation's "best" families.[40]

Boys Turning into Men in the Indies

The Nugents' patronage of Lord Buckingham's nephew, George Matthew Fortescue, illuminates several interrelated phenomena central to this chapter. First, it offers yet another testament to the dual personal and professional nature of patronage. Second, it illustrates how colonial establishments evolved in order to cater to the sons of peers. Finally, Fortescue's experiences reveal how the Indies became a viable site for the reproduction of Britain's upper classes.

No position better exemplifies the paternal aspect of military patronage than the office of aide-de-camp (ADC). In today's terms, an ADC might be described as an intern. Always filled by young men, the post involved shadowing senior commanders in the role of a personal assistant or apprentice. Because the position was filled entirely through patronage, and because it necessitated a degree of proximity between the ADC and senior officer, it was often used to place young men of rank in the custody of mentors who could be trusted to protect their interests and watch over their behavior in the absence of parental supervision. Recall that Nugent served as Lord Buckingham's ADC in Ireland. In India, he returned the favor by appointing Fortescue—a younger son of Lord Buckingham's sister, Hester Grenville, who was married to Hugh Fortescue, first Earl Fortescue—as his ADC in India. In a palpably emotional letter written to Lord Buckingham on the eve of his departure for India, Nugent characterizes his patronage of Fortescue as a means of repaying professional, filial, and affective debts: "I now come to the most painful Part of my Letter—Your uniform affectionate Attentions to me and mine, and most particularly to my dearest and most valuable Wife, have impressed themselves deeply on my Heart, and I hope to have Opportunities of proving how sensibly I feel them, by our Care of my young Aide de Camp and any Friends you may in future trust to *Our Guardianship.*"[41]

True to his promise, Nugent watched over Fortescue with a paternal level of care. At times this care was expressed in a professional medium. In the same letter quoted above, Nugent assured Lord Buckingham, "I trust having it in my power to promote him to a Company at least, without purchase, at an early period." Once in India, he complained that he was still "wait[ing] with Impatience for his Promotion," which had apparently been "Promise[d] to Lord Fortescue" by the duke of York months earlier but not yet delivered. Nugent also assumed responsibility for Fortescue in other ways, including his finances. Fortescue lived with the Nugents "at all Times," an arrangement designed to keep his living expenses minimal and subject him to their oversight. He was therefore a member of the "family party" Lady Nugent often records dining with in her daily journal entries, a group that included all of Nugent's ADCs as well as Lady Nugent's brother, who also enjoyed her husband's patronage. Before leaving for India, Nugent speculated in a letter to Lord Buckingham about Fortescue's "expences in India": "I should hope that (with the exception of the purchase of horses) he will not be obliged to draw upon his family for any money, the situation of Aide de Camp and Lieutenant of Dragoons, with the advantage of living at my table, being quite sufficient, as far as I can judge at present, to support him handsomely in that country. I shall however act in that matter according to circumstances, and in all events control *his expenditure* by endorsing his bills upon Lord Fortescue." In Calcutta, Nugent stuck to this plan, as a later letter to Lord Buckingham attests: "With his Lieutenancy, Fortescue has an income of 8 or 9 hundred pounds a Year, and as he lives with us at all Times, he cannot well spend a larger Sum. Indeed I have forbid him to draw upon his Father in future, after equipping himself for the Service, and I gave him his first Horse to diminish the Expense. If I recollect right his Draughts (all of which I endorsed) did not amount altogether to more than 300 or 350 pounds, and his second Horse and a Miniature Picture cost £200 of that sum." In addition to being familiar with the minutest details of Fortescue's expenditures, Nugent also acted as an authority in money matters, flatly "forbid[ding] him" to ask his aristocratic father for money in excess of his own (quite large) salary. Perhaps in order to ease the sting of cutting Fortescue off from the parental fount, Nugent dug into his own pockets to gift him the horse that he had earlier identified as one of his only necessary expenditures in India. At a minimum, this gesture would have cost Nugent several hundred pounds.[42]

Ever since Burke had warned of the "intoxicating" effect of the "drought of authority and dominion" consumed at too young an age by "youth in India," Britons had worried about how a young adulthood spent in the colonies might warp a young man's character. When Fortescue traveled to India he was only twenty years old—not a child, but by no means a full-grown man. The Nugents therefore did everything in their power to protect him, whether from his own intemperance, the dangers of the insalubrious climate, or the bad influence of other rowdy young officers. Lady Nugent played a particularly prominent role in this aspect of the Nugents' guardianship of Fortescue, which Nugent describes in first-person plural-possessive as "*Our Guardianship*" in the quoted letter. When Fortescue joined several other young men in "a party to hunt the wild boar," Lady Nugent anxiously awaited his safe return despite being "told he would not be in the slightest danger." She scrutinized all his affairs in the manner of a parent keeping a wary eye on a wily teenager. For example, during their first few weeks in India, she "had quite a little battle" with him on the subject of "young men smoking," which she judged "an odious custom." She was the winner of the skirmish: "he had sent off to Benares to have one [a hookah] made; however, at my request, he has given it up with a very good grace." Her victory is especially notable given how common hookah smoking was by her own estimation: "as it would be depriving half of the community of one of their greatest comforts to object to them, we have agreed to receive them" at home, she explains. She also lightly monitored Fortescue's choice of companions. When he "tiffed" (or lunched) with "Sir J. Royds," a judge on the Supreme Court, she wrote: "I am glad he has made this acquaintance, as Sir John is a most agreeable and respectable old gentlemen, and it will be an advantage to him." It seems fair to assume that Lady Nugent was thinking of the young man's morals as well as his career prospects when she wrote these lines. In short, as Nugent happily reported to Lord Buckingham, Lady Nugent "has really treated him as a Mother" and additionally wrote to his own mother, "Lady Fortescue[,] fully and repeatedly on her Son's Subject."[43]

The assiduity with which the Nugents watched over Fortescue in India was no doubt a response, at least in part, to a disaster that occurred in Jamaica a decade earlier. There, a member of the extended Grenville clan entrusted (as an ADC) to Nugent's care precipitously married a "Creole" woman. The young man in question was Anthony Gilbert Storer, the only son of the Honorable Elizabeth Proby, the daughter of the first Baron Carysfort and sister of John Joshua Proby, the second Baron and first Earl of Carysfort, who was married to Elizabeth Grenville, Lord Buckingham's sister. By the time Storer accompanied the Nugents to India, Lord Buckingham had already performed many favors for this branch of the family. When Lord Buckingham founded the Order of Saint Patrick in Ireland, he tapped his brother-in-law, Storer's uncle, Lord Carysfort, for induction in 1784. Lord Buckingham also helped maneuver Lord Carysfort's promotion in the Irish peerage to the rank of earl in 1789. His wife's family connections also promoted Lord Carysfort's political career. William Wyndham Grenville sent him to Berlin as an envoy extraordinary in 1800; and in 1806 he joined the privy council of Grenville's coalition government. As Lord Carysfort's nephew, Storer also enjoyed Grenvillite patronage, which put him in Nugent's orbit.

When Lord Buckingham found himself in the position of having to fund a regiment for Nugent to raise in Buckinghamshire, one of the commissions went to Storer.[44]

A decade later, in 1805, Storer was named Nugent's ADC, doubtless at Lord Buckingham's request. Given that the office of ADC was used to mentor and protect young men of rank from their own foolhardiness and baser instincts, Nugent's failure to prevent Storer's marriage amounted to a failure of duty. His chagrin and disappointment at the event are palpable in the letter he wrote to Lord Buckingham breaking the news: "I am sorry to say that Mr. [Storer], notwithstanding all the warnings and advice I gave him on the subject, has married a young Creole of this island. He was prevented twice before from marrying others of the same description, and he had promised to accompany me to England, so that I had made myself sure he would escape from Jamaica unfettered. I do not write to Lord Carysfort on this unpleasant occasion, but I must beg of you to break the matter to him, with my best respects and solemn assurance that it was impossible for me to prevent it." Obviously Nugent had gone to extraordinary lengths to prevent Storer from disposing of his future in a way his family would find distasteful. What Nugent does not mention here is that Storer might have wanted to stay behind on the island, having inherited a plantation in Westmoreland from his uncle, Anthony Morris Storer, in 1799. While the Grenville clan felt no qualms about profiting from plantation slavery, they did not view the West Indies as a suitable permanent residence for one of their own.[45]

Although Lady Nugent couldn't countenance a member of her family party marrying a Creole woman, she did socialize with such women regularly in an official capacity. Since sexual violence was central to slavery, many "Members of the Assembly, officers, &c. &c." had mixed-race daughters whose mothers were enslaved or free Black women. These women presented something of a conundrum for Lady Nugent. Refusing to socialize with them would anger planters, but inviting them to social events like assemblies and dinners would infuriate the planters' wives. Wright explains how Lady Nugent navigated this delicate situation by "receiv[ing] the coloured ladies apart from the rest of the company, usually in her bedroom." On one typical occasion she records: "I took tea in my own room, surrounded by the black, brown and yellow ladies of the house." Like all etiquette decisions, this one was carefully calculated to locate "mulatto" women in hierarchies of prestige and power. Often they were squeezed in at the end of a long day: "Get to my own room before ten," Lady Nugent writes, "but obliged to give audience to all the black and brown ladies in the parish, while I was undressing." Anxious to get some rest, more often than not Lady Nugent tried to "Dismiss my mulatto friends as soon as possible, and go to bed." Not snubbed entirely, these women were nonetheless made aware of their marginality.[46]

In both Indies, Lady Nugent viewed the prevention of interracial liaisons—inside and outside of marriage—as something of a personal crusade. In Jamaica, she gave the "Rev. Mr. Simcocks, from Port Royal . . . a severe lecture . . . about his marrying a young naval officer with some good-for-nothing woman there." She also went straight to potential perpetrators. Only a few days later she records: "Remonstrate with some of our young men upon the improper lives they lead, and the miseries that must result from the horrid connections they have formed." In India, the Nugents likewise did everything in their power to prevent the men under their care from marrying Indian or "half-caste" women. Nugent explains the matter plainly to Lord Buckingham's son, Lord Temple: "There is less Beauty and more of *the Brunette,* than is to be seen elsewhere. The Subaltern part of the Army are I am sorry to say marrying fast, those of the half cast Race, commonly called Mulattoes in the West Indies. When this happens to anyone with good Connections at Home, it is pitiable, as neither their Wives nor Brats can be *presentable* to Society in England." It is noteworthy that Nugent translates the new social terrain of Anglo-India into a more familiar racial lexicon by glossing "the half cast Race" as "Mulattoes." While race was surely a primary motivation in Nugent's calculations, it was not the only one: class also factored into the picture. Nugent's blasé tone in the above passage is attributable to the fact that it is principally the "Subaltern part of the Army" that is "marrying fast." It is only when someone with "good Connections at Home" (i.e., members of "Society in England") makes such a match that the result "is pitiable." To be clear, the Nugents were racist. In both her journals, Lady Nugent compares Indian and African children to "little monkeys," even though the Indian child in question is a grandson of the Mughal emperor. Still, it is worth noting that their opposition to interracial marriage did not come from concerns about purity of blood alone. They were also principally preoccupied with guarding the social reputations of the young gentlemen under their watch.[47]

The articulation of class and race is likewise evident in Lady Nugent's war on the Bengal Military Orphan Society's monthly balls. The Society was a charitable organization established in 1782 to educate the offspring of European soldiers and Indian women. As commander in chief, Nugent was "patron" of the Society, and Lady Nugent its "patroness." At first, she struck a diplomatic tone, writing: "I will not give an opinion till I am better acquainted with the institution, but I do not think I admire some of the arrangements." But after attending a "public night there" a few days later, her opinion was decided: "I cannot help being shocked, to see so many young officers dancing and flirting with these dark complexioned young ladies. It is really laying a snare for them, and cruel to their families, to arrange such meetings. The governess I do not like at all.... I asked for, but could not get a sight of, any of their works, books &c. I fancy all they learn is to dance and dress themselves to the best advantage." Lady Nugent was clearly dismayed to realize that the "dark complexioned young ladies" under the Orphan School's care were being groomed for marriages with British military personnel. Still, read closely, her remarks do not imply a blanket rejection of interracial sex or socialization. Rather, like her husband, she is specifically concerned with commissioned "officers." That Lady Nugent is thinking at the level of *class* here is evident in her concern that it is "cruel" to the "families" of these young men "to arrange such meetings." Fortescue must have been on Lady Nugent's mind when she warned that the Orphan School balls "can only lead to entrapping young and inexperienced men into half-caste marriages." Saving young gentlemen from the dangers posed by their own "inexperience" was one of Nugents' duties.[48]

Unable to secure the "abolition of the monthly balls" at the level of official policy, Lady Nugent utilized her social power to accomplish her goal by hosting competing entertainments. She lays out her reasoning in her journal: "the best plan would be, to establish something distinct from it, so as to gradually remedy the evil." To this end, she decided to begin organizing assemblies, or balls. Nugent somewhat cheekily reports on this plan in a letter home: "Lady N. is going to try Assemblies and has issued her Cards accordingly, to give the young Ladies a Chance of Husbands." Assemblies were social gatherings that featured a smorgasbord of polite leisure activities like tea, dancing, and cards. Their raison d'être, as Vickery observes, was "orchestrated heterosexual sociability." Nugent's quip was thus playful but not at all in jest. Lady Nugent's assemblies, like all assemblies, were held with the intention of steering suitable young men and women into each other's arms. In Britain, they were customarily held in public assembly rooms that were built (often by subscription) for the purpose and were open to anyone who could afford a ticket. But unlike these widely accessible gatherings, Lady Nugent's assemblies were not open to the public. By issuing cards and hosting the balls at home, Lady Nugent replicated in Calcutta a type of gathering that was already a staple of aristocratic "domiciliary sociability" in England—private assemblies.[49]

Private assemblies were popular among class elites in England as a way to guarantee a certain level of homogeneity of rank. Lady Nugent duplicated this strategy in India's satellite campus of the fashionable world in order to achieve racial homogeneity. If young men were going to go through early adulthood in India, they needed polite institutions of sociability to be made available to them so that their only options were not illicit sex or mixed-race marriages. In Chapter 4, we observed that Lord Hastings's replacement with Lord Cornwallis was greeted as a turning point toward a new era of morally upright colonial rule. One of Cornwallis's signature reforms was purging the Eurasian offspring of European officers and Indian women from Company employment. Here we find a parallel purge in the social realm. Unable to make government policy, Lady Nugent established new social norms by excluding Eurasian women from polite society. Evidence suggests that Lady Nugent's efforts were successful. During four years in India, she prevented any untoward alliances among the young men under her and her husband's supervision. What's more, she presided over at least one propitious match—that between yet another one of Nugent's ADCs, Sir Walter Raleigh Gilbert, first Baronet, and a ward of Lord Moira, Miss Isabella Ross. Under the right conditions, it was possible for the ruling class to reproduce itself in India.[50]

With this chapter, I bring the historical trajectory sketched in this book to a close. At the onset of imperial expansion at mid-century, colonial fortunes threatened to destabilize the nation's socioeconomic hierarchies, the very foundation of political and social order. Ultimately, this did not take place. Instead, new colonial wealth was absorbed into old hierarchies, and patronage was used to redirect the flow of colonial cash from upstarts to ancient families in need. Concurrently, empire's reputation got a facelift. Once established families stood to gain from colonial wealth, it ceased to be a source of shame. Now, the two Indies were turned into the very basis of the ruling class's hegemony, which as a result survived for another century.

Coda

Colonial Mentalities, Postcolonial Epistemologies

> You have made the prophecy today a fact. This is the way to India.
>
> —*Chief engineer Grenville Mellen Dodge on the completion*
> *of the transcontinental railroad, May 10, 1869*

The story this book tells begins, in the Prelude, with the Seven Years' War. Victory in 1763 catapulted Britain into a position of leadership, or what Giovanni Arrighi calls "hegemony," in the capitalist world system. In *The Long Twentieth Century,* Arrighi boils down the entire life cycle of the modern world system into "four systemic cycles of accumulation," each of which was led by a different hegemonic power. In his schema, a Genoese cycle encapsulates the fifteenth and sixteenth centuries, the Dutch dominated the seventeenth century, and the British ruled the waves from the mid-eighteenth century until the late nineteenth century, when they were displaced by the United States. Arrighi stresses that the world system is not akin to a stable territorial entity such as the British Isles; it didn't remain static as different powers seized leadership of it. In his words, "world hegemonies have not 'risen' and 'declined' in a world system that expanded independently on the basis of an invariant structure." Instead, each hegemonic power "restructure[d] the political geography of world commerce" and altered "the spatial configuration of processes of capital accumulation" to fit its own needs. Put more simply, the shape of the world system shifted depending on who was leading it. The re-shaping of the world was, in Arrighi's reckoning, the very essence of hegemonic leadership. Redacting Arrighi's argument through this book's own conceptual vocabulary, we might say that during the eighteenth century Britain reorganized "world political-economic space" in the shape of the Indies.[1]

This framework gives us a compelling way to understand the Indies mentality's demise. When the organization of global space shifted once more under the leadership of a new geopolitical world order, the two Indies ceased to be a compelling framework for organizing knowledge of the world. I locate the swansong of the Indies mentality in the 1870s, the onset of the US systemic cycle according to Arrighi. This may seem like a surprisingly late date. To be sure, the Indies mentality was residual by this time; but it was also still powerful. American desires for geopolitical dominance took shape during Britain's systemic cycle, and they bear the cultural imprint of British hegemony. One of the events that sealed the United States's rise to hegemonic status, in Arrighi's account, was the completion of the first transcontinental railroad to the Pacific. As evinced by the comments of chief engineer Grenville Mellen Dodge, the completion of the railroad also represents a chapter—the last—in the story of the Indies mentality; for its construction was widely hailed as a realization of Columbus's dream: an American passage to India.[2]

The story of the railroad begins with a down-on-his-luck New York importer of luxury goods, Asa Whitney. After making and losing his fortune, Whitney gambled on a new business model: instead of buying Asian goods from Europe, why not cut out the middleman and go straight to the source? In June 1842, he did just that, sailing for China. Although the fastest clipper ships could make the trip from New York to China in less than eighty days, Whitney's sea voyage took a hundred and fifty-three. Plagued by seasickness, painful boils, rheumatism, insomnia, and the company of the ship's captain—who filled their shared cabin with cigar smoke every evening—Whitney felt sure there had to be a better way. Inspiration hit on his return journey home two years later. Instead of traveling eastward around the Cape of Good Hope, why not travel from New York to China westward, first overland by rail, and then across the Pacific? With his fortune secured from his time in China, Whitney dedicated the next three decades to realizing this vision.[3]

Whitney and his allies campaigned for the railroad's construction —and eventually celebrated its completion—as an "American road to India." During Britain's systemic cycle of accumulation, even during its twilight, it was simply impossible to imagine geopolitical dominance outside the idiom of the Indies mentality. Indeed, railroad promoters consciously embraced the strange temporality of their project, framing it as reactivation of early modern and eighteenth-century ambitions. Walt Whitman strikes this note in the occasional poem he composed for the railroad's completion, aptly titled "Passage to India": "Tying the Eastern to the Western Sea, / The road between Europe and Asia. / (Ah Genoese thy dream! thy dream!)." Whitman here echoes the railroad's promoters. In addition to touting the railroad as the belated realization of Columbus's fantasy, they also praised it as the fulfillment of another American icon's—Thomas Jefferson's—vision. In a promotional document circulated in 1846, Whitney suggests that the "explorations of Lewis and Clark, during the administration of Mr. Jefferson, were with a view to find the commercial route across this continent to Asia." Circumstantial evidence indicates that this claim was not entirely unfounded. In *Notes on the State of Virginia*, Jefferson did speculate that "if the two continents of Asia and America be separated at all, it is only by a narrow strait." Whether it was a primary motivation or not, the Lewis and Clark expedition he authorized a few decades later tested this proposition. "When Lewis and Clark reached the shore of the Pacific in 1804," writes Henry Nash Smith in his 1950s classic *Virgin Land: The American West as Symbol and Myth*, "they reactivated the oldest of all ideas associated with America—that of a passage to India."[4]

Usually, we think of US westward expansion as an end in itself: Manifest Destiny. But for Whitney and other railroad enthusiasts, the march west was merely a means to an end, and that end was Asia. In one of his many stump speeches for the railroad, Missouri congressman Thomas Hart Benton appealed to his listeners to consider the *longue durée* of global commerce: "That trade of India which has been shifting its channels from the time of the Phoenicians to the present, is destined to shift once more, and to realize the grand idea of Columbus.... The rich commerce of Asia will flow through our center. And where has that commerce ever flowed without carrying wealth and dominion with it?" After narrating the sequential effects of the rise and fall of Alexandria, Constantinople, Genoa, Venice, Lisbon, and Amsterdam "upon the East India trade," Benton arrives at the present. "And London," he asks, "what makes her the commercial mistress of the world—what makes an island no larger than one of our first class States—the mistress of possessions in the four corners of the globe—a match for half of Europe—and dominant in Asia? What makes all this, or contributes most to make it, but this same Asiatic trade? In no instance has it failed to carry the nation, or the people which possessed it, to the highest pinnacle of wealth and power, and with it the highest attainments of letters, arts, and sciences." In the manner of a modern-day world-systems theorist, Benton adopted the perspective of the *longue durée;* and from that perspective, Asia was the open secret to geopolitical dominance. Benton didn't need Andre Gunder Frank to tell him that the world system was oriented toward the East.[5]

The eventual completion of the transcontinental railroad both proved Benton right and undercut his central premise. While the railroad *did* usher in a new age of American world systemic hegemony, it did *not* do so (at least according to Arrighi) because it connected North America to the Pacific. Instead, the expansion of the United States's domestic internal economy facilitated by the railroad was much more decisive. Nonetheless, it is remarkable that Whitney and Benton imagined the new era of US hegemony in a mold cast by the imaginative geography of British imperialism. The railroad represents the last historical instantiation of the Indies mentality. When the United States displaced Britain's leadership position in the world system, it reorganized "world political-economic space" into a new configuration.

If the historical end point of this book is the transcontinental railroad, its methodological limits are to be found in an altogether different direction. *The Global Indies* is about a hegemonic world empire—but not because I think such behemoths are the only subjects worth writing about. Nor is my method of reading cultural productions through the reconstructed lenses of their own problematics restricted in its application to world-systemic leaders, or empires, or even nations. Similarly, while this book focuses on one mentality, I do not mean to suggest that there is only one. The British empire was a powerful structure that historically remade the world in profound ways that still shape our present. But it was not all-dominating or totalizing in its power. Other mentalities, including non-European ones, persisted during and beyond the age of British world-systemic leadership.

For a long time, scholars doubted whether university-produced academic discourse was capable of grasping alternatives to modern Western Enlightenment epistemes. Dipesh Chakrabarty formulated a particularly influential version of this proposition (although Michel-Rolph Trouillot's *Silencing the Past* anticipated Chakrabarty and has been just as influential in other field formations). Chakrabarty's famous directive to "provincialize Europe" is sometimes remembered as a call to arms, but it was actually issued as a melancholy groan: Chakrabarty was doubtful his own project could ever be carried out. Three decades later, a new generation of literary critics and historians is proving that "the project of provincializing Europe" need not be attached to a "politics of despair": it is by no means impossible to realize. In Black studies and South Asia studies, scholars have begun to test the Eurocentric limits of academic knowledge production. Now it seems clear that the disciplines of literary studies and history can in fact be used to excavate, reclaim, and reinhabit non-European epistemologies.[6]

Take, for example, Anthony Bogues's *Black Heretics, Black Prophets*. In this history of the Black radical tradition, Bogues sketches out two distinct streams: "the heretic stream," which inhabits and pushes the limits of Western epistemes; and the "*prophetic redemptive*" stream, which turns away from Western colonial reason to build a base-camp for resistance in local, indigenous (often religious and/or shamanic) traditions. At one point, Bogues refers to the latter as "subaltern," a Gramscian term closely associated with South Asia, thanks to the subaltern studies collective and Gayatri Spivak's famous critique of them, "Can the Subaltern Speak?" For a long time, the answer to Spivak's question seemed like a firm *no*. But this answer now demands some texturing. It is true that the subaltern *cannot* speak in the language of the colonizer: she cannot formulate utterances that make sense according to the dictates of colonial reason. Bogues points us in this direction when he notes "the number of individuals from the redemptive prophetic stream who . . . were declared *insane* by the colonial authorities." Yet we need not follow the same logic as the "colonial authorities." Bogues's point is that if we open ourselves to the alternative epistemes that animate the "redemptive prophetic stream," what looks like insanity from the perspective of "the colonial authorities" will start to make sense. We can hear the subaltern speak if we learn to listen in the idiom of non-European epistemologies.[7]

Meanwhile, in South Asia studies, scholars have been clearing a parallel path. In her extraordinarily innovative study, *Australianama*, Samia Khatun proves that non-European epistemologies can in fact be made into a viable basis for history. Critiquing the reliance of Australian historians on English-language sources, Khatun argues that "South Asian-and aboriginal-language" materials are indispensable, not only because they add facts missing from European documents, but, more importantly, because they "have encoded within them an order of things" that is fundamentally different from English-language texts. Khatun suggests that we cull this "conceptual grid" and then turn it back on the very sources from which it came, using it to interpret them. In this way, she argues, we can recover how "knowledge traditions outside Enlightenment epistemes" historically critiqued colonial power. Transposed into the critical terms I have developed over the course of this book, Khatun suggests that we read non-European texts through the lenses of their own reconstructed mentalities. More radical still is her suggestion that we then adopt and adapt those mentalities as critical hermeneutics. British imperialism may have remade the world, but worldmaking happens at different scales, some available to non-hegemonic actors. Ning Ma makes a similar point in her comparative study of the simultaneous rise of the novel in the East and West, *The Age of Silver*: it is time to "emphasize *the worldmaking roles of non-Western civilizations*."[8]

The Global Indies is in obvious ways a literary critical addition to new imperial history. But it is also, in perhaps less obvious ways, an exercise in postcolonial studies. In this book I have used past-critical reading to try to restore to the past the gift of theory. Just because writers in the past viewed the world differently than we do does not mean that they were wrong. In the future, I would like to see this empathetic critical stance extended to non-European historical actors. At a moment when the future of planetary life seems contingent on finding an alternative to the Western Enlightenment reason that underwrote colonial modernity, it is time to steep ourselves in the non-European epistemes that might help us build a different world.

Notes

Introduction

1. St. Clair, *The Reading Nation in the Romantic Period,* 207; Davidoff and Hall, *Family Fortunes,* 162; Baird and Ryskamp, *The Poems of William Cowper,* 113. According to St. Clair, Cowper was "the most commonly read poet of the romantic period" and "probably the most popular and most read modern poet that had ever lived."

2. Some scholars have already begun to explore this pairing. See Warner, "What's Colonial about Colonial America?"; Marshall, *The Making and Unmaking of Empires;* Aravamudan, "East Indies and West Indies"; Stern, "British Asia and British Atlantic"; Stern, "Neither East nor West"; Harris, *Indography;* Nussbaum, "Between 'Oriental' and 'Blacks So Called'"; Agnani, *Hating Empire Properly;* Eacott, *Selling Empire;* Cohen, "The Global Indies."

3. Krishnan, *Reading the Global,* 1; Ramachandran, *The Worldmakers,* 5–7; Beckert, *Empire of Cotton,* 9; Shakespeare, *Merry Wives of Windsor,* 1.3.64–66; *OED Online,* s.v. "Indies, *n.*" https://www.oed-com.libproxy1.usc.edu/view/Entry/94445?rskey= fmypoo&result=2 (accessed July 16, 2019); Harris, *Indography,* 2. Beckert suggests that cotton was an underappreciated motive for Columbus's voyage and a source of his confusion, as he found the plant being cultivated in the Caribbean.

4. Williams, *Marxism and Literature,* 121–27; Bloch, *The Royal Touch,* 5.

5. Koehn, *The Power of Commerce,* 205–6.

6. Burguière, *The Annales School,* 4, 13–51; Burke, *The French Historical Revolution,* 6–31; Clark, *The Annales School,* 4:3–262; Hall, "Signification, Representation, Ideology," 91.

7. Lucien Febvre and Marc Bloch, "À nos lecteurs," *Annales d'histoire économique et social,* no. 1 (15 janvier 1929): 1, 2, quoted in Wallerstein, "*Annales* as Resistance," 6.

8. Quoted in Vovelle, *Ideologies and Mentalities*, 5; Bloch, *The Historian's Craft*, 107. Given its importance, the term *mentalités* is surprisingly difficult to define, for several reasons. First, it is more impressionistic than theoretically precise; second, it is an umbrella term for several distinct but related concepts; third, its meaning and application have evolved significantly over time; and fourth, Annalistes have tended to avoid stand-alone theorizing. My understanding of *l'histoire des mentalités* is particularly indebted to Burguière, who offers a useful synthesis of different approaches. See also le Goff, "Mentalities," 81; Birnbaum, "The *Annales* School and Social Theory," 237; Burguière, *The Annales School*, 52–78, 219–42; Duby, "L'histoire des mentalités"; Mandrou, "L'histoire des mentalités"; Airès, "L'histoire des mentalités"; Hutton, "The History of Mentalities"; Burke, "Strengths and Weaknesses of the History of Mentalities"; Chartier, "Intellectual History and the History of Mentalités"; Burke, "Reflections on the Historical Revolution in France"; Hunt, "French History in the Last Twenty Years"; Furet, "Beyond the Annales"; Gismondi, "'The Gift of Theory.'"

9. Martin and Wigen, *The Myth of Continents*, ix, xi; Lefebvre, *The Production of Space*; Arrighi, *The Long Twentieth Century*, 36; Massey, *For Space*, 84, 88.

10. Barad, *Meeting the Universe Halfway*, 46, 26, 114, 88; Hall, "Signification, Representation, Ideology," 97–100; Spivak, "Can the Subaltern Speak?," 72. Once again, I take this challenge to be central to Marx's project too. See, especially, "The German Ideology," 164–65; and the 1857 "Introduction" to the *Grundrisse*, esp. 100–105.

11. Quoted in Burguière, "The Fate of the History of *Mentalités* in the *Annales*," 410; Burguière, *The Annales School*, 59. In his candidacy statement for the Collège de France, Bloch wrote: the "interpretation of the facts of social organization *from the inside* will be the principle of my teaching, just as it is of my own work."

12. Barad, *Meeting the Universe Halfway*, 46, 49, 88 149. On literature's worldmaking capacities, see Kareem, *Eighteenth-Century Fiction and the Reinvention of Wonder*; Goldberg, Newman, and Frank, *This Distracted Globe*; Joseph, "Worlding and Unworlding in the Long Eighteenth Century"; Hayot, *On Literary Worlds*.

13. My attempt to lift Cowper's worldview from *The Task* is indebted to Kaul, *Poems of Nation*, 233–52.

14. Hall, "Signification, Representation, Ideology," 105; Anderson, *Imagined Communities*, 25–37. For Cowper's newspaper habits, see Baird and Ryskamp, *The Poems of William Cowper*, 379–84; Goodman, *Georgic Modernity and British Romanticism*, 68; Ellison, "News, Blues, and Cowper's Busy World."

15. Andrew, *Aristocratic Vice*, 37–41; Goodman, *Georgic Modernity and British Romanticism*, 72–77; O'Quinn, *Entertaining Crisis*, 5–16, 22–23.

16. Baird and Ryskamp, *The Poems of William Cowper*, 381. By October, the fighting had long since ceased in New York, but, due to the slow speed of communication in both directions between Europe and India, hostilities were ongoing in Pondicherry until May and were being reported in London newspapers until November.

17. Kramnick, *Paper Minds*, 93. In *The Task*, Cowper conjures "a world that feels within reach."

18. Williams's "structures of feeling" is heavily indebted to Lucien Goldmann's concept of "genetic structures," which was in turn deeply indebted to l'histoire des mentalités. Taken together, Williams's chapters on "Hegemony," "Structures of Feeling," and "Ideology" in *Marxism and Literature* treat the three dimensions covered by the study of mentalities: unconscious belief, affect, and reflective thought. If "structures of feeling" is taken apart from these other concepts—as it often is in new work on affect studies—then the full scope of Williams's vision is curtailed.

19. Jameson, "Cognitive Mapping," 349; Goodman, *Georgic Modernity and British Romanticism*, 8–9, 90–96.

20. Goodman, *Georgic Modernity and British Romanticism*, 69; Favret, *War at a Distance*, 24; Kaul, *Poems of Nation, Anthems of Empire*, 237. A notable exception is Kaul, who writes of *The Task*: "In pointing to those moments in 'The Sofa' in which a poetic exercise on mundane, everyday themes and objects ('I sing the SOFA') inevitably turns into an exploration of the wide world of exploration and empire, I wish to suggest the ineluctable redefinition of the 'everyday' by the latter."

21. Cowper, *The Letters and Prose Writings of William Cowper*, 1:269, 279; 2:194. For more on *The History of the Two Indies*, including its reception in England, see Agnani, *Hating Empire Properly*, 3, 12–15, 25–26, 198; Aravamudan, *Tropicopolitans*, 401. Although the *Histoire* was a collaboration between Raynal and Denis Diderot, the latter's participation was unbeknownst to many contemporary readers, including, it seems, Cowper. I thus refer to the author of the *Histoire* as Raynal.

22. Goodman, *Georgic Modernity*, 69, 81, 91; Cowper, *The Letters and Prose Writings of William Cowper*, 1:279; Mee, *Conversable Worlds*, 170–83; Raynal, *A philosophical and political history*, 1:3. The "globally telescopic eye" is Goodman's term.

23. While scholars have sifted out traces of Fielding and Lucretius in this stanza, the more substantial debt to the *History of the Two Indies* has gone unnoticed. Raynal may also reference Lucretius in the passage Cowper remediates. Compare: "For time changes the nature of the whole world, / and one state of things must pass into another, / and nothing remains as it was: all things move, / all are changed by nature and compelled to alter" to "Every thing has changed, and must change again." Lucretius quoted in Ramachandran, *Worldmakers*, 99; Raynal, *A philosophical and political history*, 1:2–3; Goodman, *Georgic Modernity and British Romanticism*, 86, 91.

24. Agnani, *Hating Empire Properly*, 42–45, 25; Raynal, *A philosophical and political history*, 1:4. Agnani explains: "Diderot's involvement in the three editions increased with each publication, and he was said to have thoroughly rewritten the third edition by spending as much as fourteen hours a day at the task."

25. O'Quinn, *Entertaining Crisis*, 20, 3. Emphasis added.

26. Criticism on the post-critical is burgeoning quickly. For touchstones and overviews, see Best and Marcus, "Surface Reading"; Hensley, "Curatorial Reading and Endless War," 64; Felski, *The Limits of Critique*; Anker and Felski, *Critique and Post Critique*.

27. Althusser, *Reading Capital*, 16–20; Jameson, *The Political Unconscious*, 60, 20, 75. For another sympathetic reevaluation of Althusser along similar lines, see Rooney, "Symptomatic Reading is a Problem of Form."

28. Althusser, *Reading Capital*, 42; Hall, "Race, Articulation, and Societies Structured in Dominance," 39. For convergences and divergences between Althusser, Marxism, and the *Annales* see Schöttler, "Althusser and Annales Historiography," 87–88; Vilar, "Marxist History"; and Birnbaum, "The *Annales* School and Social Theory," 233; Revel, "The *Annales*," 16; Eley, *A Crooked Line*, 36; Stoianovich, *French Historical Method*, 111; Braudel, "En guise de conclusion," 243–61.

29. Althusser, *Reading Capital*, 26, 42, 243, 248. The three are "Lucien Febvre, Labrousse, Braudel." Althusser calls them the day's "best historians," a compliment that some read as backhanded but I do not. For Althusser's reception among historians and the New Left, see Montag, *Althusser and His Contemporaries*, 15–35, 2; Thompson, *The Poverty of Theory*; Johnson, "Edward Thompson"; Jones, "History and Theory"; Vilar, "Marxist History"; Dworkin, *Cultural Marxism in Postwar Britain*, 219–45; Anderson, *Arguments Within English Marxism*.

There are also echoes of Bloch's *Appareil des pensées* in Foucault's notion of an episteme. Many *Annalistes* believe Foucault appropriated and simplified l'histoire des mentalités by analyzing purely mental, dematerialized, universes—especially in his later work, which focuses on prescriptive texts. Foucault also offers correctives: his emphasis on "rupture" responds to an overemphasis on continuity in l'histoire des mentalités. Burguière, *The Annales School*, 62, 153, 195–218; Burke, *The French Historical Revolution*, 131.

30. Hobsbawm, "British History and the *Annales*," 179–81, 183, 185; Birnbaum, "The *Annales* School and Social Theory," 226; Eley, *A Crooked Line*, 40, 56–57; Thompson, *The Poverty of Theory*, 26; Tilly, "Anthropology, History, and the *Annales*," 210. Hobsbawm argued that the British Marxists represented a "home-grown tradition" of "a history of mentalities"—a tradition which, while distinctly English, was also nurtured by decades of "direct influence," and indirect "confluence," and intermittent exchange with the *Annales* movement. Thompson refers to Bloch as a "formidable practitioner of historical materialism." The first issue of *Past and Present* references *Annales*.

31. For two foundational collections see Nussbaum, *The Global Eighteenth Century*, and Wilson, *A New Imperial History*. For an overview of trends in mapping imperial space, see Lester, "Imperial Circuits and Networks"; Ballantyne, "Race and Webs of Empire."

32. Raynal, *A philosophical and political history*, 1:1. This passage is echoed by Adam Smith in the *Wealth of Nations* (626), albeit without the singular declension. My approach to reading seemingly straightforward empiricist passages as moments of speculative theorizing is indebted to Kazanjian, *The Brink of Freedom*, 10–31; Kazanjian, "Hegel, Liberia."

33. Gilroy, *The Black Atlantic*, 15; Lewis and Wigen, *The Myth of Continents*, 200.

34. Greig, *The Beau Monde*; Russell, *Women, Sociability and Theatre in Georgian London*; Russell, "An 'Entertainment of Oddities'"; Russell and Tuite, *Romantic Sociability*, 20; O'Quinn, *Staging Governance*; O'Quinn, *Entertaining Crisis*.

Prelude

1. Coke and Borg, *Vauxhall Gardens;* Greig, *The Beau Monde,* 66–80.

2. Koehn, *The Power of Commerce,* 5–7.

3. *Gazetteer and London Daily Advertiser,* August 29, 1763; Coke and Borg, *Vauxhall Gardens,* 37–41, 67–8. For Bardolatry, see Anderson, *Shakespeare and the Legacy of Loss;* Ritchie and Sabor, eds., *Shakespeare in the Eighteenth Century.*

4. For the paintings, see Allen, *Francis Hayman,* 52–73; de Bolla, *The Education of the Eye,* 93–103; Coke and Borg, *Vauxhall Gardens,* 127–36; Watts, *The Cultural Work of Empire,* 65–67; Fordham, *British Art and the Seven Years' War,* 119–29. "Culture of now" quoted in Goodman, *Georgic Modernity,* 173.

5. Fordham, *British Art and the Seven Years' War,* 122–24; Russel, *Women, Sociability and Theater in Georgian London,* 104; Allen, *Francis Hayman,* 49–52. Allen similarly describes Vauxhall as "theatrical."

6. For Le Brun, see Allen, *Francis Hayman,* 67–68. I thank Zirwat Chowdhury for pointing out the reference to Le Brun, and for her insightful comments.

ONE Diagnosing the (American) Crisis in Foote's *The Cozeners* and Burney's *Evelina*

1. For 1763, see Wilson, *The Sense of the People,* 204, 193–206; Fordham, *British Art and the Seven Years' War,* 3; de Bruyn and Regan, *The Culture of the Seven Years' War,* 13–14; O'Quinn, "Facing Past and Future," 308; Marshall, "Empire and Opportunity in Britain," 111.

2. Scholars have begun to reassess the American Crisis in a global perspective. See, for example, Marshall, *The Making and Unmaking of Empires;* Bowen, "Perceptions from the Periphery"; Bowen, Mancke, and Reid, *Britain's Oceanic Empire;* Eacott, *Selling Empire.*

3. Quoted in Goodman, *Georgic Modernity,* 173n16; *London Evening Post,* July 14–16, 1774; Kelly, *Mr. Foote's Other Leg,* 107, 247; quoted in Nicholson, "The Victorian Meme Machine," 7. As Kelly explains, in his own lifetime Foote was considered David Garrick's rival and peer. In the 1770s about 12,000 people a week attended the theater in London; and in July, August, and early September they had nowhere else to go to see legitimate drama except the Haymarket. As the Haymarket's manager, principal playwright, and star actor, Foote took home £3,000–5,000 in profits each summer.

4. Jameson, "Cognitive Mapping," 349.

5. For exceptions, see Wilson, *The Sense of the People;* Russel, "An 'Entertainment of Oddities'"; O'Quinn, *Entertaining Crisis;* O'Quinn, *Staging Governance;* Scobie, "'Bunny!'"

6. Koehn, *The Power of Commerce,* 209; Sutherland, *The East India Company in Eighteenth-Century Politics,* 190–92; Lawson, *The East India Company,* 108; Eacott, *Selling Empire,* 181, 188, 207; Bowen, *Revenue and Reform;* Bowen, *The Business of Empire,* 53–83; Marshall, "Empire and Opportunity in Britain," 120–22. For the Boston Tea Party in the larger context of eighteenth-century consumer boycotts, see Sussman, *Consuming Anxieties,* 22–48.

7. Pincus, *The Heart of the Declaration,* 2, 53, 67, 86–88; Pincus, "The Rise and Fall of Empires"; Eacott, *Selling Empire,* 180–81.

8. Eacott, *Selling Empire,* 168–226; Bowen, "Perceptions from the Periphery," 293; Marshall, *The New Cambridge History of India II,* 150–51; Price, *Observations on the Nature of Civil Liberty,* 103.

9. Marshall, *The Making and Unmaking of Empires,* 205; O'Quinn, *Entertaining Crisis in the Atlantic Imperium,* 342; Colley, *Captives,* 269–72.

10. Burke, *Speech . . . on American Taxation,* 2, 10, 12, 27.

11. O'Quinn, *Entertaining Crisis,* 136, 18; Althusser, *Reading Capital,* 26. For *krinein* as the root of critique, see Heidegger, *What Is a Thing?,* 119–20; Gasché, *The Honor of Thinking,* 13–14, 108–9. From the perspective of postcolonial studies—and this book—the only "cure" for colonialism is its end, a solution that was not advocated during the American Crisis. Nonetheless, I believe that the outpouring of diagnostic critique produced during the American Crisis is still worth revisiting because a crisis is a rare and special time of clear seeing. Berlant comes close to my argument with "crisis ordinariness": "traumas of the social that are lived through collectively and that transform the sensorium to a heightened perceptiveness about the unfolding of the historical, and sometimes historic, moment." Berlant "Thinking About Feeling Historical," 5.

12. Kelly, *Mr. Foote's Other Leg,* 121–23; Dircks, Phyllis T. 2015 "Foote, Samuel (bap. 1721, d. 1777), actor and playwright." *ODNB.* 18 Jul. 2019. https://www-oxforddnb-com.libproxy2.usc.edu/view/10.1093/ref:odnb/9780198614128.001.0001/odnb-9780198614128-e-9808. The Licensing Act of 1737 confined spoken drama to London's royal patent theaters. At first, the beverage on offer at Foote's performances was chocolate; then, in 1748, he rescheduled to 6 p.m. and switched the libation to tea.

13. Foote, *The Cozeners,* 2, 33, 39–40; Scott, *The Journal of Sir Walter Scott,* 175–76; *Female Artifice,* iii–iv. For Grieve, see Moody, "Stolen Identities"; Life, Page. 2004 "Grieve, Elizabeth Harriet (b. c. 1723, d. in or after 1782), swindler." *ODNB.* 19 Jul. 2019. https://www-oxforddnb-com.libproxy2.usc.edu/view/10.1093/ref:odnb/9780198614128.001.0001/odnb-9780198614128-e-65504. The Grieve affair circulated as gossip in fashionable circles before it was reported to the public at large. Sir Walter Scott reports hearing that Fox gleefully retold the story at "Brooke's and elsewhere." The satirical poem *Female Artifice* takes for granted that those "who mix in the Great World" or belong to the "politer circle of life" will already be familiar with the story, and aims to simulate this in-the-know experience for less fortunate readers by relating "all the particulars . . . with the very same degree of Precision (I wish I could add, with the same portion of Humour) that Mr. CHARLES F-X relates them himself."

While we can surmise that Marianne was enslaved in Boston, the Mansfield Decision would complicate her legal status in London. Foote refers to the Mansfield decision in *The Nabob* (which premiered on June 29, 1772, exactly one week after it was issued): "I had some thoughts of importing three blacks from Bengal . . . but I shan't venture till the point is determined whether those creatures are to be considered as mere chattels, or men" (38).

14. *Craftsman or Say's Weekly Journal,* July 2, 1774. For *The Nabob,* see O'Quinn, *Staging Governance,* 43–73. For Foote's management of the Haymarket, see Kelly, *Mr. Foote's Other Leg,* 241–79.

15. Smith, *Plays about the Theatre in England,* 32–34; Kelly, *Mr. Foote's Other Leg,* 174; Foote, *The Commissary,* 13–15, 19; Burke, *Speech . . . on American Taxation,* 27. The *Commissary* is loosely based on Molière's *Bourgeois Gentilhomme* (1670). Fungus's music teacher is a takeoff of Drury Lane's orchestra leader, Dr. Thomas Arne, and his oratory instructor is a takeoff of Thomas Sheridan.

16. Foote, *The Cozeners,* 75; Luff, Peter. 2005 "Fox, Henry, first Baron Holland of Foxley (1705–1774), politician." *ODNB.* 19 Jul. 2019. https://www-oxforddnb-com.libproxy2. usc.edu/view/10.1093/ref:odnb/9780198614128.001.0001/odnb-9780198614128-e-10033; Luff, Peter. 2004 "Fox, (Georgiana) Caroline [née Lady (Georgiana) Caroline Lennox], suo jure Baroness Holland of Holland (1723–1774), noblewoman." *ODNB.* 19 Jul. 2019. https:// www-oxforddnb-com.libproxy2.usc.edu/view/10.1093/ref:odnb/9780198614128 .001.0001/odnb-9780198614128-e-48888; Sutherland and Binney, "Henry Fox as Paymaster General of the Forces"; Harling, *The Waning of Old Corruption,* 72; Mitchell, *Charles James Fox,* 16; *Public Advertiser,* April 26, 1773, quoted in Holzman, *The Nabobs in England,* 31.

John Calcraft was Henry Fox's agent and protégé; his net worth at death was £600,000. Memory of Fox's embezzlement was kept alive by Parliament's refusal to clear his official accounts. In 1788, a satirical cartoon about the Hastings impeachment trial pictures Charles James Fox saying, "Egad it would have been a devil of a Job for me, if my Fa—r had made *such* an *Atonement* for—*Unaccounted Millions.*" See Robinson, *Edmund Burke,* 103.

17. Sutherland and Binney, "Henry Fox as Paymaster General," 252; *Middlesex Journal and Evening Advertiser,* Nov. 30–Dec. 2, 1773; *Morning Chronicle and London Advertiser,* March 5, 1774. Charles James Fox's elder brother Stephen was also a gambler.

18. Andrew, *Aristocratic Vice,* 187; Walpole, *Letters Addressed to the Countess of Ossory,* 105–7; *London Chronicle or Universal Evening Post,* Nov. 2–4, 1773. The *St. James Chronicle* took a particularly hard stance: "let not the People be deterred from their Endeavors to detect those Traitors to their Country, who make a private Emolument by the Sale of public Employments. I hope Mrs. Greeve [sic] will be brought to confess; and if it is true she has a Partner in her Guilt, that we shall see the Fox brought forth from his lurking Place; notwithstanding she has made her Boast that she shall get more by disowning her Connections with the Great, than she did by claiming Men of the first Rank and Fortune for her Relations" (November 16, 1773).

19. Tony Lumpkin is a character from Oliver Goldsmith's *She Stoops to Conquer.* Toby was also judged to be a "'Tony Lumpkin" in a review of *The Cozeners* in the *London Evening Post* (July 14–16, 1774). Carter, *Men and the Emergence of Polite Society,* 88; quoted in Cannon, John. "Stanhope, Phillip Dormer, fourth earl of Chesterfield." *ODNB.* 9 May 2013. http://www.oxforddnb.com/themes/theme.jsp?articleid=92738. For the aristocracy's failure of leadership during the American Crisis, see Andrew, *Aristocratic Vice;* Colley, *Britons,* 147–55; O'Quinn, *Entertaining Crisis;* Russell, *The Theatres of War,*

38–47; Wilson, *The Sense of the People,* 179–89. For the transition to a martial style of masculinity ushered in by the American War, see Russell, *The Theatres of War;* O'Quinn, *Entertaining Crisis,* 243–301. For a detailed account of Burney's engagement with Omai, see Scobie, "Bunny!"

20. Kinservik, *Disciplining Satire,* 10–11, 134–71; Scott, *The Journal of Sir Walter Scott,* 175–76; *London Evening Post,* July 12–14, 1774. Foote's next play, *A Trip to Calais,* was rejected by the Lord Chamberlain on account of the aristocratic pedigree of its subject, Elizabeth Chudleigh, duchess of Kingston—who was on trial for bigamy before the House of Lords—an episode that ruined Foote's career and life. See Kelly, *Mr. Foote's Other Leg,* 285–372; Russell, *Women, Sociability and Theatre in Georgian London,* 153–77.

21. *Female Artifice,* 3; Foote, *The Cozeners,* 94; *London Evening Post,* Oct. 30–Nov. 2, 1773; *The Westminster Magazine,* March 1774, 145; *Morning Chronicle and London Advertiser,* July 16, 1774.

22. Bricker, "After the Golden Age," 312–13; *Morning Chronicle and London Advertiser,* July 16, 1774.

23. Foote, *The Cozeners,* 37, 69–71, 75–76. For macaronis, see Rauser, "Hair, Authenticity, and the Self-Made Macaroni"; West, "The Darly Macaroni Prints"; McNeil, *Pretty Gentlemen.*

24. Mitchell, *Charles James Fox,* 1, 6; *Middlesex Journal and Evening Advertiser,* July 14–16, 1774. For omission fees, see Andrew, *Aristocratic Vice,* 10.

25. *The Macaroni and Theatrical Magazine, or Monthly Register of the Fashions and Diversions of the Times* (London, October 1772), 1.

26. Sussman, *Consuming Anxieties,* 82; Smollett, *The Expedition of Humphrey,* 86–88; Foote, *The Cozeners,* 3. Foote was a particular favorite of George III, who despised Fox. For more on his social set, see Kelly, *Mr. Foote's Other Leg,* 195–220, 241. My focus here is London, but 1763 was a turning point in provincial cities as well. See Langford, *A Polite and Commercial People,* 71, 67–71; Wilson, *The Sense of the People,* 6; McKendrick, *The Birth of a Consumer Society.* Langford writes: "[when] one critic asked in 1767 … Why were rural folk engaging in the preposterous social custom of formal 'visits' and the consequent pointless chatter? Why did card-playing take place all the year round even in remote districts? The answer must lie in the capital. London fashions, London habits, London affectations were discerned in unlikely places."

27. For more on Soubise and the commercialization of accomplishments, see Chapter 2 and Cohen, "Fencing and the Market in Aristocratic Masculinity."

28. Stephens and Dorothy, *Catalogue of Political and Personal Satires;* Rauser, "Hair, Authenticity, and the Self-Made Macaroni," 108–9; Taylor, *The Politics of Parody,* 40–70.

29. O'Quinn, *Staging Governance,* 20–21; Taylor, *The Politics of Parody;* McNeil, *Pretty Gentlemen,* 27.

30. Kelly, *Mr. Foote's Other Leg,* 124; Scott, *The Journal of Sir Walter Scott,* 175–76. For the screen scene, see Russell, *Women, Sociability and Theatre in Georgian London,* 178–225. Charles Surface's escapades were said to be inspired by Fox; and the famous picture auction scene is a nod to Foote's *An Auction of Pictures.*

31. Foote, *The Cozeners*, 41–42; Cohn, "Representing Authority in Victorian India"; Nugent, *Lady Nugent's East India Journal*, xxxiv–xxxvii; Holzman, *The Nabobs in England*, 83; Nechtman, "A Jewel in the Crown?"; Bowen, H. V. 2008 "Clive, Robert, first Baron Clive of Plassey (1725–1774), army officer in the East India Company and administrator in India." *ODNB*. https://www-oxforddnb-com.libproxy2.usc.edu/view/10.1093/ref:odnb/9780198614128.001.0001/odnb-9780198614128-e-5697 (July 23, 2019); Clive quoted in Dirks, *The Scandal of Empire*, 5. Safely remitting an Indian fortune to Britain was so challenging that certain agents and attorneys came to specialize in this service. It was soon made illegal for Company officials to accept presents. The Nugents were scrupulous in avoiding—or at least appearing to avoid—accepting them.

32. Foote, *The Cozeners*, 67–68; Scott, *The Journal of Sir Walter Scott*, 176.

33. Foote, *The Cozeners*, 75–76. Mitchell, *Charles James Fox*, 1, 6; Wade, *Junius*, 2:384; Adams, *English Party Leaders*, 1:359; Walpole, *The Last Journals of Horace Walpole During the Reign of George III*, 270; An Heroic and Elegiac Epistle from Mrs. GRIEVE, in Newgate, to Mr. C—F—," 145; Mitchell, "Charles James Fox." It is unclear if the nickname "The Eyebrow" predates or postdates *The Cozeners*.

34. George, *Catalogue of Political and Personal Satires in the British Museum*, V. For climate and race, see Wheeler, *The Complexion of Race*. For the residual sedimentation of early modern racial discourse in later periods, see Loomba, "Periodization, Race, and Global Contact"; Loomba, "Race and the Possibilities of Comparative Critique"; Wilson, *The Island Race*, 1–15; Martinez, *Genealogical Fictions*.

35. Andrew, *Aristocratic Vice*, 5–38; O'Quinn, *Entertaining Crisis*, 13–14; Gamer and Robinson, "Mary Robinson and the Dramatic Art of the Comeback"; *London Evening Post*, July 12, 1774. For another example, see *Public Ledger*, July 12, 1774. I use "dominant" and "residual" here in conformity with Raymond Williams's schematic. Williams, *Marxism and Literature*, 121–27.

36. Foote, *The Cozeners*, 81.

37. For scholarship that does look for imperial politics in Burney, see Straub, *Evelina*, 16–17; O'Quinn, *Staging Governance*, 222–57; Hart, "Frances Burney's *Evelina*: Mirvan and Mezzotint"; Scobie, "Bunny!"; Woodworth, *Eighteenth-Century Women Writers*, 30–31.

38. Doody, *Frances Burney*, 49; Burney, *Evelina*, 210.

39. Hart, "Frances Burney's *Evelina*."

40. Burney, *Evelina*, 124. For the Black Hole, see Chatterjee, *The Black Hole of Empire*, 1–32. For Holwell's daughter, Mrs. Pleydell, see Burney, *The Early Diary Of Frances Burney*, 1:65, 120.

41. Said, *Culture and Imperialism*, 51–59; Barchas, *Matters of Fact in Jane Austen*; Jameson, *The Political Unconscious*, 60, 20, 75; Makdisi, *Romantic Imperialism*, 8–9. Saree Makdisi (along with other critics) has pointed out various ways in which Said's orientalism falls short when it comes to earlier periods. Here, I add another point: contrapuntal reading is not well suited to eighteenth-century texts. In many ways, contrapuntal reading's modus operandi recalls Jameson's symptomatic reading. Using Jameson's terms, we

might even say that Said "strongly rewrites" *Mansfield Park* according to the "single vast unfinished plot" of European imperialism.

42. Joseph, *Reading the East India Company,* 70–71. Walpole, *Letters Addressed to the Countess of Ossory,* 110; *Public Advertiser,* May 6, 1774 and May 18, 1776; *Parker's General Advertiser,* January 17, 1783; Murphy, *Know your own Mind,* 9.

43. Chatterjee, *The Black Hole of Empire,* 21; Kaul, *Poems of Nation, Anthems of Empire,* 92–112; Favret, *War at a Distance,* 4, 9, 43; O'Quinn, *Entertaining Crisis,* 16. For the centrality of sociability to English identity, see Pocock, *Virtue, Commerce, and History,* 48; Langford, *A Polite and Commercial People.*

44. Burney, *Evelina,* 125.

45. Burney, *Evelina,* 43, 53. For *Evelina's* cast of male types, see Mackie, *Rakes, Highwaymen, and Pirates,* 151–52.

46. Nussbaum, *The Limits of the Human;* "The Genius," *St. James Chronicle of the British Evening Post,* January 9, 1762. For the French associations of macaroni fashion, see McNeil, *Pretty Gentlemen,* 123–49. Colman's sketch is the first instance I have found of the Black-Hole meme.

47. Tague, *Animal Companions,* 94, 120–29. For toy dogs, see Yang, "Culture in Miniature." To name one more example, in "Out of Fashion/In Fashion," a print from 1772, two men face each other in startled amazement, one dressed in 1760s style, the other in a radically different à la mode ensemble. A monkey prancing in the background dressed as a macaroni signals the danger and folly of fashion.

48. Burney, *Evelina,* 443–48.

49. Erickson, "Esther Sleepe," 15–17, 21–22, 25; Coulombeau, "Introduction," 8.

50. Brown, "Shock Effect," 379, 404–6.

51. For Foote's friendship with Angelo, see Kelly, *Mr. Foote's Other Leg,* 93, 171, 219, 250; Angelo, *Reminiscences of Henry Angelo,* 1:450–51.

TWO A Black British Racial Formation

1. Hall, "New Ethnicities," 163–64; Lott, *Love and Theft;* Maclean, *Looking East,* 20. For "Black British," see also Gilroy, *"There Ain't No Black in the Union Jack";* and Sivanandan, *A Different Hunger.*

2. Gilroy, *The Black Atlantic,* 15; Du Bois, *The Souls of Black Folks,* 3. For critiques of the Atlantic world paradigm along these lines, see Stern, "British Asia and British Atlantic"; Stern, "Neither East nor West, Border, nor Breed, nor Birth"; Games, "Beyond the Atlantic"; Green, "Maritime Worlds and Global History"; Hofmeyr, "Universalizing the Indian Ocean"; Desai, "Oceans Connect"; Cohen, "The Global Indies."

3. Scholarship on race in British drama is too vast to cite here. See, for example, Ragussis, *Theatrical Nation;* Worrall, *Harlequin Empire;* Orr, *Empire on the English Stage;* Vaughan, *Performing Blackness on English Stages.*

4. Lambert and Lester, *Colonial Lives Across the British Empire,* 2, 23. For Soubise's biography, see Cohen, "Julius Soubise in India"; Carretta, Vincent. 2008 "Soubise, Julius [formerly Othello] (c. 1754–1798), man of fashion." *ODNB.* 27 Jul. 2019. https://www-

oxforddnb-com.libproxy2.usc.edu/view/10.1093/ref:odnb/9780198614128.001.0001/ odnb-9780198614128-e-60841. Lambert and Lester explain: "The idea of 'life geographies' evokes a sense of the spatial not simply as the location of, or backdrop to, a life, nor as a metaphor (as in the "journey" of life), but rather as co-constitutive with selfhood and identity."

5. *Public Advertiser,* January 5 and 16, 1786; For history of the committee and the colonization project, see Braidwood, *Black Poor and White Philanthropists,* 63–107; Fryer, *Staying Power,* 191–202; Fyfe, *A History of Sierra Leone;* Hall, *Macaulay and Son,* 19–49; Hanley, *Beyond Slavery and Abolition,* 55–58, 175–202; Jasanoff, *Liberty's Exiles,* 12, 127–35, 279–312.

6. Garcia, "The Transports of Lascar Specters," 55; Visram, *Asians in Britain,* 22–23, 367; Visram, *Ayahs, Lascars and Princes,* 34–54.

7. Rede, *The Road to the Stage,* 34; Felsenstein, *English Trader, Indian Maid,* 168; *Morning Herald,* August 6, 1787; Bhattacharya, "Family Jewels," 207–8; Colman, *Inkle and Yarico,* 213. Felsenstein calculates that *Inkle and Yarico* was staged 164 times between 1787 and 1800.

8. Miller, *Slaves to Fashion,* 47; O'Quinn, "Mercantile Deformities," 389; Angelo, *Reminiscences of Henry Angelo,* 452. Angelo calls Soubise "the *Black Prince,* as he was self-dubbed, and so designated in a portrait, a small whole-length, published by Darling, in Great Newport-street." The portrait is lost. Here I build on O'Quinn's argument that *Inkle and Yarico* is a key text for understanding "the racialization of class on the London stage."

9. *World and Fashionable Advertiser,* August 6, 1787; Rede, *The Road to the Stage,* 34; Anderson, *Shakespeare and the Legacy of Loss,* 27. Anderson shows that Rede's excuse was likewise used by actors like Garrick who wished to drop blackface roles in favor of tragic ones. For the parodying and impersonation of racialized and ethnic voices offstage, see Mulholland, *Sounding Imperial;* DeWispelare, *Multilingual Subjects.*

10. Kelly, "Foreword," xiii–xiv; Robinson, *Black Marxism,* 4.

11. Rede, *The Road to the Stage,* 34; Coleridge, *Coleridge's Lectures on Shakespeare,* 170; Hawkins, *The Life of Edmund Kean,* 1:221; Smith, "We are Othello," 119; Hall, "*Othello* and the Problem of Blackness," 357–58. Kean used the aforementioned excuse that burnt cork obscured facial features to justify his "bronze" *Othello.*

12. The *Tatler* quoted in Miller, *Slaves to Fashion,* 52; Bristol, "Charivari and the Comedy of Abjection in Othello." While Othello's blackface may have subjected him to ironic subversion on the early modern stage (as Bristol argues), in the eighteenth century he was a straight tragic role. For Garrick's Othello costume, see Pentzell, "Garrick's Costuming," 33; Nicoll, *The Garrick Stage;* 156–63; Furness, *Shakespeare,* 6:404. My thinking on this subject shifted during an e-mail correspondence with Kathleen Wilson, whom I thank for sharing her sources and insights. For Peg Woffington, see Cave, Richard Allen. 2004 "Woffington, Margaret [Peg] (1720?—1760), actress." *ODNB.* 28 Jul. 2019. https:// www-oxforddnb-com.libproxy2.usc.edu/view/10.1093/ref:odnb/9780198614128.001. 0001/odnb-9780198614128-e-29820; Brody, *Impossible Purities,* 98–129. Woffington was also a lover of Domenico Angelo, Soubise's fencing master. Fare, Malcolm. 2013 "Angelo, Domenico [formerly Angiolo Domenico Maria Tremamondo] (1717–1802),

fencing master." *ODNB.* 29 Jul. 2019. https://www-oxforddnb-com.libproxy2.usc.edu/view/10.1093/ref:odnb/9780198614128.001.0001/odnb-9780198614128-e-544.

13. Behn, *Oroonoko,* 12; Yang, "Asia Out of Place," 235, 238; Aravamudan, *Tropicopolitans,* 59, 65, 29–70. For more on pet slaves, see Dabydeen, *Hogarth's Blacks,* 21–34; Fryer, *Staying Power,* 21, 25, 73; Gerzina, *Black London,* 15–17, 54; Hall, *Things of Darkness,* 240–53; Miller, *Slaves to Fashion,* 48–57.

14. Watt, *British Orientalisms,* 101–6. For *Oroonoko*'s production history, see Anderson, *Shakespeare and the Legacy of Loss,* 51; Vaughan, *Performing Blackness on English Stages,* 150; Hogan, *The London Stage Part V,* vols. 1 and 2.

15. Coke, *The Letters and Journals of Lady Mary Coke,* 194–95; Angelo, *Reminiscences of Henry Angelo,* 1:447–48. Soubise was never the duke's valet, as has at times been erroneously suggested.

16. Angelo, *Reminiscences of Henry Angelo,* 1:447–52. For Soubise's stylization as a dandy, see Miller, *Slaves to Fashion,* 57–70.

17. *Nocturnal Revels,* 1:210–13; Wilson, *The Island Race,* 63–71; Carretta, Vincent. "Sessarakoo, William Ansah (b. c. 1730, d. 1770), African visitor to Britain." *ODNB.* 4 Oct. 2012; https://www-oxforddnb-com.libproxy2.usc.edu/view/10.1093/ref:odnb/9780198614128.001.0001/odnb-9780198614128-e-97280 (accessed July 30, 2019).

18. *Nocturnal Revels,* 1:228.

19. Hall, "New Ethnicities"; Castle, *Masquerade and Civilization*; Russell, *Women, Sociability and Theater in Georgian London,* 104; *Nocturnal Revels,* 1:220–32. For Islamic slaveholding practices, see Segal, *Islam's Black Slaves*; Campbell, *The Structure of Slavery in Indian Ocean Africa and Asia*; Harris, *The African Presence in Asia*; Jayasuriya and Angenot, *Uncovering the History of Africans in Asia*; Jayasuriya and Pankhurst, *The African Diaspora in the Indian Ocean.* I thank Omari Weekes for insights into how Soubise navigates "new ethnicities."

20. Blackburn, *The Making of New World Slavery*; Maclean, *Looking East*; Maclean and Matar, *Britain and the Islamic World*; Matar, *Islam in Britain*; Matar, *Turks, Moors, and Englishmen*; Garcia, *Islam and the English Enlightenment*; Sweet, "The Iberian Roots of American Racist Thought"; Loomba, "Periodization, Race, and Global Contact"; Loomba and Burton, *Race in Early Modern England*; Martinez, *Genealogical Fictions*; Segal, *Islam's Black Slaves,* 56. On the Ottoman context for *Othello,* see Vaughan, "Supersubtle Venetians." For Mungo's speech and popularity, see Carlson, "New Lows in Eighteenth-Century Theater"; Cooley, "An Early Representation of African-American English"; Miller, *Slaves to Fashion,* 27–41, 72–76; Oldham, "The 'Ties of Soft Humanity,'" 10; Wheeler, "Sounding Black-ish."

21. Cervantes Saavedra, *El zeloso estremeno,* 10.

22. Smith, *An Inquiry into the Nature and Causes of the Wealth of Nations*; Russell, *Women, Sociability and Theatre in Georgian London,* 39; Summers, *Empress of Pleasures,* 201; *General Evening Post,* April 30–May 2, 1772; Rowe, "Beckford's Insatiable Caliph," 186.

23. *Nocturnal Revels,* 1:221, 226–27; Palmer, "Brazen Cheek"; DeGalan, "Lead White or Dead White?"; Williams, *Powder and Paint*; Piper, *The English Face,* 141–43; Festa, "Cosmetic Differences."

24. Rosenthal, "Visceral Culture," 567; Fanon, *Wretched of the Earth,* 5. It's worth noting that even though we are told that Miss G— is an heiress, her use of cosmetics might flag her as a courtesan instead (prostitution is, after all, the topic of *Nocturnal Revels*), making her rejection of Soubise all the more stinging.

25. Angelo's income was thus comparable to that of Samuel Foote. *Argus,* December 29, 1789; Angelo, *Reminiscences of Henry Angelo,* 104; Aylward, *The English Master of Arms,* 198; *Gazetteer and New Daily Advertiser,* June 20, 1767. For more on Angelo's academy, see Cohen, "Fencing and the Market in Aristocratic Masculinity"; Mattfeld, *Becoming Centaur,* 113–27.

26. Angelo, *Angelo's Pic Nic,* 1:61. An earlier version of this paragraph and the following paragraph appeared in Cohen, "Fencing and the Market in Aristocratic Masculinity."

27. Nussbaum, *The Limits of the Human,* 8; Russell, *Women, Sociability and Theatre in Georgian London,* 67; Tague, *Animal Companions,* 120.

28. Soubise's celebrity coincided with a crucial decade in the evolution of British ideals of aristocratic masculinity. See Russell, *The Theatres of War;* O'Quinn, *Entertaining Crisis,* 243–301; Carter, *Men and the Emergence of Polite Society.*

29. Robb, *Sentiment and Self;* Robb, *Sex and Sensibility;* Robb, *Useful Friendship.* This paragraph and the four that follow it are adapted from Cohen, "Julius Soubise in India."

30. *Calcutta Gazette,* March 26, 1789. Soubise bore a "large Scar on the left side of the Throat" from this encounter until his death. BL Add MS 45606, 245.

31. *Bengal: Past and Present* 40, pt. 2 (1930): 157; Busteed, *Echoes from Old Calcutta,* 185; BL Add MS 45592, 21–23; BL Add MS 45590, 195–99; BL Add MS 45581, 112; BL Add MS 45588, 148, 152; BL Add MS 45589, 295–96; BL Add MS 45603, 233. In 1797 (the year before Soubise's death) Catherine Pawson "played with great applause at the Theatre."

32. BL Add MS 45590, 196–97; Gerzina, *Black London,* 21–22, 50; BL Add MS 45591, 91, 83; Robb, *Sex and Sensibility,* 213. For relationships between European men and Indian women, see Ghosh, *Sex and the Family in Colonial India.* Robb suggests that "class and social status often mattered more than race" in guiding Blechynden's treatment of women.

33. BL Add MS 45591, 109; BL Add MS 45592, 153–57; Robb, *Sentiment and Self,* 163–79. Blechynden's mixed-race children were educated as Europeans; and their descendants passed as white.

34. *Hicky's Bengal Gazette,* December 23, 1780.

35. Kapila, "Race Matters," 473; Loomba, "Racism in India," 181–84, 191; Robb, *The Concept of Race in South Asia.* Most studies of race in India focus on the post-Mutiny period. See, for example, Sinha, *Colonial Masculinity;* Ballantyne, *Orientalism and Race;* Ballhatchet, *Race, Sex and Class Under the Raj.*

36. Alam, "The Pursuit of Persian," 328; Schimmel, "Hindu and Turk," 107–11, 116; Eaton, "Introduction," 11.

37. Sancho, *Letters of the Late Ignatius Sancho,* 28, 148 205; BL Ad mss IOR/L/MAR/B/259A–D.

38. Cannadine, *Ornamentalism*, 8; Dalrymple, *White Mughals*; Sen, *Distant Sovereignty*, 18. This psychic affiliation also had important implications for caste. Viswanath argues that "a de-facto alliance between British and Indian officials and native high-caste employers of Pariah laborers" allowed caste-based forms of agrarian slavery to survive into the twentieth century. Islam generalizes this picture, arguing that an unspoken pact between British rulers and caste elites meant that the former left the caste system intact, and even protected it. Viswanath, *The Pariah Problem*, 3; Islam, "Recasting the Coolie," 165–66.

39. Hakala, *Negotiating Languages*, 8, 21–22, 33–75. I thank Walt for his generous and helpful feedback on an earlier version of this chapter.

40. Richardson, *A Dictionary, Persian, Arabic, and English*, 1269; Gilchrist, *A Dictionary of English and Hindoostanee*, xvi–xvii. The *OED* defines "negro" as "A member of a dark-skinned group of peoples originally native to sub-Saharan Africa; a person of black African origin or descent." "Negro, n. and adj." *OED Online*. June 2019. Oxford University Press. https://www-oed-com.libproxy1.usc.edu/view/Entry/125898?redirect edFrom=negro (accessed July 31, 2019).

41. Burton, *Brown over Black*; Gandhi quoted in Roy, "The Doctor and the Saint," 67. For anti-African racism in India and Gandhi's South Africa, see Loomba, "Racism in India," 181–82.

42. Gilroy, *The Black Atlantic*, 1.

43. BL Add MS 45591, 199–202; Fisher, *A Clash of Cultures*; Lee, *Virginia Woolf*, 88. For de l'Etang's employment by the Nawab, see BL IOR/F/4/508/12262.

44. Landry, *Noble Brutes*; Edwards, Enekel and Graham, *The Horse as Cultural Icon*; Allen, *Swimming with Dr. Johnson and Mrs. Thrale*; Mattfeld, *Becoming Centaur*.

45. Gommans, "The Horse Trade in Eighteenth-Century South Asia"; Meadows, "The Horse"; Lally, "Empires and Equines," 98–113; Doniger, "Presidential Address," 95; BL IOR/F/4/453; Landry, *Noble Brutes*, 16; Nugent, *Lady Nugent's East India Journal*, 139.

46. This account of Bucephalus is indebted to Donna Landry, whose generous comments greatly improved this chapter, especially my discussion of horsemanship.

47. For more on the full arc of their friendship, see Cohen, "Julius Soubise in India."

48. *Calcutta Chronicle*, December 11, 1788; Landry, *Noble Brutes*, 48–49; Mattfeld, *Becoming Centaur*.

THREE   Political Slavery and Oriental Despotism from Haiti to Bengal

1. *The Salisbury and Winchester Journal*, April 23, 1804; *The Morning Post*, July 23, 1804; *Times of London*, September 26, 1804. To my knowledge, no French original exists for this proclamation.

2. Stieber, *Haiti's Paper War*; Gaffield, *Haitian Connections*, 83–92. Stieber argues that the massacres were a well-considered strategic choice, part of "a multi-front political

strategy to maintain antislavery, anticolonial independence at all costs." She also suggests that Dessalinean rhetoric is an underappreciated origin point for the Black radical tradition.

3. Dubois, *Slaves and Other Objects* 125–26; Gibbon, *The History of The Decline and Fall of the Roman Empire*, 3:80. For the history of the word "despotism" see Koebner, "Despot and Despotism"; Nyquist, *Arbitrary Rule*, 169. My sense of political slavery in antiquity is indebted to Nyquist and DuBois.

In *Samuel Johnson's Dictionary*, "Despot. *n.f.*" is defined as "An absolute prince; one that governs with unlimited authority." "Despotical, *adj.*" is defined as "Absolute in power; unlimited in authority; arbitrary, unaccountable." "Despotism, *n.f.*" is defined as "Absolute Power." "Tyrannick, *adj.*" is defined as "a tyrant; cruel; despotick." "Tyranny" is defined as "Absolute monarchy tyrannously administered." "Tyrant, *n.f.*" is defined as "An absolute monarch governing imperiously" and "A cruel despotick and sever master; an oppressor." Given that despotism and tyranny were virtually interchangeable in the period under study, I use them that way in this chapter.

4. Dubois, *Slaves and Other Objects*, 125–26; Nyquist, *Arbitrary Rule*, 12. For the Stuarts and slavery, see my discussion below and Brewer, "Slavery, Sovereignty, and 'Inheritable Blood.'"

5. Gaffield, *Haitian Connections*, 9. My understanding of Dessalinean rhetoric is indebted to Stieber, *Haiti's Paper War*. Scholars still debate whether or not Dessalines actually proclaimed Haiti a "republic," although he certainly sought to make use of this term's caché in the Atlantic print sphere. Dessalines officially proclaimed the empire of Haiti in September 1804, but he backdated various official documents to January and February, when he signed and accepted his nomination for emperor, as Stieber explains.

6. *The English Review* quoted in Hastings, *Memoir*, 212; Dalrymple, *Retrospective View*, 70–71. For more on this way of viewing the subcontinent's past, see Sen, *Distant Sovereignty*, 27–56.

7. Ferguson, *An Essay on the History of Civil Society*, 380.

8. Ibid.; Dow, *History of Hindostan*, 3:2; quoted in Eacott, *Selling Empire*, 201.

9. Major, *Slavery, Abolitionism and Empire in India*, 9; Chatterjee, *Gender, Slavery and Law in Colonial India*; Chatterjee and Eaton, *Slavery and South Asian History*; Viswanath, *The Pariah Problem*; Arondekar, "What More Remains"; Allen, "Carrying Away the Unfortunate"; Allen, "Suppressing a Nefarious Traffic"; Kumar, "Colonialism, Bondage, and Caste in British India"; Prakash, *Bonded Histories*; Huzzey, *Freedom Burning*.

In a substantial critique of Prakash, Viswanath warns of the danger of collapsing political and chattel slavery, albeit not in these terms. Prakash confuses the rhetoric of political slavery with the practice of chattel slavery when he argues in "Terms of Servitude" that the British invented slavery in India: when "they abolished slavery in 1843 . . . what the British actually did . . . was abolish their own creations" (131). This argument is absolutely unsupportable in light of available evidence. Scholarship definitively shows that many forms of slavery predated colonial rule. Viswanath is particularly concerned with Prakash's complicity in concealing forms of agrestic caste-based slavery. See *The Pariah Problem*, 245, 274, 333–34.

10. Dobie, *Trading Places*, 9; de Man, "The Epistemology of Metaphor," 13; Ricoeur, *The Rule of Metaphor*, 18, 20; Goldstein, *Sweet Science*, 1–10; Pasanek, *Metaphors of Mind*, x, 6, 19–22.

11. Nyquist, *Arbitrary Rule*, 20–56; Dubois, *Slaves and Other Objects*, 125, 128; "despot, n." *OED Online*. June 2019. Oxford University Press. https://www-oed-com.libproxy1.usc.edu/view/Entry/51024?redirectedFrom=despot (accessed August 5, 2019).

12. Aristotle, *The Politics*, 84, 96; Nyquist, *Arbitrary Rule*, 26–28; Plutarch quoted in Koebner, "Despot and Despotism," 278.

13. Orme, *Historical fragments*, 437, 425; Chapelain quoted in Armitage and Subrahmanyam, "Introduction," xv.

14. Wheeler, *The Complexion of Race*, 188–92; McLaren, "From Analysis to Prescription"; Montesquieu, *The Spirit of Laws*, 1:325, 279; Dow, *History of Hindostan*, xxii. For more on geographic and climatic determinism see *The Complexion of Race*, 1–48.

15. Fullarton, *A view of the English interests in India*, 247; Montesquieu, *The Spirit of Laws*, 1:328; Sen, *Distant Sovereignty*, 94.

16. Sen, *Distant Sovereignty*, 13.

17. Prior to the eighteenth century, the Ottomans were often considered a part of Europe. Ingram, *Writing the Ottomans*, 1, 3; Osterhammel, *Unfabling the East*, 2, 38–65; Goffman, *The Ottoman Empire and Early Modern Europe*, 18–20; Ingram, "English Literature on the Ottoman Turks," 1–2; Knolles, *The Generall Historie of the Turkes*, 1154. For more on the Ottomans and early modern England, see Barbour, *Before Orientalism*; Maclean, *Looking East*; Maclean and Matar, *Britain and the Islamic World*; Matar, *Islam in Britain*; Matar, *Turks, Moors, and Englishmen*. For the eighteenth century, see O'Quinn, *Engaging the Ottoman Empire*.

18. Ingram, *Writing the Ottomans*, 59; Ingram, "English Literature on the Ottoman Turks," 165–5; Knolles, *The Generall Historie of the Turkes*, 1155; Nyquist, *Arbitrary Rule*, 82–84. Knolles's *Commonweale* was not a straight translation of Bodin; it was a synthesis of French and Latin editions. I thank Ania Loomba for the insight about premodern empires.

19. Bodin, *The six bookes of a common-weale*, 212, 202.

20. Cedric, *Black Marxism*, 9–28; Kelley, "Foreword," xiii; Bodin, *The six bookes of a common-weale*, 201–3. Robinson also draws connections between classical precedents and the racialization of poverty under European feudalism.

21. Di Palma, *Wasteland*, 14; Hill, *The World Turned Upside Down*, 19; Thompson, *The Making of the English Working Class*, 87.

22. Sieyès, *Emmanuel Joseph Sieyès*, 47, 117, 45; Nyquist, *Arbitrary Rule*, 148; Bailyn, *The Ideological Origins of the American Revolution*, 81–83. Nyquist notes that radicals indicted the monarchy and "landowners responsible for enclosing the commons" on the charge of reducing "their subjects to abject 'slavery'" during the Civil War. The "Norman Yoke" also featured in American Patriot writings.

23. Guha, *A Rule of Property for Bengal*, 17–24; Dow, *History of Hindostan*, lxxxv; Grant, *An Inquiry*, 2–3; Rouse, *Dissertation concerning the Landed Property of Bengal*, iv, 94–95; Marx, *Karl Marx on Colonialism and Modernization*, 427, 233, 295. Elsewhere I

have argued that the events of 1857 led Karl Marx (who covered Indian affairs as a journalist for the *New York Tribune*) to revise his so-called Asiatic Mode of production, arguing that ultimate property ownership lay not with the so-called despot but with "village corporations."

24. Pettit, *Republicanism*, 31–32; Eacott, *Selling Empire*, 209; Dorsey, "To 'Corroborate Our Own Claims,'" 355; Priestley, *The Present State of Liberty in Great Britain and her Colonies*, iv; Price, *Observations on the Nature of Civil Liberty*, 28–29. Pettit does not mention India a single time in his history of the Euro-American republican tradition. Perhaps this oversight stems from his downplaying of republicanism's Athenian roots, since despotism is less strongly associated with Asia in Roman sources. Mary Nyquist corrects this oversight, insisting that Roman anti-tyranny discourse is in fact "much indebted to its Greek originators." The historiography of the American Crisis might also be to blame for Pettit's oversight: prior to the past few years, it generally overlooked India. For example, Bailyn does discuss the Asian connections of despotism, but he does not make the link to colonial India. Similarly, in his seminal book on American slavery, Davis discusses Aristotle at length without mentioning Asia or the context of the Persian wars. See Lovett, Frank, "Republicanism," *The Stanford Encyclopedia of Philosophy* (Summer 2018 Edition), Edward N. Zalta, ed. https://plato.stanford.edu/archives/sum2018/ entries/republicanism/; Bailyn, *The Ideological Origins of the American Revolution*, 63–65; Nyquist, *Arbitrary Rule*, 13; Davis, *The Problem of Slavery in Western Culture*, 69–72.

25. Nash, "Sparks from the Altar of '76," 6–8, 12; Johnson quoted in Gerzina, *Black London*, 45.

26. Hey, *Observations on the Nature of Civil Liberty*, 24; Johnson's dictionary quoted in Pasanek, *Metaphors of Mind*, 19.

27. Brown, *Moral Capital*, 243; Davis, *The Problem of Slavery in the Age of Revolution*, 386; Equiano, *The Interesting Narrative*, 144, 243; Koebner, "Despot and Despotism," 288–89; Nyquist, *Arbitrary Rule*, 169.

28. Bodin, *The six bookes of a common-weale*, 201; Brewer, "Slavery, Sovereignty, and 'Inheritable Blood,'" 1049, 1056. The Stuarts also attempted to pursue imperialism in India as a part of their absolutist agenda, but they were defeated. See Vaughan, "John Company Armed."

29. Gray, *Doctor Price's Notions*, 22; Ferguson, *Remarks on a Pamphlet*, 25.

30. Price, *A Discourse on the Love of Our Country*, 31.

31. Ibid., 39–40, 50.

32. Burke private correspondence quoted in Dreyer, "The Genesis of Burke's Reflections," 466.

33. Dessalines quoted in Gaffield, *Haitian Connections*, 53.

34. Sulivan, *An analysis of the political history of India*, 290–91; Campbell, *A narrative of the extraordinary adventures*, 264. For plays about Tipu Sultan, see O'Quinn, *Staging Governance*, 312–48.

35. Corbet quoted in Gaffield, *Haitian Connections*, 74. All quotes about Christophe in this paragraph are from McIntosh and Pierrot, "Capturing the likeness of Henry I of Haiti," 6, 9, 17. For Nugent's diplomacy with Haiti, see Gaffield (61–181).

36. Thompson, *The Making of the English Working Class*, 90; Spence, *Pig's meat*, 3:150; Makdisi, "Immortal Joy," 23-24.

37. *Authentic memoirs of Tippo Sultaun*, 2; Nugent, *Lady Nugent's Journal of her Residence in Jamaica*, 48; Hill, *The Jamaican Stage*, 229-39; Burton, *Afro-Creole Power*, 65-67, 74, 82-83.

38. The decision to feature Tipu's children is not as idiosyncratic as it might seem: they loomed fairly large in the European imagination, as they were famously held captive by Lord Cornwallis following the Third Anglo-Mysore War. Indeed, one of Tipu's sons is a central character in "Lame Jervas," a story by Maria Edgeworth discussed in the next chapter.

FOUR The Geography of Freedom in the Age of Revolutions

1. Patrick C. Lipscomb III, "Stephen, James (1758–1832), lawyer and slavery abolitionist." *ODNB*. 23 Sep. 2004. https://www-oxforddnb-com.libproxy2.usc.edu/view/10.1093/ref:odnb/9780198614128.001.0001/odnb-9780198614128-e-26373 (accessed Sept. 10, 2019).

2. Dow, *History of Hindostan*, 3:2; Marshall, "The Moral Swing to the East"; Harlow, *The Founding of the Second British Empire*; Davis, *The Problem of Slavery in the Age of Revolution*, 62; Brown, *Moral Capital*, 209-12.

3. Marshall, "The Moral Swing to the East," 81; Chatterjee, *Gender, Slavery and Law in Colonial India*; Chatterjee and Eaton, *Slavery and South Asian History*; Viswanath, *The Pariah Problem*. For more on slavery in India, see Chapter 3.

4. Hartman, *Scenes of Subjection*, 7; Lowe, *The Intimacies of Four Continents*; Holt, *The Problem of Freedom*, 6; Sell, "Capital Through Slavery." Along similar lines, Zach Sell argues: "projects to universalize free labor often depended upon the proliferation of coercion."

5. Lowe, *The Intimacies of Four Continents*, 45–46.

6. Parker, *Evidence of Our Transactions in the East Indies*, vii.

7. Ibid., 26-27. For Burgoyne, see Hargrove, *General John Burgoyne*, 59-62.

8. Marshall, *The Writings and Speeches of Edmund Burke*, 5:26, 378-80; Cannon, *The Fox-North Coalition*, 142-53, 166. Sir George Nugent's patron, George Grenville, played a key role in this constitutional crisis by announcing that MPs who voted for Fox's bill would be considered enemies of the king. This was an unconstitutional use of the king's name, or "secret influence," a capital crime. Terrified of prosecution, Grenville resigned; and George III hinted at abdication.

9. Marshall, *The Writings and Speeches of Edmund Burke*, 6:1-2; Suleri, *The Rhetoric of English India*, 49-74; Aravamudan, *Tropicopolitans*, 223-29; O'Quinn, *Staging Governance*, 164-221; Taylor, *Theatres of Opposition*, 67-118; Agnani, *Hating Empire Properly*, 109-32.

10. Burke, "Speech on Opening of Impeachment," in Marshall and Todd, eds., *The Writings and Speeches of Edmund Burke*, 6:346-47; Dalrymple, *Retrospective View*, 70-71.

11. O'Quinn, *Staging Governance*, 271; Aravamudan, *Tropicopolitans*, 227. For the gendered and sexual dimensions of Oriental despotism, see Watt, *British Orientalisms*, 79–122.

12. Starke, *Sword of Peace*, 6–7, 49.

13. Ibid.; "congee|congé, n," *OED* Online. July 2018. Oxford University Press. http://www.oed.com.libproxy1.usc.edu/view/Entry/39046?rskey=4dqZyQ&result=1 (accessed September 7, 2018); O'Quinn, *Staging Governance*, 290–92.

14. Sharp quoted in Brown, *Moral Capital*, 243; Roach, "The Global Parasol." For so-called pet slaves in English portraiture, see Aravamudan, *Tropicopolitans*, 34–39; Miller, *Slaves to Fashion*, 50–51; Hall, *Things of Darkness*, 211–53.

15. Starke, *Sword of Peace*, 20–22; Watt, *British Orientalisms*, 82. Watt advances a related argument: "In thus invoking these different notions of slavery, *The Sword of Peace* helps us to think about the terms on which Britons could imagine themselves as possessed of free will and agency."

16. Cox, *Slavery, Abolition, and Emancipation*, 130; Nussbaum, "Between 'Oriental' and 'Blacks So Called,'" 141; Brown, *Moral Capital*, 162; Marshall, *The Writings and Speeches of Edmund Burke*, 6:4–5.

17. Starke, *Sword of Peace*, 32; Adolphus, *Memoirs of John Bannister*, 1:167–68.

18. Starke, *Sword of Peace*, 12, 32, 57; O'Quinn, *Staging Governance*, 273–76, 387 n15, 297; Dirks, *The Scandal of Empire*, 123.

19. Dirks, *The Scandal of Empire*, 21, 85; Brown, *Moral Capital*, 29. For Crown patronage, see Cohen, "The 'Aristocratic Imperialists,'" 8–10; Marshall, "Empire and Opportunity," 125–26.

20. Burke, *Reflections on the Revolution in France*, 10; Pitts, *A Turn to Empire*.

21. It's worth noting that by 1804, Napoleon had reinstalled slavery in the French colonies, losing Haiti in the process. *Morning Chronicle*, June 13, 1804; Rigg, J. M., and Rebecca Mills. "Ellis, George (1753–1815), writer." *ODNB*. 23 Sep. 2004; https://www-oxforddnb-com.libproxy2.usc.edu/view/10.1093/ref:odnb/9780198614128.001.0001/odnb-9780198614128-e-8692 (accessed Sept. 14, 2019); Davis, *The Problem of Slavery in the Age of Revolution*, 364–65, 380. Radicals continued to support abolition on both sides of the Atlantic. See Drescher, "Cart Whip and Billy Roller"; Hollis, "Anti-Slavery and British Working-Class Radicalism"; Foner, "Abolitionism and the Labor Movement."

22. Butler, *Maria Edgeworth*, 96, 111, 124, 138; Boulukos, "Maria Edgeworth's 'Grateful Negro,'" 12–13; Dunne, "'A gentleman's estate,'" 104; Kim, "Maria Edgeworth's *The Grateful Negro*," 105–6, 119–22; Kelly, "Class, Gender, Nation, and Empire," 89–93. Critics have sometimes overstated Edgeworth's radicalism; but, as Butler observes, she identified more with her class interests than her father did, and she even tried to obfuscate the extent of his radicalism after his death.

23. Edgeworth, "On the Education of the Poor," 6–7, 51. For more on this essay, see Cohen, "Wage Slavery," 197–201; Smyth, "'That *This Here* Box.'"

24. Kim, "Maria Edgeworth's *The Grateful Negro*," 105–6; Paine, *Rights of Man*, 130. One of the few books that attempts to treat the 1790s in a global framework is Armitage and Subrahmanyam, eds., *The Age of Revolutions in Global Context*. Tipu Sultan

never actually founded a Jacobin club. See Smith, Blake, "The Citizen-Sultan? A Jacobin Club In India," *The Age of Revolutions*. https://ageofrevolutions.com/2016/05/09/the-citizen-sultan-a-jacobin-club-in-india/(accessed Dec. 28, 2018).

25. Cohen, *Lady Nugent's East India Journal*, 10–11, 48, 97; Jasanoff, *Liberty's Exiles*, 338; Butler, *Maria Edgeworth*, 97–98, 208, 229–30; Dodwell and Miles, *Alphabetical List*, 154–55, 370–71.

26. Payton, *The Making of Modern Cornwall*, 75, 73–81; Deacon, *A Concise History of Cornwall*, 106–10; Nandy, Somendra C. "Amir Chand [Omichund, Umichund] (d. 1758), merchant." *ODNB*. 23 Sep. 2004. https://www-oxforddnb-com.libproxy2.usc.edu/view/10.1093/ref:odnb/9780198614128.001.0001/odnb-9780198614128-e-63551 (accessed Sept. 14, 2019). Cornwall's "culture of technical ingenuity was attracting some of the most inventive minds in Britain," including the inventor of the safety lamp, Sir Humphrey Davy, from whom Edgeworth learned about Cornish mining. For Edgeworth's blending of fact and fiction, see Gamer, "Maria Edgeworth and the Romance of Real Life."

27. Edgeworth, *Popular Tales*, 1:85, 105.

28. Stokes, *The English Utilitarians and India*, 45; Otto, *The Life and Letters of Lord Macaulay*, 240; Edgeworth, "On the Education of the Poor," 11–13; Fanon, *The Wretched of the Earth*, 3–4.

29. Edgeworth, *Castle Rackrent and Ennui*, 215–16; Edgeworth, *Popular Tales*, 1:91, 122.

30. Edgeworth, *Castle Rackrent and Ennui*, 215–16; Edgeworth, *Popular Tales*, 1:98–100, 116.

31. Edgeworth, *Popular Tales*, 3:184–85, 192, 198–99, 206, 224; Richardson, *Literature, Education, and Romanticism*, 226.

32. *Morning Chronicle*, June 7, 1804; Edgeworth, *Popular Tales*, 1:116. In "The Grateful Negro," Edgeworth also draws attention to the risk posed by slaves born in Africa, as both rebel leaders were survivors of the middle passage.

33. Mallipeddi, *Spectacular Suffering*, 109–45; Edgeworth, *Popular Tales*, 3:195; Holt, *The Problem of Freedom*, 34, 38.

34. Edgeworth, *Popular Tales*, 1:6–7.

35. Ibid., 1:24, 26–28, 129, 3:224. In India, Jervas's life is saved by a slave: "The grateful Saheb."

36. Islam, "Recasting the Coolie," 88; Hartman, *Scenes of Subjection*, 7; Edgeworth, *Popular Tales*, 7.

37. Holt, *The Problem of Freedom*, 39; Hartman, *Scenes of Subjection*, 137–38; Bentham, *The Works of Jeremy Bentham*, 7:188; Sell, "Capital Through Slavery." Hartman's discussion of Bentham is indebted to Davis, *The Problem of Slavery*, 456. Zach Sell similarly argues, in an antebellum US context: "abolitionists relied upon divisions which marked slavery and freedom as diametrically opposed. Yet, such oppositions left unconsidered forms of expropriation and dispossession outside of this dichotomy."

38. Baptist, *The Half Has Never Been Told*, 130; Hobbes, *Leviathan*, 3–4; Edgeworth, *Practical Education*, 228; Crimmins, "Bentham and Hobbes." The literature on the subject of labor management and colonial slavery is growing quickly, upending the

conventional wisdom of an earlier generation of scholars that management strategies were developed to oversee free laborers in the metropole. See, for example, Cooke, "The Denial of Slavery"; Rosenthal, "Slavery's Scientific Management"; van der Linden, "Reconstructing the Origins of Modern Labor Management"; Esch and Roediger, *The Production of Difference*. Although Esch and Roediger focus on the twentieth century, they draw connections between the plantation overseer and the factory supervisor.

39. Bentham, *An Introduction to the Principles of Morals and Legislation,* i, 1; Bentham, *The Works of Jeremy Bentham,* 10:216. In the preface to his *Introduction,* Bentham attributes the delay in publication to finding himself "unexpectedly entangled in an unsuspected corner of the metaphysical maze," another relatively transparent reference to the liberty and necessity debates. For example, Richard Hey, in his response to Richard Price's *Observations on the Nature of Civil Liberty* similarly refers to the liberty and necessity debates as "that ocean of controversy into which Metaphysicians, Moralists, Philosophers, Divines, have launched in great numbers." Bentham prepared notes on Hey's pamphlet for his close friend John Lind, who was writing his own rebuttal to Price (in line with Hey's) with Bentham's help. Hey, *Observations on the Nature of Civil Liberty,* 22; Bentham, *The Correspondence of Jeremy Bentham,* 1:310n158.

40. Pettit, *A Theory of Freedom,* 1; Ulmer, "William Wordsworth and Philosophical Necessity," 172; Molivas, "Richard Price, the Debate on Free Will, and Natural Rights," 106; Burke, *Reflections on the Revolution in France,* 61.

41. Bentham, *The Works of Jeremy Bentham,* 10:216; Pettit, *A Theory of Freedom,* 124–51; Pettit, *Republicanism,* 35–37, 45; Crimmins, "Bentham and Hobbes"; Stokes, *The English Utilitarians and India,* xvi, 72. For Edgeworth's relation to Bentham, see Hausermann, *The Genevese Background,* 49–59. She most admired Bentham's translator and mouthpiece in continental Europe, Etienne Dumont, whom she met in Paris in 1802 and subsequently corresponded with for decades.

Pettit's account does need to be amended on one point: the whitewashed picture he paints of the revolutionary age. For example, he explains Hobbes's renewed appeal thusly: "it became clear, towards the end of the eighteenth century, that with citizenship extended beyond the realm of propertied males, it was no longer possible to think of making all citizens free in the old sense: in particular it was not feasible, under received ideas, to think of conferring freedom as non-domination on women and servants." In point of fact, one of the strongest impetuses for rethinking freedom came from the uprising on Saint-Domingue, which made it seem inevitable that liberty would eventually be extended to—or forcibly seized by—enslaved Africans all over the Atlantic.

42. Price, *Observations on the Nature of Civil Liberty,* 3; Hey, *Observations on the Nature of Civil Liberty,* 22; Price and Priestley, *A Free Discussion,* 145–46.

43. Kramnick, *Actions and Objects,* 6, 35–37; Price and Priestley, *A Free Discussion,* 145–46.

44. Johnson, "On Agency," 114–15; Price and Priestley, *A Free Discussion,* 145–46; Pettit, *Republicanism,* viii, 8–9, 22; Kramnick, *Actions and Objects,* 6, 35–36.

45. Price and Priestley, *A Free Discussion,* 152; Edgeworth, *Practical Education,* 1:244, 57. Priestley uses "voluntary" to signal that humans can choose, to a degree, what

circumstances they put themselves in, thereby participating in the formation of the association of ideas, the "internal" mechanism for Priestley's determinism. Edgeworth was especially attracted to Priestley's combination of necessitarianism and association-ism. See Price, *Revolutions in Taste*, 109–16; Butler, *Maria Edgeworth*, 62; Oliver, *A Study of Maria Edgeworth*, 529–30.

46. Edgeworth, *Popular Tales*, 1:49–51.

47. Price and Priestley, *A Free Discussion*, 342, 139, 143, 158.

48. Kramnick, *Actions and Objects from Hobbes to Richardson*, 35, 40–41; Price and Priestley, *A Free Discussion*, xxiv, 177–78.

49. Oliver, *A Study of Maria Edgeworth*, 536; quoted in Brunon-Ernst, *Beyond Foucault*, 1.

50. Williams, *Capitalism and Slavery*, 123.

51. Edgeworth, "On the Education of the Poor," 3; Lowe, *The Intimacies of Four Continents*, 6; "Minute of the board of trade," August 7, 1792, in *East-India Sugar*, 52–53. These positions are echoed in Henry Grey's critique of Henry Taylor's plan for emanci-pation: "The essential difference between the slave & the free labourer is that the latter is induced to work by motives which act upon his reason the former by the fear of bodily pain." Quoted in Holt, *The Problem of Freedom*, 47.

52. Edgeworth, *Popular Tales*, 3:194, 226, 239; Edgeworth, *Practical Education*, 1:254.

53. Hartman, *Scenes of Subjection*, 5; Holt, *The Problem of Freedom*, xix, xxii.

54. Guha, *A Rule of Property for Bengal*, 40; Stokes, *The English Utilitarians and India*, 39; Harvey and Moten, *The Undercommons*, 57.

55. Colebrooke, *Remarks on the Husbandry*, 79–81; *The Anti-Jacobin Review and Magazine* 25 (1807): 70–79; Marshall, "The Moral Swing to the East," 81; Chatterjee, *Gender, Slavery and Law in Colonial India*, 6; Hartman, *Scenes of Subjection*, 110–12, 119, 233n3. For Colebrook's biography, see Rocher and Rocher, *The Making of Western Indology*; and Gombrich, Richard F. 2004 "Colebrooke, Henry Thomas (1765–1837), administrator in India and scholar." *ODNB*. 1 Jul. 2019. https://www-oxforddnb-com.libproxy2.usc.edu/view/10.1093/ref:odnb/9780198614128.001.0001/odnb-9780198614128-e-5866.

56. Viswanath, *The Pariah Problem*, 4–5, 8, 241, 331.

57. Rocher and Rocher, *The Making of Western Indology*, 96–99; Viswanath, *The Pariah Problem*, 5–8.

58. Lowe, *The Intimacies of Four Continents*, 46; Islam, "Recasting the Coolie," 1, 3, 7–8, 12–13, 78–79, 161; Kumar, "Colonialism, Bondage, and Caste in British India," 125; Sell, "Capital Through Slavery." Sell adds yet another experiment to this list: "from 1839 to 1849, the East India Company brought ten white U.S. plantation overseers to India to introduce an 'American system' of cotton cultivation capable of competing in 'quantity and quality' with the United States." At least one British abolitionist, Thomas Clarkson, supported the scheme, which he described as providential. Like Colebrooke before him, Clarkson emphasized the low cost of labor in India. For those involved in this scheme, Sell argues, "the condition of colonial labor was assumed to be free."

59. For a nuanced account of formal freedom's shortcomings, see Kazanjian, *The Brink of Freedom*.

FIVE A Sociable and Aristocratic Empire

1. The Huntington (HEH) Stowe Temple Grenville (STG) Correspondence 8(50); Foucault, *Society Must Be Defended,* 164, 228.

2. Lambert and Lester, *Colonial Lives;* Brown, "Inter-colonial migration," 206.

3. "Indies, n." *OED Online.* September 2019. Oxford University Press. https://www-oed-com.libproxy1.usc.edu/view/Entry/94445?rskey=u7s2bh&result=2 (accessed Sept. 21, 2019).

4. Greig and Vickery, "The Political Day in Georgian London"; Joseph, *Reading the East India Company,* 15.

5. Elias, *The Court Society,* 96.

6. For colonial lives, see Anderson, *Subaltern Lives,* 12–16; Lambert and Lester, *Colonial Lives;* Hall, *Civilising Subjects,* 23–65; Hall, *Macaulay and Son;* Colley, *Captives;* Colley, *The Ordeal of Elizabeth Marsh;* Rothschild, *The Inner Life of Empires;* Jasanoff, *Liberty's Exiles;* Ogborn, *Global Lives;* "Biography and History: Inextricably Interwoven," a special issue of the *Journal of Interdisciplinary History* 40, no. 3 (2010); "Critical Feminist Biography," a special issue of *Journal of Women's History* 21, no. 3–4 (2009); *The American Historical Review* 114, no. 3 (2009); *Journal of British Studies* 53, no. 3 (2014).

7. Our bourgeois distinctions are easier to leave behind as our own society's wealth gap widens, making inherited wealth and connections increasingly vital to career success. Latour, *Reassembling the Social,* 165–71; Elias, *The Court Society,* 18, 52–53, 74, 96–97; Goodman, "Public Sphere and Private Life"; Smith, "The Court in England"; Greig, *The Beau Monde.* Greig points out that the beau monde and the ruling elite overlapped almost entirely.

8. Marshall, "The Moral Swing to the East," 70, 85; Marshall, "Empire and Opportunity in Britain," 125–26. For an extended argument about the role of the empire in the aristocracy's rebounding fortunes, see Cohen, "The 'Aristocratic Imperialists.'"

9. Colley, *Britons,* 177–93; Nugent, *Lady Nugent's Journal of her Residence in Jamaica,* 1; Bayly, *Imperial Meridian,* 133, 155. Colley uses the term "service elite" to indicate that "Heroes" like General Wolfe were of service to the state. My point here is that the late Georgian/Regency state did not serve all Britons equally; rather, it was predatory, corrupt, and parasitic. Nor did it serve Africans and Indians who were captured, enslaved, and colonized for profit by British subjects and trading companies.

10. Namier, *The Structure of Politics,* 220–25; Cannon, *Aristocratic Century,* 97–99; Thompson, "Eighteenth-Century English Society," 141; Hume, "The Value of Money," 377; Harling, *The Waning of Old Corruption,* 72; Cannon, *The Fox-North Coalition,* 132–70; Beckett, *The Rise and Fall of the Grenvilles,* 71–72; quoted in Dyck, *William Cobbett,* 72. In truth, Lord Buckingham was politically incompetent. His Achilles's heel was his dogged loyalty to George III. In 1783 he offered the most infamous proof of his devotion by unconstitutionally using the king's name in order to defeat Charles James Fox's India Bill (see Chapter 4). After this episode, he was a persona non grata so far as the ministry was concerned; his serious political career was effectively over. Nonetheless, he managed to repeat his misstep only a few years later. In 1789, when he was lord lieutenant of

Ireland, he seriously undermined his own authority by refusing to transmit the Irish parliament's vote to invest the Prince of Wales with full regency powers during the king's illness. The king's speedy recovery robbed this foolhardy sign of fidelity of any political utility, so that he once again appeared in the guise of a politically incompetent royal lackey. Moreover, he earned the resentment of the Prince of Wales, which may explain the latter's treatment of Nugent when he gave away Nugent's job to Lord Moira.

11. Marx, *Karl Marx on Colonialism*, 91, 222–25; Namier, *The Structure of Politics*, 224; Nugent, *Lady Nugent's Journal of her Residence in Jamaica*, 28, 63; Finn and Smith, *The East India Company at Home*; Wade, *The Black Book*, 344–72; Hannah Young, "Researching Female Slave-owners at the Huntington Library," blog post, *Legacies of British Slave-Ownership*, 30 May 2014, https://lbsatucl.wordpress.com/2014/05/30/researching-female-slave-owners-at-the-huntington-library/. In 1835, following emancipation, Young reports, Lady Temple claimed compensation for 379 enslaved people living on the estate, to the tune of over £6,000.

12. Jasanoff, *Liberty's Exiles*, 338; Shammas, "British Investing in Financial Assets Before 1800," 6; Allen, "Class Structure and Inequality," 105–10.

13. Wright, "Introduction," xii–xiv; Woodland, Patrick. "Nugent, Robert Craggs, Earl Nugent (1709–1788), politician and poet." *ODNB*. 23 Sep. 2004. https://www-oxforddnb-com.libproxy2.usc.edu/view/10.1093/ref:odnb/9780198614128.001.0001/odnb-9780198614128-e-20399 (accessed Sept. 21, 2019); Boyden, Peter B. "Nugent [formerly Fennings], Sir George, first baronet (1757–1849), army officer." *ODNB*. 23 Sep. 2004. https://www-oxforddnb-com.libproxy2.usc.edu/view/10.1093/ref:odnb/9780198614128.001.0001/odnb-9780198614128-e-20390 (accessed Sept. 21, 2019). Philip Wright suggests that Nugent and his brother inherited their grandfather's personal estate (£200,000), but I can find no evidence that this was the case; indeed, it seems unlikely given the disarray of Nugent's finances before his departure for India, discussed below.

14. Purvis, Thomas L. "Skinner, Cortlandt (1727–1799), politician and army officer in America." *ODNB*. 23 Sep. 2004. https://www-oxforddnb-com.libproxy2.usc.edu/view/10.1093/ref:odnb/9780198614128.001.0001/odnb-9780198614128-e-53720 (accessed Sept. 21, 2019); Raza, Rosemary Cargill. "Nugent [née Skinner], Maria, Lady Nugent (1770/71–1834), diarist." *ODNB*. 23 Sep. 2004. https://www-oxforddnb-com.libproxy2.usc.edu/view/10.1093/ref:odnb/9780198614128.001.0001/odnb-9780198614128-e-47677 (accessed Sept. 21, 2019); Jasanoff, *Liberty's Exiles*, 28–29; Nugent, *Lady Nugent's East India Journal*, xiv; MacGregor, *History of the Clan Gregor*, 299–301.

15. Elias, *The Court Society*, 96; Beckett, *The Rise and Fall of the Grenvilles*, 83; Robson, "Purchase and Promotion," 60; Sack, *The Grenvillites 1801–1829*, 45.

16. Cannon, *Aristocratic Century*, 119; Bruce, *The Purchase System*; Nelson, *Francis Rawdon-Hastings*, 144–49; Cohen, "The 'Aristocratic Imperialists,'" 8–9; Nugent, *Lady Nugent's East India Journal*, 279. Francis Rawdon-Hastings was desperately in debt, largely as a result of loans made to the Prince of Wales. In lieu of repayment, the Prince Regent appointed him governor-general *and* commander-in-chief on November 18,

1812, only sixteen months after the Nugents had sailed for India. These were the two most profitable positions in the empire, and Lord Moira expected to receive both salaries. To his dismay, he did not. We might speculate that the Prince Regent's snubbing of Nugent was partly motivated by his antipathy to Lord Buckingham, who had taken the side of George III during the regency crisis of 1789 (see n. 10 above).

17. Centre for Buckinghamshire Studies D-FR/233/1; Kettering, "Friendship and Clientage"; Tadmor, *Family and Friends*, 11, 167–68; Nugent, *Lady Nugent's Journal of her Residence in Jamaica*, 256, 259–60, 268; Nugent, *Lady Nugent's East India Journal*, 202.

18. Tadmor, *Family and Friends*, 28; Lambert and Lester, *Colonial Lives*, 26; Sack, *The Grenvillites 1801–1829*, 46–47; Robson, "Purchase and Promotion in the British Army in the Eighteenth Century," 60.

19. HEH STG Correspondence 9(5)(9). "The fact is," Lady Nugent explains, "Col. O— commands at a Place on the very borders of Cashmere from where all the fine shawls are brought. The Sovereign of the district that Col. Ochterloy [*sic*] commands has lately made war against and conquered the King of Cashmere. In consequence all the beautiful manufacture of that place is of easy access and Col. O— has been able to make the beautiful selection he has sent you. All of my shawls now look like Frumpery and I shall be ashamed to show them by the side of yours. You have 4 scarlet and gold, 2 plain Scarlet, and 2 most beautiful black, 2 very plain white and 2 white with a running Pattern all over the edge. This is very uncommon and much esteemed by *Judges of Shawls*." I am grateful to Naomi Tadmor and Vanessa Wilkie for conversations about how patronage benefited the dignity of the patron.

20. Wright, "Introduction," xv; Robins, *Champagne and Silver Buckles*, 13.

21. Wright, "Introduction," xv, xxii; Nugent, *Lady Nugent's Journal of her Residence in Jamaica*, 18, 20, 184, 273; HEH STG Correspondence 44(12); BL Add MS 59004 f.18.

22. Nugent, *Lady Nugent's Journal of her Residence in Jamaica*, 47, 277; Peers, *Between Mars and Mammon*, 49; BL Add MS 59004 f.30; HEH STG Correspondence 48(11). For Crown patronage, see Marshall, "The Moral Swing to the East," 78; Cohen, "The 'Aristocratic Imperialists.'" In December 1801, Lady Nugent wrote in her journal: "Confess my misery, that the dear name of mother will never greet my ear probably."

23. HEH STG Correspondence 48(11)(13), 8(48); Nugent, *Lady Nugent's Journal of her Residence in Jamaica*, 252, 259.

24. Wright, "Introduction," xv; Nugent, *Lady Nugent's Journal of her Residence in Jamaica*, 1, 276; Nugent, *Lady Nugent's East India Journal*, 40.

25. HEH STG Correspondence 8(50). An earlier version of this paragraph and the three that follow were published in Cohen, "The 'Aristocratic Imperialists.'"

26. HEH STG Correspondence 9(2)(9)(10).

27. Elias, *The Court Society*, 96; HEH STG Correspondence 9(2), 48(12); Sack, *The Grenvillites 1801–1829*, xiii.

28. Seccombe, Thomas, and H. C. G. Matthew. "Fremantle, Thomas Francis, first Baron Cottesloe, and Baron Fremantle in the nobility of the Austrian empire (1798–1890), politician and civil servant." *ODNB*. 23 Sep. 2004. https://www-oxforddnb-com.libproxy2.

usc.edu/view/10.1093/ref:odnb/9780198614128.001.0001/odnb-9780198614128-e-10160 (accessed Sept. 21, 2019). The fact that a number of Fremantle's close kin were Catholics must have been another cause for concern, as the Nugents had long feared that Lady Buckingham's influence would lead Louisa to convert to Catholicism. Seccombe mistakenly indicates that the Nugents were Catholics; they were not. See Nugent, *Lady Nugent's East India Journal*, xxvi–xxvii, 371–81.

29. Colley, *Britons*, 177–93; Elias, *The Court Society*, 8.

30. Nugent, *Lady Nugent's Journal of her Residence in Jamaica*, 92, 256, 266; National Library of Scotland-Minto Correspondence 11307 f.67; Elias, *The Court Society*, 92.

31. BL Add MS 59004 f.18, f.21; Nugent, *Lady Nugent's East India Journal*, 351–53; Elias, *The Court Society*, 52–53; Lord Buckingham, quoted in Beckett, *The Rise and Fall of the Grenvilles*, 70. It is worth noting that Nugent's thoughts on the issue appear to have been shaped by Lord Buckingham, who was scrupulous on the point of honors. When the latter was lord lieutenant of Ireland, he similarly pestered Grenville for reward, going so far as to send him a list of men who received various rewards (peerages, pensions, and the Garter) as "marks of the King's satisfaction" for similar postings, and asked "would it be improper or impossible to state that I am returning [from Ireland] (such as I am) without any feather?" Lord Buckingham also appears to have been in the background in 1806, egging on Nugent's sense of injustice, as the latter explained to Grenville: "I have been induced to trouble your Lordship with this Application, by the Conversations which I have had with the Marquis of Buckingham upon the Subject, and my very sore Feelings in consequence."

32. Elias, *The Court Society*, 52–53; Nugent, *Lady Nugent's Journal of her Residence in Jamaica*, xi.

33. Nugent, *Lady Nugent's Journal of her Residence in Jamaica*, 2, 12, 218; Nugent, *Lady Nugent's East India Journal*, 331, 339.

34. Elias, *The Court Society*, 52–53; Nugent, *Lady Nugent's Journal of her Residence in Jamaica*, 97; Nugent, *Lady Nugent's East India Journal*, 187.

35. Nugent, *Lady Nugent's Journal of her Residence in Jamaica*, 17, 69, 171–72.

36. Quoted in Wright, "Introduction," xiv; Nugent, *Lady Nugent's Journal of her Residence in Jamaica*, 30, 34, 89, 106, 133, 182, 200, 220; Nugent, *Lady Nugent's East India Journal*, 292; Ashelford, *The Art of Dress*, 130, 146–47; Greig, *Beau Monde*, 99–130; Skeehan, "Caribbean Women," 120.

37. Nugent, *Lady Nugent's Journal of her Residence in Jamaica*, 81, 214; Nugent, *Lady Nugent's East India Journal*, 40, 319, 329; Cohen, "The 'Aristocratic Imperialists,'" 15–16.

38. Nugent, *Lady Nugent's East India Journal*, 311, 324, 338–39, 461; Nugent, *Lady Nugent's Journal of her Residence in Jamaica*, 69.

39. Nugent, *Lady Nugent's Journal of her Residence in Jamaica*, 259, 263–64. Sir George Nugent also sent back political information in letters. See, for example, Nugent, *Lady Nugent's East India Journal*, 354–59.

40. In 1783, Burke counted "two hundred and fifty young gentlemen" who worked under the governor general of India, "some of them of the best families in England." Burke, *The Writings and Speeches of Edmund Burke*, 5:434.

41. HEH STG Correspondence 44(14).

42. Nugent, *Lady Nugent's East India Journal,* 64; HEH STG Correspondence 44(14)(18). Nugent explained to Lord Buckingham: "I don't write to Lord Fortescue about him, as he might think it necessary to answer my Letter and it would give him Trouble."

43. Burke, *The Writings and Speeches of Edmund Burke,* 5:402–3; HEH STG Correspondence 44(18); Nugent, *Lady Nugent's East India Journal,* 48–49, 52.

44. G. F. R. Barker and E. A. Smith. "Proby, John Joshua, first earl of Carysfort (1751–1828), politician." *ODNB.* Sept. 23, 2004. https://www-oxforddnb-com.libproxy2. usc.edu/view/10.1093/ref:odnb/9780198614128.001.0001/odnb-9780198614128-e-22832 (accessed Sept. 22, 2019).

45. HEH STG Correspondence 44(12); Nugent, *Lady Nugent's Journal of her Residence in Jamaica,* 221; "Anthony Gilbert Storer," *Legacies of British Slave-ownership database,* http://www.depts-live.ucl.ac.uk/lbs/person/view/1320236682 (accessed Sept. 13, 2016).

46. Nugent, *Lady Nugent's Journal of her Residence in Jamaica,* 65, 78, 83; Wright, "Introduction," ixxx.

47. Nugent, *Lady Nugent's Journal of her Residence in Jamaica,* 42, 171–72; Nugent, *Lady Nugent's East India Journal,* 101; HEH STG Correspondence 82(14). An earlier version of this paragraph and the two following appeared in Cohen, "The 'Aristocratic Imperialists.'"

48. Nugent, *Lady Nugent's East India Journal,* xlviii–xlix, 54–55, 306–7, 310–11, 439. Lady Nugent enlisted Lady Loudon as an ally in this cause. Working together, the two ladies undertook "a tedious investigation of the Orphan School establishment" and wrote up their findings.

49. HEH STG Correspondence 82(14); Vickery, *The Gentleman's Daughter,* 239–41; Nugent, *Lady Nugent's East India Journal,* 310–11; Russell, *Women, Sociability, and Theatre,* 11.

50. Nugent, *Lady Nugent's East India Journal,* 295–96, 314; Greig, *Beau Monde,* 201; Clark, *British Clubs and Societies,* 427. The transition to fashionable forms of private sociability on the part of Calcutta's Anglo elite is noted in passing by Clark. For Cornwallis, see V. E. R. Anderson, "The Eurasian Problem in Nineteenth Century India." The young couple were both from a social class located just below the Nugents. However, their fortunes were on the rise. Gilbert was the son of a vicar, but managed, by his military service, to be made a baronet. Ross was the daughter of an army officer. It is unclear how she became Lord Moira's ward; perhaps she was a relation.

Coda

1. The epigraph is quoted in Bain, *Empire Express,* 666; Arrighi, *The Long Twentieth Century,* xi, 9–14, 30–31, 49.

2. Arrighi, *The Long Twentieth Century,* 240.

3. This paragraph is based on Bain, *Empire Express,* 3–15.

4. Whitman, "Passage to India," 63–67; Smith, *Virgin Land,* 20–29; Mapp, *The Elusive West,* 101; Jefferson, *Notes on the State of Virginia,* 107; Whitney, *Project for a Railroad to the Pacific,* 1.

5. Benton quoted in Smith, *Virgin Land,* 28–29.

6. Chakrabarty, "Provincializing Europe," 353.

7. Bogues, *Black Heretics, Black Prophets,* 16–17. Although she is a poet rather than a scholar, M. NourbeSe Philip has given us an astonishing illustration of this unlearning (of colonial reason) and relearning (of alternative epistemologies) in her poem *Zong!*

8. Khatun, *Australianama,* 14, 23; Ma, *The Age of Silver,* 3. Stieber's work does this for a Dessalinian strand of Haitian thought that has been systematically overlooked in favor of republicanism.

Bibliography

Abu-Lughod, Janet L. *Before European Hegemony: The World System A.D. 1250–1350.* New York: Oxford University Press, 1989.

Adams, William Henry Davenport. *English Party Leaders and English Parties from Walpole to Peel.* London: Tinsley Brothers, 1878.

Adolphus, John. *Memoirs of John Bannister, Comedian.* London: Richard Bentley, 1839.

Agnani, Sunil M. *Hating Empire Properly: The Two Indies and the Limits of Enlightenment Anticolonialism.* New York: Fordham University Press, 2013.

Airès, Philippe. "L'histoire des mentalités." In *La nouvelle histoire,* edited by Jacques Le Geoff, 402–23. Paris: Éditions Complexe, 1978.

Alam, Muzaffar. "The Pursuit of Persian: Language in Mughal Politics." *Modern Asian Studies* 32, no. 2 (May 1998): 317–49.

Allen, Brian. *Francis Hayman.* New Haven, CT: Yale University Press, 1987.

Allen, Julia. *Swimming with Dr. Johnson and Mrs. Thrale: Sport, Health and Exercise in Eighteenth-Century England.* Cambridge: Cambridge University Press, 2012.

Allen, Richard B. "Carrying Away the Unfortunate: The Exportation of Slaves from India during the Late Eighteenth Century." In *Le Monde Créole: Peuplement, sociétés et condition humaine, Xviie–Xxe siècles: Mélanges offerts à Hubert Gerbeau,* edited by Hubert Gerbeau et al. Paris: Indes savantes, 2005.

———. "Suppressing a Nefarious Traffic: Britain and the Abolition of Slave Trading in India and the Western Indian Ocean, 1770–1830." *William and Mary Quarterly* 66, no. 4 (2009): 873–94.

Allen, Robert C. "Class Structure and Inequality During the Industrial Revolution: Lessons from England's Social Tables, 1688–1867." *The Economic History Review* 72, no. 1 (2019): 88–125.

Althusser, Louis, Etienne Balibar, Roger Establet, Pierre Macherey, and Jacques Rancière. *Reading Capital: The Complete Edition.* Translated by Ben Brewster and David Fernbach. New York: Verso, 2015.

Anderson, Benedict. *Imagined Communities: Reflections on the Origins and Spread of Nationalism.* New York: Verso, 2006.

Anderson, Clare. *Subaltern Lives: Biographies of Colonialism in the Indian Ocean World, 1790–1920.* Cambridge: Cambridge University Press, 2012.

Anderson, Emily. *Shakespeare and the Legacy of Loss.* Ann Arbor: University of Michigan Press, 2018.

Anderson, Perry. *Arguments Within English Marxism.* New York: Verso, 1980.

Anderson, Valerie E. R. "The Eurasian Problem in Nineteenth Century India." PhD diss., SOAS (School of Oriental and African Studies), 2011.

Andrew, Donna T. *Aristocratic Vice: The Attack on Duelling, Suicide, Adultery, and Gambling in Eighteenth-Century England.* New Haven, CT: Yale University Press, 2013.

Angelo, Henry Charles William. *Reminiscences of Henry Angelo.* London: Henry Colburn and Richard Bentley, 1830.

Anker, Elizabeth A., and Rita Felski, eds. *Critique and Post Critique.* Durham, NC: Duke University Press, 2017.

Aravamudan, Srinivas. "East Indies and West Indies: Comparative Misapprehensions." *Anthropological Forum* 16, no. 3 (2006): 291–309.

———. *Enlightenment Orientalism: Resisting the Rise of the Novel.* Chicago: University of Chicago Press, 2012.

———. *Tropicopolitans: Colonialism and Agency, 1688–1804.* Durham, NC: Duke University Press, 1999.

Armitage, David, and Sanjay Subrahmanyam, eds. *The Age of Revolutions in Global Context, c. 1760–1840.* Basingstoke: Macmillan, 2010.

Armitage, David, and Sanjay Subrahmanyam. "Introduction: The Age of Revolutions, c. 1760–1840: Global Causation, Connection, and Comparison." In Armitage and Subrahmanyam, eds., *The Age of Revolutions in Global Context*, xii–xxxii.

Aristotle. *The Politics and the Constitution of Athens.* Edited by Stephen Everson. Cambridge: Cambridge University Press, 1996.

Arondekar, Anjali. "What More Remains: Slavery, Sexuality, South Asia." *History of the Present: A Journal of Critical History* 6, no. 2 (Fall 2016): 146–54.

Arrighi, Giovanni. *The Long Twentieth Century: Money, Power, and the Origins of Our Times.* London: Verso, 1994.

Ashelford, Jane. *The Art of Dress: Clothes and Society, 1500–1914.* London: National Trust, 1996.

Authentic memoirs of Tippo Sultaun. Including his cruel treatment of English prisoners. London: M. Allen, 1799.

Aylward, J. D. *The English Master of Arms, from the Twelfth to the Twentieth Century.* London: Routledge and Kegan Paul, 1956.

Bailyn, Bernard. *The Ideological Origins of the American Revolution.* Cambridge, MA: Belknap Press, 1967.

Bain, David Haward. *Empire Express: Building the First Transcontinental Railroad.* New York: Viking, 1999.

Baird, John D., and Charles Ryskamp, eds. *The Poems of William Cowper: 1782–1785.* Oxford: Clarendon Press, 1995.

Ballantyne, Tony. *Orientalism and Race: Aryanism in the British Empire.* New York: Palgrave Macmillan, 2002.

———. "Race and Webs of Empire: Aryanism from India to the Pacific." *Journal of Colonialism and Colonial History* 2, no. 3 (2001).

Ballaster, Ros. *Fabulous Orients: Fictions of the East in England 1662–1785.* Oxford: Oxford University Press, 2005.

Ballhatchet, Kenneth. *Race, Sex and Class Under the Raj: Imperial Attitudes and Policies and Their Critics 1792–1805.* London: Palgrave Macmillan, 1980.

Baptist, Edward E. *The Half Has Never Been Told: Slavery and the Making of American Capitalism.* New York: Basic Books, 2014.

Barad, Karen. *Meeting the Universe Halfway: Quantum Physics and the Entanglement of Matter and Meaning.* Durham, NC: Duke University Press, 2007.

Barbour, Richmond. *Before Orientalism: London's Theatre of the East, 1576–1626.* Cambridge: Cambridge University Press, 2003.

Barchas, Janine. *Matters of Fact in Jane Austen: History, Location, and Celebrity.* Baltimore: Johns Hopkins University Press, 2012.

Bayly, C. A. *Imperial Meridian: The British Empire and the World 1780–1830.* London: Longman, 1989.

Beckert, Sven. *Empire of Cotton: A Global History.* New York: Vintage Books, 2015.

Beckett, John. *The Rise and Fall of the Grenvilles: Dukes of Buckingham and Chandos.* Manchester: Manchester University Press, 1994.

Behn, Aphra. *Oroonoko and Other Writings.* Oxford: Oxford World's Classics, 1994.

Bentham, Jeremy. *The Correspondence of Jeremy Bentham.* Edited by Timothy L. S. Sprigge. London: UCL Press, 2017.

———. *An Introduction to the Principles of Morals and Legislation.* London: T. Payne, 1789.

———. *The Works of Jeremy Bentham.* Edinburgh: William Tait, 1840.

Berlant, Lauren. "Thinking About Feeling Historical." *Emotion, Space and Society* 1 (2008): 4–9.

Best, Stephen, and Sharon Marcus. "Surface Reading: An Introduction." *Representations* 108, no. 1 (2009): 1–21.

Bhattacharya, Nandini. "Family Jewels: George Colman's '*Inkle and Yarico*' and Connoisseurship." *Eighteenth-Century Studies* 34, no. 2 (2001): 207–26.

Birnbaum, Norman. "The *Annales* School and Social Theory." *Review (Fernand Braudel Center)* 1, no. 3/4 (Winter–Spring, 1978): 225–35.

Blackburn, Robin. *The Making of New World Slavery: From the Baroque to the Modern, 1492–1800.* London: Verso, 1997.

Bloch, Marc. *The Historian's Craft.* Translated by Peter Putnam. New York: Vintage Books, 1953.

———. *The Royal Touch: Sacred Monarchy and Scrofula in England and France.* Translated by J. E. Anderson. London: Routledge and Kegan Paul, 1973.

Bodin, Jean. *The six bookes of a common-weale.* Translated by Richard Knolles. London: G. Bishop, 1606.

Bogues, Anthony. *Black Heretics, Black Prophets: Radical Political Intellectuals.* New York: Routledge, 2003.

de Bolla, Peter. *The Education of the Eye: Painting, Landscape, and Architecture in Eighteenth-Century Britain.* Stanford, CA: Stanford University Press, 2003.

Bolt, Christine, and Seymour Drescher, eds. *Anti-Slavery, Religion and Reform: Essays in Memory of Roger Anstey.* Kent: Dawson, 1980.

Booth, Marilyn, and Antoinette Burton. "Editor's Note: Critical Feminist Biography." *Journal of Women's History* 21 (2009): 7–12.

Boulukos, George E. "Maria Edgeworth's 'Grateful Negro' and the Sentimental Argument for Slavery." *Eighteenth-Century Life* 28 (1999): 12–29.

Bowen, H. V. *The Business of Empire: The East India Company and Imperial Britain, 1756–1833.* Cambridge: Cambridge University Press, 2006.

———. "Perceptions from the Periphery: Colonial American Views of Britain's Asiatic Empire, 1756–1783." In *Negotiated Empires: Centers and Peripheries in the Americas, 1500–1820,* edited by Christine Daniels and Michael V. Kennedy, 283–300. New York: Routledge, 2002.

———. *Revenue and Reform: The India Problem in British Politics, 1757–1773.* Cambridge: Cambridge University Press, 2002.

Bowen, H. V., Elizabeth Mancke, and John G. Reid, eds. *Britain's Oceanic Empire: Atlantic and Indian Ocean Worlds, c. 1550–1850.* Cambridge: Cambridge University Press, 2012.

Braidwood, Stephen J. *Black Poor and White Philanthropists: London's Blacks and the Foundation of the Sierra Leone Settlement 1786–1791.* Liverpool: Liverpool University Press, 1994.

Braudel, Fernand. "En guise de conclusion." *Review (Fernand Braudel Center)* 1, no. 3/4 (Winter–Spring, 1978): 243–61.

Brewer, Holly. "Slavery, Sovereignty, and 'Inheritable Blood': Reconsidering John Locke and the Origins of American Slavery." *American Historical Review* 122, no. 4 (October 2017): 1038–78.

Bricker, Andrew Benjamin. "After the Golden Age: Libel, Caricature, and the Deverbalization of Satire." *Eighteenth-Century Studies* 51, no. 3 (2018): 305–36.

Bristol, Michael D. "Charivari and the Comedy of Abjection in Othello." *Renaissance Drama* 21 (1990): 3–21.

Brody, Jennifer DeVere. *Impossible Purities: Blackness, Femininity, and Victorian Culture.* Durham, NC: Duke University Press, 1998.

Brown, Christopher Leslie. *Moral Capital: Foundations of British Abolitionism.* Chapel Hill: University of North Carolina Press, 2006.

Brown, Laura. "Shock Effect: *Evelina*'s Monkey and the Marriage Plot." *The Eighteenth-Century Novel* 6–7 (2009): 379–407.

Brown, Laurence. "Inter-colonial Migration and the Refashioning of Indentured Labor: Arthur Gordon in Trinidad, Mauritius and Fiji (1866–1880)." In Lambert and Lester, *Colonial Lives Across the British Empire*, 204–27.

Bruce, Anthony. *The Purchase System in the British Army, 1660–1871*. London: Royal Historical Society, 1980.

Brunon-Ernst, Anne, ed. *Beyond Foucault: New Perspectives on Bentham's Panopticon*. Surrey: Ashgate, 2012.

Bruyn, Fran de, and Shaun Regan, eds. *The Culture of the Seven Years' War: Empire, Identity, and the Arts in the Eighteenth-Century Atlantic World*. Toronto: University of Toronto Press, 2014.

Burguière, André. *The Annales School: An Intellectual History*. Translated by Jane Marie Todd. Ithaca, NY: Cornell University Press, 2009.

———. "The Fate of the History of *Mentalités* in the *Annales*." In Clark, *The Annales School*, 2:404–17.

Burke, Edmund. *Speech of Burke, Esq; on American Taxation, April 19, 1774*. 3rd ed. London, 1775.

———. *Reflections on the Revolution in France*. Edited by L. G. Mitchell. Oxford: Oxford University Press, 1993.

Burke, Peter. *The French Historical Revolution: The* Annales *School, 1929–2014*. Cambridge, UK: Polity Press, 2015.

———. "Reflections on the Historical Revolution in France: The *Annales* School and British Social History." *Review (Fernand Braudel Center)* 1, no. 3/4 (Winter–Spring 1978): 147–56.

———. "Strengths and Weaknesses of the History of Mentalities." In Clark, *The Annales School*, 2:442–56.

Burney, Frances. *The Early Diary Of Frances Burney*. Edited by Annie Raine Ellis. London: George Bell and Sons, 1889.

———. *Evelina, or The History of a Young Lady's Entrance into the World*. New York: Penguin Books, 1994.

Burton, Antoinette. *Brown over Black: Race and the Politics of Postcolonial Citation*. Gurgaon (India): Three Essays Collective, 2012.

Burton, Richard D. E. *Afro-Creole Power, Opposition, and Play in the Caribbean*. Ithaca, NY: Cornell University Press, 1997.

Busteed, H. E. *Echoes from Old Calcutta: Being Chiefly Reminiscences of the Days of Warren Hastings*. Calcutta: Thacker, Spink, 1897.

Butler, Marilyn. *Maria Edgeworth: A Literary Biography*. Oxford: Clarendon Press, 1972.

Campbell, Donald. *A narrative of the extraordinary adventures, and sufferings by shipwreck & imprisonment, of Donald Campbell, Esq. of Barbreck*. London: Vernor and Hood, 1796.

Campbell, Gwyn. *The Structure of Slavery in Indian Ocean Africa and Asia*. London: Frank Cass, 2004.

Cannadine, David. *Aspects of Aristocracy: Grandeur and Decline in Modern Britain*. New Haven, CT: Yale University Press, 1994.

———. *Ornamentalism: How the British Saw Their Empire.* Oxford: Oxford University Press, 2001.

Cannon, John. *Aristocratic Century: The Peerage of Eighteenth-Century England.* Cambridge: Cambridge University Press, 1984.

———. *The Fox-North Coalition: Crisis of the Constitution, 1782–4.* Cambridge: Cambridge University Press, 1969.

Carlson, Julie A. "New Lows in Eighteenth-Century Theater: The Rise of Mungo." *European Romantic Review* 18, no. 2 (2007): 139–47.

Carter, Phillip. *Men and the Emergence of Polite Society.* London: Longman Group, 2001.

Castle, Terry. *Masquerade and Civilization: The Carnivalesque in Eighteenth-Century English Culture and Fiction.* Stanford, CA: Stanford University Press, 1986.

Cervantes Saavedra, Miguel de. *El zeloso estremeno: The Jealous Estremaduran. A novel.* Translated by J. Ozell. London: D. Midwinter, 1709.

Chakrabarty, Dipesh. "Provincializing Europe: Postcoloniality and the Critique of History." *Cultural Studies* 6, no. 3 (1992): 337–57.

Chartier, Roger. "Intellectual History and the History of Mentalités: A Dual Reevaluation." In Clark, *The Annales School,* 2:457–87.

Chatterjee, Indrani. *Gender, Slavery and Law in Colonial India.* New Delhi: Oxford University Press, 1999.

Chatterjee, Indrani, and Maxwell Eaton, eds. *Slavery and South Asian History.* Bloomington: Indiana University Press, 2006.

Chatterjee, Partha. *The Black Hole of Empire: History of a Global Practice of Power.* Princeton, NJ: Princeton University Press, 2012.

Clark, Peter. *British Clubs and Societies 1580–1800: The Origins of an Associational World.* Oxford: Oxford University Press, 2000.

Clark, Stuart, ed. *The Annales School: Critical Assessments.* London: Routledge, 1999.

Cohen, Ashley L. "The 'Aristocratic Imperialists' of Late Georgian and Regency Britain." *Eighteenth-Century Studies* 50, no.1 (Fall 2016): 5–26.

———. "Fencing and the Market in Aristocratic Masculinity." In *Sporting Cultures, 1650–1850,* edited by Daniel O'Quinn and Alexis Tadie, 66–90. Toronto: University of Toronto Press, 2018.

———. "The Global Indies: Historicizing Oceanic Metageographies." *Comparative Literature* 69, no. 1 (2017): 7–15.

———. "Julius Soubise in India." In *Britain's Black Past,* edited by Gretchen Gerzina, 215–33. Liverpool: Liverpool University Press, 2020.

———. "Wage Slavery, Oriental Despotism, and Global Labor Management in Maria Edgeworth's *Popular Tales.*" *The Eighteenth Century: Theory and Interpretation* 55, nos. 2–3 (2014): 193–215.

Coke, David, and Alan Borg. *Vauxhall Gardens, A History.* New Haven, CT: Yale University Press, 2011.

Colebrooke, Henry Thomas. *Remarks on the Husbandry and Internal Commerce of Bengal.* Calcutta, 1804; reprinted 1884.

Coleridge, Samuel Taylor. *Coleridge's Lectures on Shakespeare and Other Dramatists.* Edited by Ernest Rhys. London: J. M. Dent, 1907.

Colley, Linda. "The Apotheosis of George III: Loyalty, Royalty and the British Nation 1760–1820." *Past & Present* 102 (1984): 94–129.

———. *Britons: Forging the Nation 1707–1837.* New Haven, CT: Yale University Press, 2005.

———. *Captives: Britain, Empire and the World, 1600–1850.* London: Random House, 2002.

———. *The Ordeal of Elizabeth Marsh: A Woman in World History.* New York: Anchor Books, 2007.

Colman, George, the Younger. "Inkle and Yarico." In *English Trader, Indian Maid: Representing Gender, Race, and Slavery in the New World,* edited by Frank Felsenstein, 167–233. Baltimore: Johns Hopkins University Press, 1999.

Cooke, Bill. "The Denial of Slavery in Management Studies." *Journal of Management Studies* 40, no. 8 (December 2003): 1895–1918.

Cooley, Marianne. "An Early Representation of African-American English." In *Language Variety in the South Revisited,* edited by Cynthia Bernstein, Thomas Nunnally, and Robin Sabino, 51–58. Tuscaloosa: University of Alabama Press, 1997.

Coulombeau, Sophie. "Introduction." *Eighteenth-Century Life* 42, no. 2 (April 2018): 1–11.

Cowper, William. *The Letters and Prose Writings of William Cowper.* Edited by James King and Charles Ryskamp. Oxford: Clarendon Press, 1979.

Cox, Jeffrey, ed. *Slavery, Abolition, and Emancipation: Writings in the British Romantic Period, Volume 5, Drama.* London: Pickering and Chatto, 1999.

Crimmins, James E. "Bentham and Hobbes: An Issue of Influence." *Journal of the History of Ideas* 63, no. 4 (2002): 677–96.

Dabydeen, David. *Hogarth's Blacks: Images of Blacks in Eighteenth-Century English Art.* Manchester: Manchester University Press, 1985.

Dalrymple, Alexander. *Retrospective View of the Antient System of the East-India-Company, with a Plan of Regulation.* London: John Sewell, 1784.

Dalrymple, William. *White Mughals: Love and Betrayal in Eighteenth-Century India.* New York: Viking, 2002.

Davidoff, Leonore, and Catherine Hall. *Family Fortunes: Men and Women of the English Middle Class.* Chicago: University of Chicago Press, 1987.

Davis, David Brion. *The Problem of Slavery in the Age of Revolution, 1770–1823.* Ithaca, NY: Cornell University Press, 1999.

———. *The Problem of Slavery in Western Culture.* Ithaca, NY: Cornell University Press, 1966.

Deacon, Bernard. *A Concise History of Cornwall.* Cardiff: University of Wales, 2007.

DeGalan, Aimée Marcereau. "Lead White or Dead White? Dangerous Beauty Practices of Eighteenth-Century England." *Bulletin of the Detroit Institute of Arts* 76 (2002): 38–49.

DeWispelare, Daniel. *Multilingual Subjects: On Standard English, Its Speakers, and Others in the Long Eighteenth Century.* Philadelphia: University of Pennsylvania Press, 2017.

Desai, Gaurav. "Oceans Connect: The Indian Ocean and African Identities." *PMLA* 25, no. 3 (May 2010): 713–20.

Dirks, Nicholas B. *Castes of Mind: Colonialism and the Making of Modern India.* Princeton NJ: Princeton University Press, 2001.

——. *The Scandal of Empire: India and the Creation of Imperial Britain.* Cambridge, MA: Belknap Press of Harvard University Press, 2006.

Dobie, Madeleine. *Trading Places: Colonization and Slavery in Eighteenth-Century French Culture.* Ithaca, NY: Cornell University Press, 2010.

Dodwell, Edward, and James Samuel Miles. *Alphabetical List of the Honourable East India Company's Bengal Civil Servants. . . .* London: Longman, Orme, Brown and Co., 1839.

Doniger, Wendy. "Presidential Address: 'I have Scinde': Flogging a Dead (White Male Orientalist) Horse." *The Journal of Asian Studies* 58, no. 4 (1999): 940–60.

Doody, Margaret Anne. *Frances Burney: The Life in the Works.* Cambridge: Cambridge University Press, 1988.

Dorsey, Peter A. "To 'Corroborate Our Own Claims': Public Positioning and the Slavery Metaphor in Revolutionary America." *American Quarterly* 55, no. 3 (2003): 353–86.

Dow, Alexander. *History of Hindostan.* London: John Murray, 1772.

Drescher, Seymour. "Cart Whip and Billy Roller: Anti-Slavery and Reform Symbolism in Industrializing Britain." *Journal of Social History* 15 (1981): 3–24.

——. "On James Farr's 'So Vile and Miserable an Estate.'" *Political Theory* 16, no. 3 (1988): 502–3.

Dreyer, Frederick. "The Genesis of Burke's Reflections." *The Journal of Modern History* 50, no. 3 (1970): 462–79.

Dubois, Page. *Slaves and Other Objects.* Chicago: University of Chicago Press, 2003.

Du Bois, W. E. B. *The Souls of Black Folks.* Edited by Brent Hayes Edwards. Oxford: Oxford World's Classics, 2007.

Duby, Georges. "L'histoire des mentalités." In *L'Histoire et ses methodes: Encyclopedie de la Pleide,* edited by Charles Samaran, 436–38. Paris: Gallimard, 1961.

Dunne, Tom. "'A gentleman's estate should be a moral school': Edgeworthstown in Fact and Fiction, 1760–1840." In *Longford: Essays in County History,* edited by Raymond Gillespie and Gerard Moran, 95–121. Dublin: Lilliput Press, 1991.

Dworkin, Dennis. *Cultural Marxism in Postwar Britain: History, the New Left, and the Origins of Cultural Studies.* Durham, NC: Duke University Press, 1997.

Dyck, Ian. *William Cobbett and Rural Popular Culture.* Cambridge: Cambridge University Press, 1992.

Eacott, Jonathan. *Selling Empire: India in the Making of Britain and America, 1600–1830.* Chapel Hill: Omohundro Institute and University of North Carolina Press, 2016.

East-India Sugar: Papers Respecting the Culture and Manufacture of Sugar in British India. London: Printed by order of the Court of Proprietors of the East-India Company by E. Cox and Son, 1822.

Eaton, Richard M. "Introduction." In Chatterjee and Eaton, *Slavery and South Asian History.*

Edgeworth, Maria. *Castle Rackrent and Ennui.* New York: Penguin Classics, 1992.

———. *Popular Tales.* London: J. Johnson, 1804.

———. *Practical Education.* London: J. Johnson, 1798.

———. "On the Education of the Poor." Unpublished manuscript, University of Oxford, Bodleian Library, MS. Eng. misc. e. 1461.

Edwards, Peter, Karl A. E. Enekel, and Elspeth Graham. *The Horse as Cultural Icon: The Real and the Symbolic Horse in the Early Modern World.* Leiden: Brill, 2012.

Eley, Geoff. *A Crooked Line: From Cultural History to the History of Society.* Ann Arbor: University of Michigan Press, 2005.

Elias, Norbert. *The Court Society.* Translated by Edmund Jephcott. New York: Pantheon Books, 1983.

Ellison, Julie K. "News, Blues, and Cowper's Busy World." *Modern Language Quarterly* 62, no. 3 (2001): 219–37.

Equiano, Olaudah. *The Interesting Narrative of the Life of Olaudah Equiano, or Gustavus Vassa, the African. Written by Himself.* In *The Classic Slave Narratives,* edited by Henry Louis Gates, Jr., 15–247. New York: Signet Classic, 2002.

Erickson, Amy Louise. "Esther Sleepe, Fan-Maker, and Her Family." *Eighteenth-Century Life* 42, no. 2 (April 2018): 15–37.

Esch, Elizabeth, and David Roediger. *The Production of Difference: Race and the Management of Labor in U.S. History.* Oxford: Oxford University Press, 2012.

Fanon, Frantz. *The Wretched of the Earth.* New York: Grove Press, 1963.

Favret, Mary. *War at a Distance: Romanticism and the Making of Modern Wartime.* Princeton, NJ: Princeton University Press, 2010.

Felsenstein, Frank, ed. *English Trader, Indian Maid: Representing Gender, Race, and Slavery in the New World: An Inkle and Yarico Reader.* Baltimore: Johns Hopkins University Press, 1999.

Felski, Rita. *The Limits of Critique.* Chicago: University of Chicago Press, 2015.

Female Artifice; or, Charles Fox Outwitted. London: J. Ridley, 1774.

Ferguson, Adam. *An Essay on the History of Civil Society.* Dublin: Boulter Grierson, 1767.

———. *Remarks on a Pamphlet Lately Published by Dr. Price. . . .* London: T. Cadell, 1776.

Festa, Lynn. "Cosmetic Differences: The Changing Faces of England and France." *Studies in Eighteenth-Century Culture* 34 (2005): 25–54.

Finn, Margot, and Kate Smith, eds., *The East India Company at Home, 1757–1857.* London: UCL Press, 2018.

Foner, Eric. "Abolitionism and the Labor Movement in Antebellum America." In Bolt and Drescher, eds., *Anti-Slavery, Religion and Reform,* 254–71.

Foote, Samuel. *The Commissary.* London: P. Vaillant, 1765.

———. *The Cozeners.* London: T. Sherlock and T. Cadell, 1778.

———. *The Nabob.* London: T. Sherlock and T. Cadell, 1778.

Fordham, Douglas. *British Art and the Seven Years' War: Allegiance and Autonomy.* Philadelphia: University of Pennsylvania Press, 2010.

Foucault, Michel. *Society Must Be Defended: Lectures at the Collège de France 1975–1976*. New York: Picador, 2003.

Frank, Andre Gunder. *Reorient: Global Economy in the Asian Age*. Berkeley: University of California Press, 1998.

Fryer, Peter. *Staying Power: Black People in Britain Since 1504*. Atlantic Highlands, NJ: Pluto Press, 1984.

Fullarton, William. *A view of the English interests in India; and an account of the military operations in the southern parts of the peninsula, during the campaigns of 1782, 1783, and 1784*. London: T. Cadell, 1787.

Furet, Françoise. "Beyond the Annales." In Clark, *The Annales School*, 2:509–29.

Fyfe, Christopher. *A History of Sierra Leone*. Oxford: Oxford University Press, 1962.

Gaffield, Julia. *Haitian Connections in the Atlantic World: Recognition After Revolution*. Chapel Hill: University of North Carolina Press, 2015.

Gamer, Michael. "Maria Edgeworth and the Romance of Real Life." *Novel* 34, no. 2 (2001): 232–66.

Gamer, Michael, and Terry F. Robinson, "Mary Robinson and the Dramatic Art of the Comeback." *Studies in Romanticism* 48, no. 2 (2009): 219–56.

Games, Alison. "Beyond the Atlantic: English Globetrotters and Transoceanic Connections." *William and Mary Quarterly* 63, no. 4 (October 2006): 675–92.

Garcia, Humberto. *Islam and the English Enlightenment, 1670–1840*. Baltimore: Johns Hopkins University Press, 2012.

———. "The Transports of Lascar Specters: Dispossessed Indian Sailors in Women's Romantic Poetry." *The Eighteenth Century: Theory and Interpretation* 55, nos. 2–3 (2014): 255–72.

Gasché, Rodolphe. *The Honor of Thinking: Critique, Theory, Philosophy*. Stanford, CA: Stanford University Press, 2007.

Gerzina, Gretchen. *Black London: Life Before Emancipation*. New Brunswick, NJ: Rutgers University Press, 1995.

Ghosh, Durba. *Sex and the Family in Colonial India: The Making of Empire*. Cambridge: Cambridge University Press, 2006.

Gibbon, Edward. *The History of The Decline and Fall of the Roman Empire*. London: W. Strahan and T. Cadell, 1783.

Gilroy, Paul. *"There Ain't No Black in the Union Jack": The Cultural Politics of Race and Nation*. Chicago: University of Chicago Press, 1991.

———. *The Black Atlantic: Modernity and Double Consciousness*. Cambridge, MA: Harvard University Press, 1993.

Gismondi, Michael A. "'The Gift of Theory': A Critique of the *histoire des mentalités*." In *The Annales School: Critical Assessments*, 2:418–41. New York: Routledge, 1999.

le Goff, Jacques. "Mentalities: A New Field for Historians." In Michael Fineberg, trans., *Social Science Information, International Social Science Council* 13, no. 1 (1974): 81–97.

Goffman, Daniel. *The Ottoman Empire and Early Modern Europe*. Cambridge: Cambridge University Press, 2002.

Goldberg, Jonathan, Karen Newman, and Marcie Frank. *This Distracted Globe: World-making in Early Modern Literature.* New York: Fordham University Press, 2016.

Goldstein, Amanda Jo. *Sweet Science: Romantic Materialism and the New Logics of Life.* Chicago: University of Chicago Press, 2017.

Gommans, Jos. "The Horse Trade in Eighteenth-Century South Asia." *Journal of the Economic and Social History of the Orient* 37, no. 3 (1994): 228–50.

Goodman, Dena. "Public Sphere and Private Life: Toward a Synthesis of Current Historiographical Approaches to the Old Regime." *History and Theory* 31, no. 1 (February 1992): 1–20.

Goodman, Kevis. *Georgic Modernity and British Romanticism: Poetry and the Mediation of History.* Cambridge: Cambridge University Press, 2004.

Grant, Charles. *An Inquiry into the Nature of Zemindary Tenures in the Landed Property of Bengal, &c.* London: J. Debrett, 1790.

Gray, John. *Doctor Price's Notions of the Nature of Civil Liberty Shewn to be Contradictory to Reason and Scripture.* London: T. Becket, 1777.

Green, Nile. "Maritime Worlds and Global History: Comparing the Mediterranean and Indian Ocean through Barcelona and Bombay." *History Compass* 11, no. 9 (2013): 513–23.

Greig, Hannah. *The Beau Monde: Fashionable Society in Georgian London.* Oxford: Oxford University Press, 2013.

Greig, Hannah, and Amanda Vickery. "The Political Day in Georgian London." *Past and Present* (forthcoming).

Guha, Ranajit. *A Rule of Property for Bengal: An Essay on the Idea of Permanent Settlement.* Durham, NC: Duke University Press, 1996.

Hakala, Walter N. *Negotiating Languages: Urdu, Hindi, and the Definition of Modern South Asia.* New York: Columbia University Press, 2016.

Hall, Catherine. *Civilizing Subjects: Colony and Metropole in the English Imagination, 1830–1867.* Chicago: University of Chicago Press, 2002.

———. *Macaulay and Son: Architects of Imperial Britain.* New Haven, CT: Yale University Press, 2012.

Hall, Kim F. "*Othello* and the Problem of Blackness." In *A Companion to Shakespeare's Works: The Tragedies,* edited by Richard Dutton, Jean Howard, and Jean E. Howard, 357–74. London: Blackwell Publishing, 2003.

———. *Things of Darkness: Economies of Race and Gender in Early Modern England.* Ithaca, NY: Cornell University Press, 1995.

Hall, Stuart. "New Ethnicities." In *Black British Cultural Studies, A Reader,* edited by Houston A. Baker, Jr., Manthia Diawara, and Ruth H. Lindeborg, 163–72. Chicago: University of Chicago Press, 1996.

———. "Race, Articulation, and Societies Structured in Dominance." In *Black British Cultural Studies,* edited by Houston A. Baker Jr., Manthia Diawara, and Ruth H. Lindeborg, 16–60. Chicago: University of Chicago Press, 1996.

———. "Signification, Representation, Ideology: Althusser and the Post-Structuralist Debates." *Critical Studies in Mass Communication* 2, no. 2 (June 1985): 91–114.

Hanley, Ryan. *Beyond Slavery and Abolition: Black British Writing, c. 1770–1830.* Cambridge: Cambridge University Press, 2019.

Hargrove, Richard J., Jr. *General John Burgoyne.* Newark: University of Delaware Press, 1983.

Harlow, Vincent T. *The Founding of the Second British Empire, 1763–1793.* London: Longmans, 1964.

Harris, Jonathan Gil, ed. *Indography: Writing the "Indian" in Early Modern England.* New York: Palgrave Macmillan, 2012.

Harris, Joseph E. *The African Presence in Asia: Consequences of the East African Slave Trade.* Evanston, IL: Northwestern University Press, 1971.

Hart, John. "Frances Burney's *Evelina:* Mirvan and Mezzotint." *Eighteenth-Century Fiction* 7, no. 1 (October 1994): 51–70.

Hartman, Saidiya V. *Scenes of Subjection: Terror, Slavery, and Self-Making in Nineteenth-Century America.* New York: Oxford University Press, 1997.

Harvey, Stefano, and Fred Moten. *The Undercommons: Fugitive Planning and Black Study.* New York: Wivenhoe, 2013.

Hausermann, H. W. *The Genevese Background: Studies of Shelley, Francis Danby, Maria Edgeworth, Ruskin, Meredith, and Joseph Conrad in Geneva, with hitherto unpublished letters.* London: Routledge and Paul, 1952.

Hawkins, Frederick William. *The Life of Edmund Kean.* London: Tinsley Brothers, 1869.

Hayot, Eric. *On Literary Worlds.* New York: Oxford University Press, 2012.

Heidegger, Martin. *What Is a Thing?.* Translated by W. B. Barton and V. Deutsch. South Bend, IN: Regnery/Gateway, 1967.

Hensley, Nathan K. "Curatorial Reading and Endless War." *Victorian Studies* 56, no. 1 (2013): 59–83.

Hey, Richard. *Observations on the Nature of Civil Liberty, and the Principles of Government.* London: T. Cadell, 1776.

Hill, Christopher. *The World Turned Upside Down: Radical Ideas During the English Revolution.* London: Penguin Books, 1972.

Hill, Errol. *The Jamaican Stage, 1655–1900.* Amherst: University of Massachusetts Press, 1992.

Hobbes, Thomas. *Leviathan: With selected variants from the Latin edition of 1668.* Edited by Edwin Curley. Indianapolis: Hackett Publishing, 1994.

Hobsbawm, Eric. "British History and the *Annales:* A Note." In *On History.* London: Weidenfeld and Nicolson, 1997.

Hofmeyr, Isabel. "Universalizing the Indian Ocean." *PMLA* 25, no. 3 (May 2010): 721–29.

Hogan, Charles Beecher. *The London Stage, 1660–1800; A Calendar of Plays, Entertainments & Afterpieces, Together with Casts, Box-Receipts and Contemporary Comment.* Carbondale: Southern Illinois University Press, 1960.

Hollis, Patricia. "Anti-Slavery and British Working-Class Radicalism in the Years of Reform." In Bolt and Drescher, eds., *Anti-Slavery, Religion and Reform,* 294–315.

Holt, Thomas. *The Problem of Freedom: Race, Labor, and Politics in Jamaica and Britain, 1832–1938.* Baltimore: Johns Hopkins University Press, 1992.

Holzman, James M. *The Nabobs in England: A Study of the Returned Anglo-Indian, 1760–1785.* New York: Columbia University Press, 1926.

Hume, Robert D. "The Value of Money in Eighteenth-Century England: Incomes, Prices, Buying Power—and Some Problems in Cultural Economics." *Huntington Library Quarterly* 77, no. 4 (Winter 2014): 373–416.

Hunt, Lynn. "French History in the Last Twenty Years: The Rise and Fall of the *Annales* Paradigm." In Clark, *The Annales School,* 1:24–38.

Hutton, Patrick H. "The History of Mentalities: The New Map of Cultural History." In *The Annales School: Critical Assessments,* 2:381–403. New York: Routledge, 1999.

Huzzey, Richard. *Freedom Burning: Anti-Slavery and Empire in Victorian Britain.* Ithaca, NY: Cornell University Press, 2012.

Ingram, Anders. "English Literature on the Ottoman Turks in the Sixteenth and Seventeenth Centuries." PhD diss., University of Durham, 2009.

——. *Writing the Ottomans: Turkish History in Early Modern England.* London: Palgrave Macmillan, 2015.

Islam, Najnin. "Recasting the Coolie: Racialization, Caste, and Narratives of Asian Indentureship." PhD diss., University Pennsylvania, 2018.

Jameson, Fredric. "Cognitive Mapping." In *Marxism and the Interpretation of Culture,* edited by Cary Nelson and Lawrence Grossberg. Urbana and Chicago: University of Illinois Press, 1988.

——. *The Political Unconscious: Narrative as a Socially Symbolic Act.* Ithaca, NY: Cornell University Press, 1981.

Jasanoff, Maya. *Liberty's Exiles: The Loss of America and the Remaking of the British Empire.* London: Harper Collins, 2011.

Jayasuriya, Shihan de Silva, and Jean-Pierre Angenot. *Uncovering the History of Africans in Asia.* Leiden: Brill, 2008.

Jayasuriya, Shihan de Silva, and Richard Pankhurst. *The African Diaspora in the Indian Ocean.* Trenton, NJ: Africa World Press, 2003.

Jefferson, Thomas. *Notes on the State of Virginia.* New York: Penguin Books, 1999.

Johnson, Richard. "Edward Thompson, Eugene Genovese, and Socialist-Humanist History." *History Workshop* 6 (1978): 79–100.

Johnson, Walter. "On Agency." *Journal of Social History* 37, no. 1 (2003): 113–24.

Jones, Gareth Stedman. "History and Theory." *History Workshop* 8 (1979): 198–202.

Joseph, Betty. *Reading the East India Company 1720–1840: Colonial Currencies of Gender.* Chicago: University of Chicago Press, 2003.

——. "Worlding and Unworlding in the Long Eighteenth Century." *Eighteenth-Century Studies* 52, no. 1 (Fall 2018): 27–31.

Kareem, Sarah Tindal. *Eighteenth-Century Fiction and the Reinvention of Wonder.* Oxford: Oxford University Press, 2014.

Kaul, Suvir. *Poems of Nation, Anthems of Empire: English Verse in the Long Eighteenth Century.* Charlottesville: University of Virginia Press, 2000.

Kazanjian, David. *The Brink of Freedom: Improvising Life in the Nineteenth-Century Atlantic World.* Durham, NC: Duke University Press, 2016.

——. "Hegel, Liberia." *Diacritics* 40, no. 1 (2012): 6–39.

Kelley, Robin D. G. "Foreword." In C. J. Robinson, *Black Marxism,* xi–xxiii.

Kelly, Gary. "Class, Gender, Nation, and Empire: Money and Merit in the Writing of the Edgeworths." *Wordsworth Circle* 25, no. 2 (1994): 89–93.

Kelly, Ian. *Mr. Foote's Other Leg.* London: Picador, 2012.

Kettering, Sharon. "Friendship and Clientage in Early Modern France." *French History* 6, no. 2 (1992): 139–50.

Khatun, Samia. *Australianama: The South Asian Odyssey in Australia.* London: Hurst and Co., 2018.

Kim, Elizabeth S. "Maria Edgeworth's *The Grateful Negro:* A Site for Rewriting Rebellion." *Eighteenth-Century Fiction* 16, no. 1 (2003): 103–26.

Kinservik, Matthew J. *Disciplining Satire: The Censorship of Satiric Comedy on the Eighteenth-Century London Stage.* Lewisburg, PA: Bucknell University Press, 2002.

Knolles, Richard. *The Generall Historie of the Turkes.* London: Printed by Adam Islip, 1603.

Koebner, R. "Despot and Despotism: Vicissitudes of a Political Term." *Journal of the Warburg and Courtauld Institutes* 14, no. 3/4 (1951): 275–302.

Koehn, Nancy F. *The Power of Commerce: Economy and Governance in the First British Empire.* Ithaca, NY: Cornell University Press, 1994.

Kramnick, Jonathan. *Actions and Objects from Hobbes to Richardson.* Stanford, CA: Stanford University Press, 2010.

——. *Paper Minds: Literature and the Ecology of Consciousness.* Chicago: University of Chicago Press, 2018.

Krishnan, Sanjay. *Reading the Global: Troubling Perspectives on Britain's Empire in Asia.* New York: Columbia University Press, 2007.

Kumar, Dharma. "Colonialism, Bondage, and Caste in British India." In *Breaking the Chains: Slavery, Bondage, and Emancipation in Modern Africa and Asia,* edited by Martin A. Klein, 112–30. Madison: University of Wisconsin Press, 1993.

Lally, Jagjeet. "Empires and Equines: The Horse in Art and Exchange in South Asia, ca.1600–ca.1850." *Comparative Studies of South Asia, Africa and the Middle East* 35, no. 1 (2015): 96–116.

Lambert, David, and Alan Lester, eds. *Colonial Lives Across the British Empire: Imperial Careering in the Long Nineteenth Century.* Cambridge: Cambridge University Press, 2006.

Lambert, David, and Alan Lester. "Missionary Politics and the Captive Audience: William Shrewsbury in the Caribbean and the Cape Colony." In Lambert and Lester, eds., *Colonial Lives Across the British Empire,* 88–112.

Landry, Donna. *Noble Brutes: How Eastern Horses Transformed English Culture.* Baltimore: Johns Hopkins University Press, 2009.

Langford, Paul. *A Polite and Commercial People: England 1727–1783.* Oxford: Oxford University Press, 1989.

Latour, Bruno. *Reassembling the Social: An Introduction to Actor-Network-Theory.* Oxford: Oxford University Press, 2005.

Lawson, Philip. *The East India Company: A History.* London: Routledge, 1993.

Lee, Hermione. *Virginia Woolf.* New York: Alfred A. Knopf, 1997.

Lefebvre, Henri. *The Production of Space.* Translated by Donald Nicholson-Smith. Oxford: Blackwell, 1991.

Lester, Alan. "Imperial Circuits and Networks: Geographies of the British Empire." *History Compass* 4, no. 1 (2006): 124–41.

Lewis, Martin W., and Karen E. Wigen. *The Myth of Continents: A Critique of Metageography.* Berkeley: University of California Press, 1997.

van der Linden, Marcel. "Re-constructing the Origins of Modern Labor Management." *Labor History* 51, no. 4 (2010): 509–22.

Loomba, Ania. "Of Gifts, Ambassadors, and Copy-Cats: Diplomacy, Exchange, and Difference in Early Modern India." In *Emissaries in Early Modern Literature and Culture: Mediation, Transmission, Traffic, 1550–1700,* edited by Brinda Charry and Gitanjali Shahani, 41–76. Surrey: Ashgate, 2009.

———. "Periodization, Race, and Global Contact," *Journal of Medieval and Early Modern Studies* 37, no. 3 (2007): 595–620.

———. "Race and the Possibilities of Comparative Critique." *New Literary History* 40, no. 3 (2009): 501–22.

———. "Racism in India." In *The Routledge Companion to the Philosophy of Race,* edited by Paul C. Taylor, Linda Martin Alcoff, and Luvell Anderson, 181–99. New York: Routledge, 2018.

Lott, Eric. *Love and Theft: Blackface Minstrelsy and the American Working Class.* Oxford: Oxford University Press, 2013.

Lowe, Lisa. *The Intimacies of Four Continents.* Durham, NC: Duke University Press, 2015.

Lucas, Paul. "A Collective Biography of Students and Barristers of Lincoln's Inn, 1680–1804: A Study in the 'Aristocratic Resurgence' of the Eighteenth Century." *The Journal of Modern History* 46 (1974): 227–61.

Lyttelton, George Baron. *Letters from a Persian in England, to his Friend at Ispahan.* London: J. Millan, 1735.

Ma, Ning. *The Age of Silver: The Rise of the Novel East and West.* Oxford: Oxford University Press, 2016.

MacGregor, Amelia Georgianna Murray. *History of the Clan Gregor from Public Records and Private Collections.* Edinburgh: William Brown, 1901.

Mackie, Erin. *Rakes, Highwaymen, and Pirates: The Making of the Modern Gentleman in the Eighteenth Century.* Baltimore: Johns Hopkins University Press, 2009.

MacLean, Gerald. *Looking East: English Writing and the Ottoman Empire Before 1800.* London: Palgrave Macmillan, 2007.

MacLean, Gerald, and Nabil Matar. *Britain and the Islamic World, 1558–1713.* Oxford: Oxford University Press, 2011.

Major, Andrea. *Slavery, Abolitionism and Empire in India, 1772–1843.* Liverpool: Liverpool University Press, 2012.

Makdisi, Saree. "Immortal Joy: William Blake and the Cultural Politics of Empire." In *Blake, Nation and Empire,* edited by Steve Clark and David Worrall, 20–39. New York: Palgrave Macmillan, 2006.

——. *Romantic Imperialism: Universal Empire and the Culture of Modernity.* Cambridge: Cambridge University Press, 1998.

Mallipeddi, Ramesh. *Spectacular Suffering: Witnessing Slavery in the Eighteenth-Century British Atlantic.* Charlottesville: University of Virginia Press, 2016.

de Man, Paul. "The Epistemology of Metaphor." *Critical Inquiry* 5, no. 1 (Autumn 1978): 12–30.

Mandrou, Robert. "L'histoire des mentalités." *Encyclopædia universalis,* 8:436–8. Paris: Encyclopaedia Universalis France, 1968.

Mapp, Paul W. *The Elusive West and the Contest for Empire, 1713–1763.* Chapel Hill: University of North Carolina Press, 2011.

Marx, Karl. "The German Ideology." In *The Marx-Engels Reader.* Edited by Robert C. Tucker. New York: W. W. Norton and Company, 1978.

——. *Karl Marx on Colonialism and Modernization.* Edited by Shlomo Avineri. Garden City, NJ: Doubleday, 1968.

Marshall, P. J. "Empire and Opportunity in Britain, 1763–75: The Prothero Lecture." *Transactions of the Royal Historical Society* 5 (1995): 111–28.

——. *The Making and Unmaking of Empires: Britain, India, and America c. 1750–1783.* Oxford: Oxford University Press, 2005.

——. "The Moral Swing to the East: British Humanitarianism, India and the West Indies." In *A Free Though Conquering People: Eighteenth-Century Britain and Its Empire,* 69–95. Burlington, VT: Ashgate, 2003.

——. *The New Cambridge History of India II. Bengal: The British Bridgehead, Eastern India: 1740–1828.* Cambridge: Cambridge University Press, 1987.

Marshall, P. J., and William B. Todd, eds. *The Writings and Speeches of Edmund Burke, Vol. 5: India: Madras and Bengal: 1774–1785.* Oxford: Oxford University Press, 1981.

——. *The Writings and Speeches of Edmund Burke, Vol. 6: India: The Launching of the Hastings Impeachment: 1786–1788.* Oxford: Oxford University Press, 1991.

Martínez, María Elena. *Genealogical Fictions: Limpieza de Sangre, Religion, and Gender in Colonial Mexico.* Stanford, CA: Stanford University Press, 2008.

Massey, Doreen. *For Space.* London: Sage, 2005.

Matar, Nabil. *Islam in Britain, 1558–1685.* Cambridge: Cambridge University Press, 1998.

——. *Turks, Moors, and Englishmen in the Age of Discovery.* New York: Columbia University Press, 1999.

Mattfeld, Monica. *Becoming Centaur: Eighteenth-Century Masculinity and English Horsemanship.* State College: Penn State University Press, 2017.

McIntosh, Tabitha, and Grégory Pierrot. "Capturing the Likeness of Henry I of Haiti (1805–1822)." *Atlantic Studies* 14, no. 2 (2016): 1–25.

McKendrick, Neil. *The Birth of a Consumer Society: The Commercialization of Eighteenth-Century England.* Bloomington: Indiana University Press, 1982.

McLaren, Martha. "From Analysis to Prescription: Scottish Concepts of Asian Despotism in Early Nineteenth-Century British India." *International History Review* 15, no. 3 (1993): 469–501.

McNeil, Peter. *Pretty Gentlemen: Macaroni Men and the Eighteenth-Century Fashion World*. New Haven, CT: Yale University Press, 2018.

Meadows, Monica. "The Horse: Conspicuous Consumption of Embodied Masculinity in South Asia, 1600–1850." PhD diss., University of Washington, 2013.

Mee, Jon. *Conversable Worlds: Literature, Contention, and Community 1762 to 1830*. Oxford: Oxford University Press, 2011.

Miller, Monica. *Slaves to Fashion: Black Dandyism and the Styling of Black Diasporic Identity*. Durham, NC: Duke University Press, 2009.

Minuti, Rolando. "Oriental Despotism." *European History Online* published by the Leibniz Institute of European History, Mainz 2012-05-03. http://www.ieg-ego.eu/minutir-2012-en (accessed July 26, 2017).

Mitchell, L. G. *Charles James Fox*. Oxford: Oxford University Press, 1992.

Molivas, Gregory I. "Richard Price, the Debate on Free Will, and Natural Rights." *Journal of the History of Ideas* 58, no. 1 (1997): 105–23.

Montag, Warren. *Althusser and His Contemporaries: Philosophy's Perpetual War*. Durham, NC: Duke University Press, 2013.

de Montesquieu, M. de Secondat Baron. *The Spirit of Laws*. London: S. Crowder, 1777.

Moody, Jane. "Stolen Identities: Character, Mimicry and the Invention of Samuel Foote." In *Theatre and Celebrity in Britain, 1660–2000*, edited by Mary Luckhurst and Jane Moody, 65–89. New York: Palgrave and Macmillan, 2005.

Mulholland, James. *Sounding Imperial: Poetic Voice and the Politics of Empire, 1730–1820*. Baltimore: Johns Hopkins University Press, 2013.

Murphy, Arthur. *Know your own Mind: A Comedy*. London: T Becket, 1776.

Namier, Lewis. *The Structure of Politics at the Ascension of George III*. London: Palgrave Macmillan, 1978.

Nash, Gary B. "Sparks from the Altar of '76: International Repercussions and Reconsiderations of the American Revolution." In Armitage and Subrahmanyam, *The Age of Revolutions in Global Context*, 1–19.

Nechtman, T. W. "A Jewel in the Crown? Indian Wealth in Domestic Britain in the Late Eighteenth Century." *Eighteenth-Century Studies* 41, no. 1 (2007): 71–86.

Nelson, Paul David. *Francis Rawdon-Hastings, Marquess of Hastings: Soldier, Peer of the Realm, Governor-General of India*. Madison, NJ: Fairleigh Dickinson University Press, 2005.

Nicholson, Bob. "The Victorian Meme Machine: Remixing the Nineteenth-Century Archive." *19: Interdisciplinary Studies in the Long Nineteenth Century* 21 (2015): 1–34.

Nicoll, Allardyce. *The Garrick Stage: Theatres and Audience in the Eighteenth Century*. Manchester: Manchester University Press, 1980.

Nocturnal Revels: or, The History of King's-Place, and other Modern Nunneries. London: M. Goadby, 1779.

Nugent, Maria. *Lady Nugent's East India Journal: A Critical Edition*. Edited by Ashley L. Cohen. Delhi: Oxford University Press, 2014.

——. *Lady Nugent's Journal of her Residence in Jamaica from 1801 to 1805.* Edited by Philip Wright. Kingston: University of the West Indies Press, 2002.

Nussbaum, Felicity A. "Between 'Oriental' and 'Blacks So Called,' 1688–1788." In *The Postcolonial Enlightenment: Eighteenth-Century Colonialism and Postcolonial Theory,* edited by Daniel Carey and Lynn Festa, 38–70. Oxford: Oxford University Press, 2013.

——. *The Limits of the Human: Fictions of Anomaly, Race, and Gender in the Long Eighteenth Century.* Cambridge: Cambridge University Press, 2003.

——, ed. *The Global Eighteenth Century.* Baltimore: Johns Hopkins University Press, 2005.

Nussbaum, Felicity, and Saree Makdisi, eds. *The Arabian Nights in Historical Context Between East and West.* Oxford: Oxford University Press, 2008.

Nyquist, Mary. *Arbitrary Rule: Slavery, Tyranny, and the Power of Life and Death.* Chicago: Chicago University Press, 2013.

Ogborn, Miles. *Global Lives: Britain and the World, 1550–1800.* Cambridge: Cambridge University Press, 2008.

Oldham, J. R. "The 'Ties of Soft Humanity': Slavery and Race in British Drama, 1760–1800." *Huntington Library Quarterly* 56, no. 1 (1993): 1–14.

Oliver, Grace Atkinson. *A Study of Maria Edgeworth.* Boston: A. Williams, 1882.

O'Quinn, Daniel. *Engaging the Ottoman Empire: Vexed Mediations, 1690–1815.* Philadelphia: University of Pennsylvania Press, 2019.

——. *Entertaining Crisis in the Atlantic Imperium, 1770–1790.* Baltimore: Johns Hopkins University Press, 2011.

——. "Facing Past and Future: Joshua Reynolds's Portraits Of Augustus Keppel." In de Bruyn and Regan, eds., *The Culture of the Seven Years' War,* 307–38.

——. "Mercantile Deformities: George Colman's *Inkle and Yarico* and the Racialization of Class Relations." *Theatre Journal* 54, no. 3 (2002): 389–409.

——. *Staging Governance: Theatrical Imperialism in London 1770–1800.* Baltimore: Johns Hopkins University Press, 2005.

Orme, Robert. *Historical fragments of the Mogul empire.* London: F. Wingrave, 1805.

Orr, Bridget. *Empire on the English Stage 1660–1714.* Cambridge: Cambridge University Press, 2001.

Osterhammel, Jürgen. *Unfabling the East: The Enlightenment's Encounter with Asia.* Princeton, NJ: Princeton University Press, 2018.

Paine, Thomas. *Rights of Man. Part the Second.* London: J. S. Jordan, 1792.

Palma, Vittoria Di. *Wasteland, A History.* New Haven, CT: Yale University Press, 2014.

Palmer, Caroline. "Brazen Cheek: Face-Painters in Late Eighteenth-Century England." *Oxford Art Journal* 31, no. 2 (2008): 197–213.

Parker, Thomas. *Evidence of Our Transactions in the East Indies with an Enquiry into the General Conduct of Great Britain to Other Countries, From the Peace of Paris, in 1763.* London: Printed for Charles Dilly, 1782.

Pasanek, Brad. *Metaphors of Mind: An Eighteenth-Century Dictionary.* Baltimore: Johns Hopkins University Press, 2015.

Payton, Philip. *The Making of Modern Cornwall*. Exeter: Dyllansow Truran and Co., 1992.

Peers, Douglas M. *Between Mars and Mammon: Colonial Armies and the Garrison State and Early 19th-Century India*. London: Tauris Academic Studies, 1995.

Pentzell, Raymond J. "Garrick's Costuming." *Theatre Survey* 10, no. 1 (1969): 18–42.

Pettit, Philip. *Republicanism: A Theory of Freedom and Government*. Oxford: Oxford University Press, 1997.

———. *A Theory of Freedom: From the Psychology to the Politics of Agency*. Oxford: Oxford University Press, 2001.

Pincus, Steven. *The Heart of the Declaration: The Founders' Case for an Activist Government*. New Haven, CT: Yale University Press, 2016.

———. "The Rise and Fall of Empires: An Essay in Economic and Political Liberty." *Journal of Policy History* 29, no. 2 (2017): 305–18.

Piper, David. *The English Face*. Edited by Malcom Rogers. London: National Portrait Gallery, 1992.

Pitts, Jennifer. *A Turn to Empire: The Rise of Imperial Liberalism in Britain and France*. Princeton, NJ: Princeton University Press, 2005.

Pocock, J. G. A. *Virtue, Commerce, and History: Essays on Political Thought and History, Chiefly in the Eighteenth Century*. Cambridge: Cambridge University Press, 1985.

Prakash, Gyan. *Bonded Histories: Genealogies Of Labor Servitude in Colonial India*. Cambridge: Cambridge University Press, 1990.

———. "Terms of Servitude: The Colonial Discourse on Slavery and Bondage in India." In *Breaking the Chains: Slavery, Bondage, and Emancipation in Modern Africa and Asia*, edited by Martin A. Klein, 131–49. Madison: University of Wisconsin Press, 1993.

Price, Fiona. *Revolutions in Taste, 1773–1818: Women Writers and the Aesthetics of Romanticism*. Surrey: Ashgate, 2009.

Price, Richard. *A Discourse on the Love of Our Country*. London: George Stafford, 1789.

———. *Observations on the Nature of Civil Liberty*. London: T. Cadell, 1776.

Price, Richard, and Joseph Priestley, *A Free Discussion of the Doctrines of Materialism, and Philosophical Necessity, In a Correspondence Between Dr. Price, and Dr. Priestley*. London: J. Johnson, 1778.

Priestley, Joseph. *The Present State of Liberty in Great Britain and her Colonies*. London: Johnson and Payne, 1769.

Ragussis, Michael. *Theatrical Nation: Jews and Other Outlandish Englishmen in Georgian Britain*. Philadelphia: University of Pennsylvania Press, 2010.

Ramachandran, Ayesha. *The Worldmakers: Global Imagining in Early Modern Europe*. Chicago: University of Chicago Press, 2015.

Rao, Anupama. *The Caste Question: Dalits and the Politics of Modern India*. Berkeley: University of California Press, 2009.

Rauser, Amelia. "Hair, Authenticity, and the Self-Made Macaroni." *Eighteenth-Century Studies* 38, no. 1 (2004): 101–17.

Raynal, Guillaume Thomas François, Abbé. *A philosophical and political history of the settlements and trade of the Europeans in the East and West Indies* ... , translated by J. O. Justamond. London: W. Strahan and T. Cadell, 1783.

Rede, Leman Thomas. *The Road to the Stage, or, The Performer's Preceptor.* London: J. Onwhyn, 1827.

Revel, Jacques. "The *Annales:* Continuities and Discontinuities." *Review (Fernand Braudel Center)* 1, no. 3/4 (Winter–Spring, 1978): 9–18.

Richardson, Alan. *Literature, Education, and Romanticism: Reading as Social Practice 1780–1832.* Cambridge: Cambridge University Press, 1994.

Richardson, John. *A Dictionary, Persian, Arabic, and English.* Oxford: The Clarendon Press, 1777–80.

Ricoeur, Paul. *The Rule of Metaphor: Multi-Disciplinary Studies of the Creation of Meaning in Language.* Translated by Robert Czerny. London: Routledge, 2003.

Ritchie, Fiona, and Peter Sabor, eds. *Shakespeare in the Eighteenth Century.* Cambridge: Cambridge University Press, 2012.

Roach, Joseph. "The Global Parasol: Accessorizing the Four Corners of the World." In Nussbaum, *The Global Eighteenth Century,* 93–106.

Robb, Peter, ed. *The Concept of Race in South Asia.* Delhi: Oxford University Press, 1995.

——. "Credit, Work, and Race: Early Colonialism through a Contemporary European View." *Indian Economic and Social History Review* 37, no. 1 (2000): 1–25.

——. *Sentiment and Self: Richard Blechynden's Calcutta Diaries, 1791–1822.* Delhi: Oxford University Press, 2011.

——. *Sex and Sensibility: Richard Blechynden's Calcutta Diaries, 1791–1822.* Delhi: Oxford University Press, 2011.

——. *Useful Friendship: Europeans and Indians in Early Calcutta.* Delhi: Oxford University Press, 2014.

Robins, Joseph. *Champagne and Silver Buckles: The Viceregal Court at Dublin Castle 1700–1922.* Dublin: Lilliput Press, 2001.

Robinson, Cedric J. *Black Marxism: The Making of the Black Radical Tradition.* Chapel Hill: University of North Carolina Press, 2000.

Robinson, Nicholas K. *Edmund Burke: A Life in Caricature.* New Haven, CT: Yale University Press, 1996.

Robson, Eric. "Purchase and Promotion in the British Army in the Eighteenth Century." *History* 36, no. 126–27 (February and June 1951): 57–72.

Rocher, Rosane, and Ludo Rocher. *The Making of Western Indology: Henry Thomas Colebrooke and the East India Company.* London: Routledge, 2012.

Rooney, Ellen. "Symptomatic Reading Is a Problem of Form." In Anker and Felski, eds., *Critique and Post Critique,* 127–52.

Rosenthal, Angela. "Visceral Culture: Blushing and the Legibility of Whiteness in Eighteenth-Century British Portraiture." *Art History* 27, no. 4 (2004), 563–92.

Rosenthal, Caitlin. "Slavery's Scientific Management: Masters and Managers." In *Slavery's Capitalism: A New History of American Economic Development,* edited by Sven Beckert and Seth Rockman, 62–86. Philadelphia: University of Pennsylvania Press, 2016.

Rothschild, Emma. *The Inner Life of Empires: An Eighteenth-Century History.* Princeton, NJ: Princeton University Press, 2011.

Rouse, Charles William Boughton, Esq. *Dissertation concerning the Landed Property of Bengal.* London: John Stockdale, 1791.

Rowe, Samuel. "Beckford's Insatiable Caliph: Oriental Despotism and Consumer Society." *Eighteenth-Century Studies* 52, no. 2 (2019): 183–200.

Roy, Arundhati. "The Doctor and the Saint." In *Annihilation of Caste: The Annotated Critical Edition,* edited by S. Anand, 17–179. New York: Verso, 2016.

Russell, Gillian. "An 'Entertainment of Oddities': Fashionable Sociability and the Pacific in the 1770s." In Wilson, ed., *A New Imperial History,* 48–70.

——. *The Theatres of War: Performance, Politics, and Society, 1793-1815.* Oxford: Oxford University Press, 1995.

——. *Women, Sociability and Theatre in Georgian London.* Cambridge: Cambridge University Press, 2007.

Russell, Gillian, and Clara Tuite. *Romantic Sociability: Social Networks and Literary Culture in Britain, 1770-1840.* Cambridge: Cambridge University Press, 2002.

Sack, James J. *The Grenvillites 1801-1829: Party Politics and Factionalism in the Age of Pitt and Liverpool.* Urbana: University of Illinois Press, 1979.

Said, Edward W. *Culture and Imperialism.* New York: Vintage Books, 1994.

Sancho, Ignatius. *Letters of the Late Ignatius Sancho, an African.* Edited by Vincent Carretta. New York: Penguin Books, 1998.

Schimmel, Annemarie. "Hindu and Turk: A Poetical Image and Its Application to Historical Fact." In *Islam and Cultural Change in the Middle Ages,* edited by Speros Vryonis, Jr., 107–26. Wiesbaden: Otto Harrassowitz, 1975.

Scobie, Ruth. "'Bunny! O! Bunny!': The Burney Family in Oceania." *Eighteenth-Century Life* 42, no. 2 (April 2018): 56–72.

Scott, Julius S. *The Common Wind: Afro-American Currents in the Age of the Haitian Revolution.* New York: Verso, 2018.

Scott, Sir Walter. *The Journal of Sir Walter Scott, from the original manuscript at Abbotsford.* New York: Harper and Brothers, 1890.

Segal, Ronald. *Islam's Black Slaves: The Other Black Diaspora.* New York, Farrar, Strauss and Giroux, 2001.

Sell, Zach. "Capital Through Slavery: U.S. Settler Slavery and the British Imperial World." Unpublished manuscript, last modified June 24, 2019.

Sen, Sudipta. *Distant Sovereignty: National Imperialism and the Origins of British India.* New York: Routledge, 2002.

Shakespeare, William. *The Merry Wives of Windsor.* Edited by T. W. Craik. Oxford: Oxford University Press, 1990.

Shammas, Carole. "British Investing in Financial Assets Before 1800." Unpublished manuscript, presented to the EMSI/Chicago Summer Reading Group, July 17, 2019.

Sharpe, Christina. *In the Wake: On Blackness and Being.* Durham, NC: Duke University Press, 2016.

Sieyès, Emmanuel Joseph. *Emmanuel Joseph Sieyès: The Essential Political Writings*. Edited by Oliver W. Lembcke and Florian Weber. Leiden: Brill, 2014.

Sinha, Mrinalini. *Colonial Masculinity: The 'Manly Englishman' and the 'Effeminate Bengali' in the Late Nineteenth Century*. Manchester: Manchester University Press, 1995.

Sivanandan, A. *A Different Hunger: Writings on Black Resistance*. London: Pluto Press, 1982.

Skeehan, Danielle C. "Caribbean Women, Creole Fashioning, and the Fabric of Black Atlantic Writing." *The Eighteenth Century* 56, no. 1 (2015): 105–23.

Smith, Adam. *An Inquiry into the Nature and Causes of the Wealth of Nations*. Indianapolis: Liberty Fund, 1982.

Smith, Dane Farnsworth. *Plays About the Theatre in England, 1737–1800*. Lewisburg, PA: Bucknell University Press, 1979.

Smith, Hannah. "The Court in England, 1714–1760: A Declining Political Institution?." *History* 90, no. 1 (January 2005): 23–41.

Smith, Henry Nash. *Virgin Land: The American West as Myth and Symbol*. Cambridge, MA: Harvard University Press, 1978.

Smith, Ian. "We Are Othello: Speaking of Race in Early Modern Studies." *Shakespeare Quarterly* 67, no. 1 (Spring 2016): 104–24.

Smollett, Tobias. *The Expedition of Humphrey Clinker*. Oxford: Oxford World's Classics, 2009.

Smyth, Andrew J. "That *This Here* Box Be in the *Nature* of a Trap: Maria Edgeworth's Pedagogical Gardens, Ireland, and the Education of the Poor." In *Time of Beauty, Time of Fear: The Romantic Legacy in the Literature of Childhood*, edited by James Holt McGavran, Jr., 40–55. Iowa City: University of Iowa Press, 2012.

Solkin, David H. *Painting for Money: The Visual Arts and the Public Sphere in Eighteenth-Century England*. New Haven, CT: Yale University Press, 1993.

Spence, Thomas. *Pig's meat; or, Lessons for the swinish multitude*. London: Printed for T. Spence, 1794–95.

Spivak, Gayatri Chakravorty. "Can the Subaltern Speak?" In *Marxism and the Interpretation of Culture*, edited by C. Nelson and L. Grossberg, 271–313. Basingstoke: Macmillan Education, 1988.

Starke, Mariana. *The Sword of Peace; or, A Voyage of Love*. London: J. Debrett, 1789.

St. Clair, William. *The Reading Nation in the Romantic Period*. Cambridge: Cambridge University Press, 2004.

Stephen, James. *The Dangers of the Country*. London: J. Butterworth, 1807.

Stephens, Frederic George, and Mary Dorothy George, *Catalogue of Political and Personal Satires in the Department of Prints and Drawings in the British Museum*. London: BMP, 1870.

Stern, Phillip J. "British Asia and British Atlantic: Comparisons and Connections." *William and Mary Quarterly* 63, no. 4 (2006): 693–712.

——. "Neither East nor West, Border, nor Breed, nor Birth: Early Modern Empire and Global History." *Huntington Library Quarterly* 72, no. 1 (2009): 113–26.

Stieber, Chelsea. *Haiti's Paper War: Post-Independence Writing, Civil War, and the Making of the Republic (1804–1954)*. New York: New York University Press, 2020.

Stoianovich, Traian. *French Historical Method: The* Annales *Paradigm*. Ithaca, NY: Cornell University Press, 1976.

Stokes, Eric. *The English Utilitarians and India*. Oxford: The Clarendon Press, 1959.

Straub, Kristina, ed. *Evelina*. Boston: Bedford Cultural Editions, 1997.

Suleri, Sara. *The Rhetoric of English India*. Chicago: University of Chicago Press, 1992.

Sulivan, Richard Joseph, Esq. *An analysis of the political history of India. In which is considered, the present situation of the East, and the connection of its several powers with the empire of Great Britain*. London: T. Becket, 1784.

Summers, Judith. *Empress of Pleasures: The Life and Adventures of Teresa Cornelys*. London: Penguin Books, 2003.

Sussman, Charlotte. *Consuming Anxieties: Consumer Protest, Gender, and British Slavery, 1713–1833*. Stanford, CA: Stanford University Press, 2000.

Sutherland, Lucy S. *The East India Company in Eighteenth-Century Politics*. Oxford: Clarendon Press, 1952.

Sutherland, Lucy S., and J. Binney. "Henry Fox as Paymaster General of the Forces." *The English Historical Review* 70, no. 275 (April 1955): 229–57.

Swaminathan, Srividhya, and Adam R. Beach. "Introduction: Invoking Slavery in Literature and Scholarship." In *Invoking Slavery in the Eighteenth-Century British Imagination*, edited by Swaminathan and Beach, 1–20. Surrey: Ashgate, 2013.

Sweet, James. "The Iberian Roots of American Racist Thought." *William and Mary Quarterly* 54, no. 1 (1997): 143–66.

Tadmor, Naomi. *Family and Friends in Eighteenth-Century England: Household, Kinship, and Patronage*. Cambridge: Cambridge University Press, 2001.

Tague, Ingrid H. *Animal Companions: Pets and Social Change in Eighteenth-Century Britain*. University Park: Pennsylvania State University Press, 2015.

Taylor, David Francis. *The Politics of Parody: A Literary History of Caricature, 1760–1830*. New Haven, CT: Yale University Press, 2018.

——. *Theatres of Opposition: Empire, Revolution, and Richard Brinsley Sheridan*. Oxford: Oxford University Press, 2012.

Thompson, E. P. "Eighteenth-Century English Society: Class Struggle Without Class?." *Social History* 3 (1978): 133–65.

——. *The Making of the English Working Class*. New York: Vintage Books, 1966.

——. *The Poverty of Theory: Or an Orrery of Errors*. London: Merlin Press, 1995.

Toledano, Ehud R. *As If Silent and Absent: Bonds of Enslavement in the Islamic Middle East*. New Haven, CT: Yale University Press, 2007.

Trenchard, John, and Thomas Gordon, eds. *Cato's Letters, Vol. 1 November 5, 1720 to June 17, 1721*. Indianapolis: Liberty Fund, 1995.

Trevelyan, George Otto. *The Early History of Charles James Fox*. New York: Harper and Brothers, 1881.

——. *The Life and Letters of Lord Macaulay*. London: Longmans, Green, 1876.

Ulmer, William A. "William Wordsworth and Philosophical Necessity." *Studies in Philology* 110, no. 1 (Winter 2013): 168–98.

Valensi, Lucette. *The Birth of the Despot: Venice and the Sublime Porte*. Translated by Arthur Denner. Ithaca, NY: Cornell University Press, 1993.

Vaughan, Virginia Mason. *Performing Blackness on English Stages, 1500–1800*. Cambridge: Cambridge University Press, 2005.

———. "Supersubtle Venetians: Richard Knolles and the Geopolitics of Shakespeare's *Othello*." In *Visions of Venice in Shakespeare*, edited by Laura Tosi and Shaul Bassi, 19–32. Surrey: Ashgate, 2011.

Vaughn, James M. "John Company Armed: The English East India Company, the Anglo-Mughal War and Absolutist Imperialism, c.1675–1690." *Britain and the World* 11, no. 1 (2017): 101–37.

Vickery, Amanda. *The Gentleman's Daughter: Women's Lives in Georgian England*. New Haven, CT: Yale University Press, 1998.

Vilar, Pierre. "Marxist History, a History in the Making." *New Left Review* 80 (July–August 1973): 64–106.

Visram, Rozina. *Asians in Britain: 400 Years of History*. London: Pluto Press, 2002.

———. *Ayahs, Lascars and Princes: Indians in Britain 1700–1947*. London: Pluto Press, 1986.

Viswanath, Rupa. *The Pariah Problem: Caste, Religion, and the Social in Modern India*. New York: Columbia University Press, 2014.

Vovelle, Michel. *Ideologies and Mentalities*. Translated by Eamon O'Flaherty. Chicago: University of Chicago Press, 1990.

Wade, John. *The Black Book; or Corruption Unmasked!* London: John Fairburn, 1820.

———. *Junius: Including Letters by the Same Writer Under Other Signatures. . . .* London: Henry G. Bohn, 1855.

Wallerstein, Immanuel. "*Annales* as Resistance." In *Review (Fernand Braudel Center)* 1, no. 3/4 (Winter–Spring, 1978): 5–7.

Walpole, Horace. *The Last Journals of Horace Walpole During the Reign of George III, from 1771–1783*. London: J. Lane, 1910.

———. *Letters Addressed to the Countess of Ossory: From the year 1769 to 1797*. Edited by R. Vernon Smith. London: Richard Bentley, 1848.

Warner, Michael. "What's Colonial About Colonial America?." in *Possible Pasts: Becoming Colonial in Early America,* edited by Robert Blair St. George, 49–69. Ithaca, NY: Cornell University Press, 2000.

Watt, James. *British Orientalisms, 1759–1835*. Cambridge: Cambridge University Press, 2019.

Watts, Carol. *The Cultural Work of Empire: The Seven Years' War and the Imagining of the Shandean State*. Edinburgh: Edinburgh University Press, 2007.

West, Shearer. "The Darly Macaroni Prints and the Politics of the Private Man." *Eighteenth-Century Life* 25, no. 2 (2001): 170–82.

Wheeler, Roxann. *The Complexion of Race: Categories of Difference in Eighteenth-Century Culture*. Philadelphia: University of Pennsylvania Press, 2000.

——. "Sounding Black-ish: West Indian Pidgin in London Performance and Print." *Eighteenth-Century Studies* 51, no. 1 (2017): 63–87.

Whitman, Walt. "Passage to India." In *The Collected Writings of Walt Whitman,* edited by Gay Wilson Allen and Sculley Bradley, 411–21. New York: New York University Press, 1965.

Whitney, Asa. *A Project for a Railroad to the Pacific.* New York: George W. Wood, 1849.

Williams, Eric. *Capitalism and Slavery.* Chapel Hill: University of North Carolina Press, 1994.

Williams, Neville. *Powder and Paint: A History of the Englishwoman's Toilet, Elizabeth I—Elizabeth II.* London: Longmans, Green, 1957.

Williams, Raymond. *Marxism and Literature.* Oxford: Oxford University Press, 1977.

Wilson, Kathleen. *The Island Race: Englishness, Empire and Gender in the Eighteenth Century.* London: Routledge, 2003.

——. *The Sense of the People: Politics, Culture and Imperialism in England, 1715–1785.* Cambridge: Cambridge University Press, 1995.

——, ed. *A New Imperial History: Culture, Identity and Modernity in Britain and the Empire 1660–1840.* Cambridge: Cambridge University Press, 2004.

Woodworth, Megan A. *Eighteenth-Century Women Writers and the Gentleman's Liberation Movement: Independence, War, Masculinity, and the Novel, 1778–1818.* Surrey: Ashgate, 2011.

Worrall, David. *Harlequin Empire: Race, Ethnicity and the Drama of the Popular Enlightenment.* London: Pickering and Chatto, 2007.

Wright, Philip. "Introduction." In Nugent, *Lady Nugent's Journal of her Residence in Jamaica from 1801 to 1805,* xi–xxxii.

Yang, Chi-ming. "Asia Out of Place: The Aesthetics of Incorruptibility In Behn's Oroonoko." *Eighteenth-Century Studies* 42, no. 1 (2008): 235–53.

——. "Culture in Miniature: Toy Dogs and Object Life." *Eighteenth-Century Fiction* 25, no. 1 (Fall 2012): 139–74.

Acknowledgments

Acknowledgments are a special place in a monograph: here the deceptive semblance of the solo scholar evaporates and a web of interdependencies comes into view. So many people helped make this book a thing in the world. Its existence is a testament to the generosity of countless teachers, advisors, colleagues, students, family members, and friends—more than I could possibly name in these few pages.

To begin with, I count the mentorship I received in graduate school as one of the great blessings of my life. For over a decade now my dissertation supervisors, Ania Loomba and Suvir Kaul, have been constant sources of wisdom, inspiration, and comradely sustenance. Ania and Suvir gave me models of the kind of work I wanted to do and the kind of scholar I wanted to be: rigorous, historicist, and committed to a life of the mind out of a conviction that ideas matter. I thank them both for believing in me and this project from day one; and for giving me an intellectual and ethical compass that continues to orient me today. I could not imagine writing this book without the guidance of David Kazanjian. I am profoundly grateful to him for teaching me how to think with rigor and precision, and for doing so with kindness and care.

In terms of institutional homes, my run of good luck began at Barnard College, where I was guided by Monica Miller, Rosalind Rosenberg, Ezra Tawil, and Margaret Vanderburg. At the University of Pennsylvania,

I benefited in myriad ways from the mentorship of Chi-ming Yang, who taught by example and training. I continue to admire her scholarship and feel lucky for her collegiality. I also thank David Eng, Paul Saint-Amour, Jed Esty, Michael Gamer, Tsitsi Jaji, and Nancy Bentley for their generous guidance and for giving me the opportunity to grow intellectually in a community of great minds.

A Barra Postdoctoral Fellowship at the McNeil Center for Early American Studies allowed me to join a vibrant community of historians and literary scholars led by the unflappable Dan Richter. The McNeil Center contributed in no small part to this book's evolution by hosting a manuscript workshop, where I received extraordinarily helpful feedback from Laura Brown and Danny O'Quinn.

At Georgetown University, I received institutional support for my research in the form of research leave, a course release, and several travel grants. I also received excellent mentorship from Lindsay Kaplan and Patrick O'Malley, whom I thank wholeheartedly. Caitlin Benson-Allot, Jennifer Natalya Fink, Samantha Pinto, and Nicole Rizzuto were treasured colleagues. I also enjoyed trading ideas with Nathan Hensley, Dana Luciano, Sarah McNamer, Cóilín Parsons, Seth Perlow, and Dan Shore.

Although I arrived at the University of Southern California a relatively short time ago, it already feels like home. A semester of research leave and a series of course releases have enabled me to rewrite every page of this manuscript, making it infinitely better. I thank Melissa Daniels-Rauterkus, Kate Flint, Devin Griffiths, Zakiyyah Iman Jackson, Dana Johnson, Elda María Román, Bea Sanford Russell, Meg Russert, and Karen Tongson for welcoming me to the department with open arms. David St. John has been the most supportive chair I could possibly imagine. I thank Emily Anderson for keeping the eighteenth century alive in Taper Hall, and for reading several chapters in the crunch time. Rebecca Lemon has been the Platonic ideal of a good colleague; and she gave me the confidence boost I needed to really engage with the early modern sources in my third chapter. One of the great benefits of moving to sunny Southern California is getting to take part in the eighteenth-century community here. Helen Deutsch and Felicity Nussbaum have been fabulous LA colleagues. Thanks to the SoCal Eighteenth Century

Group, and to Sarah Tindal Kareem, for giving me the opportunity to workshop Chapter 3 when I arrived in town.

Since I was a graduate student, Kathleen Wilson's scholarship has been an inspiration to me; and her consistent enthusiasm for this book has been a source of motivation to keep going. I thank her for many conversations over the years, especially about theater and race. From our first fateful meeting in Calcutta, Isabel Hofmeyr has been a favorite interlocuter. I thank her especially for the invitation to think through some of this book's framing arguments in *Comparative Literature*. Antoinette Burton has been incredibly generous to me since I was a graduate student and provided excellent feedback on some of the arguments in Chapter 5 at an earlier stage of their development. Ever since I accosted her after a performance of Paterson Joseph's *Sancho: An Act of Remembrance* at BAM, Gretchen Gerzina has been a trusted advisor for my work on Julius Soubise. I especially thank her for giving me the opportunity to publish a book chapter on Soubise's life in India in *Britain's Black Past*. Chapter 2 would have been impossible without the generosity of Peter Robb, who first helped me navigate the Blechynden diaries in 2011 and has provided valuable feedback on my work on the topic ever since.

It would be impossible to adequately thank Danny O'Quinn for his unflagging generosity as a mentor, colleague, and friend. When I first encountered Danny's work in graduate school it astonished me, setting a new high bar for what scholarship in the field could achieve. As any reader in the know will quickly recognize, this book's roots are planted in ground cleared by Danny in *Staging Governance* and *Entertaining Crisis*. From Danny's first reading of this project as a dissertation, he recognized its potential and helped me to grow it into the best possible version of itself. Over the years, he has read every page of this manuscript multiple times; and he has always been there to offer encouragement when I needed it most.

I feel so lucky to belong to a field whose practitioners are congenial and brilliant in equal measure. At ASECS, I have received sparks of insight and transfusions of intellectual lifeblood from Misty Anderson, Fiona Brideoake, Tita Chico, Lisa Freeman, Dana Gliserman-Kopans, Devoney Looser, Kathleen Lubey, Chris Nagle, Joe Roach, Laura Rosenthal, and

Janet Sorensen. I especially thank all the folks who have made the Race & Empire Caucus the best place to be, including Suvir, Chi-ming, Reggie Allen, George Bouloukos, Tony Brown, Betty Joseph, Ramesh Mallipeddi, James Mulholland, Sal Nicolazzo, Charlotte Sussman, and Gena Zuroski. At the beginning of my career, Srinivas Aravamudan was profoundly generous to me—just as he was, I know, to so many others. Although I did not know him well, I have more reason to miss his presence in the field with every passing year as I continue to learn from his brilliant scholarship.

For generously reading chapters and helping me to sharpen this book's arguments, I thank Marina Bilbija, Zirwat Chowdhury, Stephanie DeGooyer, Daniel DeWispelare, Jason Farr, Walt Hakala, John Owen Havard, Najnin Islam, Lindsay Kaplan, Donna Landry, Rebecca Lemon, Natania Meeker, David Francis Taylor, Omari Weekes, and Aaron Winslow. Megan McVay heroically copyedited the manuscript prior to review. The steady hand of my editor, Sarah Miller, guided this book to safe harbor. It has been a pleasure to work with her and her team at Yale, especially Ash Lago. I am grateful to Steve Pincus and Jonathan Kramnick for believing so fully in this project. It is an honor to publish this book under their series editorship.

The process of writing a book was more challenging than I could have ever imagined. Along the way, I was sustained by loved ones and friends. The brilliant Jason Farr has been a cherished companion at every step of this project's journey from dissertation to book—I am so pleased that we were destined to walk this academic path together. I thank my lucky stars for Chelsea Stieber, whose gold-standard comments have made every single paragraph of this book better. At a crucial moment, Devin Griffiths generously read my entire manuscript. His careful and timely interventions radically improved this book's final incarnation. I thank Devin for being the best of colleagues; and I hope to continue thinking alongside him for years to come. During the final grueling year of work on this book Jordan Allen's healing arts kept me on my feet and grounded in my heart. Annie Nugent's wisdom, so generously shared, profoundly improved this book and the life of its author.

Sociability is a keyword in this book, and it was a condition of possibility for its completion. Holly Melgard and Joey Yearous-Algozin dazzle me as poets and warm my heart as friends. Danny Snelson and

Mashinka Firunts have helped make Los Angeles feel like an instant home and make friendship feel like family. Mary Zaborskis and Omari Weekes are lights in my life: I thank them for their rock-solid friendship and for being so much fun. Since our summer in Jaipur a decade ago, Chris Sherman has been the best *dost*, comrade, conversation partner, and *bhai* I could ever imagine. I thank him and Neha Bhardwaj for being my chosen family, and for adding Simran Rani to it.

My family has always been my biggest support and supporters. Erick Brownstein, Amanda Enclade, Solomon, Jules, and Austen have always made their home feel like mine; and they have lived with this book for as long as anyone. I thank them for helping gestate it, and for bringing me home to California. Karen and Bruce Borger's kvelling has buoyed me over the years; and I thank Bruce for that first fateful trip to India. Erika Weiss has always been like a sister; and I know this book will make her proud. Ben Cohen, Brooke Rehman, Kaitlin Winslow, and Freddie Rivas have made time off from this manuscript loads of fun in recent years. Kenny Mopper has always been a sagacious and caring academic dad; and time spent with him as well as Weiwei and Eliana Jin over the past few years has been precious and buoying. Brian and Judi Winslow never ceased to be encouraging even when my work made things difficult. My beloved grandparents, Samuel and Adele Borger, sustained my education in spiritual and material ways. I wish they could have seen this book enter the world; I know they would have been beaming. This book is dedicated to my parents, Michael Cohen and Hara Borger Cohen, who never doubted me and always empowered me to follow my passions, no matter how far off the beaten track they took me.

More than anyone else, Aaron Winslow has made the writing of this book possible. I thank him for feeding me in body, mind, and heart, and for making me laugh at every turn. Most of all, I thank him for building a world with me, and for filling it with so much joy.

Index